Adult Development, Therapy, and Culture
A Postmodern Synthesis

The Plenum Series in Adult Development and Aging

SERIES EDITOR:
Jack Demick, *Suffolk University, Boston, Massachusetts*

ADULT DEVELOPMENT, THERAPY, AND CULTURE
A Postmodern Synthesis
Gerald Young

THE AMERICAN FATHER
Biocultural and Developmental Aspects
Wade C. Mackey

HANDBOOK OF PAIN AND AGING
Edited by David I. Mostofsky and Jacob Lomranz

PSYCHOLOGICAL TREATMENT OF OLDER ADULTS
An Introductory Text
Edited by Michel Hersen and Vincent B. Van Hasselt

Preface

s volume proposes a theoretical integration of several major streams in ntemporary psychological theory about adult development and therapy. t adopts the perspective that there are steps in development throughout the adult period, and that they are characterized by a union of the cognitive and affective, the self and the other, and idea with idea (in second-order collective abstractions). That is, they are at once postformal in terms of Piaget's theory, sociocultural in terms of Vygotsky's theory, and postmodern— with the latter perspective providing an integrating theme. The affirmative, multivoiced, contextual, relational, other-sensitive side of postmodernism is emphasized. Lévinas's philosophy of responsibility for the other is seen as congruent with this ethos.

The neopiagetian model of development on which the current approach is based proposes that the last stage in development concerns collective intelligence, or postmodern, postformal thought. Kegan (1994) has attempted independently to describe adult development from the same perspective. His work on the development of the postmodern mind of the adult is groundbreaking and impressive in its depth. However, I analyze the limitations as well as the contributions of his approach, underscoring the advantages of my particular model.

Therapy is considered from a narrative, coconstructive, developmental perspective. In particular, Michael White's approach of problem externalization/agency internalization is described and elaborated into a model where precipitating stresses are considered first-order external factors that can create bad habits, or second-order externalizations. I use a graphic approach with my clients that emphasizes the personal control they can acquire over their externalized problems. Therapy is considered a developmental process, and examples of the optimal (and nonoptimal) stories that clients can recount about each developmental step are offered.

To be more specific, the current model maintains that development is marked by a succession of 25 substages or levels that cover the lifespan through the organization of 5 substages that recur cyclically within 5 stages (see Table P.1, with 4 sublevels within each substage); the stages and substages integrate the cognitive and the socioaffective acquisitions of development (e.g., self and family development) by describing parallels in their emergence; they are spurred by multiple developmental transition mechanisms, subsumed in a sociocultural model of coappropriation, which involves the developing individual in context (e.g., parents as sociocultural buffers; see Figure 8.1). Therapy is practiced best as a conversational coconstruction aimed at freeing clients toward transition or the normative path to freedom along the sequence of the 25 major steps in development that are proposed (see Young, submitted, for a detailed description of the 25 steps in development).

The book has been influenced by postmodern conceptions and at the same time it may speak to some substantive issues that are inherent to that perspective. Thus, a major goal of the book is to describe the contemporary postmodern program in psychology, and to show the manner in which the synthetic theory that is being proposed bears a reciprocal relation to it. This underscores my effort to instill a unity or overarching vision in the current work; the postmodern comparison brings a solder that binds its innovations together in a coherent framework. The fact that its companion volume (Young, submitted) describes the 25-step developmental progression at the base of the current work in terms of dynamic systems theory does not represent a contradiction, for postmodernism and chaos theory share many characteristics (T. R. Young, 1995).

The synthetic aspect of the model on human development outlined in this volume should make it relevant to a broad spectrum of researchers, academics, clinicians, other professionals, and advanced undergraduate and graduate students interested in adult development and psychotherapy. Also, it should appeal to workers-students in developmental psychology, in general, and in specialized developmental areas such as infant, child, adolescent, family, and lifespan psychology; developmental psychopathology; developmental therapy or counseling; psychiatry; family and couples therapy; education; social work; and child care. In addition, it relates to other pertinent areas in psychology such as cognition, personality, and relationships, and to social and clinical psychology. Finally, its extension into the area of sociocultural and historicopolitical influences on development may make the book appealing to sociologists, political theorists, and anthropologists.

Acknowledgments

Three individuals have contributed to the writing of sections of the book, and their astute observations are gratefully appreciated. Sylvana Santalupo Macdonald is the first author of Chapter 13. Edward S. Meade is the second author of the sections "Tomm's Systemic Therapy" and "Externalization" in Chapter 9 on pages 197–200 and 205–207, respectively. Carina M. Young is the second author of the section "Disney as a Film of Society" in Chapter 8 on pages 184–186. Also, she designed and drew the artwork on the front cover, following an idea that I presented to her. The editors with whom I dealt at Plenum, Jack Demick and Eliot Werner, provided expert advice and warm encouragement. The editorial supervision process was handled both very efficiently and personally by Herman Makler. Over the years many colleagues, clients, and students have shared with me conversations and ideas, and this book constitutes my thanks to them. My past supervisors, Thérèse Gouin Décarie and Peter H. Wolff, sought to delineate parallels across piagetian cognitive and psychodynamic development (Gouin Décarie, 1962, and Wolff, 1960, respectively), and I thank them for their inspiration.

My parents, my wife, and our children—Samuel, Rosalind, Lélia, Carina, Joy, and Victoria—have been a constant source of encouragement and affection, and to them I dedicate this book. They, and my wife, in particular, have informed and educated all aspects of the book.

Contents

PART III. SOCIOCULTURAL DEVELOPMENT

PART V. THERAPY AND EPISTEMOLOGY

PART V. CONCLUSIONS

A 25-Step Developmental Model

COGNITION

Introduction

Young (1990a, 1990b, submitted) has proposed a 25-step model of development that is neopiagetian in its cognitive origin and neoeriksonian in its socioemotional one (see Table P.1). It describes parallels in the two domains across the lifespan. The cognitive model integrates the work of current neopiagetian theorists, and as such borrows their concept of a cyclic recursion of substages within stages of development. I found that I had to add to these models cognitive steps especially at the level of adult development. Aside from its basis in current neopiagetian work, the current model also manifests a deep respect for the notion that fractals permeate the psychological developmental field. In Chapters 7 and 12, I describe the concept of fractalization (concerned with self-similarity across different system levels), and the manner in which the current theory speaks to it.

As for the construction of the socioemotional component of the current theory, Erikson's (1980) eight-stage lifespan theory proved instrumental. Other stage theorists, such as Loevinger (1976), also were consulted. Their work is reviewed in Chapter 3. Given that Erikson described eight developmental stages and the construction of the current theory required 25, I had to create 17 others. Erikson's were matched to their appropriate cognitive mate, and the 17 others were elaborated upon the basis of the cognitive level underlying them and the literature on socioemotional development. In the end, 25 socioemotional systems were described, with the same four particular dimensions seen as organizing each of them. Even Erikson's stages are shown to be organized around these dimensions. In the present chapter, the 25 steps in socioemotional development are not de-

Table P.1. A Neopiagetian Theory
of Cognitive Development Consisting of 25 Levels

Level	Stage	Substage	Age range
1	Reflex	Coordination	Earlier fetal life
2		Hierarchization	Quite premature
3		Systematization	Somewhat premature
4		Multiplication	Full-term newborn
5		Integration	0–1 month
6	Sensorimotor	Coordination	1–4 months
7		Hierarchization	4–8 months
8		Systematization	8–12 months
9		Multiplication	12–18 months
10		Integration	18–24 months
11	Perioperational	Coordination	2–3.5 years
12		Hierarchization	3.5–5 years
13		Systematization	5–7 years
14		Multiplication	7–9 years
15		Integration	9–11 years
16	Abstract	Coordination	11–13 years
17		Hierarchization	13–16 years
18		Systematization	16–19 years
19		Multiplication	19–22 years
20		Integration	22–25 years
21	Collective	Coordination	25–28 years
22	Intelligence	Hierarchization	28–39 years
23		Systematization	39–50 years
24		Multiplication	50–61 years
25		Integration	61– years

scribed in depth. They are presented only in terms of their underlying challenges and crises, which nevertheless gives an ample picture of their substance. A fuller presentation of them can be found in Young (submitted).

Piaget

Piaget (1972) described four major stages of cognitive development, with the second and third often grouped together. In the sensorimotor period from birth to 2 years, infants derive knowledge of the environment by relating perception and direct action. At first, basic reflexes are used. These reflexes undergo metamorphosis into voluntary, organized patterns of behavior (schemes). Next, in the preoperational stage 2- to 7-year-olds represent objects and events in the world with symbols, words, images, and gestures. Mental processes become increasingly structured, but still lack complete fluidity. For example, there is egocentric perspective-taking and no reversal in thought pathways. Then, older children come to think logically in the physical situations confronting them by using "concrete" mental operations. These are interiorized action patterns that allow non-egocentric perspective-taking and reversibility in thought. Finally, adolescents embark on abstract, experimental hypothesis-testing in their imagination when they are faced with problems to solve and in dealing with the possible, the future, and so on.

Case (1985) sees the preoperational stage as one in which children acquire an understanding of second-order relations of primary relations, or bipolar patterns of organization among actions, objects, people, or events in the environment. In Case's balance scale task, preoperational children grasp the relation between the difference in weight between two objects and the effect of this difference on the relative position of the arms of the scale. They understand that in using the scale, the heavier the objects' difference in weight, the more the heavier object lowers and the more the lighter one rises. Case describes concrete operations in terms of skills in using dimensions during thought. Dimensions are continuous qualities which characterize the world, such as height and width. For Piaget, the hallmark of concrete operations is found in children's mastery of conservation problems, where they realize that physical transformations do not alter objects (e.g., in pouring water from one container to another). Case emphasizes the way children who conserve compare dimensions (e.g., of changing height and width) in understanding that objects in conservation problems have not been altered in the course of transformation. Finally, Case describes formal thought in adolescence in terms of vectors in an abstract multidimensional thought field.

In short, Piaget describes a structural model of cognitive development consisting of four major stages: sensorimotor, preoperational (representation driven), concrete operational (logical), and formal (abstract) operational thought.

Neopiagetians

Each of the neopiagetians, Case (1985, 1996) and K. W. Fischer (1980; Fischer & Hencke, 1996), have described a 13- to 15-level cognitive developmental theory involving four to five stages with three cyclically recurring substages. In both theories, the cyclic substages begin with single entities (unifocal, set substages for Case and Fischer, respectively), which come to coordinate in pairs (bifocal, mapping substages), and then become even more complex (elaboration, system substages). Moreover, one substage in each cycle has a dual character, for it functions both in its own right and as a transition substage, being a compound of the prior level (consolidation for the elaboration substage of Case, system of systems for the set substage of Fischer).

A major difference between Case's and Fischer's theories concerns the modal ages when the substages are supposed to emerge. The only time that similar substages are seen to develop at comparable ages across the two theories is in the sensorimotor period between 4 and 18 to 20 months of age. In contrast, the 2-year-old for Case uses interrelational coordinated bifocal relations but in Fischer uses representational single entity sets. Another example is that the 16-year-old uses abstract thought in both Case and Fischer, but at a complex elaboration level in Case and at a coordinated mapping level in Fischer. Inconsistencies such as these may speak to basic lacunae in the theories.

Mounoud (1986) presents a clearer dividing line between the various cognitive levels, because 15 levels are seen to derive from the repetition of five substages in each of three stages, with no transitional, compound substage. In Mounoud's system, initial global codes emerge and then are applied separately. Following this, codes are globally related. Then, the relations are partly analyzed, leading to complete synthesis. (This summary is a simplification from tables in Mounoud. See Young [1990a].)

THE CURRENT THEORY

Recursions

The current theory shares the fundamental assumption of Fischer, Case, and Mounoud that cognitive development witnesses a repetition of identical structural steps from stage to stage in a cyclic recursion of substages. This concept is related to Piaget's notion of "vertical decalage," but is more stringent and operational than it (Case, 1987; K. W. Fischer, 1980). Despite this shared starting point with three prior theories, the current theory differs from each of them in that I borrowed only one salient aspect from each of them, in turn, as I considered the nature of the three major aspects necessary in the construction of a neopiagetian theory. That is, in constructing the current neopiagetian theory, Fischer's stage model proved the most beneficial, Case's age ranges for each of the substages were deemed the most appropriate, and Mounoud's model of substage progression was judged the most pertinent.

Stages

First, the current model of cognitive development is based on Fischer's model of four major stages in cognitive development—reflexive, sensorimotor, representational, and abstract. Following Piaget, Fischer combined the preoperational and concrete operational stages into one stage, which he called the representational stage. When this step of combining two stages into a superordinate one is taken by a cognitive theorist, it is not with the goal of altering the essence of the description of either of the two stages involved; rather, it is performed in order to reflect their shared attributes. A major difference between my approach and that of Fischer's in this regard is that for two reasons I label the combined preoperational-concrete operational stage "perioperational" instead of "representational." First, in effect the beginnings of representational thought emerge at the end of the prior sensorimotor stage. Second, by using the label "periopera-tional," with its meaning of "around" or "about," a way has been found to use one adjective with ties to both of the original labels (preoperational and concrete operational) used by Piaget to characterize the childhood stages of cognitive development.

Fischer's cognitive stage progression has been modified in the current theory by the addition of a stage concerning postformal thought, called collective intelligence. Although Fischer referred to a system of systems substage beyond the abstract period, he did not give it the status of a separate cognitive stage with its own three-step substage cycle. The concept of collective intelligence appears in the postformal literature in several guises. Labouvie-Vief (1992) reminds us that the concept of the collective was important to Piaget, who wrote that adolescents feel for "collective ideals" and assign themselves goals and roles "in social life." However, this attitude was derived from their new formal operational potentials, and did not refer to a collective style of cognition, like the one suggested here. For Labouvie-Vief, postformal thought is characterized in part by a genuine interaction between individual and community or self and other, because truth does not reside in any sphere alone, but is constructed cooperatively in an interpersonal social process among (partially) self-organized (auton-omous) beings. She also describes this stage as one in which there is an interaction or fusion involving cognition and emotion.

Sinott (1994) has a similar view of the postformal stage of cognitive development. It includes a subjective, self-referential meta-awareness that the world is filtered through our emotions and cognitions, an awareness that is honed in the everchanging interpersonal realm. This leads to the ability to operate with or orchestrate different abstract systems while seeking a superordinate, unitative one, to form abstract metasytems or metatheo-ries (like Commons & Richards, 1990). Also, postformal thought involves the ability to choose or commit to, through self-referential, pragmatic, and relativistic thought processes, one abstract system among many (contra-dictory) ones, and to know and accept that one is performing at this sometimes difficult level. The social implication here is that one realizes that the other must make equally part-subjective reality choices so that

adults need cooperative group or collective cognition, exploration, consensus, and solution-making in system-fitting to reality.

Others are beginning to describe a "group" intelligence, based on
socially shared or distributed collective processes, where communal cognition is greater than and/or qualitatively different than the individual part
cognitions involved (e.g., Wertsch, Tulviste, & Hagstrom, 1993; Williams &
Sternberg, 1988). All these conceptualizations are quite consistent with the
current one where the situated, dialogic, multiple nature of second-order
cognitive systematizations are emphasized.

To summarize, in the collective intelligence mode of thought, intel-
ligent adults can expand their intellectual limits by symbiotically sharing
with and contributing to collective knowledge. They realize the limits of
their individual cognition and seek a metaintegration of the certain and
uncertain, the absolute and relative, the personal and the shared, the
mental and the emotional, the self and the other, and so on, in the communal crucible. They know that cognitive and affective giving and taking are
cofunctions in being. Their will to grow motivates the use of their formal
thinking skills in this process, so that metasystems, second-order abstractions, and the like can be constructed with the fusion in parameters previously mentioned. Thus, the substages of coordination/hierarchization,
systematization, and multiplication in the collective intelligence stage of
cognitive development may concern subdiscipline, discipline, and interdisciplinary levels of collective intelligence or the like, respectively. Similarly, the integration substage would concern the larger collective level.

Age Ranges

The current theory builds on Case's age ranges for the substage levels
that he presented. Case is the theorist who best respected the original age
ranges corresponding to Piaget's stages and substages in development.
That is, apparently Case added new substages to Piaget's developmental
cognitive model mostly by splitting Piaget's stages and their respective age
ranges. Perhaps this is why in Case, after the age of one month, there is an
orderly increase in the age range of successive levels (one to several levels
involving ⅓, ½, 1½, 2, and 3 years, in turn).

Substages

The present theory was constructed upon a five-step substage cycle
with no compound substage included, as in Mounoud. This seemed justified, in part, by the possible confusion in Fischer and Case about whether
compound levels are truly distinct from the three-substage cycle within
each stage.

A five-step cyclic recursion of cognitive substages seemed preferable to other options not only because of Mounoud's model but also for the following reason: A cycle with this property could preserve intact much of Piaget's account of the sensorimotor stage. He described a six-step progression of sensorimotor substages—reflex exercise, primary circular reactions, secondary circular reactions, coordination of secondary schemes, tertiary circular reactions, and invention of new means through mental combination. Researchers still work with his original six-substage model (cf. Desrochers, Ricard, & Gouin Décarie, 1995; Rast & Meltzoff, 1995).

However, there is one major change in Piaget's approach to the sensorimotor stage that is made in the current model, and it can be justified with ease. That is, his first sensorimotor substage, which begins at birth, has been placed at the end of my reflexive stage, which is seen to develop prior to the sensorimotor stage. Because Piaget's first sensorimotor substage involves reflex exercise for the most part, this decision seems well-founded. Thus, the last five substages in Piaget's account of sensorimotor intelligence are left after this decision, and their uniform nature on the sensorimotor plane dictates that they remain as a unit in the current theory.

With this initial logic, I determined the five terms or labels that correspond best to Piaget's original description of the last five substages of the sensorimotor stage. It was kept in mind that the five labels also had to fit simultaneously simpler reflexive behaviors which develop earlier and more complex thoughts which emerge later in development. Moreover, it was kept in mind that the five-step recursion had to be phrased in terms general enough to incorporate a diverse array of developmental phenomena at any one level. The five terms for the substages that I thought best fit these requirements are called coordination, hierarchization, systematization, multiplication, and integration.

Coordination refers to an interrelation of two different cognitive control units (acquired in the previous substage for the most part). However, the interrelation does not specify which of the units has ascendancy in terms of either a temporal order or a dominant–subordinate relationship. The units exist in a reciprocal balance (pairing, addition, juxtaposition, opposition, and the like) of a back and forth nature, and if hierarchies are established they are tentative, tenuous structures. With development of the substage of hierarchization, the deficiencies in the just-described coordinations are countered, for paired cognitive control units evidence a strengthened dominant–subservient relation and/or a fixed sequence in time.

Systematization is marked by both an expansion and simplification of hierarchized control units. On the one hand, component units add (recruit) refinements (feedback, extra adaptive behaviors), which permit better on-target adjustment at the onset of the behavior, at its end-point, etc. On the other hand, the new structure meshes into a smoothly operating, more unified whole through a less fixed, hierarchical, and more complementary coordination of the component units. Multiplication refers to the combination of systems, even more than two at a time. This is accomplished both by chaining them over time (either repetitively, but more important, by using different ones in each slot), and/or by embedding, where primary systems are subserved by secondary ones (less elaborate than the primary ones). This produces an element of reversibility in behavior, but not as clearly as in the next substage of integration.

The last substage of integration in the current model of cognitive substage recursion finds multiple cognitive units more precisely differentiated in flexible branching as they are applied. This produces linear sequences or chains comprised of strings of component systems different from each other, with some embedded in others. An embedded component system may be just as elaborate as any constituent system of the main string. Moreover, it may unfold in parallel with movements or behaviors of the main string, i.e., it and the main string may unfold simultaneously. In short, the reversibility evident in the organization of this substage is a mature, efficient one. To use Fischer's language, elements of subsets can be paired without compromising the integrity or continuity of the subsets.

Sublevels

Up to this point, 25 steps or levels in development have been emphasized. Like Fischer, I raise the possibility of sublevels within levels. Fischer described sublevels within cognitive levels, but he viewed these as variable from one task to another and as potentially limitless in number within any one level. My approach has been to seek a cyclic repetition at the sublevel and not only substage level. Thus, in the current model it is suggested that sublevels may consist of a sequence of initiation, application, maturation, and transition, or the like. However, it would be premature to try to enunciate a definitive model here because of the paucity of prior theory and data on the topic. Nevertheless, the proposed sequence is straightforward and some research has been found which seems to support it, as shown in Young (submitted).

It will be recalled that I have rejected the possibility that particular developmental epochs in cognitive development may contain both the final step in one substage cycle and the first one of the next. However, it is probable that at the microlevel of sublevels within substages, this scenario does take place. Thus, the suggested sublevel sequence of initiation, application, maturation, and transition may really be a five-step cycle, with the last two occurring simultaneously. In this regard, I suggest that the transition phase is marked by the dual attribute of full synthesis of one substage and tentative beginning of its successor. Thus, on the surface a fourfold sublevel sequence appears, but in essence a five-step pathway is inherent in it. This speaks to the notion that just as five substages are contained in each of five stages in development, fractal geometry in the developmental process must assure that there are five sublevels within each of the substages of development. Thus, the sublevel sequence of tentative beginning, initiation, application, maturation, and synthesis corresponds to the coordination, hierarchization, systematization, multiplication, integration sequence in substage development, and likely functions in very similar ways.

SOCIOEMOTIONS

Erikson

A new socioemotional system (25 in all) is hypothesized to emerge at each of the 25 cognitive substages described in the current model. Erikson's (1980) eight steps in psychosexual development (see Table P.2) are embedded in the 25 systems, placed at the juncture of the second and fourth substages of each of the last four stages. It is as if specific socioemotional acquisitions during odd-numbered substages prepare the groundwork for spurts in eriksonian personality development during even-numbered substages.

The Current Model

It is proposed that the 25 cognitive substages in development described in the current theory bring with them 25 emergent socioemotional potentials that have to be parlayed into mastered skills. However, at any one substage, if there is no supportive environment, if remnants of prior crises linger, this developmental task may prove overwhelming; in lieu of pulsion to growth one may find struggle. The specific nature of the 25 socioemotional systems corresponding to the 25 cognitive substages dictates the precise danger in each developmental period. Tables P.3–P.7 present the hypothesized 25 problematic challenges and oppositions in behavioral potential that individuals must confront as they develop to fulfillment, at least according to the current theory. Noam (1992) underscores that the dangers in functioning at lower levels of development are not necessarily more dangerous than those at higher levels. Moreover, the latter's increased complexity does not necessarily guarantee increased maturity. Therefore, individuals may adopt lower levels of functioning as a protective mechanism so that in their development lower levels may

Table P.2. The Issues–Crises in Erikson's Psychosocial Developmental Stages

Stage (and normative age)	Issue–crisis
1. *Trust vs. Mistrust* (0–1)	First year devoted to acquiring sentiment of trust in self and environment. Mothers, in particular, satisfy infants' basic needs, creating this feeling of positive self-worth. Inconsistent, discontinuous, or rejecting care may result in a sense of loss, perception of the world as dangerous, and view of the world as unreliable.
2. *Autonomy vs. Shame/ Doubt* (1–3)	In the following years, toddlers and young children learn the tasks of self-sufficiency such as feeding, dressing, cleaning self. They separate from the parents and learn the rules of their culture. Problems in attaining a sense of independence may produce self-doubt in capacities, expectation of defeat in a struggle involving will, and feelings of shame.
3. *Initiative vs. Guilt* (3–6)	Preschoolers' energy and imagination lead not only to communication, curiosity, pretend play, acceptance of responsibility, trying to act grown-up, but also intrusive activities, consuming fantasies. The latter happenings can lead to conflicts with family members and also guilt. Excessive guilt can dampen initiative, so a balance of initiative and respect of others' requirements is needed. Children's conscience emerge here.
4. *Industry vs. Inferiority* (6–12)	The school-age period before puberty sees children master complex social and academic skills. Comparisons with peers are made. The reward for accepting instruction is praise for success, producing a sense of efficacy and self-assurance. The potential crisis is that a sense of personal inadequacy can develop if these skills escape children in their life at school or at home, causing them to avoid new activities.
5. *Identity vs. Identity Diffusion* (12–18)	Adolescents integrate childhood identifications to create a self-identity concerning their pubertal drives, skills, social roles, and potential work roles. They choose whom to become from among the multiple possible selves available. They may want to try out many selves but must be moderate. Confusion at these levels is temporarily unavoidable, and the risk is of role ambiguity, diffusion, or negativity (oppositional behavior against peers' and parents' wishes).
6. *Intimacy vs. Isolation* (20s)	Young adults secure in their identity can establish a feeling of intimacy with the inner self and the outer world (friends, love partner). They can share all aspects of oneself with others without fearing the loss of identity. A deep sentiment of loneliness may be incurred if individuals cannot fully enter into an intimate relationship due to a fear of losing their identity.

Table P.2. (*Continued*)

Stage (and normative age)	Issue–crisis
7. *Generativity vs. Self-absorption* (20s +)	In middle adulthood, mature individuals strive to establish and guide the following generation. Responsibilities concern family, work, the role of mentor, and whatever standards the culture defines. Problems here yield self-centered, self-absorbed behavior and a feeling of interpersonal emptiness.
8. *Ego Integrity vs. Despair* (50s +)	With intimacy and acceptance of one's efforts at generativity, older persons can look back at their lives as meaningful, productive, satisfying, happy. They actively reminisce about the past, enthusiastically anticipate the future, and seemingly possess wisdom. At issue is whether the dominant mood will be one of contentment or disappointment with unfulfilled goals, leading to sadness, displeasure, disgust.

Note. Adapted from Erikson (1980).

Table P.3. Dangers in Development in the Reflex Substages

Level	Danger and opposition in substage
1. *Distance acts vs. no stance*	Distance regulation to target is irregular, too forward, or rarely "near." Without a primary base, behavior is undifferentiated.
2. *Nursing vs. rootless acts*	Basic reflexive survival mechanisms are awry, e.g., in reacting to stimuli or in nursing. Given an absence of physical alimentation, behavior is without orientation or stability.
3. *Outcome vs. outcast acts*	Target-related appetitive behavior is contextually inappropriate, over- or underenergized, too negative (e.g., avoidance, crying), etc. Because of this foundation, behavior may promote rejection.
4. *Caregiving vs. careless giving acts*	The caregiver system is not activated appropriately (e.g., newborn is too passive or tests caregivers' limits with too much crying, colicky behavior). Caregivers bring their own agenda, and this may be maladaptive (e.g., indifference, postpartum depression, abuse). The will to live may be compromised by long-term, ineffective, nonoptimal, or emotionally absent caregiving due to problems with infants, caregivers, or their match.
5. *Emotional vs. malemotional acts*	Evaluations along emotion-related dimensions (e.g., whether goals being interfered with) are inaccurate. Component emotional reactions are problematic. In short, emotional scripts are not functioning normatively (e.g., too damped, too negative). For example, infants manifest distress in unpredictable ways, are not soothed in a normal manner, are too fussy, are never engaged by sensorily interesting spectacles/objects. The same extremes may be evident in other emotions as they emerge in the succeeding substages. As in prior substage (and in all subsequent substages), caregivers may contribute to these difficulties.

Table P.4. Dangers in Development in the Sensorimotor Substages

Level	Danger and opposition in substage
6. *Dyadic vs. dysdyadic acts*	Social dialogue is marked by poor synchrony with partner, incorrect reading of partner, misplaced actions, variable reactions, too demanding bids, excessive turning off, deficient learning skills, etc. The pleasure and joy typically inherent in a dyadic interaction with caregivers instead may be replaced by much frustration, gaze aversion, and disinterest.
7. *Trust vs. mistrust acts*	A sense of mistrust in oneself and the social world takes hold, for caregiving is unreliable, intermittent, or otherwise negative (e.g., rejecting, overintrusive, smothering). Infants cannot create a normal, mutually regulated, hierarchical integration with the caregiver where at times they are dominant and at other times subordinate in a reciprocal balance of play. Emotions that emerge involve fear, sadness, crankiness, and the like.
8. *Sociability vs. unsociability acts*	A lack of sociability pervades social intercourse with the caregiver, family, strangers. Insecurity in the attachment relationship solidifies in either an anxious avoidant or anxious ambivalent-resistant (mixed) fashion (Bowlby, 1980). Infants do not share with caregivers sitting as a secure base, fail to adapt to their departure, ignore them, or are ambivalent on their return, and are not optimally interactive or are negative with strangers. Thus, we see emotions such as worry, dislike, aggressive displacement, and displacement escape.
9. *Autonomy vs. doubt acts*	A sense of autonomy is stifled, for toddlers develop pervading, overly dependent behavior, doubt, hesitation, inertia, or lack of self-confidence. Deliberate trial-and-error exploring becomes chaotic, trying, erroneous, imploring (dependency), flat in affect, or with exaggerated fear. Dependent behavior brings with it emotions such as jealousy, greed, and defiance.
10. *Interdigitational vs. dedigitational acts*	Mutuality in play is impossible, for young children cannot partake in prolonged, reciprocal, peaceful exchanges, have no facility in entering smoothly such social relations, and are either too overpowering/possessive or too submissive/subjugated when participating in them. Thus, give-and-take social behavior may be avoided. Children evaluate others with contempt, not appreciation, and evalute themselves with the same and a sense of rejection, not pride.

continue to be problematic even when the individual is involved in higher level functioning.

The model that has been developed incorporates the work of Erikson on the crises in development which correspond to his eight developmental levels, but of course adds 17 more. Moreover, although the current concep-

Table P.5. Dangers in Development in the Perioperational Substages

Level	Danger and opposition in substage
11. *Superordinate vs. discoordinate acts*	Disjointed, inappropriately juxtaposed oppositions in social behavior manifest. Children seem incoherent, fragmented, and without refined social skills. Language does not fit context, actions mismatch intentions, and emotions improperly contrast. This may be evident (in different ways) both over long stretches and neighboring behaviors. The normal egocentrism of children is inappropriate or compromised, for the "ego" is dispersed or fractionated.
12. *Initiative vs. guilt acts*	Initiative is damped by (familial) conflict deriving from too intrusive impositions or fantasies. This may even result in the Oedipus conflict. The nascent superego is saturated with guilt related to repressed wishes. Adoption of the same-sex parental identity in a nonvolatile manner is affected.
13. *Identification vs. problematic identification acts*	Identification with the primary characteristics of the parents is undermined, for the process may be limited to frontal negative attributes (e.g., anger, rejection, confused signals) or dismissed, producing a frontal negativity (aggressivity, advoidance, depression). This attitude may carry over into peer- and school-related activity (e.g., disobeying parental wishes, compensatory overinclusion of negative peer models in behavior, resistance, underachievement in schooling). Self-devaluation is seeded.
14. *Industry vs. inferiority acts*	The problems above are magnified, resulting in a sense of rebelliousness, inferiority, or inadequacy. Chains of fight and/or flight become linked in children's minds, overwhelming their ego's image of itself. A propensity to overcontrol may develop as a defense mechanism, leading to exploitation, manipulation, deception, and the like.
15. *Role vs. role confusion acts*	The social roles imagined in the context of family, friends, school, and other institutions are limited and limiting. These roles are restricted ones, overreactions, compensations of lack, etc., befitting the sense of rebelliousness and/or inferiority developed previously. This emotional cauldron may produce a social (external), role-oriented individual trying to mask internal conflicts.

tion of the nature of a stage and its challenges borrows from Erikson, his theory has been modified in several ways. First, I have reduced the age range to which some of his stages apply. This facilitates their insertion into the current model. Second, the oppositions involved are presented as a dialectic of competing *acts* in order to highlight their external social con-

Table P.6. Dangers in Development in the Abstract Substages

Level	Danger and opposition in substage
16. *Conscious vs. contraconscious acts*	Young adolescents can lapse into conscious self-depreciation, a closure to freeing represeed thoughts, cynical ridicule of others and their constructive efforts, and "turning off" free thinking altogether. One reaction to this confusion may be to conform excessively, and adopt the role identifications perceived as preferred by parents, peers, and teachers.
17. *Identity vs. identity diffusion acts*	The search for identity can be subverted, postponed, meander, or lead to back alleys, as Erikson described.
18. *Nurturing vs. misnurturing acts*	Responsible adult roles cannot be envisioned. Decisions are not subjected to critical, personal standards. Social relations are more undirectional or parallel than reciprocal. Work and school activities are not future-directed and may be demeaned. Any nurturing is superficial and considered superfluous.
19. *Intimacy vs. isolation acts*	This pattern continues, but more so, for multiple adult roles may be foisted on the individual by society. Abandonment of any such roles already undertaken, or other self- and other-destructive behavior becomes possible, yielding sentiments of loneliness and isolation. Instead of a relativist, unique, yet mutual self, there is an absolute, desolate one.
20. *Universal vs. self-singular acts.*	Rather than encouraging others' development, the self implodes in self-indulgent acts, or worse.

Table P.7. Dangers in Development in the Collective Intelligence Substages

Level	Danger and opposition in substage
21. *Postmetaphysical vs. disillusionment acts*	Disillusionment with society, with groups, and with constructive activity can pervade the individual, for the notion of profiting from collective symbiosis is not entertained.
22. *Generativity vs. self-absorption acts*	Generative role models with family, at work, and in the community are sacrificed for self-absorption, a sense of emptiness, and stagnation.
23. *Catalytic vs. midlife crisis acts*	Midlife crisis develops; instead of emerging as a force in whatever collective is of concern, the adult pays the price for having skirted the collective. The confusions and changes engendered are unconscious attempts to return to prior levels through misapplied catalytic discoveries, shifts, inversions, and the like in thought.
24. *Ego integrity vs. despair acts*	Disappointment with the meaningless felt in life sets in.
25. *Cathartic vs. abandonment acts*	The elderly unwisely shut out spiritual experiences, denying any fellowship with humanity, the unknown, and infinity.

textual aspect compared to their internal psychodynamic one. Third, the particular labels that Erikson used to indicate the oppositions concern emergent characteristics that develop either optimally or nonoptimally in a variety of ways. But the particular adjective that he chose for the nonopti- mal condition can be too specific (e.g., problems in trust need not concern only mistrust). I have tried to accommodate to this concern in the descrip- tions of the 17 new oppositions created in the current model.

Conclusion

In the current theory, the 25 socioemotional systems that develop in parallel with the cognitive ones culminate in those that accompany the collective stage of intelligence in the adult. This stage concerns sym- biotically constructed sociomotions with transabstract intelligence com- plexes. Thus, the socioemotional systems that correspond to this stage of development are especially other-oriented (e.g., Erikson's stage of gener- ativity, and other levels that are cosmic, cathartic, and catalytic in a social sense as much as any other).

The dangers or crises inherent in each of the 25 steps in development are oppositions grounded in the social and not the internal world. That is, each of the 25 steps in development of the synthetic theory are thought to offer the developing individual socioemotional challenges in how to grow toward and into the other. Both the self and other are constructed in the meeting ground between the developing individual and the other through the opportunities that new potentials in growth offer.

PART I

INTRODUCTION

CHAPTER 1

Overview

SYNTHESES

The current work builds on a neopiagetian model of cognitive development across the lifespan consisting of 25 steps, as described in the Prologue. A dominant theme linking all others in the current work is that human development is postmodern in its core, e.g., in its adult collective intelligence stage, its coappropriation transition mechanism, its coconstructive, narrative therapeutic approach, its lévinasian philosophy of responsibility for the other, its constructs of Relational Meaning Worlds, "the IWEMEUS," and comemes, and its heterological epistemology.

The integrated nature of the theory also is reflected in several specific models that I created based on it, e.g., on the cognitive (mis)perception of the other (see Table 7.1). In this model, it is hypothesized that in parallel with the 25 general developmental levels that are described, 25 steps evolve in the way others (including one's children or partner) are perceived or misperceived by each developing self (or larger unit such as society). These perceptions lead to particular behaviors associated with them (e.g., if a child is seen as at best reflexive in nature, child abuse is potentiated), which in turn elicit predictable reactions.

Also, the theory reveals itself as synthetic in its major model of the transition mechanism in development. This function, called coappropriation, borrows the vygotskian notion of internalization–appropriation and marries it with the piagetian one of equilibration. It emphasizes the mutual coconstruction of cognitive coschemes that takes place with adequate social buffering.

Furthermore, the synthetic nature of the current work is indicated in its approach to therapy. The transition therapy approach that I have adopted expands Michael White's concept of postmodern narrative therapy (agency internalization/problem externalization) to include a diachronic, developmental perspective. In particular, for each of the 25 steps of the current theory, appropriate agency-internalizing and problem-externalizing story themes have been created so that the specific developmental substages that are the locus of client's difficulties can be addressed directly.

Finally, the synthetic nature of the current work is indicated by the diverse range of issues to which it has been applied beyond those already mentioned (e.g., story telling, censorship, the unconscious, possible interspecies intelligences).

CHAPTER SUMMARIES

In the following summary of the book's chapters, I will underscore both the nature of the theory being proposed and its relationship to other workers-models in the field.

In Chapter 1, after an outline of the book (above) and chapter summaries (below), comments are provided. The synthetic nature of the model being proposed is emphasized, and its contributions are highlighted. At the general level, the integrative postmodern foundation of the book is underscored, and at the specific level its models of adult thought, psychotherapy, the cognitive (mis)perception of the other, and the coappropriation transition process are considered significant.

In the first part of Chapter 2, the approach of postmodernism and its applicability to psychology are discussed. First, modernism and its totalizing nature is described. Then, postmodernism is examined, in particular, its deconstructive, analytic side and its constructive, affirmative side. In essence, postmodernism seeks to parse truths depicted as unitary into its underlying assumptions, and constituent situated verities (primary and hidden narratives), and speaks to our intrinsic other-sensitivity. It is argued that the postmodern approach is not antithetical to the current stage-oriented one on the nature of human development. That is, even if I describe one sequence of universal steps in the developmental process, they are seen to form a scaffold on which individual differences can be woven, they culminate in an adult mind that thinks in a postmodern fashion, and they reflect postmodernism's ultimate imperative toward moderate foundationalism, or universalism with contextualism.

This leads to a discussion of Lévinas's profound philosophy of responsibility for the other. The current theory is considered complementary to Lévinas's, for it is seen to provide a description of the developmental pathway that unfolds into the dwelling in alterity that characterizes the mature, moral adult of Lévinas.

In the second part of the chapter, Kegan's (1994) postmodern model of adult development is described in detail. It is neopiagetian like the current one. Six stages in development across the lifespan are described, with the last three called the traditional, modern, and postmodern stages. The richness of his descriptions of the last three stages, in particular, is outstanding. However, in contrast to the current theory, Kegan does not consider the collective nature of adult thought, does not include substages within stages, and errs in his labels for the stages. That is, his modern stage reads like a postmodern one, so that the last three stages should have been termed *modern, early postmodern*, and *late postmodern*, or the like.

In the first part of Chapter 3, competing theories of adult development are presented and compared with the current one, and the latter's implications for self development are examined. In particular, the 25-step developmental model is expanded to include parallels in self development across the lifespan. The 25-level model of self development derived from the theory incorporates the work of Loevinger (1976, 1987, 1993, 1994), Selman (1980), and Sroufe (1990), for infants, children-adolescents, and adolescents-adults, respectively. In a related extension of the current model to the question of self development, self-efficacy (introduced by Bandura, e.g., 1989) is examined in terms of the way it may develop in line with the cognitive substages of the model.

In Chapter 4 the model of parenting or family development that issues from an extension of the 25-step model of development is presented. It describes the stance that a family should adopt in order to foster optimal development in light of the developing person's corresponding cognitive and socioemotional development. Other theorists on the family lifecycle (e.g., Carter & McGoldrick, 1989; Wapner, 1993) present fewer steps, are too milestone-oriented, and/or do not start from the developing individual's perspective, in particular, unlike the case here. Also, a model on the development of the marital cycle that is derived from the current synthetic model of development is presented as a complement to the one on family development, with its five stages involving attraction, attachment, commitment, growth, and mutuality.

The chapter concludes with some applied issues. The steps in development of the self and the family that are presented may have import for understanding the way the normal developmental pathway can go awry.

In Chapter 5, after introducing the concepts of coconstructivism, culture, and environmental structure (Bronfenbrenner, 1993a, 1993b), Vygotsky's sociocultural model of cognitive development is described in depth. Topics include the genetic or historical analysis of developing behavior; the genetic law, which underscores the sociocultural base of developing behavior; the zone of proximal development, concerning the scaffolding that adults and culture provides the developing individual; higher mental function, the product of the developmental process; and mediating devices, especially that of language; and internalization, which permits the transformation of sociocultural material. Following Vygotsky, I emphasize the mutuality of the developing individual and the sociocultural milieu in fostering development in individual ways in the movement from the intermental to the intramental plane.

Contemporary elaborations of vygotskian theory are reviewed. These include the work of Wertsch (1991, 1993, 1994a, 1994b, 1995a, 1995b, 1995c) on sociocultural influences in development and on the multivoicedness of mind; Rogoff (1990, 1992, 1993, 1994, 1995) and Granott (1993) on interactional learning situations, e.g., apprenticeship, guided participation, imitation, mutual collaboration; Sigel (1993) on distancing, Moss (1992) on affect, and Saxe (1991, 1994) on practice participation; and Rogoff on internalization and the related concept of appropriation.

An ongoing study with children is described which speaks to Vygotsky's model. In a study of storytelling in children and their mothers, it was found that the cognitive complexity of the mothers' stories was negatively correlated with that of their child. This result could be interpreted in several ways, but one interesting possibility is that the more the mothers restrained themselves from giving too complex stories, the more their child could give an optimally complex one in his or her turn. Thus, the results of the study speak to Moss's (1992) concept of the zone of inhibited development, and the current emphasis on the role of activation/inhibition coordination in development.

A section on information processing is included in the chapter as well as one on intersubjectivity. The former section helps clarify the process of internalization and appropriation. The latter introduces the work of Clinchy and Belenky, in particular. They describe women's epistemological positions in understanding truth, knowledge, their acquisition, and their sources (Belenky, Clinchy, Goldberger, & Tartule, 1986; Clinchy, 1993). Five epistemological positions or women's ways of knowing are outlined, and they are seen to form a developmental series—silence, received knowing, subjective knowing, procedural knowing, and constructive knowing.

In conclusion, three apparent lacunae in the vygotskian approach are mentioned. Neovygotskian theory needs to consider (1) the way specific societal ideologies, values, and practices are transmitted to the child through the parents in a process of incubation if not inculcation; (2) the way neopiagetian stage theory can provide an axis on which individual differences develop through processes described by Vygotsky; and (3) the way the concept of appropriation as it is now defined only begins to address the nature of the product and the process involved in its functioning.

In Chapters 7 and 8 each of the latter three lacunae in vygotskian theory are addressed, in turn. First, in Chapter 7, I speculate that activation/inhibition coordination fractals may characterize equally the world and developing mind/brain, with equivalent fractals in the parent sphere serving as buffers between these two spheres. In this regard, a model of caregiving in terms of the (mis)perceived cognitive level of the child is elucidated (after Sameroff, e.g., Sameroff & Feil, 1985). It is hypothesized that parents differentially treat their child according to her or his perceived level of cognitive functioning (i.e., within the 25 developmental steps of the current theory). Specific reactions by the child to each perceived developmental level, including negative ones when poorly perceived, also are described. The work of Belenky and Clinchy, in particular, is incorporated in this section. Their work is noteworthy because there appears to be a one-to-one correspondence between the current model of five stages in the development of the cognitive (mis)perception of the other and their model on the development of five epistemological positions.

The current model on the cognitive (mis)perception of the other is generalized to the way adult partners may treat each other in relationships, and the way societies treat their individual members and/or subgroups. For example, if treated in a reflexive fashion by absolutist regimes, individuals in a population feel obliterated or they react with nihilism or anarchy. A sensorimotor perception of individuals by an authoritarian regime leads to either dominating sterilization or revolution. A preoperational perception of the population leads to assimilation or resistance. If perceived abstractly, the population's individuals should be able to avoid involution for evolution and proceed to develop the ultimate collective, empathic, emancipated intelligence. This sociocultural application of the current theory brings us full circle to the vygotskian concern for the constitutive construction of the child's developing mental function, for it serves to specify the variegated ways that sociocultural messages are infused into the developmental program.

The second lacuna in vygotskian theory listed in Chapter 6 and dealt with in Chapter 8 concerns the tension between universals in development and individual differences in development. In the current view, individual differences in cognitive development are considered to be intrinsic to the 25-step framework of development. This structure is seen as providing a scaffold or trunk on which different developmental webs can be woven on its branches depending on sociocultural, contextual factors (Case and Fischer have developed similar points of view, and these are presented as points of comparison).

The third vygotskian limit, also treated in Chapter 8, concerns the concept of appropriation in cognitive development. It is expanded in order to provide a powerful model of the change process in cognitive development. In terms of more specific models of transition in development, among other points of view, Piaget emphasizes the twin processes of accommodation and assimilation in equilibration, information theorists propose an array of mechanisms related to resources, mental space, etc., and vygotskians refer to internalization or appropriation of shared socio-cultural activity. My particular modification of the appropriation function specifies that the product involved is a "coscheme" because of the shared nature of cognitive development. Also, I suggest that the process involved should incorporate the piagetian notion of equilibration. Finally, I empha-size that the environment provides sociocultural buffers to protect the child's equilibrium in a potentially hostile world. In order to highlight the constitutive nature of this transition mechanism, it is labeled "coappro-priation."

To be more specific, it is hypothesized that the developing individual develops coschemes in mutuality with her or his surround by engaging in a cyclical dialectic with it. Coschemes are considered the product of the appropriation process, and they are seen to be actively applied to the environment by the developing individual, causing self-induced disequil-ibration. If sociocultural buffers in the environment act to provide the appropriate protective buffers to any negative element in the environment, then equilibration can occur, leading to coscheme (re)organization. The coappropriation process may involve a (potentially) hostile world, and so disequilibration normally is buffered by the parent, and, with develop-ment, by other sociocultural elements and eventually by the child her or himself, facilitating a return to equilibrium. However, when sociocultural buffers are inadequate or absent, for example, due to parents' poor percep-tions of the cognitive level of their child because of their own affective experiences, smooth (re)equilibration and subsequent cognitive develop-ment are compromised.

A study with adolescents which addresses these issues is summarized at the end of the chapter. The study suggests that certain scales derived from the current synthetic theory can lead to interesting results relative to comparable scales not based on it. The study is described in full in Chapter 13. Finally, recent Disney animated films are analyzed according to the current theory about the cognitive (mis)perception of the other for the type of message they send about male–female relationships.

A form of brief systemic familial therapy used by White (e.g., M. White, 1993a, 1993b, 1993c, 1994; M. White & Epston, 1990; O'Hanlon, 1994) is presented in Chapter 9. It is explicitly postmodern, coconstructive, and narrative in nature. In dealing with clients, it seeks to balance internal-ization of a narrative about a competent self and externalization of the clients' problematic behavior. The ultimate goal is to free the client toward continual transformation and sensitivity in relations. The sequence of interventive questions that is used in the internalization–externalization procedure is documented. This procedure is an example of the way activa-tion and inhibition processes can be coordinated in therapy. Parry and Doan (1994) have systematized the narrative approach to therapy espoused by White, and their work is summarized. They present 16 authoring and 12 revisioning tools for use in narrative therapy.

Recent developments in family therapy are related to a model of the classification of therapies based on two axes, one concerning the processes of activation–inhibition coordination and the other the viewpoints of constructivism and objectivism. Some of the other therapeutic positions examined in the chapter include attachment (e.g., Byng-Hall, 1995) and emotion-focused, dialectical–constructivist (e.g., Greenberg & Pascual-Leone, 1995) therapies.

I have been using a variant of White's approach in my clinical work, and it is described in Chapter 10. It is called transition therapy because of its emphasis on the continual change process in human growth. Presenting problems are considered as vicious circles of bad habits around a core of competent, caring characteristics. Moreover, the problems themselves are viewed as products of external stresses (e.g., familial, societal), in a function called second-order externalization. Thus, presenting problems are considered second-order externalizations originating in outside influences, such as past or present stresses, and are considered controllable by personal strengths and skills which have been masked but are available. Graphs are drawn placing the vicious circles in clients' behavior around a list of client-generated positive attributes and resources which can be brought to bear in controlling and going beyond presenting problems. The graphs function as visual aids in the coconstruction with the clients of alternative narratives, beginning with the minority of times that their primary narratives did not dominate them but were controlled.

The developmental aspect of the therapeutic approach that I employ addresses the lack of a diachronic perspective in White's approach to therapy. That is, in maneuvering during the agency internalization/problem externalization process, I may attempt to show for several appropriate steps of the 25 steps of the current synthetic model of development the extent to which the positive stories that are associated with them have emerged or are struggling to emerge relative to any negative, dominant old stories. Specifically, appropriate agency-internalizing and problem-externalizing story themes have been created for each of the 25 developmental substages of the current model, and the most relevant ones for any particular client, that may be at the origin of her or his issues, are consulted in the therapeutic encounter. (This recent innovation in the current therapeutic approach should constitute its most important contribution; see Table 10.1.)

Additional components of my therapeutic approach use sayings, a poem, and diagrams of families, again with implicit messages of internalized self-agency and externalized problematic behavior.

Chapter 11 examines epistemological stances, and explains the coexistential one advocated in the current theory. It analyzes each of six different approaches in the constructivist school (radical constructivism, critical constructivism, existentialism, efficient constructivism, social constructivism, and coconstructivism). I organize the schools according to a two-dimensional model, relating to whether empirical and social considerations enter into the constructive equation. It is argued that in order to understand the process of knowledge acquisition, all six schools need to be seen as complementary. Lyddon (1995) independently came to the same conclusion with respect to four of the schools. Thus, the label *synthetic* has been applied to both the ontological and epistemological pursuits of the current theory, adding to its sense of parsimony. The schools are seen as reflections of the ethos of being-becoming-world/world-becoming-being, where Lévinas's concept of responsibility for the other, or in my terms, "world love" and "world work," are considered the hallmark of mature adult psychology.

The first part of Chapter 12 deals with elaborations and speculations based on the proposed model of five stages in development, I suggest that it can be applied to a wide spectrum of areas (e.g., personality development; censorship; institutions; the biological approach to mate selection; the nature of reproductive strategies). The model that has been developed for the latter examples concerns the way five different evolutionary pressures (natural individual-level selection, kin selection, selection of group for individual behavior, reciprocal altruism, group selection) have molded the five stages of development in the current theory and their parallel reproductive parental strategies. Also, I speculate upon the nature of the development of intelligence in the future when the lifespan will be significantly longer than that of today.

It is suggested that the proper study of psychology concerns fractal generation and propagation in behavior, a process labeled "fractalization." Codevelopmental fractalization would refer to this process as it applies to the particular domain of development. The concepts of group selection, emergenesis, and complexity speak to the possibility that complex behaviors such as collective intelligence behaviors are emergent properties of the human gene pool, and lead toward Gaialike behavior.

One manner in which the diverse conceptions of the current theory can be integrated is through the construct of Relational Meaning Worlds. They can be defined as individual or (sub)collective emergent emotional–cognitive integrations of socially-constructed realities. They are constituted by comemes, or collective emotional–cognitive meaning units, which influence but also are influenced by individuals. Comemes vary in developmental complexity and maturity, and they are very powerful mediational devices in the cocreation of reality. They vehicle cognitive (mis)-perceptions of the other from individual and collective to individual and collective. It behooves us as individuals and collectives to optimize comeme development.

The second part of the chapter offers a summary of and conclusions about postmodernism. The nature of adult thought from the postmodern perspective is described. Also, postmodern therapy is examined in terms of *multiplicity man*, a client for whom I was consulted.

In Chapter 13, a scale on the cognitive complexity of narratives that was derived from the current 25-step developmental theory is used to analyze the quality of thought of a sample of adolescents who were asked to reason about political topics with their mothers. Also, the model of the cognitive (mis)perception of the other derived from the current theory was used to create a scale of discourse support which is applied to the dialogue between the adolescents and their mothers. The transcripts that were analyzed were taken from a project that had already been published, but with certain predictions not confirmed (Santolupo & Pratt, 1994). Thus, the goal of the reanalysis was to show that the current synthetic model of development can lead to effective tools that can be applied to relevant data.

Results of the application of the two scales derived from the current theory to the dialogue study appear promising. For example, the cognitive complexity score of the adolescents' discourse was positively correlated with their age–education level and with their score on a related measure of discourse complexity. Also, the mothers' cognitive complexity score was positively correlated with their score on the discourse quality scale. One result showed that the mothers seem to set up a zone of inhibition development; the less they gave support to their adolescents in the dialogue, the more the adolescents showed cognitive complexity in their reasoning. Thus, the cognitive complexity scale and the discourse support scale derived from the current theory give results that suggest that it has face validity.

The postscript in Chapter 14 reviews the most recent literature on the major themes covered in the book. There are sections on postmodernism, adult development, culture, therapy, philosophy, and a model on the development of cultural identity. The section on postmodernism highlights the need for a moderate foundationalism respective of experienced reality. The section on adult development examines the validity of stage theories and their contextualist counterparts. In the culture section, the role of the individual and community in identity development and social organization are discussed. I describe, in particular, Etzioni's (1996) moderate communitarian model that the I&WE is the basic social unit. The philosophy section presents two views on whether Lévinas's concept of the individual's unconditional responsibility for the other speaks to a practiced everyday morality. In terms of psychotherapy, postmodern therapy is shown to be both growing yet criticized. As for my personal contributions,

Table 1.1. Summary of Key Contributions of the Synthetic Theory: Structure

Area	Contribution
Levels	5 stages (reflexive, sensorimotor, perioperational, abstract, collective intelligence) × 5 substages (coordination, hierarchization, systematization, multiplication, integration; and perhaps × 4 sublevels; initiation, application, maturation, transition, with the latter in two phases) = 25 substages and up to 100–125 levels in development
Applied to	In particular, the stages describe developmental progressions in cognition and language (e.g., storytelling), on the one hand, and socioemotions, on the other hand. The socioemotional parallel refers to the 25 socioemotional systems structured around three dimensions of appraisal related to goal compatibility (positive, negative), activity-reactivity, and context (figure-ground, Young, submitted). But the parallels range across diverse domains (this volume), e.g., self, family, parenting strategies, couples, personality, the unconscious, institutions, censorship. For example, 5 stages in the evolution of adult relationships are seen to develop as reflections of the 5 general developmental stages; they are attraction, attachment, commitment, growth, and mutuality
Stage	The fifth stage of collective intelligence is defined as involving a cognitive–emotional symbiotic fusion, where the individual contributes to and takes from communal interaction, e.g., in brainstorming, especially in terms of forming superordinate metasystemic principles. It is seen as a postmodern intelligence
Underpinnings	Each substage has neurological and phylogenetic bases. Moreover, each stage is shown to have evolved through a particular evolutionary pressure. These pressures also were seen to be associated with specific parenting styles: Reflexive stage = style of physical parenting, early reptilian in origin, due to natural selection; Sensorimotor stage = attachment–promotion parenting, early mammalian, due to evolutionary pressure of kin selection; Perioperational stage = educational parenting, early ape, group for individual level of pressure; Abstract stage = parenting to promote immediate community linkage, *Homo sapiens sapiens*, due to reciprocal altruism; Collective intelligence stage = parenting to promote wider community linkage, contemporary humans, due to group selection
Individual differences	A quantum model of development permits individual differences on the universal scaffold provided by the 25-step model of development
Scales	Two scales derived from the 25-step model of development created for discourse contexts. One examines the degree of cognitive complexity of texts, whereas the other looks at the degree of social support that is offered by others in producing texts (e.g., mothers of children). Two studies are described which support the empirical value of the scales and the face validity of the theory

I elaborate a model of cultural identity development based on Etzioni (1996). Essentially, I add the subjective me and us to his objective I and we, leading to the concept of the IWEMEUS. Also, I show how the scale of the cognitive (mis)perception of the other can be applied to politicians' speech within the dialogue that they engage us. It is shown how they act to modulate the development of our cultural identities toward their political goals. Finally, a metaphorical description of postmodern therapy is offered for client use.

CONCLUSION

The current synthetic theory of development aims to make a significant contribution to adult development and therapy, in particular, and to

Table 1.2. Summary of Key Contributions of the Synthetic Theory: Transition Processes

Area	Contribution
Neopiagetian	*Cognitive control units*: Mechanisms such as schemata, schemes, operations. One per substage = 25 in all
Neoeriksonian	*Psychosocial affectivity*: Erikson's 8 stages are embedded in the 25-step sequence of socioemotional systems that develop in parallel with the cognitive substages. All the 25 systems are marked by eriksonian crises-challenges that influence cognitive development
Neobowlbian	*Social self-working schemata*: Internal working models, with social embeddedness emphasized (Young, submitted). Also, 25 levels of them. They carry attachment experiences into the developing individual's cognition
Neobanduran	*Self-efficacy in levels*: A sense of self-competence also develops in concert with the 25 steps, and influences cognitive development
Neosystemic	*Fractalization*: The five cyclic substages show a parallel with the five stages in which they recur. This self-similarity across different levels may mark development and psychology, in general. Complexity: Transitions across substages and levels may be frequent (up to 100) because they function as self-organizing attractors which reach controlling parameter thresholds at the "edge of chaos," or system balance of disorder and order (Young, submitted)
Neovygotskian	*Coappropriation*: In a process that includes sociocultural buffers in a potentially negative or hostile world, the developing individual internalizes sociocultural material through the equilibration of mutually derived coschemes
Activation–inhibition coordination	Underlying both of the structure and transition mechanisms in development may be a metric where activation and inhibition processes coordinate in dynamic interplay

Table 1.3. Summary of Key Contributions of the Synthetic Theory: Other Areas

Area	Contribution
Cognitive (mis)perception of the other	Each child is perceived as being capable of developing at best to one or the other of the 25 substages in development, depending on the affective lens that parents use to filter the world, which usually is based on their own parenting experiences, in a process of intergenerational transmission. Each level of (mis)perception elicits a particular reaction in the child (e.g., being raised with a misperception of being capable of functioning at the perioperational stage at best, and so open to manipulation, can lead to resistance). Adults may be perceived by their partners or their cultures in the same way (e.g., reflexive at best in a despotic regime) and manifest reactions similar to the child (e.g., revolt in this case).
Therapy	A type of activation–inhibition coordination therapy that I use is outlined in terms of internalization of agency and externalization of the problem (after Michael White). The therapy is narrative, coconstructive, and postmodern. It is labeled *transition therapy* because of its integration of the current synthetic developmental theory and its emphasis on the continual change function in human growth. Graphic representations are employed. The 25 dangers–crises–challenges in the 25 steps in development can be used in this therapy when needed. Thus, for example, externalizations in therapy are presented in terms of story themes reflective of the particular 25 developmental levels of the current theory. The five-stage model of couple development that I have developed is used in marital counseling.
Attachment	A model of 14 different qualities of caregiving and consequent attachment types is presented (Young, submitted). Links to the substages in development are discussed.
Emotions	A model of emotional development is included among the 25 socioemotional systems (Young, submitted). It argues that there are at least 48 basic emotional families organized along 4 dimensions, including one involving the 6 cognitive substages in the first 2 years of life.
Epistemology	A synthetic model of six different constructivist, postmodern schools is presented.
Universe	The adult mind develops into a collective symbiotic thought process. Postmodernism leads to a sensitive empathy for the other. It is grounded in relational mutuality, as is the vygotskian approach. Levinas speaks of a responsibility for all others. Systems theory implies the presence of a suprasystem of the individual in the cosmos. Fractals transmit patterns from one laminar structure of substance organization to the next. Quantum theory speaks of correlated states even when particles move at the speed of light in opposite directions. Gaia refers to a self-correcting planet Earth that ensures life. I describe supraindividual Relational Meaning Worlds with constituent comemes (e.g., on cultural identity, the IWEMEUS) that vibrate with living attributes and mediate human development as much as we mediate their development. The human task of becoming being in the world is world work and world love. Development is transformation toward facilitating universal developing transformation.

Table 1.3. (*Continued*)

Area	Contribution
Overall	A comprehensive, multidomain integration based upon a 25-stage theory of human development within the context of postmodern themes is described. It is a rigorous, empirically grounded theory based on the theory and work of other researchers. It has been tested in some studies, and leads to testable, falsifiable predictions in areas where I have yet to study it.

developmental psychology, in general. The specific contributions made by this book and its companion (Young, submitted) are highlighted in the accompanying tables (Tables 1.1–1.3).

ON READING THE BOOK

The hardest part for the reader will be letting go of the lenses or blinders that he or she brings to the task. If one adheres to one particular perspective in developmental psychology and therapy, this book will disappoint and deceive, for it comes with its own perspective. For example, even neopiagetians will notice that my approach does not follow the traditional theorists in the field even though it is neopiagetian in its stage conception. And the postmodern umbrella that I bring to the synthetic task is not always standard. For example, it not only deconstructs but also constructs, and it does this from relational fields that sometimes are unique and dialogical with extant perspectives.

The book is diverse in its topics and theoretical stances so that it may seem that it is lacking in coherence, but in this regard I remind the reader of its dual nature. On the one hand, it attempts to show the web of relations across its many theoretical faces so that their systemic relationship reflects an integration. On the other hand, its postmodern theme provides an overarching vision of development, and this despite the fact that there is no one version of postmodernism. Nevertheless, postmodernism by definition asks us not to seek one source from which all answers flow. It accepts a dynamic tension across multiple perspectives on truth, and knows that better forms of truth lie in the emergence beyond such tension. I hope the current theory will help render the equilibration of this tension a more graceful, less turbulent process. In conclusion, I believe that the current book poses more challenges than it resolves, and merits more criticisms for its limits than compliments for its successes, but nevertheless raises and speaks to fundamental issues in the study of human development and therapy.

CHAPTER 2

The Postmodern Adult

POSTMODERNISM AND
THE SYNTHETIC THEORY

Modernism

Modernism is a perspective on humans and their world that reached its zenith at the beginning of the current century. (For recent understandings of postmodernism, see Brewster Smith, 1994, 1995; C. T. Fischer, 1992; K. Gergen, 1994a, 1994b, 1995; M. Gergen, 1995; Gülerce, 1995a, 1995b; Kegan, 1994; Kvale, 1992; Misra, 1993; Neimeyer, Neimeyer, Lyddon, and Hoshmand, 1994; Neimeyer and Mahoney, 1995; Packer, 1992; Parry, 1993; Russell and Gaubatz, 1995; D. White and Wang, 1995; for specialized postmodern topics in psychology, see Danziger, 1991 and the book series edited by K. Gergen that is reviewed in Neimeyer et al., 1994.)

Modernism prescribed unified, monological, specifying, "ultimate" truths through religions, political belief systems, and other hegemonies or colonizing instruments, and through the sociocultural and artistic institutions that mirrored and served them. Thus, in terms of the individual's development in the modern climate, the self (e.g., the freudian ego) became the pantheon of cultural concerns; it could be known because the world was considered inevitably knowable and it became the locus of will, choice, gratification, and so on. Ultimately, this led to an exclusion of the self from others, in the sense of not acknowledging them and not joining with them for mutual growth, but rather recognizing their overwhelming collective power in controlling the self (via powerful others and their ideologies).

Postmodernism

In midcentury, after the Second World War and the Holocaust, the fallacies of modernism could no longer support its weight. In its place has developed the perspective of postmodernism (or late modernism; Brewster Smith, 1994; or *postmodernity*, a term which is more general in focus compared to the term *postmodernism*; but the latter one is used more often in the psychological literature). In the next section, the tenets of post-modernism are explored.

I have encountered resistance to the term itself, which probably dis-colors people's perception of it. However, I believe the term is here to stay so I will continue to employ it. Its prefix is both its weakness and its strength. On the one hand, it (and similar terms such as deconstruction-ism) implies that it is defined solely in terms of a reaction against modern-ism and that it does not have its own unchanging basic assumptions and postulates. The strength of the term *postmodernism*, however, is this very absence of set characteristics, its continually changing nature, and its ever-increasing refinement and nuanced sensitivity to the human condition.

Postmodernism and the Arts

Postmodernism has its origins in the artistic domain, and it is beyond the scope of the current work to examine that origin (see Gergen, 1994a, 1994b; Parry, 1993; Trachtenberg, 1995). Below, the contemporary novels of Thomas Pynchon are examined from a postmodern perspective. In the current section, the recent short stories of Grace Paley (in Aarons, 1995) are described for their postmodern turn. They are particularly salient for the therapeutic approach that I describe later in the book because of their emphasis on the changing and changeable nature of stories that authors and narrators, and thus also clients, can tell.

In general, postmodern literature is reflexive, indeterminate, elastic, fluid, multioptional, fragmented, context-mediated, epistemically humble instead of arrogant, and ambiguous in temporality and structure. In Paley, in particular, this unconventionalism takes the form of battles among author, narrator, and other characters for authorial control in a "rhetoric of voices." For example, the narrator may say, "I want to go on with the story ...," "I like your paragraphs ...," or "I see you can't tell a plain story." As Paley's characters tell stories, they continually self-invent from within their sociopolitical community and their relations with each other, for they do not emerge from some linear story line (e.g., one character says, "I want ... to be a different person." "There is thus in Paley's fiction a constant building up of interpretive possibilities, as characters become the processes they tell" (Aarons, 1995, p. 204). There is no controlling metanarrative, but only a storytelling process where stories give way to one another without traditional boundaries. The subject of the story is its telling, and it acts to make options beckon, invite, and ultimately concretize in life at least in part (e.g., "She could be a hundred different things ..."; "[E]very one, real or invented, deserves the open destiny of life"; or "Reality? A lesson in reality? Am I a cabdriver? No. I drive a cab but I am not a cabdriver.").

Postmodernism and Psychology

Gergen (1994a, 1994b) describes postmodernism well as presented in psychology. He characterizes postmodernism as relational rather than representational in that truths, realities, and knowledges are heterogenous, interpreted, local, situated, provisional, and political. Postmodernism is a contextual, nonfoundational paradigmatic approach derived from Wittgenstein's philosophical perspective that language obtains its meaning through its application in social and cultural practice rather than through a referential basis. Thus, for postmodernism humans need to adopt a reflexive or reflective stance toward language, or become aware of its potentially (modernistic) totalizing, moralizing, truth-creating, and divisive nature. For example, a postmodernist would ask who profits from the current epidemic in the diagnosis of the psychiatric label of "depression" and the recent boom in the prescription for it of the psychiatric drug Prozac? Thus, postmodernism objects to homogenous theories because the world is heterogenous. It is oversimplifying and even dangerous to reduce "the blurred variety of things to misleading singularities and dominating centers" (Fairlamb, 1994, p. 246). In this atmosphere, the marginalized perspective is centered, ground becomes figure, muffled constructs obtain voice, and oppressed, disqualified knowledges are rewritten into consciousness.

Frosh (1995) explains well the reason why postmodernism is not representational. In its disavowal of the subject–object dichotomy which permits the reification of perceived reality as absolute truth, postmodernism implies that there is no distance between reader and text, or self and other. Thus, texts are penetrated, not symbolized, and the real, exciting lived moment is when attempts at symbolization become impossible in genuine relatedness with text.

According to Gergen, postmodernism does not have one face, and it is evolving itself. On the one hand, it has a deconstructive, skeptical, or negative side, where suffocating modernism is demythified so that the individual can be liberated from its constricting tenets. Thus, truth is perceived as shifting, fragmentary, and without foundation. Consequently, the self, as it is deconstructed in postmodernism, no longer can be characterized as having a sense of certain freedom, agency, will, and inner coherence. Instead, when the contemporary self is examined, multiple, polyform, polyvocal, dispersed, and fragmented entities, and decentered inner fixation or inertia is evident, with the result that personal control is abdicated in favor of control by corporate, political, and media conglomerates. As for the self's conception of the other, as deconstructed in postmodernism, in contemporary society there appears to be a preoccupation with the internal, which can lead to a neglect of the external, which includes the other, and thus it can lead to spiritual bankruptcy.

On the other hand, postmodernism has a constructive, reconstructive, affirmative, or positive component, where truth is respected for its inherent uncertainty, ambiguity, diversity, and complexity. It is seen as embedded, contingent, contextual, pragmatic, interpreted, and re-presented. That is, it is considered locally constructed, open-ended, changing, and practiced in communal context in a web of background assumptions, circumstances, motivations, oppressions, invitations, and possibilities. This opens truth construction to continual wonderment. In this forum, the individual is seen as the composer of her or his own particular utilitarian, pragmatic story. Thus, in this constructive sense of postmodernism, the self becomes multiple, continuously redefined in situated linguistic and historicopolitical, sociocultural practices, and potentially the source of a profound respect for the other, the disenfranchised, and the marginalized, and of activist actions to promote justice and redress modern ills.

Finally, affirmative postmodernism does not reject outright the possibility of increasing complexity, differentiation, novelty, emergence, integration, and organization in development, despite its antiuniversal stance. That is, it can conceive of increased order, direction, and nonclosed cycles (spirals) in development (Organic Arrows in time) (Overton, 1994a, pp. 226–227). This supports my primary contention that neopiagetian stage theory in development offers a valid theoretical framework, and leads to the development of an adult stage that is at once postformal, collective, and postmodern.

Beyond this juxtaposition of skeptical and affirmative meanings in postmodernism, there is a proliferation of related and synonymous terms that are used to describe and characterize it. For example, it has been or can be construed as constitutive, narrativist, rhetorical, semiotic, contextualist, relativist, perspectivist, pragmatic, nonessentialist, nonfoundational, nonabsolutist, antiparticularist, antirepresentational, nontechnical, humanistic, hermeneutical, interpretationist, discursive, dispersive, dialogical, and dialectical. It has many aspects, just as the individual it describes is modular or multiple in level, texture, voice, relations, connections, separateness, self, and mind.

M. White (1993a, 1993b, 1993c) captures well the constructionist turn in postmodernism in his concept of constitutionalism, where truths are "negotiated over time within contexts of communities" and "are not representations or reflections of life as lived, but are directly constitutive of life" and "do not correspond with the world, but have real effects in the shaping of life" (M. White, 1993b, pp. 124–125). Overton (1994a, 1994b) also describes the interpretationism implicit in postmodern thought. He highlights the vehicular role of metaphor in the process of the constitution of knowledge. It is seen to continually embody, enact, form, and inhabit knowledge and the process of its construction in the dialogical web that is mind.

Heterological Epistemology

Fairlamb (1994) argues that postmodernism may be creating its own hegemony in rejecting and not accommodating to modernism. That is, postmodernism's contest of universalisms in "interpretive communities" is mediated in the social matrix of language from which it springs, and it can be ruthlessly totalizing in its rejection of objectivist, foundationalist thought. To deeply defend localism and to rail against generalities, which are postmodern preoccupations, are themselves dogmatic activities. Fairlamb claims that certain objective realities, such as in science, transcend historical and cultural borders so that one must adopt a "heterological" epistemology involving constraints on meaning creation. This does not mean that there are no hermeneutical, contextualist practices which locally transform universal rationality into contingent, situated outcomes. Rather, the givens of objectivity provide necessary constraints on which interpretations must be built. Thus, for example, he argues against literary critics who believe that in working with *Hamlet*, they do not merely improve it, they create it because each individual has her or his own *Hamlet*. As he states, "[T]he mind is not its own place."

Fairlamb guides us through the Habermas–Gadamer debate on modernism (universalism) versus postmodernism (hermeneuticism), reminding us at first that to some extent there are blends inherent in their points of view. For Habermas, there are necessary, nonarbitrary, formal, rational, critical, specifiable, but pragmatic preconditions, constraints, or grounds for understanding that transcend hermeneutic questionability and openness or the "linguistic enclosure of truth." For Gadamer, "the only critical force that can be intelligible is that within the horizon of understanding" (Fairlamb, 1994, pp. 113–114). "[T]he essence of the question is the opening up, and keeping open, of possibilities" (Gadamer, 1988, p. 266). Coherent understanding is derived from the experiential movement of concentric circles of interpretation guided by a vision of the whole. "There is always a world already interpreted ... into which our experience steps" (Gadamer, 1976, p. 15).

However, for Fairlamb, Gadamer inadvertently adopts a form of critical transcendence through his invariant constraint that there is a "perpetual possibility of questionability." If the reductionism inherent in abstraction is moderated by practical, situated contingencies in a "semiotic formalization of the thought process," then it poses no totalizing danger. And for Fairlamb, Habermas's assertion that formal conditions exist and can be discovered in a given objective domain does not take into account that there are multiple overlapping domains. "[T]here may be a tension between multiple universalities within the same context that impinge on the absoluteness of each" (Fairlamb, 1994, pp. 213–214). The two opposing points of view are not intransigent, mutually exclusive antinomies but dwell inside each other or "intermediate" each other. Objective generalities on possibility can coexist with particular indeterminate interpretations in (historical) context. They constitutively comerge to create new significations in meaning in a dialectic of the general and the particular. Similarly, according to Harré (1995), Wittgenstein called for a "moderate foundationalism." Ultimately, to describe the intermediating process in critical inquiry, Fairlamb (1994) uses, perhaps without realizing it, the language of dynamical systems theory. He describes the manner in which "the whole has its own reality" created in a relational process ("[P]atterns ... have their own systemic–causal force—an objective reality", p. 259).

Fairlamb's account of heterology presages some of the themes that mark the current work. I agree with him that the contextualization of generalizations in combination with the generalization of contextualizations form the bedrock of the critical process. One inheres in the other, as necessary conditions for their reciprocal emancipation from the inchoate. The ultimate postmodernism is one that is sensitive to the modern roots from which it derives.

In this regard, there is no contradiction when in the present work I argue that there can be a universal normative trajectory in development consisting of 25 steps, and that they culminate in adult postmodern, postformal collective thought. Through a universal program develops a mind that comes to question universality but without abandoning it for the morass of pure deconstructed contextualization. This philosophical stance of emergent contextualized universalism imbues other portions of the current work, as well. In Chapter 6, mutuality and intersubjectivity in human relationships are defined in these terms. Also, in Chapter 10, various constructivist schools of epistemology are perceived in a coexistential manner.

Postmodernism as Narrativism

Parry and Doan (1994) have written an important book on postmodern therapy, and emphasize the emergence of meanings that can be generated by story revisions. They were inspired by Michael White, "who has finally brought family therapy into the postmodern world," as will be shown in Chapter 9. They contend that the plurivocity of a person's or a culture's stories stand in contrast to the grand or metanarratives that are imposed on storytellers. Stories shape meaning in listeners and tellers, and so come to be believed as true; it is not that they are meaningful because they are true. Living outside shared stories invites disconnection, incoherence, and uncertainty. Inhabiting a story landscape without the crux of one "true" guiding narrative lets one perceive that any one story becomes but one possibility. Thus, new stories may be created to provide the meaning, direction, and intentionality necessary to life. But the delegitimization or destroying of universal metanarratives in our postmodern times has brought with it its own dangers. Without the salve of given truth, many adults and clients are in *story shock*, if I may coin a term. The postmodern therapist must help clients take back the narrator role so that they become characters in their own rather than in others' stories. People should be custodians of their own stories, and there should never be only one dominant, tyrannical version with others hidden behind it censored into oblivion. When there is an intentional identification with a multivocal narrative thread, the stories involved offer direct, interpretive mediating codes for living. "A story told by a person in his/her own words of his/her own experience does not have to plead its legitimacy in any higher court of narrative appeal, because no narrative has any greater legitimacy than the person's own" (pp. 26–27).

If this perspective is valid for any one individual, then each individual should realize its validity for all other persons. Thus, if an individual seems bound to one dominant misreading of life, then the appropriate approach is not correction but compassion. Psychological growth is potentiated by an attitude such as this. We participate inescapably in each other's stories. "As each person expands that sense of participation to embrace all life—that is to say, every being capable of suffering—each can develop her/his own metanarrative" (p. 30). Given the development of this type of metanarrative, inevitably responsibility toward the other is called forth. Parry and Doan cite the philosopher Emmanuel Lévinas, in particular, in this regard. He argues that throughout the history of Western philosophy, the other has been demeaned in comparison to the self. However, for Lévinas, the ethical relationship of an individual to the mystery of the other constitutes the foundation of the self and precedes in development the acquisition of the self.

Lévinas's Philosophy of the Other

Closer reading of Lévinas reveals a splendid philosophy (Hand, 1989; Poirié, 1987; Rosmarin, 1991). Out of the anonymous, impersonal, and horribly neutral *there is* ("il y a"), we subjects are born to oppose it, to go beyond. We are born into an eternal responsibility for the other, for otherness, for alterity, even before we acquire liberty, and are responsible for the other's peace, mistakes, suffering, and death even before our own. In this regard, Lévinas often would quote from Dostoevsky's *The Brothers Karamazov*, "We are all responsible for everyone else—but I am more responsible than all the others." He also would cite a Jewish commentary about the "responsibility of responsibility."

Language mediates proximity to the other, who is infinity, unicity. Thus, face, which is the manner by which we present to the other, and the other to us, signifies infinity, is not totality. In the primordial encounter with the face of the other, especially as stranger, lies our moral existence. Face is obligation, signification, precondition for our moral responsibility for other; responsibility is the "essential, primary, and fundamental structure of subjectivity" (Lévinas, 1985, p. 95, in M. Freeman, 1995). There is a multiplicity in being which refuses to totalize the other, and see each other as normative. Thus, there is infinity in the other and in our endless obligation to the other. In this sense, for example, Lévinas speaks to postmodernism.

The for-the-other ("le pour-l'autre") is an irreplaceable, asymmetric responsibility to which we were elected without giving consent, to which we are forever hostage without respite, without reward, from which derives the will to substitute for the other in her or his misery, and so which leads to suffering for and even by the other. Suffering for the unjustifiable suffering of the other is just. Love is a gathering, a gift, an expression of we-all rather than we-two; it is living with the other as other, where the other is seen as an other for others ("autre pour les autres"). Justice derives from the injustice of servitude to the other. Equality in everything is borne by our inequality, by the excess of our helping obligations. We have political responsibilities that derive from this ethic, and if society would apply it in full, then society would be transformed into a community. In this perspective, God is a revelation, the absolute alterity in the sanctity of unconditional, endless, unfulfillable other-responsibility.

Lévinas and Postmodernism

Is Lévinas arguing that self-abnegation and self-sacrifice lie at the heart of the human condition? I think not, for goodness and abnegation precede self in Lévinas's philosophy and, moreover, the ultimate hope an other-responsible self can have for others receiving from the self is that in their turn they develop to be capable of becoming fully responsible for others. In each other's alterity inhabits a potential sensitivity to all others. Also, self-affirmation and limit-setting are the natural accompaniments to affection and attachment in good parenting or shepherding, and at times this requires not self-sacrifice but the demand on the other to perform in a particular, limited manner for her or his own long-term benefit.

Lévinas valorizes the I-for-the-other, and at one level this concept seems similar to Buber's (1970) conception of the I–Thou authentic relationship. However, there are several differences between these two perspectives. First, Buber describes the fullness derived in genuine sharing between persons, whereas Lévinas describes an asymmetric type of self-giving to the other. Second, Buber's Thou may be singular but Lévinas's never is, for one act of helping the other always implies the necessity of more, and any one other is meant to be an other for all others.

Is Lévinas's concept of responsible-for-other comparable to Heidegger's construct of "Dasein" (being-in-the-world), which denotes "the openness of existence to being and its meaning, that is, to the being and meaning of all encountered phenomena" (Dallmayr, 1993, p. 238)? For Heidegger, Dasein can be self-reflexive (it can choose itself) despite its attribute of concernfulness, and it involves a relationship of being to the other which includes, in part, a responsibility for the other, but it is not a responsibility for the other, per se. Thus, Lévinas's concept of human nature is more othercentric than Heidegger's. It is based on a forgetfulness of the self, rather than on the celebration of its being.

If humans are born with a preoriginal responsibility for the other, the question becomes how that responsibility is lost through developmental time. Here is where the current theory meets Lévinas's work, where it becomes responsible for it as other. On the one hand, it describes the steps in the development toward the postmodern mind, which includes this very morality of responsibility for the other. On the other hand, it describes the manner in which full developmental potential may be subverted by inappropriate, limited cognitive misperceptions of the other that parents and culture bring to the task of raising and educating children.

Rosmarin (1991) describes the manner in which the sense of responsibility for the other develops in the individual according to Lévinas. In this developmental pathway, there is no mention of the child or adolescent, for it is seen as an adult phenomenon. The first step out of living life in the horror of the nightmarish, quality-annihilating, interior *there is* ("il y a") is the vital, egoistic pursuit of happiness in the exterior world. Needs nourish the growth away from the interior psychological uterus and the exterior world to form an individuated, independent being. The person becomes aware of his or her self, its satisfactions, its frustrations when not satisfied, and the appropriate strategies needed to overcome problems in self-satisfaction. In this regard, in particular, material objects are appropriated through work. Through the development of this psychological indepen-dence, totalizing systems of which the self is a part are distinguished. Also, the independence of others is accepted in order to have allies and better subvert any totalizing independence-nullifying practices in the system. At this juncture, the individual realizes the incompleteness of material pleni-tude and of the self, and manifests deep spiritual desire to meet infinity in the face of the other.

Despite the preoriginal, elected nature of the responsibility to the other, at this point the individual can choose voluntarily to open fully to the other or can choose not to do so. In the former case, a vital, "sensual," respectful communication with the other begins and builds where the other's opacity and vulnerability are understood, leading to *goodness*. This is the step in the process that leads to self-disinterest, self-transcendence, and self-sacrifice, where the self is "denucleated," or exiled and becomes a vulnerable hostage to the other's welfare. The unending suffering of the entire universe is assumed humbly without respite and with unlimited patience by the self. As the title of Lévinas's cardinal work implies ("Autre-ment qu'être"), other than being means to be otherwise. Rather than loving the other like the self, we should love the other, for this is ourselves. In bearing the other's suffering, we become the messiah.

Perils and Potentials

Brewster Smith (1994, 1995) fears that the postmodern approach leads to a rejection of "objective" scientific investigation and at the same time its potential salutary repercussions for the perils confronting humankind. My perspective is that when postmodernism is used by less than very mature thinkers or societies, then there are increased dangers of it being abused for nefarious ends. For example, its relational theme about language and thought can be misused to justify willy-nilly ethical relativism, on the one hand, or dogmatic ethical absolutism, on the other hand, depending on the oppressive needs of the moment.

However, in and of itself postmodernism does not contain the seeds for these ends. Rather, in the hands of mature adults it should be used with the sensitivity that is at its base (and therefore, for example, would include science as part of its condition). For me, postmodernism is appealing because of its optimism. Humans are not to be trapped by prefigured truths, but should continuously refigure their emergent truth configurations about the self, the other, and the world in a contextually sensitive manner. The dangers of abandon are countered by doable moralities. Living with and through the other in an authentic, empathic, respecting, responsible, agency-promoting (dare I say loving?) communion becomes the linchpin process in developing the self, the other, and the earth in their constitutive mutuality. We as a species have our own destinies and those of others in our collective hands. This is the quasi-ultimate truth that derives from postmodernism; no one can do it but ourselves, and it must be done and continuously so. The peril of postmodernism is that we live in its deconstructive and not in its constructive mode, and thereby fail to act on the perils that modernism hid and that we denied.

Conclusion

Parry (1993) captures well this positive potential of postmodernism in his analysis of Thomas Pynchon's (e.g., 1973) novels with its concept of "We-system." For Pynchon, "through connecting with each other in the We-system ..., the heart's real satisfactions will be found and we will not ... continue to assume that our desires are being met when they are only being counterfeited" (Parry, 1993, p. 452). The means of entry into this process is through "penetration of the moment, ... attention to what is happening around oneself—the very opposite of the modernist entry *into* oneself— attention, in other words, to the other ... in order to experience ... concrete connectedness with all others" (p. 453).

Gergen (interviewed in Misra, 1993) calls postmodernism a generative theory, for it continually offers new alternatives, different procedures, theoretical innovations, and creative ruptures. It prizes theory before data, but adheres to no one theory. Its relativism is considered less dangerous than that of any fixed modernism, for it forever queries and is open to query, forever doubtful and curious, and forever free and interactive.

In the spirit of its tenet that knowledge is practical, pragmatic, praxic, situated, and embodied in everyday life, and acquired "at the dangerous edge of things" (Bevan & Kessel, 1994), I offer you this snippet of conversation with Lester Kreiger, carpenter/farmer/college dropout ("specialization seemed constricting") from both Toronto and Mobray, Manitoba, who spent one week at our house constructing door frame/doors and coconstructing knowledge.

> For me, carpentry is a means of creation. There are many roads to the spirit. The artist working to create the masterpiece and the physicist trying to place all of creation in one formula are inspired by a spiritual understanding. They are trying to achieve the impossible, but still try because they are listening to the dictates of the spirit. This spirit is the essence of the human journey.
>
> So there is no single formula or universe, but, if I may coin a term, only multiple *relaverses*.

> The universe is fundamentally unfathomable, so that the possibility of
> multiple universes should not be surprising. Scientists tell the story they want
> us to hear. It's time that they began to listen to other narratives.

But even multiple universes exist within one supersystem. Multiplicity conjoins in unicity, living and nonliving together. Postmodernism recognizes this when it argues against artificial dualisms. Similarly, system elements form patterns in systems theory, and are altered by those patterns. Thus, when I argue for the fusion of self and other, cognition and emotion, and (abstract) idea and (abstract) idea in the stage of postmodern collective thought, I am arguing for the return of a universal verity or a lost innocence, if you will. William Blake (in Falck, 1994) captures this fusion well, in describing poetic language. According to him, it

> is vitally metaphorical; that is, it marks the before unapprehended relation of
> things and perpetuates their apprehension, until words, which represent them,
> become through time, signs for portions or classes of thought, instead of pictures
> of integral thoughts: and then, if no new poets should arise to create afresh the
> associations which have been thus disorganized, language will be dead to all the
> nobler purposes of human intercourse. (p. 199)

For Falck (1994), this view suggests an "original unity of emotional and descriptive meaning" in the "before unapprehended relation of things."

Finally, it might be possible to argue that the current theoretical project is antipostmodern despite its postmodern trappings. That is, it describes universal steps and transition mechanisms in development even if they are individual-sensitive and contextualized. But there is no contradiction here, for postmodernism in its affirmative strivings does not dismiss the possibility of a universal/objective-relativistic/constructivist rapprochement in psychological theory. It is especially a changing movement, with deconstructive and reconstructive sides, so that a paramodern (Larner, 1995) or moderate foundational (Wittgenstein) integration of the classic modern and postmodern perspectives is in character with its profoundest aspirations.

Relations to the Current Work

Introduction. The current work has been influenced by postmodern thinking, especially in its concept of the postformal adult developmental stage of collective intelligence, in its emphasis on the vygotskian approach to sociocultural transition mechanisms in development (and my corollary concept of the development of cognitive coschemes through coappropriation and the cognitive (mis)perception of the other), and in its particular therapeutic and epistemological models. The stage of collective intelligence refers to the constitutive sharing in which adults engage in their communal intellectual activities, and thus could be called the *stage of postmodern intelligence* for all intents and purposes. The vygotskian perspective, and the concepts of coschemes, coappropriation, and the cognitive (mis)perception of the other describe the negotiated, situated, sociocultural mutuality involved in cognitive development. Again, these notions fit the postmodern program, and could be called *postmodern transition mechanisms* in cognitive development. Finally, the brief family therapeutic approach that I describe is a quintessential *postmodern therapy*, and the synthetic epistemological stance that I defend is a *postmodern epistemology*, for each is based, in particular, on the constructivist, constitutive approach that underlies postmodernism. Again, the postmodern enterprise matches the current endeavor. And there are other parallels between the current and postmodern positions that will become evident as we proceed.

Does this mean that the current work simply is a replication and extension of the postmodern position into the developmental realm? Not at all. It has messages in and of itself for postmodernism. The latter is not a unitary, hulking intellectual monolith, but a responsive, emerging perspective, and thus could share in some of the current ideas without losing its identity. That is, it should be able to live the constitutive negotiation that it prescribes because it is a spiraling embodiment of the collective intelligence processes from which it emanates.

In essence, the current work adds to the postmodern perspective by helping to understand better the path the postmodern individual follows in development, to where (to what stage) the postmodern individual develops, and the manner in which this development takes place, can go awry, and can be treated therapeutically. And in so doing, it qualifies and extends our understanding of the postmodern perspective itself.

The Postmodern Adult.   Much of the current work is oriented to defining the nature of the mature adult's developing postmodern mind. I argue that optimally the adult is in a continual state of transformation or its preparation. There is constant change toward complexity, being, becoming, and evolution. Adult thought is relativistic, nonessentialist, multiplicitous, differentiated, constructive, accepts possibility, options, contradiction, and conflict, and rejects objectivist or unidimensional perspectives of reality. It is marked by fusion in traditional oppositions such as cognition and emotion, self and other, and abstract values and their opposites (i.e., it forms abstract second-order thought). Adult thought is self-created, or narrates its own stories and constructions, and ultimately becomes aware of this process.

Through this reflexive awareness of self-authorship and the interpreted nature of truths, the adult mind grasps that others' realities also are constructed. The shared social context of behaving prepares the way for empathy and sensitivity to others. Thus, the mature adult symbiotically communes with the surround (dyadic and collective worlds) with wonderment and worship. He or she is activist, and feels responsible for others, manifesting world work and world love. Wisely, others are seen as developmental beings who deserve to grow to the state of continual transformation.

KEGAN'S THEORY
OF ADULT DEVELOPMENT

Introduction

The most important theory on the application of postmodern conceptions to adult development is that of Robert Kegan (1982, 1994). In the following sections, first I describe his theory and then I turn to a critique, preparing the way for the alternative view contained in the current work.

Kegan's theory builds on the structural foundations of Piaget's cognitive developmental theory in that he describes the equivalent of Piaget's four major stages of cognitive development (sensorimotor, preoperational, concrete operational, formal operational), and adds to that lattice by subdividing the last formal operational period into three phases (early, full, post) which stretch cognitive development throughout adulthood. The six-step developmental sequence that derives from this process is numbered 0 to 5 by Kegan, reflective of the equivalent status the later periods are given relative to the first ones (i.e., each of the last periods are considered separate stages in development like the first ones). Kegan uses the labels *incorporative*, *impulsive*, and *imperial* for the first three preformal stages, and uses the labels *interpersonal*, *institutional*, and *interindividual* for the three formal ones. He chose these particular encapsulating terms because he sought to amplify the cognitive underpinnings of the stages into their affective and interpersonal derivatives.

The major characteristic of each stage is presented by Kegan in terms of its underlying subjective–objective structure. That is, the self focus at each of the first five stages becomes the object focus of the ensuing one, and the first stage is seen as bereft of any object focus. Thus, the sequence at the level of self focus involves a movement through the following six foci of psychological embeddedness: (0) reflexes (sensing, moving); (1) impulses, perceptions; (2) needs, interests, wishes, competencies, enduring dispositions; (3) interpersonal concordance, shared subjective experience, mutuality; (4) personal self-system autonomy, independence, authorship, identity, psychic administration, ideology; and (5) interindividuality, interpenetration of self systems, and interdependent self-surrender and self-definition. Also, Kegan emphasizes the culture of embeddedness that is associated with each of the stages. In this regard, the sequence concerns (0) primary caretaking (e.g., comfort, protection); (1) parenting (e.g., attachment, peer play promotion); (2) role differentiation (family, school, peer); (3) encouraging mutual, reciprocal dyadic relationships; (4) cultivating self-identity and self-authorship in love and work settings; and (5) genuine intimacy in these settings.

For each stage of development, Kegan seeks to describe the underlying consciousness (principle of mental organization, form or order of mind, experience- or meaning-constructive capacities, mental stance before the sociocognitive surround). Moreover, he describes the demands of the cultural surround on the individual's developing cognitive–affective apparatus in terms of these cognitive stages and their orders of consciousness. Society's agenda or curriculum of claims, demands, prescriptions, and expectations are understood to be not only in the form of what humans should know but also on *how* we should know, or what level of complexity or frame in consciousness we should bring to the task of meaning making. Thus, one could hypothesize that "the historical evolution of cultural mentality" parallels the ontogenetic growth of the individual in terms of the six stages described above. Gradually, human society is evolving through to the last stage of the series, and perhaps a century ago it was only at the fifth level.

Each of the stages are considered to pass through five transition levels. Thus, each new stage (1) emerges and reflects upon the prior stage, which clearly remains primary in the developing person; (2) becomes more in evidence but still finds developing cognition dominated by the prior level; (3) becomes predominant but not exclusive, with the lower-order stage still used; (4) becomes the primary focus, but only through lower-level inhibition of intrusion by the prior stage; and (5) ends up securely established. Note that the type of cyclic recursion in levels of cognitive development described here fits with the theories of Case (1985) and K. W. Fischer (1980).

Comparison with the Current Theory

In Kegan (1994), the last three developmental stages are referred to as the traditional, modern, and postmodern, respectively, and he focuses especially on them. Thus, his theory exhibits several important similarities compared to the present work. First, both attempt to describe cognitive–socioaffective correspondences in development in terms of a modification of piagetian cognitive–developmental theory, and both fixate on the adult period. Second, both maintain that the developmental trajectory depicted is applicable not only to the individual but also to the wider societal entity. Finally, both characterize the final stage in the series as a postmodern one.

However, for each of these three similarities between Kegan's work and mine, there are corresponding differences, as well. First, the developmental scaffold of universal cognitive phases on which my theory is constructed consists of five stages which manifest a cyclic recursion of five substages, with four sublevels within each of these. Thus, the sequence of steps in cognitive development postulated in my version of neopiagetian theory resembles his with its concept of six stages and five transitional steps. However, through my description of sublevels within substages, the current theory is much more differentiated than Kegan's. Moreover, his transitional levels resemble the nature of my sublevels within substages and not the substages themselves. Thus, his two-tiered structure of stages and levels seems to be lacking the current emphasis on an intermediate tier of substages between them in developmental structure.

Additionally, Kegan makes no provision for a reflexive stage prior to the sensorimotor one, unlike the case here, and he splits the childhood period into the preoperational and concrete operational periods, following many others, but unlike the case here. More important, for the central focus of his book, which is development in the adult period, he splits the adult period into two stages where only one seems justified. I believe that he took this decision because he does not integrate substages (in the sense of Fischer, Case, or myself) into his model, and the differentiation afforded in the developmental trajectory by this absent theoretical tier had to be compensated in other ways. (The same argument applies to his need to have two childhood stages where according to me one would suffice so long as substages could account for the developmental shifts evident in the ontogenetic trajectory.)

Second, although I agree that individuals and society pass through the same stages in their growth in complexity, I do not agree with Kegan's assumption that the latter are often in advance of the former even in our relatively progressive society. Culture does not impose its demands impartially on our individual psyches, waiting as a neutral wash in which we can bathe ourselves in its multilayered wisdom, like a concerned parents behaving in Vygotsky's zone of proximal development when with their child. To the contrary, society can be insidiously invasive and undermining or even overtly repressive and manipulative in its tentacled hold on us, depending on the historical context, issue, etc., and I think that Kegan underemphasizes this point. Thus, our culture's demands may not be for us to adjust to an ever increasingly complex frame of cognitive maturity presented benignly or benevolently to us but to comply or submit to an implicit or explicit sabotage of such. One culture or one of its components may not demand that we develop forward to its higher states but backward to its entrapping or entrapped one(s). In this volume, the conceptual vehicle that translates this message is called the cognitive (mis)perception of the other. I attempt to show the manner in which the individual or any social unit (e.g., couple, subcollective, society) may not construct or address the other from the full potential revealed by its regular level of cognitive advance because of affective limits or contextual–historical contingencies.

As for the third major difference between Kegan's and my theory of adult development, we have different perspectives on when the mature mind can be characterized as postmodern. In Kegan's schema of the stages of development, the last stage emerges in the midlife age period of the forties, and only then are the enslaving certainties of modernism's mentality transformed into the hermeneutical multiplicity of postmodernism. In contrast, in the current perspective, postmodern cognition begins to emerge in the twenties when the young adult develops a collective mode of abstract thought. To be sure, this stage is marked by the five-step substage progression mentioned previously, so that the nature of postmodern thought is seen to develop continually. The issue is to what extent do young adults show nascent signs of the postmodern turn in their thought and affect, and I think that the answer is that signs of postmodern thinking are present in the adult mind younger than Kegan would have us believe.

In fact, careful reading of Kegan reveals that his modern stage of development in the young adult is quintessentially postmodern in characteristics. That is, he describes the young adult's mental life in postmodernistic rather than modernistic terms, as will become evident later on. But because he has been entrapped by his creation of a six-step schema in cognitive stage development without intermediate substages, when the time came to choose the appropriate correspondence across his theory to the traditional–modern–postmodern sequence, Kegan had but one choice, and it led him to the error described. Nevertheless, the error is but a semantic one, for his cognitive and socioaffective description of the young adult is excellent. Had he used the appropriate terminology to begin with, there would be little difference in his understanding of the cognitive nature of the young adult compared to the one he has, and thus in essence it resembles my own despite the major difference in the labels used to represent it. If Kegan could relabel his stages in light of my critique, he might opt for the sequence—traditional-modern, early postmodern, and advanced or late postmodern, or something to this effect. Of course, a better option may have been to construct at the outset a model equivalent to the current one.

The Stages in Childhood

Kegan (1994) spends little time addressing the first stage of cognitive development in the sensorimotor period. In the preoperational period, the preschooler is considered to function according to the principle of independent elements. There is no conceptual coherence in the child's thought processes. Consequently, thought at this level is illogical, cognitively egocentric, and impulsive. The child is presented as having a superficial, immediate, momentary, single point, atomistic way of knowing that is appearance/perception-dominated and need/wish/want/desire/fantasy/impulse-oriented. Thus, the child of this age fails to distinguish self from other in terms of distinct categories even though both are understood as separate, independent, permanent objects. For example, a father who comes home late due to work-related reasons is considered "mean" by a 3-year-old.

The principle that organizes the concrete operational child's mentation is described in detail. At this stage, the child is viewed as a categorical knower who can mentally create "durable categories," or "property-bearing classes" with rules about what constitutes properties. Attributes are considered properties of a set with governing regularities, and this same principle applies across diverse domains such as those concerning objects, social relations, and introspections. For example, self and other are seen to possess the properties of enduring distinct mind, interests, intentions, plans, strategies, roles, preferences, points of view, habits, and abilities, and are seen to live in a logical cause–effect, narratively sequenced, social tit-for-tat, reciprocal concrete world.

The Traditional Stage

The beginning formal operational period of the adolescent is described in terms of cross-categorical or transcategorical knowing or meaning making. In this stage, thinking is abstract, generalized, metaphenomenal, reasoning about reasoning, reflective, inferential, hypotheticodeductive, inductive, propositional, combinatorial, connotative, thematic, with ideals and values, and insightful. The durable categories developed in the prior stage become elements of a higher order superordinate principle of mental organization where they are subordinated, regulated, integrated, and related simultaneously. And the adolescent realizes consciously that personal preferences are being subordinated to wider perspectives.

Thus, the deeply held point of view of the preadolescent becomes in the adolescent subordinate to an integrated or corelational, coconstructed perspective which is based on the internalization of the opinions of her/his caregivers (e.g., "I worry that if I mess up, others will worry"). The other is distinguished from internalizations of her or his point of view, and comes to matter intrinsically as part of a coconstruction of the self out of the relationship between the categories of self and other. Thus, the self is constructed in terms of a subordinated identification with the parental relationship or a coordination of points of view within the self rather than as a category in and of itself. Dyadic social relations and even one's relationship with society come to acquire an interpersonal sense of sharing, bonding, connection, mutuality, trustworthiness, empathy, concern for welfare, and intrinsic value which go beyond the personal frame. Emotions are experienced as inner psychological states or interior reflections-motivations-subjectivities. Values, ideals, and broad beliefs are enabled by internalized identifications which subordinate facts to possibilities, even if opposite in tenor to the facts.

The Modern Stage

The adult organizes thought according to higher order systemic structures where the abstract ideas of the adolescent are systematized into a relational field or systematic whole. All possible combinations of constructed conceptual relations can be combined systematically to construct a generalized regulative, mediating system of relationships of cognitive relationships. Because cross-categorical structures become objects rather than subjects of knowing, enough distance from them is obtained to be able to weave them as parts into new, more complex supervening whole structures. The adult mental structure subtends, subordinates, coordinates, acts upon, controls, directs, mediates, integrates, and actually invents or generates the meaning of (social) mentalization. Abstract conceptions are about abstract ideas, ideals, and values, where each is relativized in a more complex, integrated network (e.g., a set of ideas about abstract ideas) instead of capturing us. The whole of which one is part can be examined from the "outside in," or in terms of the relations of its parts, including our relation to it, rather from the "inside out," or only in terms of ourselves.

Consequently, for the adult, the self is constituted by interacting selves of which it is the administrator, and it is the author of its interior psychological realities. Thus, one finds self-authorship, internal identity, self-regulation, self-initiation, self-correction, self-evaluation, self-formation, self-critique, and self-reformulation. The self realizes that experiences do not define but belong to each self and other, and so can be related to, subordinated, and regulated, rather than constituting each self and other. Ideologies are formulated and beliefs are authored from deeply held convictions, so that the individual is no longer created by rigid values. Because there are values about values, mechanisms are in place which can regulate conflicts between them. There is less the need for vision than the ability to organize epistemology in order to allow its personally derived creation. Multiplicities in realities are recognized (e.g., awareness of one's multiple-role consciousness of place in institutional settings). Phenomena are liberated from their "received meanings." The way realities are constructed and who authorizes them are understood (e.g., the relationship-regulating forms of self and institutions are cognized). It is understood that one applies one's own meaning-making and meaning-regulative principles in order to construct, pattern, shape, select, and invent reality without being embedded in it. Thus, one cognitively seizes and revels in personal authority, guidance by one's own vision, or internal judgment over reality authorship. Responsibility is taken for the present and future, no matter what the constraining circumstance, rather than abdicating responsibility to the external.

Different ideas, beliefs, values, and roles are not merely evaluated, but also understood as assumptive, as objects to deidentify with or deconstruct rather than subjects which construct oneself. Because the self is not its mental constructions nor identifies with them, but *has* them, agreement about ideas, values, and beliefs no longer constitutes the criterion of intimacy in a couple. Rather, closeness in a couple now reflects a reciprocal acceptance by the partners that each partner can self-create and regulate these abstract concepts and exist apart from the relationship despite the relationship's importance to both of them. We can reject our partner's request or opinion without rejecting our partner, and give succor to our partner even when our partner's discontent is about us. In general, interpersonal relationships form a relational network, where one stands in relationship or connection to relationships and roles rather than to persons themselves. The loyalty felt for the community's creed is tempered by knowledge of a needed pluralism in its practice. Adults create internally an order of consciousness equivalent to the "community's collective intelligence," where they enculture themselves, recreating community from the perspective of a higher order plane where they are charged to become their own gods.

Kegan (1994) clarifies that his concept of self-authorization or its lack (embeddedness) in development is orthogonal to Gilligan's (1982) concept of separateness versus connectedness in relationships. The former is a developmental acquisition where one comes to decide for oneself instead of having decisions externally decided, whereas the latter is a stylistic difference where one decides by oneself or in a union. Thus, one could decide for oneself either separately or in union, and one could have decisions made for oneself either separately or in union. Similarly, one could become more autonomous, self-regulated, self-governing, or differentiated and decide that particular connections and attachments are precious and need to be kept open to interchange and change or that they are not worth maintaining at this level, depending on circumstance; or one could stay at the level where relationships are externally constructed or make up the self in the social world rather than get made by the self according to personal standards; and one could live at this level in a collaborative relational or separate instrumental fashion, depending on style or experience.

Applications to Therapy

A major application of Kegan's theory of adult development is to therapy. He perceives the therapist's task as the facilitation of movement to more complex orders of consciousness, in particular, from a traditional adolescent to a modern young adult mentality. Individuals and families must learn that they are active creators of their realities and not constructed by them or simple repositories of them. But families cannot change if at least one of its members does not. (Many therapists would contest this absolute all-or-none conviction.)

To escape the captive relationship to the group mind, adults in therapy must depart epistemologically from their parents' mind. They must aim for the following principles, and be guided toward them in therapy. That is, standards of experiential judgment reside in the self. Choices are made internally for the self, based on personal resources. Self-assuredness is developed through meeting self-constructed standards. The meaning ascribed to events is under personal authority. Family values are taken as objects to critique. As authors of their own experience, clients (re)write myths, scripts, and plays in a manner that is theirs, that write a new future, that transform.

One way to facilitate this evolution in the client's mentality is to have the therapist serve as an axis of external standards to which the client adheres instead of having the family of origin serve that role. Thus, the therapist serves as a bridge from family-derived standards to self-derived standards. Another manner would be to put an appropriate gloss or alternate perspective on the standards of the family of origin in order to facilitate the shift in basis of standard construction. Finally, the therapist can hint at an alternate set of standards already within the individual, and provoke a psychological mitosis, differentiation, or distinction construction. In each scenario, the self must become separate from its story, with the story seen as object and not only alterable but also self-authored.

Several steps are involved in this process (after Robbins, 1990). First, the client begins therapy and is diffusely upset, and one or more of the strategies mentioned above are implemented. Next, conflict between the old and new perspectives is engendered. The client experiences fear, disorientation, guilt, and divided loyalties. Leaving the cosmic protection afforded by family loyalties is forestalled by the client in order to avoid spiritual exile or death of soul, even when the family functions along life-stealing dimensions of personal history. But, metaphorically speaking, an internal committee emerges, which lets each voice speak, and it coordinates, regulates, and integrates the voices into one team. Nevertheless, the self still is not yet the leader of the team. In the next phase of therapy, the client expresses anger at the old schemas, and comes to know what he or she is not (or at least what he or she does not want to be) even if the schemas still serve as powerful magnets in her or his psychology. Next, the client can come to terms with old schemas, turning to them without capitulating, and so constructing a new relationship with them. The client may realize that "[t]he critical, demanding voice is nonetheless a loving, companionable voice that means well" (pp. 265–266). The client may apprehend that the prior devotion to the terms of the family's religion was a major accomplishment rather than a recipe for incompetence. Self powers now are acknowledged and can be redirected. Previously discounted self parts can become foci of transformation.

Applications to University Education

Kegan also examines self-directed learning from the viewpoint of mental modernity. First, he argues that universities should promote better student learning experiences by treating students as self-governing adults needing challenge. Thus, they should be asked to make decisions, design programs, relate in groups, master their discipline, and "contend with competing values, theory, and advice."

Second, Kegan describes students who are self-directed learners, or in the modern stage of thought. Fitting the frame of young adults' ways of knowing, self-directed learners use critical thinking, manifest individual initiative, set their own goals, take responsibility for their learning, and acquire a sense that they are cocreators of their educational experience. They develop personal perspectives over their thinking, reading, writing, and knowledge making. Moreover, they develop systematic procedures not only for generating and evaluating concepts, but for formulating more complex wholes and understanding that concepts are but mechanisms for further conceptualization and critique rather than crucibles of truth. In learning through this philosophy, inevitably relations in the personal field are revisioned and transformed, whether these relations are supportive or not, so that self-directed learners grow not only in their educational setting but also outside it.

Similarly, Barr and Tagg (1995) describe the need for a paradigm shift in university education. For them, universities must move from an instructional to a learning mode. Instead of conceiving themselves as instructional providers transferring knowledge to students, universities should act to produce learning and empowered learners, where students discover and construct knowledge in cooperative, collaborative, and supportive environments. In the same vein, Halonen (1995) argues that universities should aim to develop in students the collaborative construction of complex skills such as theory building and decision making, along with metacognition, or cognitive self-assessment, and appropriate attitude (e.g., skepticism, tolerance of ambiguity and difference).

The Postmodern Stage

As much as young adults embark on a journey toward and within maturity along the lines just described, where their parenting, couplehood, work life, extra schooling, citizenship, and, if needed, their therapy are defined in terms of full formal and modern parameters, according to Kegan, their voyage does not begin to reach harbor until they enter the stage of postformal or postmodern thought in the midlife period. The mental organizational principle that coalesces in this period concerns across-system mental complexes called transsystems or cross-forms, multiforms, or cross-theories.

Transsystems are dialectical structures that take as object the abstract systems, formulations, and ideologies constructed in the prior stage of development. These objects are integrated into transcomplexes such as trans- or postideologies which inherently contain paradox, contradiction, oppositeness, or conflict. But the dialectical tension involved promotes a complementarity of the component opposites leading to collaborative wholeness, interpenetration, interform structuration, or synthesis at the level of thought (transformulations), social relations (interinstitutional perspectives), and intrapersonal feelings (interpenetration of selves, interindividuation). The parts that were in opposition do not remain intact, but transform as their relationship is constituted, for they no longer are whole, distinct elements themselves.

Thus, different ways of constructing reality or different realities can be visited impartially and tried out so that new vistas of the self may be explored in consequence. The exterior no longer is considered an opposite to an internal singularity, because internal opposites as systems are acknowledged and even created, leading to their multiple interaction. Ultimately, the transsystems of the postformal, postmodern period are, on the one hand, fluid structures forever incomplete and, on the other hand, are not the focus, per se, of one's way of knowing. That is, the process itself of transsystem construction assumes primordial contemplation, and systemic knowing is relativized or subordinated as object in construction. That is, the process of interaction is constructed as prior to the existence of form or system. Plans, even collectively created ones, live in incompleteness, and should be continually nourished by contradictions so that they can live growth and ongoing reconstruction. Or, the relationship which creates the elements contained within it is taken a priori in mental organization, rather than the elements themselves.

The first phase of postmodern thought is deconstructive, where the objective truth claims of any internally consistent, universal system, theory, metanarrative, discourse, or form are dismissed, for truth is recognized as the product of constructive processes. Thus, reification of ideology-saturated absolutes is rejected because of their danger for hegemony and stagnation. In the reconstructive phase of postmodernism, deconstructed tenets are recaptured, reelaborated, reformulated, reappropriated, reintegrated, and reconnected on less absolutist grounds. In their diversity and nonhomogeneity, they are understood to be equally important, polysemous, and plural.

Postmodern thought is constituted by the insight that thought is a product of a constructive mechanism which does not privilege any of its products even if a superb metatheory. The best theories are generative procedures for the reconstruction of themselves, even at the level of their generative procedures. This is the only universal generalization that issues from postmodernism, the only legitimate judgmental valorization where none seem permitted, that the presence of continual transforming processes of meaning making, of a "reinterpretive ideology for authorizing reality," is the epitome of postmodern thinking in the mature adult.

In conclusion, I cite Kegan (1994) who contends that postmodern thought stands for

> the recognition of our multiple selves, for the capacity to see conflict as a signal of our overidentification with a single system, for the sense of our relationships and connections as prior to and constitutive of the individual self, for an identification with the transformative process of our being rather than the formative products of our becoming .... (p. 351)

For these reasons, postmodern adults accept the differences in people around them and the differences in their multiple selves (e.g., separate male and connecting female components). They are tolerant and giving, differentiating and integrating, and passionately engaged and disengaged in recuperation in an endless reverberation of fascination.

Conclusion

Kegan's account of the postmodern mind is progressive because it speaks of the different types of postmodernism, of its empathic aspects, and of its emphasis on the transformative process in mature living. However, it fails to emphasize the collective element in adult thinking. In my own theory, the adult is considered to develop a socially collective intelligence, where Kegan's transsystems (called generalized abstractions and the like) are created. That is, transsystem formation is facilitated when the individual lives a symbiotic group intelligence with others in the social surround. Moreover, in this theory the postmodern mind experiences a fusion of cognition and emotion, mind and body, and subjective and objective in its psychological praxis. Kegan hints at these principles, e.g., in discussing the collective nature of work and leadership activities, and in discussing the interpersonal and intrapersonal sides of mind. However, these hints need more expansion and the collective aspect of the postmodern adult is considered in more depth here than in Kegan. This takes place especially through my emphasis on the vygotskian program in developmental psychology.

As I alluded at the beginning of this section on Kegan, it seems to me that Kegan's modern stage of development has many attributes of postmodernism. For example, it discounts identification with universals, relativizes thought, personally self-invents or authors thought and identity, makes and regulates meaning, engages in metaevaluation, analyzes the subjective (e.g., values) as objects, is polyvocal or multiple, and goes beyond single abstract thoughts, thus facilitating the avoidance of totalizing ideas. In this regard, it appears that the point of emergence of postmodern thought in development in Kegan's theory is at the beginning of adulthood, and not in its midcourse. Thus, Kegan's postmodern stage should termed an advanced or late postmodern one or the like, because his modern one is essentially postmodern. I hope to show that the current theory presents a clearer course of adult development than the one Kegan describes, although the rigor and depth of his analysis is masterful, it should be consulted when a good summary of the development of postmodern thought is needed, and it has served my theoretical evolution in good stead.

Note that I believe that Kegan's confusion about the traditional, modern, postmodern sequence has led him to make two other errors in the description of the stages of development. First, he mentions that the postmodern stage emerges in two phases, the deconstructive and reconstructive periods. However, now knowing that his modern stage is really an early postmodern one, it makes more sense to place the deconstructive postmodern phase in his modern one. Careful reading shows that there is

Table 2.1 The Postmodern, Postformal Collective Intelligence Substages
and Corresponding Socioemotional Acquisitions

	Cognition	Socioemotion
Coordination	Subdomain (generic theory/ procedure, Pascual-Leone, 1990) coordination (metatheory, supra-abstraction, overarching principle, second-order logical system or hypothesis, etc., building) occurs. It refers to contextualized, multiplistic generalizations in scientific, professional, religious, moral, artistic, complex practical/technical, and other knowledge domains (even oral folk traditions).	Attempted collective subdomain coordination is accompanied by subtle speculation on principles (postmetaphysical reasoning), which not only engenders superior perspicacity, but also a sense of awe about flux, ideas, and uncertainty.
Hierarchization	Subdomain hierarchization can manifest, for dominant/ subordinate relations established across contextualized, multiplistic generalizations.	Progress in this endeavor is accompanied by feelings of generativity. For example, one can become a mentor of some sort to younger individuals.
Systematization	Domain systematization can be attempted through mutuality in subdomain regulation over contextualized, multiplistic generalizations.	People can master an entire domain, catalyzing personal transformation. This can occur through a train of quantitative additions (emergent discoveries) or by a major qualitative change in foundation (paradigmatic shift). When these advances are radically different from existing direction, we can speak of chaotic attractors and catastrophic inversions, respectively. [Terms loosely borrowed from systems theory.]
Multiplication	Interdomain efforts may be undertaken (multiplication of contextualized, multiplistic generalizations).	Older adults who span whole domains may experience a sense of ego integrity or satisfaction and acceptance of their life flow.
Integration	Perhaps knowledge domains are integrated.	In the final phases of life, often there is a wider knowledge which is accompanied by cathartic or purifying experiences. The elderly become impregnated by a holistic sense of wisdom and also feel communion or reverence with what they regard as holy. In their most meditative moments, they hope to transcend, and feel one with mystery.

little difference between them at any rate. Also, his traditional stage was not described as a modern one, but possesses all of its attributes. However, Kegan did not emphasize the modern, totalizing nature of adolescent thought in his traditional stage, given his error in not realizing that it is modern. Thus, an appropriate modification of his theory would add this aspect to the description of the adolescent mind.

Finally, one could ask what is missing in Kegan's theory given that in the end he has a two-step sequence in adult development of postmodern thought and I have a five-step sequence. It will be recalled that the sequence that I describe concerns the substages of coordination, hierarchization, systematization, multiplication, and integration within the postmodern stage. Thus, for me postmodern thought goes from an initial stage where there is both deconstructive and constructive elements simultaneously to four other increasingly more complex substages. In this regard, Kegan's modern stage corresponds to the current postmodern coordination substage and his postmodern stage should be subdivided into four substages corresponding to the current hierarchization to integration series. The closest match between the manner in which he describes his postmodern stage and the four remaining postmodern substages of the current theory seems to be with the current substage of systematization. Thus, he seems to be missing a substage where postmodern coordinations in thought are hierarchized before becoming systemic, and missing substages where systems are constructed into more complex multiplications and integrations after they become systemic. Thus, in the current work, there are five substages in the development of postmodern adult thought in comparison with Kegan's more limited model (see Table 2.1; Young, 1990b). However, the description of the current substages does not possess the richness that characterizes Kegan's work, and I refer the reader to his work as a primary reference source.

Now we turn to the development of the self and of parenting or the family from the perspective of the current theory to show that its extension can be rewarding for understanding the development toward and into the adult period. We begin by examining in the next chapter the development of the self from infancy into the elderly period. This sets the stage for the following chapter on an analysis of the stages in parenting or family development that adults pass through as their children develop.

PART II

SELF AND FAMILY DEVELOPMENT

CHAPTER 3

Self Development

INTRODUCTION

In this chapter and the next, current theory is applied to the domains of self and family–marital development. Implications of the chapters for postmodernism are treated at the end of the next chapter. (This same procedure of commenting on postmodernism is followed after each of the ensuing three parts of the book.)

The self is considered to be comprised of at least two components: the implicit, functioning *I* self and the explicit, self-evaluative *me* self (see Young, submitted). Following many theorists in the area, for the most part the I self is treated in the current work. (Hereafter, the discussion of self refers to this component, unless otherwise specified.) Using the proposed 25-step model of development as a base, a model of self development across the lifespan is extrapolated. The works of Sroufe (1990, 1996), Selman (1980), and Loevinger (1976, 1987, 1993, 1994) on infants, children-adolescents, and adolescents-adults, respectively, are taken into account in this process. In the last part of the chapter, the 25-step model of the self that is created is extended to one particular component of the me self, one's sense of self-efficacy.

Santostefano (1991) also has attempted to show a parallel between cognitive developmental levels and self developmental levels, but in a more limited way compared to the current approach. He showed how passage through the traditional piagetian sensorimotor substage series in infancy may help promote the development of the four phases in self development described by Stern (1985; presented in the next section). Lewis (1990) proposed a model of the development of intentionality in infancy, but it is not included in the current discussion because the levels that he describes do not relate to Piaget's sensorimotor substages for the most part and there are definitional problems with his work (Ricard & Gouin-Décarie, 1990). Harter (1985), basing her work on K. W. Fischer

(1980), in part, has elaborated a model of self development in childhood. However, it does not lend itself to a one-to-one correspondence with the substages of the current model, and so is not described. Damon and Hart (1988; Hart, Mahoney, & Damon, 1990) have promulgated a theory of self development somewhat similar to Selman's. However, the latter's perspective seems more compatible with the current one, accounting for its emphasis here. Finally, studies on the developing self or related aspects which do not lend themselves to a developmental levels perspective are not discussed (e.g., Aloise-Young, 1993; Rochat, 1993; Stilwell, Galvin, Kopta, & Norton, 1994).

THEORIES OF SELF-DEVELOPMENT IN INFANCY

Stern's Theory

The Theory.   Stern (1985) focuses on four senses of self that are posited to develop in sequence in infancy and coexist in parallel as the developing individual grows. The self is defined as an invariant pattern of awareness which organizes psychological processes. According to Stern, the emergent self is born in the first two months of life. Infants at this age integrate their experiences, many of which are selectively goal-oriented and social. Connectedness, organization, and networks manifest and integrate affect, perception, sensorimotor events, memories, and other cognitions. A prime modality permitting such integration is amodal perception.

According to Stern, the second self to develop in infancy is the core self (from 2 to 7 to 9 months). It concerns a physical self that experiences invariant, recurrent relations over time (continuity), across domains and the body (coherence), in action (willful agency), and internally (affective patterns). Representations of social episodes are constructed, leading to anticipation of expected patterns of social relatedness or self-with-other.

The subjective self develops between 7 to 9 and 15 to 18 months of age, when affect, feelings, motives, and intentions "become the subject matter of relating ... Mental states between people can now be 'read,' matched, aligned with, or attuned to" (p. 27). Thus, intersubjective sharing characterizes the infant (e.g., following a pointed finger, responding appropriately to a request, social referencing by observing the caregiver's reaction to an ambiguous situation, responding to the caregiver's unconscious, cross-modal, multibehavioral, affective attunements, e.g., in vitality).

In the last type of self described by Stern, toddlers develop a sense of verbal self. Shareable, symbol-mediated meanings are constructed about the self and the entourage, for language permits communication, negotiation, and the cocreation of meaning.

Comment. It seems that Stern's (1985) work can serve as an important starting point in understanding the unfoldment of self development. However, his levels cover too broad age ranges, and can be differentiated in order to permit a one-to-one correspondence between the current synthetic model of substages of cognitive development and levels in self development. Stern's emergent self seems to involve two different phases, for after the initial neonatal period where behavior is integrated by amodal perception there is a more general integration of behavior which seems to take place. That is, the organizational networks that develop in the first month seem to acquire situational specificities consonant with experiences encountered, producing better approach and on-target behavior.

Similarly, Stern's core self which develops from 2 to 8 months seems to be binary. As he describes, relational patterns emerge (e.g., in social commerce), because recursive experiences with agency, continuity, coherence, and affectivity permeate development. However, it would seem that these patterns first manifest in haphazard back and forth ways or in primitive coordinations, and then develop a more functional hierarchical structure. Two-month-olds may cycle their limbs when active or cycle their rhythms of interaction with a scaffolding caregiver, but they cannot impose decisively their social agenda on the caregiver until a few months later when a separate phase appears to develop. It seems to me that concomitant with this more purposeful behavior comes a sense of trust in the world. It develops inevitably when the infants' contextually derived intentions lead to successful attainment of wanted goals.

This process accelerates in the phase when Stern's subjective late-first-year self develops, for infants become more purposeful, lead the other better, and are more receptive to the other's vitality, intonation, and signals. Note that the term *intersubjective* self seems a more appropriate one than the label of *subjective self* used by Stern for this developmental period, because of the intense attachment to the caregiver and increasing social skills that develop in this phase.

According to Stern, the verbal self develops in the second year of life. Symbol-mediated behavior explodes in this age period, but 15-month-olds are very different in this regard than 21-month-olds. Younger toddlers are experimenting deliberately in behavior in a trial-and-error fashion, using symbols as guides, whereas older toddlers have advanced to planned mental combination without action (Piaget). The verbal self should manifest a similar developmental leap, for meaning creation via symbolic word usage in older toddlers should be more complex, comprehensive, and integrated than what takes place early in the first year.

Butterworth's (1990) review of mirror and video self-recognition studies supports this two-phase distinction in self development in the second year of life. In the first part of the year, infants can use mirrors to spatially locate others and can distinguish a video image of themselves from those of others. In the latter part of the year, toddlers not only differentiate the self and others but also use particular facial features in doing so. They are not tricked by the surreptitious placement of rouge on their noses before they look in a mirror, for they raise their hand to their nose upon viewing themselves once they look into it. Also, research shows that the acquisition of the sixth piagetian sensorimotor substage in object concept development correlates with performance on such tasks.

Sroufe's Theory

Introduction.   Sroufe (1990, 1996) has elaborated a six-step model of self development in infancy which affords a one-to-one correspondence with the current synthetic model of cognitive substages in development. (The description of the phases given below follows Sroufe [1990] for the most part, but it also attempts to integrate the various stage models of different aspects of development presented in Sroufe [1996].) A more detailed analysis of Sroufe (1996) is offered in Young (submitted). Note that the age of onset for the six levels in Sroufe's theory are not always exactly equivalent to those offered by Piaget in his six-step sensorimotor model of cognitive development in infancy, but they are close enough to suggest an interesting match. However, the particular manner in which Sroufe (1996) and myself approach the issue is different, as explained in Young (submitted). Sroufe's model resembles Stern's model in some respects, but is more differentiated because six rather than four levels in self development in infancy are described. In effect, the two extra levels presented by Sroufe relate to the previous suggestions of the way Stern's theory can be refined. That is, Sroufe sees two levels of self development in the middle of the first year, and two more in the second year, unlike in Stern.

The Phases.   Sroufe's (1990, 1996) model of self development in infancy is based on the work of Sander (1975), in particular. It emphasizes the social embeddedness of the developing self early in life. In the first phase of basic regulation, newborns are physiologically regulated in the interactional matrix of smooth routines provided by the caregiver. A preferential responsiveness to the caregiver develops in the context of a turning toward the environment.

In the second phase, which begins as early as three months, infants and caregivers engage in reciprocal positive exchange or coordinated dyadic sequences involving psychological regulation. There is much affective, vocal, and motoric play as infant tension or arousal is managed. Caregivers craft these chains through sensitive, cooperative adjustment, for infants cannot represent them, intentionally initiate interaction, etc.

Nevertheless, shared joy is derived from the repetitive, organized structures that are built.

The third phase of self development in Sroufe's sequence begins as early as 6 months, and concerns "initiatory" infants who engage in directed, preferred activities. At this age, there is an upsurge in purposeful action, social initiation, active participation, mastery, emotional focus on the caregiver, etc. The infant acquires knowledge of goal achievement or failure. A particular relationship with the caregiver is emerging as part of the infant's inner organization, with the working toward the establishment of an effective attachment with her or him. In parallel, a particular sense of self is emerging, as well. Cicchetti (1991) relates the infant's emerging inner organization to her or his internalization of the history of caregiver interactions.

The next phase of self development in Sroufe's model begins as early as 9 months, and revolves around dyadic emotional regulation in the context of a specific attachment or affective bond. Infants actively focus their expanding exploration around the secure base of the caregiver, ranging away from and retreating to her or him in order to share fears and joys. The caregiver's availability and responsivity are tested through this focusing on her or him. Goals organized around the caregiver lead to back-up options in action in order to achieve them if initial means are ineffective. The working model of the attachment relationship (which emerges in the prior level) acquires a special saliency, for images of the self as wanted or unwanted permeate the heart of the self in this period. That is, infants' working models concern relationships with caregivers more than attributes of individual self. "Infants' major expectations concerning their own actions have to do with likely responses of the caregiver (and to a varying degree, others)" (Sroufe, 1990, p. 288).

The fifth phase of self development at 12 months is dominated by autonomous actions or inner aims, and is called the phase of "self-assertion." Initiative broadens, but with supervision by the caregiver. Goal success and personal gratification can be achieved even independent of the caregiver. Moreover, goals can be pursued even if in opposition to caregiver wishes. Leaving the secure base becomes a psychological and not only a physical process, but the search for a balance with engagement with the caregiver dominates. The awareness of the self as an independent actor takes hold. Inner plans dictate behavior, for self awareness comes to include the concept of self as actor.

In the final phase of self development in the first two years, at 18 months toddlers acquire an awareness of self constancy. Because of the development of appropriate symbols, toddlers realize that caregivers can be aware of their plans, especially in situations where the plans are opposed (e.g., "I do it myself"). There is a "shared awareness," for toddlers recognize that caregivers can be aware of what they themselves are aware of within themselves. A self-organizing center within is emerging in terms of self constancy. Toddlers view their selves as active initiators (or masters of their world) which can perturb their relationship with their caregivers by purposely going against their wishes. This does not overly disturb them, for they know that the general harmony maintained with caregivers will permit them to reinstitute the positive tone of the relationship, or the caregivers themselves will cooperate and do so. The toddlers coordinate their intentions with those perceived in caregivers, producing the first genuine perspective taking and roots of empathy.

Comment. Sroufe's (1990, 1996) model of self development in the first two years is superior to that of Stern's (1985) for several reasons. First, it suggests a correspondence with piagetian cognitive substages because six levels are described, like in Piaget's model. Second, some of the language used to describe the self directly relates to the terms used to describe the current synthetic model of cognitive substages in infancy (e.g., coordinations, plans). Third, some of the phases described by Sroufe provide better accounts of the psychology of the growing child compared to those derived from Stern (especially in the last two phases, in the second year of life). In consequence, Sroufe's model of self development in the first two years was incorporated extensively into the current model. Stern's model served as a ground for comparison purposes in this endeavor, except for its treatment of the youngest ages, where the description of the emergent self seemed important.

Selman's Theory of Self Development in Children and Adolescents

The Theory. Selman (1980; Selman & Demorest, 1986; Yeates, Schultz, & Selman, 1990) delineates five steps in children's acquisition of self and other understanding and social perspective taking coordination. In the first step in this process, preschoolers are considered egocentric without the capacity to differentiate the other's external, physical, objective attributes (e.g., actions, appearance) from their internal, psychological, subjective ones (e.g., feelings, motives, intentions). They do not comprehend that the other may interpret a behavior differently from them and feel differently about it.

In the next step, 5-year-olds come to adopt a subjective, unilateral (first person) perspective. Their concept of persons manifests a clear differentiation of their physical and psychological features. The other can have unique, subjective, covert feelings and thoughts. However, the other's psychological life is understood primarily from a one-way, unidimensional, personal position. For example, according to the 5-year-old, the other should be content with any gift received even if it is inappropriate.

School-age children (7 years) enter into the self-reflective/reciprocal phase of perspective taking. Their conceptual advance is found in their ability to adopt a second-person perspective, where one can contemplate one's own thoughts. This leads to the corollary observation that the other can perform the same feat. Thus, children realize that the other can deceive or act in opposition to their true purposes and feelings, including those involving the beginnings of compassion and empathy. Different perspectives are weighed in a relative way. Reciprocity emerges in the sense that the perspectives of both the self and other are appreciated. Children can put themselves in the place of the other, which helps them grasp that the other may do likewise. Thus, interactions grow beyond actions to include thoughts and feelings. The reciprocity in this phase is limited by a lack of mutual influence.

Older children (10 years) pass into a third-person perspective, a mutual stage where they can remove themselves from the self system. Both the self and the other are seen to be simultaneously actor and object with their perspectives coordinated or in need of such coordination. Thus, both the self and the other function in terms of effects (or behave and evaluate effects of actions on themselves). The coordinated perspective of self and other is viewed from a general vantage point, for one's personal perspective is seen to fit into a generalized schema of values, attitudes, etc. Mutuality prevails in the reciprocal coordination of perspectives of self and other. Children infer the way the other perceives them and their behavior, and adopt this perspective, seeing the self in light of the one imagined by the other. Relationships are judged to be mutually satisfying and with sharing.

In the last level that Selman describes on self development, the 12-year-old to adult period witnesses the acquisition of an in-depth/societal–symbolic perspective. Persons are perceived as unique complexes with both conscious and unconscious motivations. The self is enriched and entertains commitment. Relations with the others are conceived at multiple levels. Others may share basic information, have similar values, or possess comparable abstract moral notions.

Comment

Selman's model of self development informs the current one, but his sequence of four levels in self development has not been kept fully intact in the way it has been adopted in the current work. His description of the first level of self development concords with the nature of the 2-year-old child described in substage 11 of the current model. However, there seems to be no correspondence between any of the levels that he describes and the current substage 12. The next four levels in his model correspond to the current substages 13 to 16. Thus, Selman's work is fully incorporated into the current model of self development, but with a gap in the sequence that he describes, as shall be shown below.

LOEVINGER'S THEORY
OF SELF DEVELOPMENT
IN ADOLESCENTS AND ADULTS

Earlier Stages

Loevinger's model of stages in lifespan ego development (Loevinger, 1976, 1987, 1993, 1994) is derived partly from Erikson, is grounded in data, and is more general in scope than other contemporary thought on lifespan ego development. She has inspired much research on ego development in adulthood (e.g., Helson & Roberts, 1994). As can be seen in Table 3.1, Loevinger, and workers who have followed her (Cook-Greuter, 1990; Noam, 1992), describe 11 levels (stages, transition stages) of ego development, most of which are found in the adult. Other influential theorists on adolescent–adult developmental stages (e.g., Kohlberg & Ryncarz, 1990; Perry, 1970, in Blanchard-Fields, 1990, and in Smolak, 1993; Richards & Commons, 1990) are listed in Table 3.1 as points of comparison. The relative placement of the theories was deduced by consulting Richards and Commons (1990) and Commons and Grotzer (1990).

According to Loevinger, the presocial–symbiotic stage refers to adults whose answers on Loevinger's Test of Sentence Completions indicate a person who has no sense of self and is very dependent and need oriented. If one is at the next (impulsive) stage, the test answers reveal a nascent ego, but one which is still quite dependent and need-based. Others are understood in terms of dichotomies such as good-bad or what they give-withhold. The third self-protective stage concerns individuals who perceive the world through their wants, and not through any insight. They purposefully control encounters, hoping to gain advantage. In the rule-oriented stage, people learn and abide by their society's rules for the most part. An acknowledgement of the external world can lead to vacillation. Judgments are superficial, e.g., based on appearance. The conformist stage is characterized by an acceptance of group-sanctioned rules. If rules are broken, feelings of guilt and shame ensue. Interactions are action oriented, and aimed at belonging and projecting an image of niceness. Feelings are clichéd. The world is viewed in terms of palpable superficialities and stereotypes.

Table 3.1 Some Stage Theories of Development from the Concrete Operational Period Onward

Young	Kohlberg	Loevinger	Perry	Commons and Richards
Perioperational multiplication	Instrumental (transition stage)	Self-protective		Concrete
Perioperational integration		Rule-oriented		
Abstract coordination	Mutuality	Conformist		Abstract
Abstract hierarchization	Logical social	Conscientious/conformist	Dualistic construction	Formal
			Multiplicity perceived, rejected	
Abstract systemization	Social system conscience	Conscientious	Multiplicity accepted, relegated	Systematic
Abstract multiplication	Transitional postconventional	Individualistic	Immersion in multiplicity	
Abstract integration	Prior rights and responsibilities	Autonomous	Relativism viable	Metasystematic
Collective coordination	Universal processes	Postautonomous	Universal relativism; commitment foreseen	Paradigmatic
Collective hierarchization			First commitments included	
Collective systemization			Commitment implications seen	Cross-paradigmatic
Collective multiplication			Restructuring, expanding commitment	
Collective integration	Cosmic perspective	Integrated universal		

Adult Stages

Most American adults perform at the conscientious–conformist level, where there is a beginning separation of one's real and ideal selves, and personal goals and group standards. The self can be examined as a separate object and be assertive. Interpersonal relationships involve feelings as well as actions and are more reciprocal, for individuals see themselves as having some impact on others and even the whole group. Their panorama grows to include concerns about personal adjustment, reasons for acting, seeing problems, and choosing from options. However, group norms still exert their influence. For example, personal adjustment revolves around loneliness, self-consciousness, and other group-related sentiments.

In the conscientious stage, standards that are self-constructed emerge, for the self (rational, determined, with high self-esteem) and group are clearly fissioned. Personal long-term ideals, goals, and criteria for critical thought (causes, benefits, costs) are developed. In terms of the other, individuals are evaluated as different from each other and complex, and they are related to with responsibility, intensity, and reciprocal sharing. People with similar goals and values are sought. Time is consciously evaluated. For example, individuals evaluate themselves in terms of traits both back into the past and forward into the future. Humankind is conceived as perfectible, truth as discoverable.

In the individualistic stage, the self is seen as a unique entity, and is independently redefined. One's inner and outer lives are differentiated. A wide range of individual differences are tolerated. A concern for social problems develops and a sense of mutuality deepens, for relativity in thought emerges. Thus, one entertains paradoxes, accepts different roles for the same person, rejects the notion of absolute truth, recognizes problems as complex, and separates means from ends, for the former no longer justify the latter.

The autonomous phase is marked by the other's need for individualized independence within the context of mutual interdependence. Individuals seek self-fulfillment and valid commitment, and so accept the inevitability of inner conflicts (e.g., between needs and wishes) without displacing their origins in the environment. They end up tolerating these conflicts and ambiguities not only within themselves but also in others. Thus, subselves can remain separate but can be integrated, as well.

Postautonomous individuals, according to Cook-Greuter (1990), yearn to transcend their bounded ego in a web of interconnected beings or as part of an infinite wholeness. Yet they relentlessly pursue alone self-determined life courses. This existential paradox and others produce preoccupying inner conflicts. In accepting the resultant tension and continuing on with their commitments, positive equilibration is attained. Ultimate truth is judged illusory, because all knowledge is seen as constructed in contemplation.

The Final Stage. In the penultimate integrated stage in Loevinger's model of adult development, people have a universal vision and are at peace with themselves. Inner conflicts are resolved, for they are reconciled without confrontation. For example, a sense of bonding of the self with the universe is merged without problem to a sense of personal uniqueness. Multiple perspectives are adopted on issues and they are navigated readily, for individuals feel embedded in a natural global flow. For example, the connative and denotative, and the tangible and the eternal symbolic attributes of objects, are apprehended simultaneously and effortlessly. Thus, any being, whatever her or his characteristics, is experienced as someone with whom feels at one, with both self and other fully accepted in a noncontrolling fashion. Truth is immanent, accessible, but not rationally mastered.

Pascual-Leone (1990) refers to this age period as one involving a realized self partaking in a transcendental and meditative thinking which produces an open, liberally interconnected, detached unity. Thus, beliefs are considered dialectical and alternatives equally embraced, all with a serene calm in face of uncertainty. Koplowitz (1990) depicts a unitary consciousness, or direct immediate awareness knowing no time or space, no permanent object or boundary. Funk (1990) argues that there is a pervading, mystical oneness. For example, Beethoven's last symphonic works were musical holographs where each idea or phrase implied the whole, and the entirety seemed to coexist instantaneously.

Kohlberg has added a final seventh "soft" stage to his stage theory of moral development (Kohlberg & Ryncarz, 1990), and it shares the approach of the theorists just cited. Individuals sense being a part of a larger cosmos that has a natural ultimate order. The self is moral through its transcendental, mystical, intimate experience of union or bond with the universe. Sonnert (1994) has qualified the nature of this stage, arguing that it is metadiscursive. The morally mature adult exhibits a dialogue of principles and pragmatics where universalist moralistic arguments are moderated by contextualist expediencies. Moreover, multiple stage 6 moral discourses are evaluated, coordinated, and examined self-referentially, "making the moral position realistic and the realistic position moral." Moshman (1995) argues that the last two kohlbergian stages involve metaethical criteria not only of the classic kind such as the respect for persons, but also those involving communal solidarity, equilibrium, happiness, flourishing, care and alleviation of suffering, and sentiments about life's oneness and the presence of a natural order.

Comment. Blasi and Glodis (1995) have expanded Loevinger's description of the stages in the development of the self by describing the complementary subjective identities that emerge in the stages stretching from the conformist stage to a combined autonomous–integrated stage.

The authors are concerned with the subjective sense of individuality, unity, identity, and continuity that develops in one's sense of self. In the first step, a social role identity based on external appearance and social expectations develops. Next, an inner identity with self-reflection and self-feelings is observed. Then, an agentic, managed identity develops with constructed goals, standards, and ideals. Finally, an authentic identity emerges where there is independence, the acceptance of uncertainty, relativity, honesty, and universality.

The work of Blasi and Glodis (1995) illustrates the manner in which Loevinger's theory can be elaborated into a broader vision of self development. It is in this spirit that I propose the following theory.

Loevinger's model of self development in adolescence and adulthood has been integrated into the current model in the following way. The first two of her stages (presocial, impulsive) have been ignored, while the next three stages (self-protective, rule-oriented, conformist) suggested to me possible reactions that developing individuals might have to dangers which emerge in the current cognitive substages 14 to 16 (see tables on dangers in development, last line of descriptions, in the prologue to this volume). The next six stages (conscientious-conformist to postautonomous) have been incorporated into the current model of self development (level 17 to 21, 25). Loevinger's last stage of integrated being has been aligned with the current last one, breaking the one-to-one correspondence between the levels of the theories, because it and the other similar descriptions presented seem complementary to the last stage in adult development of the current model.

THE CURRENT MODEL
OF SELF DEVELOPMENT

The General Model

In constructing the current model of self development, there was only so much that could be borrowed from other theories. For the most part, I extrapolated from the 25 cognitive levels and corresponding socioemotional systems in development described in detail in Young (submitted), determining what seemed logically derivative from this base for a theory of self development. At the same time, one- or two-sentence summaries of key portions of the prior theories which seemed concordant with the current model were included. Where possible, the labels stemming from the prior theories were used to represent the 25 proposed steps in self development (presented in depth in Tables 3.2–3.6 and summarized in Table 3.7). However, new labels were created when it seemed necessary.

Table 3.2 Substages in Self and Family Development in the Reflex Stage

Self-development	Family development
1. *Fetal life*: Being not quite a self at this juncture, the moniker "elf" will do to describe the *nonself*.	*Nesting family*: Caregivers must psychologically, prepare themselves (and any siblings) for the new arrival. The physical setting is planned. Some ruminate on "ghosts" in the nursery, or their own psychological past, as their future as caregivers arrives.
2. *Premature self I*: Motor skills unexpectedly are put to test in fragile, vulnerable prematures. Even nursing acts are problematic. We can speak of a *reflexive preself*.	*Incubator family*: The family must marshall its resources to be near the endangered baby in the incubator, spending as much time as possible at the hospital.
3. *Premature self II*: Survival being more certain, the inherent openness of babies manifests. Contact and information are sought even in the precarious circumstances of the hospital. Given the grounding of behavior in primitive control schemata, there appears to be a psychological self which we can label the protoself. Since it is especially action- and target-oriented, it can be characterized as the *corporal protoself*.	*Preparatory family*: With the imminent arrival of the baby in the home, whether in terms of an impending birth of a full-term newborn of the homecoming of hospitalized preterm infant, the organizational flexibility of the family is tested. Life-styles alter to accommodate to the coming offspring (e.g., childbirth courses attended, books read, room prepared, caregiving arrangements planned).
4. *Emergent self I*: Full-term newborns manifest integrating cross-modal matching abilities tied to corresponding production schemes (e.g., imitating mouth opening) (Meltzoff & Moore, 1989). This primary perceptual/representational capacity may be affiliated with perceptual learning, simple classical conditioning, and/or priming in memory (Squire, 1987; Tulving & Schacter, 1990). Priming is a nonconscious, facilitative effect in memory and functions to improve perceptual identification of objects. Helplessness and calling behaviors elicit caregiving, making much of the intramodal world socioaffective. The emerging self seems to be a *perceptual intermodal self*. Neisser (1991) takes a similar position, for he calls the self in this period the perceptual self, and attributes to it two components—the ecological self and the interpersonal self.	*Birthing family*: The style of reception and interaction with the baby in the first few days of life may set the tone for future phases. The family is concerned, present, and caring. This matches the newborn's active need for appropriate caregiving and alimentation of her or his perceptual search.
5. *Emergent self II*: Infants in the next weeks develop the capacity to integrate separate schemes into more unified structures, building intermodal integration skills. Usually schemes function with concomitant, most basic emotional overtones and are body-focused. We can designate this self the *primary emotional self*.	*Affect/rhythm family*: The very young infant's emotional world is modulated by a cherishing, doting surveillance, for basic rhythms (sleep-wake, engage-disengage, lack-satisfaction) are established. The parents are responsive, sensitive, and interested in being interesting and provoking attention.

Table 3.3 Substages in Self and Family Development
in the Sensorimotor Stage

Self development	Family development
6. *Core, coordinated interaction self*: Young infants' scheme coordination skills lead to dyadic interchanges. Invariant patterns are established, but especially because of caregiver framing. This permits the infants' inherent active nature to achieve agency through participation in regulatory "games" played, connectedness of one's own actions and transactions, control of emotional reactions in the caregiver, etc. At this point, the self seems to be an *intercoordinated incipient social self*.	*Scaffolding family*: The parents elevate their communicative level to accommodate to the growing infant's increasingly sophisticated dyadic skills. They create holding structures in which they know when to wait, when to stimulate, when to cycle with the infant's activity, when to calm the infant, etc. Framed opportunities for optimal outreach and intercourse are provided.
7. *Core initiatory self*: At midyear, we see a more hierarchical behavior (e.g., context-created, purposeful behavior, Piaget; generalized sense of personal agency, Case, 1991b), which fosters social initiation, emotional focus, and particularities in relationships. A sense of trust in the surround, especially caregivers, develops when that surround facilitates successful goal-oriented behavior. Erikson's psychosocial stage of trust vs. mistrust also fits here, and leads me to call the self of this period the *end-focused trusting self*.	*Trustworthy family*: Self-confidence is established by an honest, accepting attitude, including empathic understanding. The infant's first overt purposeful behavior is not subverted by viewing it as too imposing, and mistrust does not develop.
8. *Subjective attachment self*: Given the emergence of primitive representational images, and the beginning of (hidden) object permanence, intentions come to guide behavior before its onset. Thus, mental states of self and other are better coordinated, producing more friendliness, sharing, referencing of the other (and indirect agency, Case, 1991b). Attachment to the caregiver becomes active (e.g., searching when the caregiver leaves, calling/protesting her or his departure). The self at this level seems an especially *permanent intersubjective self*.	*Interobjective family*: Responding reciprocally to the infant's intended intersubjectivity, parents give of themselves, share, encourage an active attachment, and become secure figures of attachment. They match the child's intersubjective sociality and attachment needs (serving as "objects" of attachment).

Table 3.3 (*Continued*)

Self development	Family development
9. *Verbal autonomous self*: Linear inner plans in year olds allow increased autonomous action even if in opposition to caregiver wishes. Also with planning capacities, infants can entertain leaving their caregivers base to explore and return in a psychological and not only a physical sense. Caregivers cocreate meaning with infants through language as they toddle about exploring and returning for refuelling. Thus, language facilitates the development of Erikson's autonomy through its distal and shared modalities. The conceptual awareness of self as an independent actor emerges. Thus, we can speak of an *independent autonomous self.*	*Autonomy-fostering family*: Parents match the toddler's exploratory and verbal gambits by accepting, supervising, explaining, answering, amplifying, extending, simplifying, correcting, etc. All this is undertaken with the appropriate emotional fuel necessary for the toddler. Topped up with feelings and words, the toddler accelerates into the fast lane of autonomous physical displacement toward psychological individuation.
10. *Verbal constancy self*: In older toddlers, symbol plans which permit mental combination underlie behavior. Also, evaluations emerge due to these plans. Thus, social interchange becomes a complex interdigitation of plans, and a mutual awareness that the other has plans and is aware, producing the beginnings of true role taking and empathy. Toddlers develop self-constancy whereby they realize that they can actively oppose caregivers and either reinstate their relationship or have caregivers cooperate. Thus, toddlers symbolize the self as a separate entity, seeing it as a willful agent of their symbolic plans. (Toddlers can use the words "I" and "Me" at this age; R. Brown, 1973). In short, the self at this age can be called an *interior implicative self.* Toddlers both implicate (evaluate) cognitively and implicate themselves (interdigitate) socially.	*"Exterior" family*: As the toddler advances in thinking and social skills, the family is called upon to be more flexible, reciprocal, and supportive, yet without denying limits. They must adopt a matching or complementary, even opposite role before the child (e.g., letting lead, control; confirming child's evaluation even if it is wrong in order to foster a sense of pride in self). Their "yesses" are either genuine and encourage, or qualified but do not discourage. "Nos" are firm, and explained. The psychological individual integrity of the toddler is fully respected; her/his separate self is acknowledged as exterior to other family members.

A Synthetic Model of Banduran Self-Efficacy

Introduction. The synthetic model of self development that has been proposed in the preceding section speaks to the development of the I self. The Me self should pass through the same developmental series as the I self (Case, 1991a). In the present section, it is suggested that a component of the

**Table 3.4 Substages in Self and Family Development
in the Perioperational Stage**

Self development	Family development
11. *Egocentric–centrated self*: Symbol plan coordination allows young children to organize cohesive, coherent wholes in behavior (e.g., in language utterances, story events, parallel tasks, and in understanding the social system of the family with its multiple roles; Case, 1991b). But coordinations involving the self are egocentrically hierarchized with no or little flexibility in thought to permit decentration on the other. This cognitive egocentrism leads to a lack of differentiation of the physical and psychosocial features of the other and a lack of appreciation of their perspective. The one self is an incorporating, coupling one, and so it is labeled the *coupling egocentric-centrated self*.	*Expanding family*: The egocentric stance of the 2- to 3-year-old as he or she expands into the world can try the most patient parents. The family's superordinate structure is tested, and a coherent, cohesive, integrated family can accommodate to the child without stifling her or him. This process is abetted by expanding out to preschool play groups, neighborhood play partners, grandparents, other family, etc. Also, at this point, the mother may be having, expecting, or planning an addition (expanding the family).
12. *Initiative self*: Preschoolers' predilection for hierarchizing symbol plans directs them to think of themselves as dominant, or with initiative in their daily challenges. The differentiation of the other is from within the children's projected perspective. This can lead to the Oedipal situation of fantasizing about the opposite-sex parent. In summary, we can refer to a *hierarchizing initiative self*.	*Initiative-fostering family*: The preschooler's abundant initiative must be counterbalanced by sensible rules explicated sensitively when the situation demands such action. The preschooler's pushing forth into the world of peers and play to master and dominate is countered by realistic restraints put in place by parents.
13. *First-person perspective taking, unilateral self*: Symbol plan systems allow rule systems to be mastered and dimensions of self- and other-ranking to be apprehended. This enables identification with parental attributes and sex-appropriate gender roles. Such perspective taking is accompanied by clear differentiation of others' psychological characteristics. But a subjective, one-way understanding of the other predominates. Thus, we can speak of a *systematizing primary-perspective self*.	*Normative-streaming family*: Parents arrange the best schooling. Rule systems, a moral ordering, etc., are provided by the family (and the school). The family continues to model appropriate sex-role behavior, channeling identification. They correct self-ranking that depreciates self-worth, and they monitor identification, assuring equilibration.

(*continued*)

Table 3.4 (*Continued*)

Self development	Family development
14. *Reciprocal, second-person perspective-taking, self-reflective self*: Concrete operations permit school-age children to think more logically, facilitating the "industry" of school. This logic is also turned inward, for children evaluate their own thoughts, and is also turned toward others, for their perspectives are evaluated. Others are understood to perform the same "other" evaluation (i.e., evaluation of the children themselves). The label *concrete operational secondary-perspective self* seems appropriate here.	*Educating family*: Parents instruct and give lessons; they help with homework and plan extracurricular activities. They protect the child from worrying too much about the opinions of others. Their forum for learning rivals that of the school in some senses.
15. *Third-person, perspective-taking, mutual self*: Subteens' logic in imagination leads to multiple exploration. They remove themselves from the self system. A different self is imagined and a mutuality in self- and other-perspective taking takes hold (third-person perspective-taking). An independence from one's own self accrues through immersion in others. At this level there seems to be a *projecting tertiary-perspective self*.	*Let-subteen-mirror family*: The relative status of the child and parents becomes more balanced or on equal footing, for actual adult roles are entertained or portrayed by the child. Parents are especially concerned that the subteen not only acquires independence (with peers) but also behaves responsibly with their freedom, without losing the perspective that he or she is still relatively young. They discuss realistic constraints in terms of the pre-adolescent's imaginings both about the self and the relation to the other and the environment. Parents act supportive. They do not feel menaced by their subteen growing toward them psychologically yet preparing distancing or independence moves. The range of the parents' reach into society (their varied activities and faces, their sense of mutuality with the surround) is mirrored in their offspring through her or his modeling function.

Me self, one's sense of self-efficacy, as described by Bandura (see Young, submitted), should develop in parallel with the general neopiagetian cognitive substages of the current model.

Table 3.8 presents the particular model of the development of a personal sense of self-efficacy that has been formulated in light of the current synthetic model of neopiagetian cognitive development. It is based on the five major stages of the current theory. However, I hint at only the general

Table 3.5 Substages in Self and Family Development in the Abstract Stage

Self development	Family development
16. *In-depth, societal–symbolic perspective-taking self*: Young adolescents can coordinate separate pathways of logic in imagination, precipitating the acquisition of formal abstract thought. Such logic enables creative conscious awareness, where adolescents have metacognitions about their cognitions and motives. Past and future are analyzed, linked, and chained, or coordinated to give a Januslike vision in the present. Conscious esteem develops for the self, the other, and ideas. Abstract logic allows one to see the self and other as complex entities functioning simultaneously at multiple conscious and unconscious levels. If confusion sets in, excessive conformity may result. At this level the self may be described as the *abstractly aware conscious self*.	*Coconscious family*: The adolescent's free exploration of internal "distances" and external realities is not inhibited, mitigated, or compromised by a lack of same in family members, either in the present or as unresolved conflicts in the past. The teenager can perceive masks, pretense, and shells, and the well-integrated family has divested itself of such vestiges for the most part. Nevertheless, parents maintain a supervisory function; they promote their standards, and try to ensure that their offspring come to self-monitor them, while acknowledging and supporting those of their offspring.
17. *Conscientious–conformist self*: Adolescents can now weigh multiple variables and logically proceed to attempt to solve problems about the self, the wider world, and their relation. Accentuated by pubertal awakening, this process can lead to an evaluation of self-identity, ideology, and place in the time course. A sense of the real self, truly personal goals, concerns about personal adjustment, and options concerning the self emerge. All this leads me to call the self in this period the *identity-seeking self*.	*Identity-fostering family*: The adolescent now sees the well-integrated family that has raised her or him as a vibrant, self-actualizing family, which infuses her or him with the sculpting vitality needed for the challenge of unfettered quest for identity and self-agency (which does not exclude a sense of familial communion and attachment; Gilligan, 1982). Parents help in this process by guiding, channeling, and setting limits on their adolescent's distancing efforts.
18. *Conscientious self*: The capacity of late adolescents for abstract systematization permits systemic understanding; personal and other perspectives can coexist in one integrated structure. Social and societal relationships are seen as components of a larger whole to which the individual must contribute. With this viewpoint comes self-constructed standards, or criteria applied in critical thought. Late adolescents seem to possess a *maturing conscientious self*.	*Letting-go family*: The late adolescent's will for a harmonious integration of self-in-system is accompanied by a parental attitude allowing much more distanced freedom from the family. Parents are nonintervening and accepting, yet give counsel, negotiate consensual goals, etc. (Barnhill and Longo [1978] use the term "letting go" in conjunction with the reencountering family, level 22 in the following table. I think that it fits better here).

Table 3.5 (*Continued*)

Self development	Family development
19. *Individualistic self*: The dialectical, relativist thought of youth permits the self to be seen as unique yet engaged in a deep mutuality with differentiated others. We can call this self the *mutual relativistic self*, for there is a profound nonabsolutist immersion in the self, the other, and their relation.	*Launching family*: Parents do all they can to promote constructive, functional, preparatory activity for the tasks of adulthood. The young person feels a profound intermutuality and cooperative distancing, and the final transition to the initiation of a new family cycle is facilitated. Parents ought to be near or in the phase of Erikson's generativity at this point, so that their own transformative reappraisal of the self is matched by their offspring's final transformation into adults.
20. *Autonomous self-sufficient self*: Adults possess abstract integration skills which enable a universal empathy. They recognize others' need for individualized independence within a framework of reciprocal interdependence. They accept others' conflicts or ambiguities as their own. This self seems an *accepting universal self*.	*Seconding family*: An adult is in consistent need of social–environmental support, complementing her or his sense of empathy for the social world/environment, in general. Parents serve as generative mediators, providing the needed support (advice, baby sitting, financial, etc.), but always trying to maintain a secondary role at a comfortable distance.

nature of the substage progression in each stage; Table 3.8. lists only the initial and final substages in each stage. The table depicts the feeling about self-efficacy that should be experienced when development is proceeding more or less normally and when it is jeopardized. The latter would obtain, for example, when the environment acts not to foster optimal development but a precarious one. For example, parents may encourage a vicious cycle of doubt and failure on cognitive tasks by negative attributions of a child's competence. In this context, the repercussions on the developing individual's sense of self should take the form indicated.

The Model. When the newborn is developing normally and is well cared for, he or she develops a sense of omnipotence before any task or challenge, which leads to a blind sense of renewal or rejuvenation before each one. If this phase is not well traversed, then a sense of annihilation at worst or stagnation at best is elicited during confrontation.

In the next stage of development, the infant developing an appropriate sense of self-efficacy should manifest security as opposed to insecurity when participating in tasks, and with increasing age will demonstrate a toddler swagger as opposed to an inhibiting stiffness.

**Table 3.6 Substages in Self and Family Development
in the Collective Intelligence Stage**

Self development	Family development
21. *Postautonomous self*: Metaphysical reasoning in subdomain or generic theory–procedure coordination engenders an appreciation of the wholeness of the web of being that allows our participation in this process. This self is termed a *holistic meta-self*.	*Extending family*: Parents strive to maintain strong links with all offspring and their children, and have them do the same, creating a familial web, or network. This often extends to inclusion of other relatives. That is, parents try to assure that familial distancing does not lead to neglect. Parents also encourage a more active participation in the wider community and world.
22. *Generative self*: With hierarchization of the coordination in the above process, a spreading generativity (e.g., mentoring) is fostered. We can speak of an *activating generative self*.	*Reencountering family*: As offspring become established and their children are born and develop, empty-nest parents have more time for tasks put on hold. The second-order distance with older grandchildren becomes more equitable as they develop toward and into adolescence. This helps foster the satisfaction and acceptance of one's life course inherent in Erikson's stage of ego integrity. Also it allows their children's unfolding generativity to develop unhindered.
23. *Midlife self*: Domain systematization parallels the transitional midlife period. Generativity is more elaborate and systemic. It is coupled with a transformative rethinking of the self and contemplation of the end of those phases where one's potential and dreams seemed to have no temporal or physical constraints. We can refer to a *catalytic midlife self*.	*Transgenerational family*: As parents approach and enter retirement, they look backward and forward, e.g., integrating their children and grandchildren into their more frequent reminiscing narratives. The distance between elder parent and adult children is marked by equality. The wisdom of the older adult can act as a solder for the entire family, and a contained instigation toward growth in their midlife offspring.
24. *Ego integrity self*: Interdomain thought is accompanied by satisfaction and acceptance of one's life course. The self appears a *satisfied ego integrity self*.	*Autumn family*: Many of the elderly are active, well-adjusted, and independent. Distance from family members is variable depending on need. Some may need support and care in their turn, a responsibility often undertaken dutifully even if it is difficult. Whether healthy or not, the elderly derive second-order satisfaction in seeing their offspring manifest satisfaction and acceptance of their life course. This second-order satisfaction becomes a second-order support for their offspring.

Table 3.6. (*Continued*)

Self development	Family development
25. *Integrated self*: In the final phases of life, often there is a wider knowledge which is accompanied by cathartic or purifying experiences. The elderly become impregnated by a holistic sense of wisdom and also feel communion or reverence with what they regard as holy. In their most meditative moments, they hope to transcend, and in consequence to be one with mystery. Self development culminates in a *purified integrated self.*	*Rested family*: Death is seen as tranquil repose, a welcome undistancing for parents who have optimally traversed life's epochal journey. Knowledge of their children's growth to integration facilitates the passage through this process.

Table 3.7 Summary of Substages in Self and Family Development

Level	Self	Family
1.	Nonself	Nesting
2.	Reflexive preself	Incubator
3.	Corporal protoself	Preparatory
4.	Perceptual intermodal self	Birthing
5.	Primary emotional self	Affect/rhythm
6.	Intercoordinated incipient social self	Scaffolding
7.	End-focused trusting self	Trustworthy
8.	Permanent intersubjective self	Interobjective
9.	Independent autonomous self	Autonomy fostering
10.	Interior immplicative self	Exterior
11.	Coupling egocentric/centrated self	Expanding
12.	Hierarchizing initiative self	Initiative-fostering
13.	Systematizing primary-perspective self	Normative-streaming
14.	Concrete operational secondary-perspective self	Educating
15.	Projecting tertiary–perspective self	Let subteen mirror
16.	Abstractly aware conscious self	Coconscious
17.	Identity seeking self	Identity fostering
18.	Maturing conscientious self	Letting go
19.	Mutual relativistic self	Launching
20.	Accepting universal self	Seconding
21.	Holistic metaself	Extending
22.	Activating generative self	Reencountering
23.	Catalytic midlife self	Transgenerational
24.	Satisfied ego-integrity self	Autumn
25.	Purified integrated self	Rested

Table 3.8 Steps in the Development of a Sense of Self-Efficacy

Stage	Self-efficacy	
	Normally developing	Compromised
Reflexive	Omnipotence	Annihilation
	Renewal	Stagnation
Sensorimotor	Security	Insecurity
	Swagger	Stiffness
Perioperational	Pretension, presumption	Presumptiousness
	Poise	Fluster (bluster)
Abstract	Assurance (certitude)	Chronic uncertainty
	Self serenity	Chronic malaise
Collective intelligence	Communal confidence	Communal cynicism
	Integrated consciousness	Collective rejection

Note. The first and last of the five substages in each stage are specified for their self-efficacy sentiments.

The perioperational child moves from an attitude of blanket pretension or presumption of success toward a preadolescent poise, but may manifest presumptuous and blustery behavior instead.

The abstract adolescent is self-assured and grows toward an adult internal serenity before life's challenges. However, there also may be a chronic uncertainty which culminates in a chronic malaise.

Finally, the maturing adult in her or his collective behavior senses a confidence and immersion in and symbiosis with the communal surround as he or she accomplishes life's complex tasks. However, instead of an increasing opening toward an integrated awareness, there may be a cynicism toward and even a rejection of collective intelligence.

Conclusion. The specific level of the sense of self-efficacy at which a developing individual is functioning should reflect her or his parents' behavior and the wider society's lens on the way he or she should approach life. Generally, parents should aim to develop an attitude that a child should be confident about her or his capabilities in all tasks, except those that are clearly (but not slightly) beyond her or his current developmental level. Moreover, they should foster a faith that they or some other significant other will be available to monitor and direct the child in an appropriate manner on such complex tasks.

However, if the developing individual is entrained to function below her or his general developmental level, and/or have confidence in a more primitive level than the one actually achieved for a particular domain, then the individual's resultant attitude may not be adaptive. That is, the adolescent or adult who carries a sensorimotor swagger or childish bluster may find these traits adaptive in some of their daily encounters. However, the flexibility of these levels of sense of self-efficacy compared to higher-order ones is limited. Moreover, they should be colored by various negative affective experiences, and thus hamper cognitive functioning.

In Chapter 7, the concept of the cognitive (mis)perception of the other is introduced and it is hypothesized that a misperception of the child can exist at different degrees and that these degrees are specified by the 25 steps of the current neopiagetian cognitive developmental model. When development is not promoted adequately by parents and/or society, it may be due to the mediating influence of this type of cognitive misperception. Thus, in terms of the promotion of development of self-efficacy in their child, parents may aim to encourage the attainment of their own or society's level rather than the optimal or the highest level possible. If a sensorimotor swagger or a perioperational bluster helped them survive in their world and/or if the world canalized them to function at this level, then surely their child should do the same in order to be well adapted. This may be true only insofar as the environment matches the child's perception of her or himself and accommodates to it, which may be difficult if the child's functioning level is well behind the one expected in normal circumstances, or if it is well ahead of the desired one in repressive circumstances.

This section completes the current presentation on the development of the self throughout the lifespan. The corollary domain of the development of the adult's optimal parenting and family stance as their children grow is discussed in the next chapter.

CHAPTER 4

Family Development

OTHER MODELS
OF FAMILY DEVELOPMENT

For each substage of self development, the growing individual's family should provide the matching fit necessary for optimal passage through the psychological challenges that life engenders. Current models of family development (e.g., Aldous, 1990; Barnhill & Longo, 1978, in Barker, 1986; Carter & McGoldrick, 1989; Combrink-Graham, 1985; Dallos, 1995; Falicov, 1988; Framo, 1994; Galinsky, 1981; Stratton, 1988; deVries, Birren, & Deutchman, 1990; Wapner, 1993; and see Birchler, 1992, and Nichols & Pace-Nichols, 1993, for models of the marital life cycle) are too global, not providing enough differentiation to help in the current search for 25 levels corresponding to the substages of self development. Moreover, the proposed family life cycle changes in these models are usually age-related milestones and not related to the developing person's psychology, per se (see Table 4.1).

The Combrinck-Graham (1985) model of family development is based on the concept of the family life spiral, where centripetal and centrifugal forces act on the family as it moves through various generational events. Some of these events occur in parallel over generations, e.g., the forties reevaluation by parents occurs simultaneously with their offsprings' adolescent challenge. As for the specific stages in her model, after the periods of birth, childhood, and adolescence come courtship-marriage, child bearing, settling down, the forties re-evaluation/middle adulthood, grandparenting, retirement planning/arrival, and late adulthood.

Barnhill and Longo (1978; modeled after Duval & Hill, 1948; in Barker, 1986) have a similar sequence which involves transition points in stage-to-stage passage. After commitment of the couple, parenting roles are adopted. Then, the child's personality must be accepted as he or she develops. Next, the child is guided into the world of institutions such as schools, scouts,

Table 4.1 Summary of Theories of the Family Life Cycle

Barnhill and Longo (1978)	Combrinck-Graham (1985)	Carter and McGoldrick (1989)	Galinsky (1981) and Wapner (1993)
Commitment of couple	Birth	Leaving home	Image making (pregnancy)
Parenting roles adopted	Middle Childhood	Single young adult	Nurturing (0–2 yr)
Acceptance of child's personality	Adolescence	The joining of family through marriage	Authority (2–5)
Guiding child in institutions	Courtship-marriage	The new couple	Interpretive (5–12)
Acceptance of adolescence, quest for independence	Childbearing	Family with young children	Interdependent (adolescence)
Preparations to launch	Settling down	Family with adolescents	Departure (e.g., young adult)
Letting go, facing each other	Forties reevaluation	Launching children/moving on	Grandparenting
Acceptance of retirement	Grandparenting	Family in later life	
Acceptance of old age	Retirement planning/arrival		
	Late adulthood		

Note. Other models exist, such as Dallos's (1995) six-step model; Courtship, Early marriage, Children, Middle marriage, Leaving home, Retirement/Old age.

and peer groups. Then, the parents must accept adolescence and the quest for independence that shortly follows. Preparations to launch a new family take place in the young adulthood of parent's offspring. This leads to parents' letting go and facing each other in the empty nest. Finally, accepting retirement and old age rounds out a productive life.

Carter and McGoldrick (1989) have a quite differentiated model of family development, even if they describe fewer phases than the other models. There are six stages in their model, and the emotional processes and second-order changes needed by the family to successfully navigate each stage are presented. The six family life stages include leaving home, marriage, having children, adapting to adolescence, launching offspring, and late life.

Galinsky (1981; updated by Wapner, 1993) proposed a model of family development that is less milestone- and more psychology-oriented than the others. In the image-making stage during pregnancy, parents-to-be create images of what is to come, prepare for future roles, and form feelings for their future child. In the nurturing stage, which lasts from birth to 2 years of age, parents become attached to the child. Next, in the authority stage from 2 to 5 years, parents use their power to select and enforce limits, communicate, and so on. Parents act to foster a sense of eriksonian autonomy in the child in this stage. In the interpretive stage from 5 to 12 years, parents help the child understand the world, values, and themselves, and function as resources to help them obtain appropriate information and instruction in order to facilitate this task. With adolescence, parents enter the interdependence stage where they promote the child's quest for self and awareness of the self's components (i.e., internal and external). With late adolescence or early adulthood comes the departure or distancing stage, where parents are confronted with the task "of accepting one's grown child's separateness and individuality, while maintaining the connection ..." (Galinsky, 1981, p. 307). Finally, with grandparenthood, the cycle becomes complete. As shall be shown in the next section, the current model borrows the general approach that Galinsky adopted, although the model of family development that is proposed encompasses 25 as opposed to seven stages.

THE CURRENT MODEL

The Model

For each of the 25 substages of self development in the current theory, a matching stance that the family must adopt in order to foster optimal development in their offspring is proposed. These levels are summarized in telegraphic form in the following (They are presented in depth in Tables 3.2–3.6 and summarized in Table 3.7.)

I. Reflexive period: (i) nesting, or preparing for baby; (ii) incubator, or proximity to vulnerable premature; (iii) preparatory, or adjusting to impending arrival at home; (iv) birthing, or bonding in first days; (v) affect-rhythm, or dancing to and with baby. II. Sensorimotor: (i) scaffolding, or framed holding of interaction; (ii) trustworthy, or supportive of goal-directed behavior; (iii) interobjective, or attachment-fostering; (iv) autonomy-fostering, or exploration facilitation; (v) exterior, or complementing interiorization of toddler. III. Perioperational: (i) expanding, or accommodating the egocentric 2-year-old; (ii) initiative-fostering, or counterbalancing the preschooler's push into the world; (iii) normative streaming, or channeling into the wider world; (iv) teaching-preaching, or helping to learn; (v) let-subteen-mirror, or encouraging adult role-playing. IV. Abstract: (i) coconscious, or consciousness-fostering; (ii) identity-fostering, or supportive of self-exploration; (iii) letting-go, or preparatory to launching; (iv) launching, or helping the adult offspring begin on own; (v) seconding, or continuing to support adult offspring. V. Collective: (i) extending, or facilitating wider family; (ii) reencountering, or promoting adult offsprings' generativity; (iii) transgenerational, or intergenerational equalization; (iv) autumn, or second-order support; (v) rested, or integrative.

Comment

Any one family stance may persist beyond the period most needed, or reappear in force when necessary. At least two of them may interface when siblings of different ages are being brought up. The constellation of necessary attitudes may become cumbersome at certain junctures of a family's evolution, but most families navigate beyond these whirlpools in raising children. Note that the description of family development being proposed is general enough to apply to most types of family structure.

In parent–offspring relations, a pushing process is not the only one involved, for families are also pulled forward in growth as they react to the challenge of children's growth. This concept seems parallel to Sameroff's (1989) environtype, where graded change in the child produces parallel change in the environment.

Self development may synchronize with cognitive development, but often there is a "horizontal décalage," or the substage of self development to which one has advanced lags behind the corresponding cognitive substage. Cognitive substage acquisition provides a necessary but not sufficient condition for self development, for myriad other factors are involved. This is true especially for the adolescent and adult levels, where there is a wide range of individual differences in décalage between cognitive and self substage development. Inevitably, this must affect the appropriate familial stance needed for the developing individual.

THE MARITAL CYCLE

Where do theories of the marital cycle fit in with the current model of the family cycle? There is no room here to review the literature on the topic (see Birchler, 1992), but its perusal revealed a rather static conception of the nature of the steps in an adult relationship. Usually, after a preliminary honeymoon period, some form of disappointment or negative emotion would set in, and this would be followed by phases of resolution. The current model follows a different tack. It describes a sequence of steps in marital development resembling the eriksonian conception of stages where each step brings with it new positive and negative potentials that may lead to either a working out toward their balance or to their conflict and a crisis.

It is suggested that adult relationships go through five phases reflective of the five stages in the current theory of development (see Table 4.2). That is, fitting the initial reflexive stage in the current synthetic model, in adult relationship development first there is a corporal, reflexive attraction, which is accompanied by an opposition of overly positive/realistic evaluations and negative ones. Second, in keeping with the next stage of infant sensorimotor development and its focus on attachment to the caregiver, in adult relationships next an emotional attachment develops, which sees the opposition of security-fostering (e.g., dialogue) and insecurity-fostering (e.g., overcontrol) behavior. In the current developmental model, in the third stage the child develops perioperations, or preoperations and concrete operations, which permit systematic representation-based thought and problem solving. Consequently, in the third phase of adult relational

Table 4.2 Steps in the Marital Cycle

Developmental stage	Relationship stage	Opposition
Reflexive	Attraction	Overpositive, realistic vs. overnegative evaluation
Sensorimotor	Attachment	Security fostering vs. insecurity fostering
Perioperational	Commitment	Cooperation, give and take vs. give or take
Abstract	Growth	Conscious unfolding vs. infolding
Collective intelligence	Mutuality	Emergent constitutiveness vs. reciprocal constraint

Note. Five substages in the cycle can be described according to the typical ones in the synthetic model of development (coordination to integration).

development a well-thought-out emotional commitment should develop in the opposition of cooperative give-and-take versus advantage-related give-or-take behavior. In adolescence, abstract formal operations-logic develops, which permits hypothesis testing, experimentation, conscious awareness, visioning the future, etc. In terms of relationships this should lead to conscious psychological growth for the partners, where an unfolding process opposes an infolding one, where each partner maximizes her or his growth in the reciprocal sharing and higher-order other-perspective taking permitted by formal operations. Finally, in the mature adult, collective intelligence and sociality develops, and this should engender transcendent mutuality in relationships, where there is emergent constitutiveness in relationship, personality, and mind.

Most research on the longitudinal course of marriage does not take a stage perspective (e.g., Karney & Bradbury, 1995). Nevertheless, the proposed model of adult relationship development has received indirect empirical support. Hecht, Marston, and Larkey (1994) factor analyzed an inventory related to love ways in couples, and five factors emerged from the data. The intuitive style involved a cluster of items more nonverbal in nature (e.g., "I express my love by the way I look at my partner"), and seems to correspond to the attraction stage of the current model. The secure and commitment factors correspond directly to the current secure and commitment stages. The traditional romantic factor (e.g., "gives me energy," strength) is somewhat equivalent to the current growth stage, and the companionate factor (e.g., "Love is the feeling of togetherness, connectedness, and sharing") corresponds to the current mutuality stage.

Moss and Schwebel (1993) have described a five-component model of intimacy in romantic relationships which also gives support to the current model of adult relationships. Their components are physical intimacy, affective intimacy, commitment, cognitive intimacy, and mutuality, which correspond to the current stages of attraction (and its bodily base), security (and its emotional base), commitment, growth (and its abstract intelligence base), and mutuality, respectively.

The model that has been described for the stages in the development of the couple can be expanded to include the five substages of the synthetic model (coordination, hierarchization, systematization, multiplication, integration). For example, only when the evaluation process of both partners in the first stage of a relationship has passed through the five substages involved (i.e., balances optimally the positive and negative of the other, leading to multiplication of coordinated, hierarchized, systematized evaluations), can that evaluation be integrated, and potentiate optimal passage through to the next stage of attachment. Similarly, only when the attachment process in a couple is reciprocally broad (integrated) across all parts (multiplied hierarchical systems) of the partner's being can optimal commitment in the next stage be fostered. The same logic applies to the way integrated commitment should engender optimal growth in the couple, and how this, in turn, should lead to optimal mutuality.

Note that the model of couple development that has been presented is not fully equivalent to the synthetic model of development from which it has been derived because it refers to a cycle that takes place in a compressed time period in the adult rather than to a lifespan developmental progression. Also, the couple model that has been presented does not deal with the interaction between the couple system and the larger family system. More work is needed in this area. Nevertheless, the model may be useful as a map of normative growth in couples. For example, I use the model of couple development with client couples that come to counseling to delineate at what stage each individual alone and the couple together may find itself for a majority of issues, how there is variation in this sense across issues, how there may even be a mixture of stages for any one issue, where the partners hope to go with respect to issues diagnosed as at lower levels and how issues with higher levels may be recruited in this regard, what complications in the past and present have impeded passage to higher levels for particular issues, and how each partner stands on the various oppositions described in the stages for each issue. As for clinical implications of the model of family development, some follow in the next sections.

CLINICAL IMPLICATIONS

The Self

The current model of self and family development may have direct clinical implications. With its description of the levels of self development and the corresponding family behavior optimal for them, a precise normative sequence is offered to which client families can be compared. Is the client family functioning at the levels of family development dictated by the ages of their children? Where do problems arise in this regard? With respect to the latter question, just as there are dangers and issues in self development with the inception of each of the 25 levels of the current developmental model, there also could be parallel crises and challenges confronting the family. Moreover, the optimal family stances described in Tables 3.2 to 3.6 have their corresponding nonoptimal and negative postures. Families are about development; but family therapy often is not, for often it is concerned with synchronous structure rather than diachronic growth (G. D. Erickson, 1988). The current theory may add to a diachronic perspective on the family in the several ways described here.

Stern (1985) diagnosed clients in terms of which of the four selves that he described seemed implicated in their problems. His basic premise that a primary locus of damaging insult resides in the developing self seems valid. However, I am hesitant to accept Stern's notion that in general all selves continue to function beyond their nascent period, so that they exist in parallel in the growing individual, and so that in one way or another early evolved selves inevitably become the focus of problematic development. This may occur, but problems in self development may concern only a later acquired self, such as with the ones suggested in the current 25-step lifespan model. Furthermore, different selves may be at the forefront for certain issues, whereas others may be involved in other issues; that is, a contextual, individual variability in self problems should be evident in clients. Recent work underscores the development of the self in adult populations, supporting the position defended here (Bacal, 1995; Basch, 1995; Brandtstädter & Greve, 1994).

Once therapists have deciphered the particular level(s) of self development that seem critical in their clients' problems, one therapeutic strategy would be to adopt the corresponding stances suggested in the current model of levels in family development. The particular self (or selves) diagnosed as problematic in the client may be reconstructed to some extent by the client and therapist working together if, through sensitive empathic action, the therapist could negotiate an appropriate coconstruction of the appropriate family functions that went awry in the client's past.

The Family

Gelcer and Schwartzbein (1989) have pointed to another way in which knowledge of cognitive levels may speak to the therapeutic process in family therapy (as practiced by Selvini-Palazzoli, 1980). They argue that client families often function at Piaget's preoperational cognitive stage when dealing with their problems and that therapy can catalyze a qualitative shift to a concrete operational level in family thought. Preoperational fixation in thought is indicated by signs of egocentrism, centration (on part of the whole, on the identified client), rigidity, distortions, irreversibility in thought, and other semiotic processes (myths, fantasies).

The therapist attempts to restructure the family's thought processes (e.g., synthesize new views of others in the family, induce new modes of cooperation, augment autonomy and subsystem (parents, children) boundaries, increase the range of expressed affect, and generate insight and awareness), perturbating their preoperational thought processes. Concrete operational thought processes (e.g., conservation, classification, class inclusion, perspective taking, decentration, and reversibility) are needed for such advances in thought and behavior. Tactics include reframing, circular (more roundabout) questions, positive connotation, and paradoxical prescriptions (aimed at effects opposite to those in the surface injunction). Equilibration is induced by a chain of progressive accommodations and assimilations, providing a shift in family epistemology.

This interesting piagetian analysis of the therapeutic process and its effects on a family's cognitive functioning can be expanded within the current model. It should be recognized that different family members may be functioning at different suboptimal levels, and not just the preoperational one. For example, concrete operational thinking itself may not be adaptive in that when more general, abstract principles are excluded from familial thought processes, different kinds of rigidities, fixations, etc., may fossilize family growth. The current neopiagetian model delineates 25 self development substages, and the full model should be consulted in determining the piagetian family problem points, as suggested above.

Attachment

Greenspan and Lieberman (1988) have developed an interesting intervention program for infants based on a stage model of socioaffective development. (The model does not really inform the current one, especially because it is not derived from a piagetian perspective, but this is not the issue.) For each stage in their theory, they describe several types of attachment patterns (e.g., equivalent to avoidant, ambivalent-resistant attachment × moderate, severe × pure, mixed). It might be advantageous to create an analogous system involving appropriate interventions for different attachment patterns at different cognitive substages. The task may not be as imposing as it seems, because individual differences in attachment security show stability from infancy to childhood and beyond (Bretherton, 1990).

REVIEW

The previous chapter extends the synthetic theory of development into the domain of self development at both the general level of the I component and the specific level of one aspect of the Me component, i.e., in terms of the developing sense of self-efficacy. Stage theorists in other traditions were consulted (Sroufe, Selman, Loevinger), and the current model incorporates their key contributions.

However, in terms of parenting and family development, discussed in the present chapter, the current procedure essentially was to ignore other models. A relatively novel perspective was adopted relative to them, that of determining the optimal stance that a family could manifest at each of the 25 steps in development in the current theory. Also, a relatively novel model of marital development was constructed through extrapolation from the current model. The chapter concludes with some applied implications, a process that continues in Chapter 9.

RE POSTMODERNISM

In terms of the implications of the current chapter for postmodernist discourse, the self of the adult developmental stage has been highlighted as multiple, perspectivist, and socially constituted. It is seen as an active construer not of singular, omniscient, universal truth but of multiple, polysemous, utilitarian truths, and as an agent not of egocentric personal pleasure but of authentic communal endeavor. The polyvocal self's perception of the other's pluralistic voices fortifies self–other mutualistic, coconstructive entwining.

This adult self is related to Erikson's mature adult living in generativity and ego integrity and Kohlberg's and Sonnert's mature metadiscursive (superordinate, contextual-pragmatic, moralistic) adult thought. Similarly, the last steps in the development of a sense of self-efficacy, and in family development and marital development in the current theory reflect this perspective (e.g., the stage of constitutive mutual growth in the marital cycle).

Let me elaborate on the last example to show the manner in which the couple in our contemporary world can be conceived as a potential pillar in any postmodern reconstruction of society. In the current model of the stages in the marital cycle, a mature couple evolves into the phase of mutual growth where each partner develops beyond her or his own individual potential had they been without a loving partner through a process of reciprocal constitutiveness or emergence. In other words, each partner serves as the catalyst for the other, or as a "zone of intimate development" for the other in a *recursive bicatalytic process*, where love's flame cyclically fuels the material that feeds it, so to speak. Conjoined authenticity is the mark of a couple's mutual growth, and itself is marked by movement toward full development of the self that was just described. Inevitably, a mutualistic couple will act constructively in the wider collective and will transfer to their children a secure attachment environment in which an intergenerational transmission of postmodern cognition, socioemotions, social relating, loving, and parenting can flourish. The outflow to a society that chooses to foster this postmodern human potential will be enormous.

PART III

SOCIOCULTURAL DEVELOPMENT

The Vygotskian Perspective on Cognitive Development

INTRODUCTION

Prolegomenon

Overview of Chapter 5. The next four chapters are meant to specify some of the particular transition mechanisms involved in cognitive development. Young (submitted) discusses the change processes undergirding the ontogenetic flow in a rather general way in terms of systems theory, and this complementary analysis in terms of vygotskian theory is required in order to obtain a fuller understanding of the forces implicated in developmental transformation. In the first two chapters, a survey of Vygotsky's theory and contemporary elaborations of it are presented. In the second two chapters, personal constructions on the perceived lacunae in the vygotskian perspective are offered.

For an in-depth presentation of Vygotsky's life work, see Newman and Holtzman (1993), van der Veer and Valsiner (1991, 1994), and Vygotsky (1987; Vygotsky & Luria, 1930/1993). For reviews of specific developmental topics in the neovygotskian literature that are not treated here, see Baker-Senett, Matusov, and Rogoff (1993a, 1993b) on planning; Gauvain (1993) on spatial thinking; Goldin-Meadow, Alibali, and Church (1993) on gestural signs of readiness for scaffolding; Nicolopoulou (1993) on play; Göncü (1993) and Lillard (1993) on pretend play; Verba (1994) on collaboration in infant interaction; Peterson and McCabe (1994) on language development; Forman, Minick, and Stone (1993), Landsmann (1991), Moll (1990), Palincsar, Brown, and Campione (1993), and Rogoff (1994) on schooling; and Sternberg and Wagner (1994; Sternberg, 1994) and Resnick (1994) on intelligence. Books by Garton (1992), Light and Butterworth (1993), and Schneider (1992) treat the question of contextual effects in development, in general. A relevant recently translated work is a 1930 book Vygotsky wrote with Luria (1993; reviewed by Kozulin, 1993). A related article is by Harris (1995) who claims that peer group socialization is a much more powerful influence on children and adolescent personality development than parental influences.

The current chapter begins with an introduction to assumptions underlying the vygotskian school, such as that of coconstructivism. Then, the structure of environment and culture are analyzed. Next, Vygotsky's theory is presented in detail. The concepts of genetic analysis, genetic law, higher mental function, internalization, unit of analysis, zone of proximal development, mediational devices, mutuality, and the development of individual differences are examined, in turn. Some recent research on the zone also is presented.

Overview of Chapter 6.   The vygotskian model of cognitive development is presented in this chapter and contemporary elaborations of it are described in the next chapter. First, Wertsch's (1991) elaboration of the wider cultural influence on the developing mind is examined. Included in this section is his concept of mediated agency (Wertsch & Bevin, 1993). Then, Rogoff's (1990, 1992, 1993) description of apprenticeship, guided participation, and appropriation is presented. These concepts deal with the cultural, interpersonal, and intrapersonal realms in cognitive development, respectively. Next, Granott's (1993; also see Granott & Gardner, 1994) systematization of Rogoff's and Vygotsky's suggested interaction types in cognitive development is examined. The zone of proximal development has received much attention, and with respect to it K. W. Fischer et al.'s (1993a) analogous concept of developmental range, Sigel's (1993) concept of distancing strategies in instruction, and Moss's (1992) work on the role of affect in the zone are presented, in turn. An important issue concerns the nature of appropriation as distinct from internalization. Here the exchange between Lawrence and Valsiner (1993) and Wertsch (1993) is presented. Then, Litowitz's (1993) emphasis on identification in internalization-appropriation is discussed. Next, Dean's (1994) presentation of Loewald's (e.g., 1980) work on affectivity in internalization is summarized. To conclude this section, Saxe's (1991, 1994) model of the way practice participation leads to cognitive development is examined. His model attempts to show the way appropriation functions in the cultural context (Biddell, 1992). Its description leads to the information and neopiagetian perspectives on transition mechanisms in development.

Following this, a section on the development of social cognition is presented. The work of Brown and Gilligan (1992, 1993) and Belenky and Clinchy (Belenky, Clinchy, Goldberger, & Tarule, 1986; Clinchy, 1993), in particular, on the development of voice in preadolescent–adolescent girls and adolescent girls–young women, respectively, is described and it is shown to be complementary to the current model of the levels of development of the cognitive (mis)perception of the other. Next, an ongoing empirical research project (Young & Young, in preparation) related to the topic of the zone of proximal development is summarized.

In the chapter's conclusion, three areas are specified where the vygotskian tradition seems yet to have adequately developed appropriate models. First, the multiple positive and negative ways that a society's ideology, dogma, ethics, and values may impinge on the shared, coconstructive process of development of its individual members have not been addressed adequately. Second, the conception of development as discontinuous, with universally present, qualitatitively distinct stages as it unfolds, has been repudiated by vygotskians in their quest for context sensitivity, variation, and individual differences in development. However, it could be that there is a healthy dialectic in development between these competing tendencies, that of context-irrelevant, universal discontinuities and context-rich, individual sensitivities, which results in their synthetic intertwining. Third, the specific manner in which the individual shares and creates meaning in the active coconstruction of knowledge with the sociocultural ecology has been called "appropriation," but, in effect, vygotskians only have begun to deal with the product and the process involved in this mechanism. (Technically, subprocess rather than process specification should be referred to, because appropriation constitutes a process in and of itself.)

Coconstructivism

A World View. According to Valsiner and Winegar (1992), vygotskian theory is quintessentially contextualist, or more synthetic than analytic and also broad in scope at the sacrifice of some precision. Contextual theories are distinct from contextualizing ones in that the role of context in the former is intrinsic to its foundation, whereas in the latter it is but one more consideration that serves to extend it. That is, contextualism seeks to explicate the interdependent, interactive, bidirectional, transactive relation between the individual and the surround, viewing neither as separate entities. In contrast, contextualizing approaches enumerate structurally independent environments as one more set of factors that influence in a unidirectional, additive, noninteractive way relatively separate, autonomous, individuals.

Contextual approaches to human development are contrasted with others such as the organic (e.g., piagetian), mechanistic (e.g., behavioral), and formal (e.g., innatist). Dixon and Lerner (1992) contend that all the

major developmental traditions that have evolved in this century, including the contextualist, stem from the darwinian paradigm that arose in the
last century. On the one hand, I am not sure that the historical sequence
that they describe is the most accurate one. In Young (submitted), I have
presented another way of organizing the major developmental schools of
thought by showing they are responses to the freudian rather than the
darwinian one. On the other hand, I did not treat the vygotskian theory in
that analysis, for I limited myself to those theories that have been predominant since the 1920s or so. As much as the contextualist approach is
influential today, particularly that of the vygotskian school, this is only a
recent phenomenon.

Vygotsky's View. The concept of coconstructivism in vygotskian theory flows from this contextualist world view. Coconstructivism (Taylor,
1995; Valsiner, 1988; van der Veer & Valsiner, 1991; Wozniak, 1992, 1993;
Wozniak & Fischer, 1993) is a metatheoretical assumption about individual
development which highlights its intersubjective nature. Coconstruction
is "the joint creation of a form, interpretation, stance, action, activity,
identity, institution, skill, ideology, emotion, or other culturally meaningful reality" (Jacoby & Ochs, 1995, p. 171, emphasis removed). It argues that
subphenomenal entities and relationships such as personal cognition and
environmental ecology undergird psychological development. The knowing, meaning-creating, interpreting mind acts in joint transactive (collaboration, cooperation, coordination) interdependence with (supportive) social and physical ecological structures to create psychological phenomena
such as experience and action. "Development is thus an emergent characteristic of the person-in-context" (Wozniak & Fischer, 1993, p. xv). Specific
components of individual phenomena (e.g., mind) and context (e.g., collective society) are reciprocally "coextensive" (Meacham, 1993) in each
other's landscape; they are catalytically conjoined in freeing and blocking
processes (or through activation–inhibition coordination, to use this volume's language [see Chapter 7]) under specific conditional configurations
(Winegar & Valsiner, 1992).

The developing individual fused in this process is not a passive recep-
tacle with a permeable boundary through which the environmental agenda
passes unhindered. Rather, within constraining limits of shared past, present, and projected future contexts, active creative contribution to and
transformative reassembly by the developing individual of any grasped
sociocultural material takes place. Thus, all culture is personal, or idiosyncratic and not mass, or monolithic. Yet a type of collective culture
emerges through negotiated, meaningful commonalities across individual
creative co-constructs.

Note that the concept of coconstructivism has been applied in a
slightly different way in the family therapy literature on epistemology

compared to its current application in the child development literature (see Chapter 11).

Culture

Even if it seems that culture evolves in shared meaning, it is not easy to define (Cole [1992a, 1992b]; for recent interesting perspectives on culture and psychology, see also Bornstein [1995], Cole [1995a, 1995b], Eckensberger [1995].) In one sense, culture refers to historically specific features of the environment. The environment has been transformed by the conceptual and material artifacts of prior generations. Yet these artifacts are not uniquely environmental, for they are products of human activity primed by both biology and environment in synergistic interaction. Through its specificity, culture contextually mediates the influence of biology and universal features of the environment on the developmental process. The mediation takes place through the twin functions of enabling and constraining (activation–inhibition coordination again). Moreover, it begins with birth, so that development is a continuous intermingling of multiple strands of coinfluence. Some modules, or self-contained units of development, may seem somewhat independent of context especially early in life, but culture acts from birth onward to influence them through its specific accumulated knowledge enablements and constraints so that they themselves are intertwined in the rope of development.

Reed (1993) presents an account of environmental mediation in terms of gibsonian theory. In the latter, the environment offers affordances for action for ourselves and for others that perceptual–cognitive development is primed to detect. Affordances, a concept promoted by the Gibsons (e.g., Gibson, 1982), do not refer uniquely to physical attributes of objects (e.g., round objects are graspable), for they also include specific socially and culturally produced properties (e.g., mailboxes are for mailing written material; also see Costnall [1995] on the sociality of affordances). Sociocultural affordances (or the field of promoted action) concern persistent, invariant patterns of direction in attention to objects, choice in activities, and use that can be made of them. Also, often they involve ways of accomplishing goals within particular scaffolds that include both encouragement of some preferred action and constraints or boundaries on others (activation–inhibition coordination again). Sociocultural affordances are contrasted with their antithesis, or individual affordances (field of free action), which are ones that the individual can realize spontaneously on her or his own and that he or she is allowed to use. Different individuals may have different intentions for the use of any one affordance. And different cultures can be defined in terms of the specific set of such affordances that they select for shared, joint attention by their members. For any one individual, the difference between the sets of sociocultural and individual affordances define Vygotsky's construct of the zone of proximal development (see below).

Environmental Structure

Bronfenbrenner (1993a). In the contextual tradition, the environment is constitutively constructed in shared interpenetration with the individual. Nevertheless, it appears to have a dynamic structure which is hierarchically arranged. It can be represented as a series of concentric circles with the individual positioned in the center. Each of its nested, interdependent levels is considered important to the developing individual (Bronfenbrenner, 1993a; see Ceci, 1993; Oppenheimer, 1991; Szapocznik & Kurtines, 1993; and Wachs, 1992, for similar models).

The most proximal level of environmental influence is the face-to-face dyadic one (e.g., family, school; the microsystem), where specific physical, symbolic, and sociocultural properties facilitate instigative and/or inhibition processes (activation–inhibition coordination once more) with the immediate environment. Next, two or more face-to-face systems may interact in a synergistic manner (the mesosystem).

The broader ecology is comprised of the exosystem and the macrosystem. The former relates to settings such as the parents' workplace, where activities take place that influence in indirect ways the more immediate settings of the developing individual. The latter involves overarching extended (sub)cultural social structures and their specific "belief systems, resources, hazards, lifestyles, opportunity structures, life course options and patterns of social interchange" (Bronfenbrenner, 1993a, p. 25). Different cultural practices may have diametrically opposite developmental consequences, depending on the dynamic organization involved in the whole system comprised of the individual with her or his disposition and the ecological context. For example, Dornbusch, Ritter, Liederman, Roberts, and Fraleigh (1987) found that different parental styles have different and sometimes opposite effects on adolescent school achievement depending on the ethnic group-sex combination involved (also see Darling and Steinberg [1993] on this topic).

Others. Feldman (1993) described broad cultural institutions or intermediaries that contribute to individual development. His sample of music prodigies was promoted or crystallized in their development by "cultural organisms," or specialized cooperative social structures with specific missions. For example, the immediate musical entourage of the prodigies formed "cocoons" around them in order to offer them optimal instruction. Also, there were "gatekeepers," organizations, such as music festivals and their judges, that mark boundaries and barriers that must be transcended before the acceptance of creative contributions, thus serving in part as a catalyst for innovation.

Sameroff and Feise (1992) define the cultural code as the regulator of the fit between the individual and the societal system, and see it as providing broad guidelines for acceptable behaviors and values. They define the family code in an analogous way and give four of its key elements— paradigms, myths, stories, and rituals. Paradigms are beliefs held about the wider world which organize information received from it and regulate behavioral attempts to deal with it. Myths are beliefs that exaggerate and highlight certain social roles, but without overt discussion. Stories are narrated texts that underscore specific morals, values, orientations, and roles. Rituals prescribe appropriate roles and ascribe particular meanings to social interactions.

The context has been laid for the proper presentation of Vygotsky's developmental theory. The environmental surround has been discussed in general terms, with its dynamic interdependence with the developing individual emphasized. Vygotsky and those who have elaborated his work have differentiated many specific processes involved in this dynamic.

THEMES IN VYGOTSKY'S
SOCIOCULTURAL THEORY

Genetic Analysis

Wertsch's (1991; Wertsch & Kanner, 1992) presentation of Vygotsky's ouevre outlines three major interrelated themes central to it. His framework is followed for the most part in the ensuing description of the core of Vygotsky's theory.

First, the theme of genetic analysis assumes that in order to fully comprehend mental function, its origins and transitions must be studied. Phenomena must be investigated *historically* in the broadest sense of the term. Vygotsky lived in a time of turmoil in Moscow, and it is clear that he was influenced by the concepts of (1) the dialectic, which describes an inherent cycle of tension and resolution in material, and of (2) the social and cultural mediation of individual development.

Genetic Law

Introduction. According to Wertsch, the second major theme in Vygotsky's work is that he maintained that many aspects of mental function originate in social life (the general genetic law of cultural development). In a 1981 translated version of an earlier work, he explained that, "[a]ny function in the child's cultural development appears twice, or on two planes. First it appears on the social plane, and then on the psychological plane" (p. 163). Thus, the configuration of an individual's specific intramental functioning can be traced back to precursors at the intermental social one.

Intramental organization is not a simple transmitted copy of social material imported into it by developing individuals. The latter are actively creative, within limits, in their internalization of sociocultural information, and create transformed products in their coconstructed mental repertoires. "[I]nternalization transforms the process itself and changes its structures and functions" (Vygotsky, 1981a, p. 163). One opinion is that the process of internalization, per se, cannot take place if one truly views cognitive development from a mutualistic vygotskian perspective, because the concept of internalization speaks to the individual's cognitive process (e.g., Rogoff, 1990). This issue is dealt with in full later in this chapter.

Higher Mental Function.   Given the intermental origin of developing cognition, higher mental function must evolve in the sociocultural matrix, and it concerns phenomena such as representation, thinking, and remembering. Moreover, the products of intermental function are shared among all its participants and are the result of their collective endeavor, even if the individuals involved end up asymmetric in their contribution.

Saxe (1991) describes how, according to Vygotsky, the developing individual in everyday life develops local, situated, "bottom-up," "spontaneous" concepts that are interlinked only gradually. In more formal institutional settings, "scientific" concepts are acquired "top-down," in that they are general structures that have to be applied to be better understood. As the child's spontaneous and scientific concepts interact to offer a unified generality and pragmatic application to thought structure, the individual and the sociocultural worlds interpenetrate in a mutual melding.

Higher mental function develops especially in a local fashion in particular shared environments. However, there are also general revolutionary breakthroughs or crises that emerge periodically in development. Vygotsky eschewed the piagetian concept of stages, but according to him, in developmental revolutionary periods, transformation of existing and emergence of different higher mental functions is facilitated (Valsiner & Van der Veer, 1993). Vygotsky enumerated six major crisis periods in development: at the newborn moment, and at the 1st, 3rd, 7th, 13th, and 17th years. He proposed that each follows the dialectical cycle of thesis (a stable period), antithesis (crisis involving involution, disintegration), and synthesis (evolution, culmination, reorganized mental structure, higher mental function). Yet at other points in his writing Vygotsky emphasized a three/four-step progression in the development of higher mental function (Glassman, 1995). The stages involved concerned prespeech/primitive thinking, instrumental thinking, and internalized thinking. Also, at most other points in his writing, he did not emphasize particular transition periods. Rather, he highlighted the means which potentiated change, in general. That is, he described how the incorporation of new mediational means transforms and organizes action along "entirely new lines," inducing a series of unspecified qualitative shifts (Wertsch & Sommer, 1995). His reluctance to endorse a stage view of development was partly a reaction to the action-removed, cerebral-primacy perspective inherent in Piaget's account of the stages of cognitive development (Glassman, 1995).

Unit of Analysis

This section turns to the question of the way to analyze the mental product of the shared relationship between the individual and the wider social context. Vygotsky described dialectical pairings such as biology and culture and individual and society as fused, mutually interpenetrated, coincident, convergent, interwoven factors in the development of mental function (Tudge & Winterhoff, 1993). Thus, he argued that the best way to study the development of the individual's mental function in the social milieu is to take a unit of analysis that would encapsulate both.

Any chosen unit of analysis must possess "all the characteristics of the whole" (Vygotsky, 1987, p. 46, cited in Rogoff, 1990). In this regard, meaning in mediating devices such as words was the principal unit that he chose because meaning such as this is shared or coconstructed in the joint, collaborative relation of the developing individual and the social context of which the individual is part. The Laboratory of Comparative Human Cognition (1983) perceives the unit of analysis as socially assembled situations, or cultural contexts for shared action emanating from joint human construction. Similarly, Rogoff (1990, 1992, 1993, 1995; Rogoff & Chavajay, 1993; Rogoff, Mosier, Mistry, & Goncú, 1993) sees the unit as the shared sociocultural activity or event. Rogoff and Chavajay (1995) refer to shared sociocultural endeavors with inherited yet transformable cultural tools and practices having particular histories and organization. Gallimore and Goldenberg (1993), Goodnow (1993), and Tharpe (1993) emphasize the notion that the appropriate unit of analysis of psychological study is the activity setting, which includes the objective aspects of the context and of the participants' behavioral processes and the subjective aspects of the latter. This concept permits a unification of dyadic, small-group, and cultural context components of shared context in mental development (Minick, 1985). Similarly, Nicolopoulou and Cole (1993) refer to an activity system, or collective reality. Finally, Wertsch (1991, 1993, 1994a, 1994b, 1995a, 1995b, 1995c; Wertsch & Bevins, 1993; Wertsch, del Río, & Alvaraz, 1995; Wertsch & Kanner, 1992; Wertsch & Sohmer, 1995; Wertsch, Tulviste, & Hagstrom, 1993) refers to mediated action as the appropriate unit of socio-cultural cognitive analysis where neither the individual nor the social serves as focus (see "Mediation" below and Chapter 14 for my concept of the IWEMEUS). For Vygotsky, shared meaning is created especially in the zone of proximal development, a construct which is presented next.

Zone of Proximal Development

Description. Vygotsky described the practical ramifications of his genetic law in terms of the "zone of proximal development." He defined it as the difference between the developing individual's performance in "independent problem solving" and in "problem solving under adult guidance or in collaboration with more capable peers" on tasks that have not yet been mastered (Vygotsky, 1978, p. 86, in Wertsch & Kanner, 1992). Thus, adults who tutor during problem solving by instructing, giving examples and demonstrations, and asking leading questions, all slightly ahead of the child's actual level of mental development, act to accelerate that development. The motivated child who is open to the shared context with the tutoring adult comes to learn through the process of imitation, in particular, according to Vygotsky. "[I]nstruction is possible only when there is a potential for imitation (1987, pp. 211–212, cited in Newman & Holtzman, 1993).

The zone continues to be a primary focus of vygotskian theorizing. Stone (1993) describes the prolepsis and conversational implicature that take place in the zone (defined respectively as speaker presuppositions which challenge the listener and speaker implications conveyed contex-tually, not logically). For Rogoff (1990), relative to the adult, the child may have the prime responsibility for structuring and managing the situation and for determining the appropriate level of her or his participation, de-spite the greater skills of the former. That is, collaborative structuring is involved. Rogoff, Mosier, Mistry, and Göncü (1993) describe the negotia-tion in the zone as a bridging or stretching. Rogoff also emphasized that tacit observational learning as much as actual tutoring comprise efficient means of learning in the zone. Minick (1985) and Moll and Whitmore (1993) describe the zone in terms of the larger cultural setting; it is seen as the locus of the development of mind in social practice. In this regard, Rogoff (1990, pp. 46–47) qualifies the zone as "a dynamic region of sensi-tivity to learning the skills of culture," and because of its mutuality and the active participation of the child in the constructive process she adds that it is "a crucible of development and of culture." Youniss (1994) describes how Vygotsky extended the concept of the zone to the cultural level, with more "primitive" societies amenable to advance through the experience of contact with more advanced ones.

Research. Studies are investigating not only the tutoring function in the zone by the adult but also the way the adult withdraws support as the child reaches mastery thresholds in joint problem solving (e.g., Pratt, Green, MacVicar, & Bountrogianni, 1992; Wood, 1980). Moreover, this work also is investigating the nature of quality instruction in the zone. For example, Portes (1991) reported that maternal verbal guidance (e.g., in order to direct attention) predicted academic achievement such as mathematics skills. Scholnick and Wing (1992) found that parents helped children learn "if-then" arguments by providing initial premises, prompts for inferences, and feedback. Pederson and McCabe (1993) determined that different parental styles of narrative elicitation related to different child narrative skills. That is, contextual versus event elaboration questions by parents were associated, respectively, in children with better contextual orientation and better plot structure narratives. There is much research on the role of (expert) children as tutors in the zone of proximal development, and the similarities and differences between this situation and the situation where child peers of equal cognitive level act to accelerate their cognitive development through collaborative discourse about piagetian problems (e.g., Azmitia & Hesser, 1993; Duran & Gauvain, 1993; Kruger, 1992, 1993; Rogoff, 1993; Tudge, 1992). However, it is beyond the scope of this chapter to review the ample amount of research on the topic. Finally, van Geert (1994) points out that the nature of the developmental transformations that take place in the zone have not been specified by vygotskian research. He applies dynamical systems theory to the question, and with mathematical modeling shows that it can be continuous or nonlinear, progressive or regressive, constant or variable, and oscillatory, cyclical, and chaotic. Valsiner (1994) adds that these processes may be altered by self-reflective or self-reconstructive mechanisms.

Mediation

According to Wertsch, the third major theme in Vygotsky's model of cognitive development is that higher mental functioning is assisted in its development by sociocultural mediating devices such as material tools and psychological signs. The latter, in particular, are important and pervasive. Thus, sign systems such as languages (1) are the vehicles of the sociocultural message; (2) are reflections of sociocultural genesis; and

(3) are used in social interactions within particular cultural settings. Furthermore, sign systems mediate mental development by the particulars of their nature, just as specific labor tools channel problem solving to their particular structural and functional properties. The language system more than facilitates and streamlines mental actions, for it transmutes the essential course, organization, and even quality of mental activities according to its intrinsic parameters.

Contemporary vygotskians emphasize the meaning making that mediational devices permit (Wertsch; also Chang-Wells & Wells, 1993). Participants in the zone of proximal development form hypotheses, test them, modify them, negotiate, etc., through mediational devices. Wertsch argues that they permit "semiotic uptake."

Language may be the major mediational device according to Vygotsky, but he described others (e.g., drawings). Contemporary vygotskians also are referring to artifacts (e.g., textbooks) in this regard (Chang-Wells & Wells, 1993; Griffin, Belyaeva, Soldatova, & the Velikhov-Hamburg Collective, 1993; Hatano, 1993; Moll & Whitmore, 1993). Artifacts create contexts, influence, constrain, and can be instruments of power.

Vygotsky attributed a major self-development function to mediational devices, in general, and to language, in particular. He argued that a primary goal in development is to gain self-control, and that language first serves as a social agent of influence over the self and a personal agent of influence over the other. However, eventually it "becomes a means of influencing oneself" (Vygotsky, 1981a, p. 157). This process is manifested especially in the period of development of intramental private speech from intermental social speech, where the young child shows emergent self-regulative functions tied to such inner speech.

Wertsch (Wertsch & Bevins, 1993; Wertsch, Tulviste, & Hagstrom, 1993) points out that for Vygotsky the centrality of mediational means in cognitive development led him to imply that human agency is not inherent in individuals in isolation, for it is always mediated. Thus, Wertsch spoke of "mediated agency" (Wertsch, 1991, 1993, 1994a, 1994b, 1995a, 1995b, 1995c; Wertsch & Bevins, 1993; Wertsch, del Río, & Alvaraz, 1995; Wertsch & Kanner, 1992; Wertsch & Sohmer, 1995; Wertsch, Tulviste, & Hagstrom, 1993). Individuals are responsible for their actions, but are influenced by sociocultural mediational means or tools in formulating problems and their solutions. These means are acquired in a process involving transition from the intermental to the intramental plane, and thus reflect a communal, socially distributed origin that allows for individual differences. Wertsch (1994b) describes the dialectical tension that exists in the universal, repetitive forms of mediational means and individual, unique, particular, nonrepeatable, contextualized, concrete adaptations implicit in their instantiations. Similarly, for Wertsch (1995a, Wertsch, del Río, & Alvarez,

1995) culture is imported into individuals by means of mediational devices used, while sociocultural settings are cyclically (re)created through their use. Thus, the tools shape or transform action, constraining and empowering, "altering the entire flow" (Vygotsky, 1981b, p. 137), but they do not determine or cause it, for they leave room for unpredictability and creativity. In fact, culture appropriates them from their original contexts in unanticipated ways, reflexively showing the same creativity seen at the individual level.

The advantage of the mediated aspect of cognitive development for the developing individual's sense of agency is that he or she does not have to reinvent de novo the collective knowledge implicit in the adopted mediational means (e.g., language). However, at the same time the preformulated packets in adopted mediational means may constrain instead of empower. Thus, the creative process that the developing individual brings into the internalization function is fundamental in countering these constraints (Valsiner, 1988). If children come to resemble each other in aspects of their sociocultural knowledge and tools, it is because of a collective social sharing and negotiation which channels but does not nullify their individual creativity in absorbing sociocultural messages.

Wertsch (1991) adds an interesting note about the semiotic potentials of mediational devices. On the one hand, they can be decontextualized, or become generalized abstract means, e.g., a dictionary-type definition taught in formal schooling. On the other hand, they can undergo recontextualization, e.g., when language serves as a metacontext to itself, as in discourse where the meaning of successive utterances increasingly is clarified by anaphoric linkage(s) to prior text.

Newman and Holtzman (1993) dispute Wertsch's emphasis on mediation in Vygotsky's theory. While their argument is beyond the scope of the present work, in it they introduce an interesting concept. They see a dialectic between the processes of socialization and societization in individual development. The former refers to the developing individual's increasing sociality and knowledge of rules governing behavior. The latter refers to the individual's adaptation to and assimilation by society. Again, a shared mutuality is seen in the development of mental function, which leads to the next section.

Mutuality

Rogoff (1990, 1992, 1993) has analyzed the concept that there is a primal interrelatedness of the developing individual and the sociocultural context. Constitutive mutuality, collaborative joining, inseparable interdependence, shared boundedness, integrated embeddedness, reciprocally defining unification, and fused process are some ways of characterizing this interrelatedness. She adds that the context includes both interpersonal and sociocultural activities. "[I]ndividual, interpersonal, and sociocultural processes constitute each other and cannot be separated" (Rogoff, Chavajay, & Matusov, 1993, p. 533).

In response to Valsiner's (1991a) review of her 1990 book, Rogoff (1992) points out that she is advocating more than a position of inclusive separation where the individual, the context, and their link exist separately but obligatorily fused in dialectical synthesis. Rather, she maintains that there is one whole process where one component, such as individuals or their contexts, may be backgrounded or foregrounded as a temporary procedure of convenience, but because the components are mutually defining in a constitutive manner without being reducible one to the other, then they cannot be described separately without sight lost of their inherent participation in the whole. Moreover, an approach such as this obviates the need for a separate description of links between the individual and the context, for inclusion of the dimension of links into a model of individual-context interrelations presupposes that each of the constituents may exist separately.

Blatt and colleagues (Blatt, in press; Blatt & Blass, 1996; Guisinger & Blatt, 1994) present a somewhat similar argument, but allow for the development of a separate sense of self development in conjunction with the development of a sense of interpersonal, communalistic relatedness. These two aspects of the growing individual's sense of integrity are seen to develop in a transactional, reciprocal, mutualistic, interactive, interrelated, dialectical manner with higher levels of development in one arena necessary for higher levels of development in the other.

Similarly, Fogel (1993) speaks of a coregulated, dialogical process in cognitive and social development that produces an embodied, participatory cognition. His metaphor about development is "being-in-relation" or "life-in-the-world," where in coregulation there is a "dynamically changing individual at the very moment of transaction with others" (p. 61), with behavior and goals emerging creatively from social discourse.

Moll (1994) explores a similar line of thought about the natural (biological, material, physical, neurological, lower psychological process) and cultural (ensemble of social interactions and relations) mechanisms of development in vygotskian thought. The former mechanisms are not determined by or dissolved in the latter ones, but are manifested in, conditioned by, acted upon by, transformed by, and provide the ground for the formation of and emergence of them. At the same time, they provide developmental constraints and possibilities. They exist in a relational dialogue as development unfolds, without a cartesian separation. Wertsch (1994a) adds that the natural and cultural enjoin in a dialectical contact and mutual influencing and transformation in development. In another context, Wertsch (1994b) describes the individual–society antimony as antithetical to the continual, irreducible dialectical tension that governs individual–society interrelatedness and the growth or alteration of the entire flow and structure of higher mental function.

Individual Differences

The final comment in this chapter on basic vygotskian theory speaks to the issue of individual differences in development. Given the intimate, emergent coconstruction of developing cognition and culture, ontogenesis should be marked by an inherent variability in content pathways and outcome (Rogoff, 1990). But Vygotsky describes the development of "higher" mental functions, which implicates an ordering in complexity of representational acquisitions over developmental time that leads to an ideal endpoint. Rogoff suggests that a more contextualist approach would underscore that mental development varies in goals, purposes, and values according to local aspirations and circumstances, and that the development of increasingly "higher" mental function is not inevitable. This issue is one of the most fundamental in developmental psychology, and is discussed in full in Chapter 8.

CONCLUSION

Vygotsky has given to psychology a rich vein of theory and practical implications. His emphasis on the sociocultural and historical context in which development takes place proved to be a needed counterpoint to the essentializing, cartesian, self-centric perspectives in the developmental psychology of his time. The concepts of context and mutuality were not valued in those developmental theories, viz., the mechanicism of behaviorism, the internal cognitive stage view of Piaget, the interior yet imposed affective dramas of psychodynanism. His most respected contribution lies in his concept of the zone of proximal development, which in its most basic form examines the difference between learning with and without socially mediated instructional scaffolding.

In the next chapter, we see how the field of developmental psychology has profited from Vygotsky's instruction; Vygotskian theory is dynamically expanding its theoretical map. In this chapter, contemporary elaborations of vygotskian theory are elucidated. Where appropriate, comments and criticisms are made, preparing the way for my own refinements of this approach to cognitive development.

CHAPTER 6

Contemporary Elaborations of Vygotskian Theory

VYGOTSKIAN DEVELOPMENTS

The Multivoicedness of Minds

Wertsch (1991; also see Miller, 1994) has extended Vygotsky's theory by applying Bakhtin's (e.g., 1981) concept that "dialogic interanimation" characterizes the voices of any one speaker and the discourse of partners in communication. When we listen, volleys of answering or counter words are elicited in mentation by each utterance. This principal of dialogicality applies to both inner and public speech. The speaker's culture is one of the voices that speaks through the speaker, in that a social language or speech genre (e.g., social class, professional grouping) qualifies presentation style. Thus, speech is inherently historical, cultural, and institutional. It is a coexistential "heteroglot" (in Cazden, 1993). It has a "stylistic aura," a generic meaning, or a sociocultural intentional denotation.

According to Bakhtin (as described by Wertsch, 1991), when one voice speaks through another via a social language, "ventriloquation" is taking place. "The word in language is half someone else's" (Bakhtin, 1981, p. 293). Meaning is a product of and is owned by multiple voices in both the speaker and the listener, or all parties in a dialogue. Even in the interchange between a very scaffolding mother and her baby, there is a "hidden" dialogicality.

Wertsch (1991) contends that, in effect, Bakhtin is describing a hierarchy of mediational means that developing individuals have at their disposal. Certain ones such as social language are privileged or preferred in particular sociocultural contexts. A major goal in development, then, is to acquire efficiency in the process of ventriloquating, or having one voice speak through another, and to learn to recognize specific mediational means and their patterns of privileging in context.

Apprenticeship, Guided Participation, Appropriation

Rogoff (1990–1993, 1995) has scrutinized the nature of sociocultural activity at each of three interrelated levels which she considers important. First, at the level of community, Rogoff analyzes organized cultural activity in terms of the metaphor of apprenticeship, where novices actively learn skills and values from more expert, supportive individuals, either through direct mentoring-sponsorship or through more tacit, implicit observation, such as takes place in scouting. In the latter there are several levels of relative expertise, so that in activities such as girl scout cookie sales peers both compete and collaborate, guide and are guided, and work within and modify prior traditions and procedures.

Second, at the interpersonal level, Rogoff describes the concept of guided participation, which refers to the face-to-face or side-by-side inter-action, involvement, communication, and collaboration of individuals as they perform a culturally valued activity. There is a mutual, active partici-pation in determining engagements, arrangements, and shared meaning even if, for example, momentarily one partner is more active in leading and another in following. Often activity such as this takes the form of routine problem solving or daily activities so that the guiding style may be tacit or indirect and the goal is have the less experienced party achieve self-management.

Third, at the intrapersonal level, Rogoff emphasizes the concept of appropriation, also called participatory appropriation. It was introduced by Leont'ev (1981), in particular. Dewey described it in 1916 in the follow-ing way.

> [In] the degree to which an individual shares in some conjoint activity ... the individual appropriates the purpose which actuates it, becomes familiar with its methods and subject matters, acquires needed skill, and is saturated with its emotional spirit. (Dewey, 1916, p. 26, in Wozniak and Fischer, 1993)

For Rogoff (1990–1993, 1995), appropriation is a dynamic, ongoing, creative intrapersonal process. It takes place in a common, shared socio-cultural activity where there is task-, context-, or domain-specific change or transformation in skill preparatory to anticipatory adaptation of that skill to future circumstances. She adds that the appropriation process takes place in each participant through their active participation in, understand-ing of, and adjustment to such activity. Mercer (1993) points out that appropriation is a reciprocal process with each participant deriving understanding through their meeting, but that the child, in particular, gains an enormous advantage because of the sociocultural packaging provided by the adult.

This conceptualization of the process underlying cognitive development differs from that of the more traditional perspectives of imitation or internalization in its emphasis on the mutually constitutive and creative nature of the process. The cognitive transformation process is neither a passive copying of nor an active importation of an external template or model, but is an "intersubjective engagement in the shared problem solving process" (Rogoff, 1993, p. 149). "Hence, the process is inherently *creative* with the individual actively seeking meaning and making links ..." (p. 145) beyond the shared activity itself.

Rogoff (1995) reemphasizes that appropriation is used in three ways as a concept, and that her manner of usage is the only one that distinguishes it from internalization. First, it is used as a synonym for internalization, but the quagmire here is that an external mental aliment is seen as imported across some fictitious boundary separating developing individual and milieu into some distinct mind. Second, sometimes appropriation is seen as a two-step process involving internalization then transformation. Again, the pitfall is that mental item importation and copying is considered important in mental function. Third is Rogoff's usage of the term, where the issue of participant–surround boundary is circumvented, for active participation is considered both the process and the product. "Appropriation occurs in the process of participation," and appropriation itself is a transformative activity, rather than a preparation for it, through the creativity required to comprehend, adjust, and contribute to relationship. In this perspective, time also is boundary-free or seamless, for activity is an extension of the past in the present toward the future.

Types of Sociocultural Interaction

Introduction. In effect, Rogoff (1990–1993, 1995) has attempted to expand Vygotsky's model of efficacious adult participation in the child's mental development by discussing cultural apprenticeship and interpersonal guided participation in addition to the zone of proximal development. Granott (1993; Granott & Gardner, 1994) has carried this process one step further by describing in a systematic way diverse types of sociocultural interaction within the space of a two-dimensional model.

First, interactions can vary along a continuum of degree of collaboration. At the positive pole, they can be highly mutual in the vygotskian sense of deriving shared meaning in an event, task, or situation of common focus. At the negative end, interactions can be highly disruptive. Moder-

ately high levels of this dimension would involve collaborations that have
some united effort and sharing, with little independent activity. The latter
behavior characterizes the neutral point of the scale.

The second orthogonal dimension that one finds in sociocultural interaction concerns the relative degree of knowledge and expertise that
participants bring with them into the particular context of their interaction. This dimension may vary from highly asymmetric (e.g., an adult
tutoring a child) to symmetric (e.g., child peers) interaction. Other dimensions (e.g., motivation, experience, familiarity) are relevant but not treated
in the model; also, although the model includes negative collaboration,
this type of interaction is not treated in depth.

The Model. In Granott's (1993) model of sociocultural interaction
types, highly asymmetric expertise in conjunction with highly mutual
collaboration defines scaffolding, which represents the traditional vygotskian context of the zone of proximal development. Here, guidance by the
scaffolder is supportive, sensitive, subtle, approving, and is marked by a
gradual shift of dominance to the partner. For the most part, the knowledge
construction that is generated by this interactive style is not coconstructive, for the scaffolder orients her or his activity to the constructive process
in the novice.

Highly asymmetric expertise in conjunction with moderate collaboration produces the situations of apprenticeship and guided participation
(e.g., schooling, parent advising) as described by Rogoff. In these cases, the
asymmetric guidance is not continuous, leaving much room for independent activities or symmetric discussions. When it does take place, it is
more directive, unidirectional, and informative than in scaffolding. Again,
one finds a relative absence of mutual coconstruction of knowledge, because the focus is on the novice's construction of knowledge.

When highly asymmetric expertise is coupled with independent activity involving a high degree of interest in the expert's actions instead of
any overt collaboration, it results in imitation or substantial observational
learning through modeling as described by Bandura (1989). As in the
previous interactive styles, the knowledge construction process is marked
by a lack of synchrony and balance.

An interactive context that involves a moderate degree of relative
asymmetry in participant expertise associated with highly mutual collaboration produces an asymmetric collaboration, as with two children coop-
erating in a shared task where one is more expert than the other and gives
relatively more directives and advice. Knowledge coconstruction does
take place in this interactive context, though it is more or less unbalanced.

If a collaboration moderate in scope is coupled with some asymmetry
in participant expertise, then the style that manifests is called asymmetric

counterpoint interaction, as when a heterogeneous group of children work together on a particular activity. This sociocultural activity is characterized by moderately asymmetric partners sharing feedback in a common activity, but with the more expert one(s) directing the flow of the interaction more often than the less expert one(s). Also, there is independent meaning construction of the activity by the partners, and thus possible cognitive comparison and conflict.

In the combination of moderately asymmetric participant expertise and independent noncollaborative activity, the interaction type of swift imitation is potentiated. It involves independent behavior interspersed with brief bouts of partial imitation of the actions of a moderately more capable participant, even if no verbal interchange takes place (e.g., as in the interactions of preschoolers on the playground or in drawing activities). Thus, the knowledge construction that derives from this type of interaction is quite separate, and partial cognitive comparison or conflict is possible.

Interactive contexts that derive from symmetric participant expertise are described. Mutual collaboration indicates that there is a high degree of collaboration in concert with an equivalent level of expertise in the partners. Thus, the interaction takes the form of a reciprocal sharing in a simultaneous coconstruction of knowledge.

In symmetric counterpoint interaction, such as occurs in group problem solving or discussion, where one individual at a time has the floor and leads, the parallel nature of the participants' expertise is accompanied by a moderate degree of collaboration. There is a shifting dominance and an alternation between common activity and independent activity with observation. The knowledge construction that takes place is separate and not mutual (e.g., each individual tries to find her or his own solution to a problem without too much information sharing), leading to cognitive comparison and possible similar individual outcomes, but also possible cognitive differences or confrontation.

In parallel activity, there is equal expertise and no collaboration, with some cross-observation and exchange to interrupt parallel self-absorption. Knowledge construction is separate and unsynchronized, with partial cognitive comparison or confrontation possible.

Conclusion.   Granott (1993; Granott & Gardner, 1994) has provided an indispensable framework for the comprehension of the way knowledge is constructed in all participants in the full range of sociocultural interactions that can take place. She has contrasted the traditional situation of the zone of proximal development (scaffolding) not only with Rogoff's situations of apprenticeship and guided participation but also with others that involve varying degrees of relative participant expertise and collaboration. Knowledge may be coconstructed by the developing individual and the context in which he or she is interacting, but it does not necessarily follow that individuals are always cross-coordinated with each other in their knowledge coconstruction as they participate in interaction.

Tomasello, Kruger, and Ratner (1993) have developed another model of important situations in cultural learning. They emphasize imitative learning, instructed learning, and collaborative learning. (Similarly, in an evolutionary context, Donald [1993] speaks of the stages of mimetic skill, language, and external, cultural symbols and Raethel [1994a, 1994b] describes a sequence of mimetic, discursive, and object-cultural symbolic communication.) Although the Tomesello et al. scheme is less complete than that of Granott (1993), they attempted to specify the developmental order of these acquisitions (the order is the one given in the list), unlike the case for Granott (1993). A fruitful line of inquiry would be to formulate a complete developmental model of the diverse interactional or cultural learning situations in which children participate, perhaps by combining the different perspectives to date.

Developmental Range

K. W. Fischer and his colleagues (Bidell & K. W. Fischer, 1992; K. W. Fischer, Bullock, Rotenberg, & Raya, 1993a; K. W. Fischer, Knight, & Van Paris, 1993b; Kitchener, Lynch, K. W. Fischer, & Wood, 1993) have described a concept related to the zone of proximal development, i.e., the developmental range. Normally, developing individuals manifest systematic differences in cognitive performance level according to the degree of contextual support that they receive for resolving cognitive problems. The lower and upper limit of this range define the developmental range. The functional level in the individual's cognitive performance is the one shown spontaneously when there is no special support; for example, spontaneously in free play or when asked to produce the best story possible. The optimal cognitive level is the one normally obtained with moderate degrees of support, such as with instruction, modeling, or task familiarization. Key information may be presented to the child without direct intervention, e.g., a gist of a story, or a story may be modeled or acted out and explained in detail before asking the child to make up a similar one. Or stories may be practiced repeatedly before their formal presentation. With scaffolded, direct coparticipation by the adult or expert peer, the developing individual may manifest the highest or optimal cognitive performance level of which he or she is capable.

Fischer points out what seems to be a contradiction between the concepts of zone of proximal development and developmental range. With increasing age, the former seems to decrease in the distance between minimum and maximum levels whereas for the latter the opposite seems to be the case. That is, in proximal zone scaffolding the developing child becomes increasingly capable of autoregulative control of the mental structures involved so the zone gradually diminishes or even disappears with increasing age. In contrast, the research shows that the developmental range is larger later in life relative to earlier on. However, it may be that the comparison made by Fischer is not a valid one in that as the child grows older and is given more complex tasks at each age, the challenge is the same throughout development and the need for a temporarily supportive environment in the zone of proximal development does not decrease with increasing age. All that decreases is its need on any one task over age because of the child's growing competencies relative to the task.

In general, for Fischer the developing child is in constant need of contextual support of her or his cognitive development in any one domain because the higher order automization of the skills involved proceeds at a relatively slow pace. This process in cognitive development assures that there is not premature foreclosure in the search for adaptive strategies and premature fixation on inappropriate ones. The developing child seems to manifest both the ability to form automatic generalizations at a higher level, and to delay the formation of generalizations such as these in order to better permit local lower-level learning. Thus, depending on the context, the developing child can manifest the most appropriate option in learning strategy to maximize learning. Consequently, the developmental range exhibited by any one child is as much a product of her or his own adaptive functioning to contextual conditions as it is a straightforward response to their imposed nature.

The last point raised about Fischer's work concerns the relationship between the extreme two levels of the developmental range, the functional and optimal levels, and the issue of whether there is continuity or stagelike discontinuity in cognitive development. According to Fischer, the cognitive performance level that manifests under no or low support conditions, such as in spontaneous performance, produces developmental patterns in cognitive development that are continuous in form, or without evidence of stages. In contrast, when contextual support is optimal, the resultant pattern of cognitive performance suggests stagelike growth with sudden shifts in cognitive level after periods of stasis.

Distancing

The Concept. Sigel and his colleagues (Cocking & Renninger, 1993; Sigel, 1992, 1993; Sigel, Stinson, & Kim, 1993; Sigel & Vandenberg, 1994) have examined in detail the nature of teaching strategies that adults use in the socialization of the developing cognition of children. Through procedures in discourse in everyday activities, adults act to promote children's representational competence and their understanding of the representational rule (i.e., events, objects, and persons can be represented by some sign or symbol and still retain their original meaning). More specifically, adults employ distancing acts, strategies, or behaviors that place cognitive demands on children to use their own thought functions in the contexts before them. This encourages the children to think or reason, mentally separate themselves from the cognitive situations before them, project to some other temporal plane (past, future, or nonpalpable present), anticipate outcomes, reconstruct past experiences, seek options, and represent (with symbol or sign systems) events, objects, and persons in their current context in meaningful ways.

Cognitive discrepancies arise through the mismatch between two representations, with one being more advanced or more appropriate than the other. They may be two that are juxtaposed in the children's internal representational space, or two that have been presented externally by the adult, or a combination of an internal and an external one. The resultant cognitive tension, conflict, and contradiction may engender dialectical opportunities for resolving the cognitive discrepancies. Cognitive disequilibrium, decentration, and activity are set in motion, inducing mental (representational) differentiation, restructuring, and transformation. Among other factors, internal affect, beliefs, and values and external dialogue help determine whether cognitive gains are incorporated into the representational system or ignored-rejected. These changes are part of the source of learned meta-awarenesses about the distancing cycle. Moreover, they lead to reciprocal, mutual effects in the tutor. For example, if I may complete Sigel's thought, feedback about what distancing acts work best with a child reinforces their future use. Learning about the way distancing opens the child is an opening experience.

The specific acts that adults utilize when encouraging distancing in children vary in their level, format, effectiveness, direction, and directedness. They may include attention getting, giving information, directly helping by structuring or correcting, modeling, taking over, and so on. These disparate behaviors can be classified into three levels of distancing ranging from high to low. High level distancing encourages evaluation, inference, generalization, transformation, planning, reconstruction, comparing, concluding, seeing options, and resolving conflicts. Thus, demands are abstract, open, and allow alternatives. Medium level distancing promotes sequencing, describing similarities and differences, classifying, enumerating, etc. For example, a parent may provide an explanation, or give a reason with a command or with information, but without too much encouragement of representational distancing from the immediate present.

Low level distancing facilitates labeling, information production, defining, demonstration, observation, etc. In short, demands are concrete, focused, and closed, as when parents give an order or make a rule or factual statement.

In terms of format, statements-imperatives versus questions have differential distancing effects, with the latter considered generally more effective in eliciting better distancing. Also, emotional support (e.g., approval, disapproval) has a cardinal influence on the effectiveness of distancing acts. Finally, distancing acts may be self-directed (e.g., when solving a problem alone) as well as other-directed (e.g., manipulating the problem's context), and they may be indirect as well as direct.

Research. Research on the short- and long-term effects of different qualities of parental distancing on children's cognitive development reveals that this factor plays an important role in cognitive development (McGillicuddy-De Lisi, 1992; Roberts & Barnes, 1992; Sigel et al., 1993). For example, the initial 2-year-old assessment in Sigel et al.'s 5-year follow-up study showed that in young children low-level distancing strategies (e.g., didactic controlling) were associated with lower general mental ability, seriation, memory, and anticipatory imagery. Later on at the follow-up, high-level distancing by the mother on a structured task was positively correlated with the children's mathematical achievement. In contrast, reading achievement was not associated with any distancing measure or with any contemporaneously measured variable, but with parental approval when the parents read stories to their children at the younger age. On the one hand, the results show that the representational demands of mathematics competence requires appropriate distancing strategies for optimal mastery in children, especially if the mother is the parent effecting the strategy. On the other hand, the data indicate that for reading achievement (1) affective encouragement is more important than distancing in promoting optimal performance; (2) both parents are involved in the process; and (3) the early prereading period is the most important, for there are sleeper effects later on, when children transform from listeners of reading material to actual readers.

Socioaffectivity in Sociocultural Contexts

The Concept. Moss (1992) adds to Sigel's observation that the affective dimension in the adult–child learning encounter is its cardinal underpinning. She argues that as a skill is acquired in the zone of proximal development, it passes through three successive dialectical phases—acquisition, consolidation, and inhibition. The latter refers to the suppression, disintegration, and decomposition of the habitual, immature, and less advanced, less challenging, less efficient, or less adaptive skill in order to permit reintegration of its components within other more advanced, adaptive mental functions, leading to greater diversification and application in problem solving.

For example, in a study of gifted compared to nongifted preschool children in joint problem solving, she found that mothers of gifted children showed restraint by permitting their children to verbalize before they responded with a metacognitive, self-aware strategy. The behavior of these mothers is indicative of the way self-control, inhibition, and consequent intellectual creativity are cultivated in the zone by sensitivity to their dynamics. Thus, Moss speaks of the zone of *inhibited* development.

Moss also undertook a study on scaffolded problem solving in securely and insecurely attached 18- to 30-month-olds. Securely attached toddlers and their mothers exhibited (1) less of the immature, nonchallenging exchange patterns, such as simple joint labeling or subgoal sequencing; (2) less poorly collaborative, disorganized interactions; and (3) less negative affect and negative social regulation. It seemed that the presence of inhibition in their shared behavior bore direct positive consequences in the joint construction of the toddler's higher order mental function. Moss concludes that for the process of internalization of cognitive gains to continue to progress, the developing individual should experience a scaffolding milieu that manifests a flexible concern for the developmental process "in both a cognitive and affective sense."

Comment. Other vygotskians also are emphasizing the role of affect, motivation, and values in cognitive development (e.g., Forman & McPhail, 1993; Stone, 1993). In this regard, Minick, Stone, and Forman (1993) wrote that

> To say that ... cognition develops as part of an integral system in connection with motivation, affect, and values does not merely imply the need for an addendum to earlier theoretical formulations. A fundamental conceptualization of mind and its development in social practice is needed. (p. 7)

Other studies have related certain attitudinal and affective behaviors of parents in the zone of proximal development to children's cognitive outcome. Pratt et al. (1992) found that authoritative parenting (Baumrind, 1991) was positively correlated with more effective (e.g., direct) styles of parental scaffolding of fifth-graders' mathematics homework. Diaz, Neal, and Vachio (1991) reported that high-risk mothers (for child abuse and neglect) of 3-year-olds relative to controls showed more controlling verbal didactic strategies, fewer attributions of competence in their children, and less distancing. They conclude that positive affect and motivation given by mothers in the context of positive attributions of competence of their children seems the most important mediating variable in fueling collaborative responsibility in the zone of proximal development.

To conclude, I underscore the prominence that Moss (1992) gives to the mutual coconstruction of inhibitory skills needed in concert with complementary facilitating ones in the zone. Her concept of the zone of inhibited development speaks to my own emphasis on the importance of activation–inhibition coordination in all phases of cognitive development. In this sense, it would be best to refer to it as the *zone of activation–inhibition coordination.*

Internalization

The Concept.   Previously, the concept of internalization in cognitive development was introduced and contrasted with the concept of appropriation. Lawrence and Valsiner (1993) and Wertsch (1993, 1995c) have continued the debate on the topic under a slightly different guise. For Lawrence and Valsiner, traditionally internalization refers to the continually ongoing, dynamic, active intramental importation and creative, open-ended, indeterminate transformation, either immediately or later on, of intermentally encountered sociocultural material. This process results in more intercoordinated, adaptive, flexible, and potentially higher forms of coconstructed mental functions. Thus, the latter involve a mental emergence not only in the sense of the mental reconstruction of the conjoined internal and external but also in the sense of the transmutation of the old into the new. "[W]e have a new structure, a new function of formerly applied methods and an entirely new composition of psychological processes" (Vygotsky & Luria, 1930/1993, p. 110, cited in Lawrence & Valsiner, 1993).

Lawrence and Valsiner add to the basic description of internalization in the following ways. They enumerate the types of social others involved in holding out material for internalization, i.e., people, social institutions, or culturally constructed external mediating devices. They contend that internalization involves not only a cognitive incorporation but also an incorporation into the affective processes intertwined with the intramental ones. The intramental plane is one where subjective experience or personal sense colors and is colored by the interiorization process. Valsiner (1992) adds that in the process of internalization the social other involved in the social negotiation may even have its agenda countered or overcome. Finally, for Lawrence and Valsiner (1993) internalization is seen to participate in a cyclical process with the complementary function of externalization, where it is posited that internal mental structures are injected back into the social environment. The reconstituted external in the internal becomes the aliment for the reconstitution of the external, as the sociocultural context and the individual engage in a spiral of recreation of the other.

Comment. Wertsch (1993) maintains that the concept of internalization should be discarded for the one of mastery, because the former contains the implicit assumption of a type of dualism involving the internal and the external. "What is lost by speaking of mastering a skill, concept, or structure?" (p. 169). The concept of mastery in mental development is especially appealing to Wertsch because it carries with it the corollary that there must be sociocultual mediational means that participate in the mastery process, as we have seen. "[T]hey do part of our thinking, speaking, and acting" (p. 170). This functions to add to the developmental equation the cumulative weight of cultural, institutional, and historical forces, so that it comes to reflect an inextricable dialectic between the mediational tools appropriated by individuals and the individuals-in-context wielding them.

Previously, it was shown that Rogoff (1990–1993, 1995) also has called for the replacement of the concept of internalization, in this case by the constitutive concept of appropriation. Wertsch argues that Rogoff's concept of appropriation relative to his own concept of mastery does not attribute enough influence to the mediational cultural tools that carry the sociocultural milieu with them to the individual. (For a critique of both points of view, see Arievitch and van der Veer [1995] on Gal'perin's conception of internalization as material-sensitive yet material-independent appropriated mental actions.) Although this may be true, I have a more fundamental criticism that applies to all the concepts that have been described in this chapter about the way intramental functions are formed in the encounter of the developing individual and the sociocultural context. That is, it appears to me that whether one is referring to internalization, appropriation, or mastery, neither the specific cognitive product (e.g., How is mental function represented by the cognitive system?) nor the specific process involved (e.g., How does cognitive transformation take place?) is well described. Later on, I describe my own model on the process of mental function development, and how it responds to these apparent lacunae.

The Self in Internalization. Recent conceptions of internalization or appropriation emphasize the role of the self in the process (Cazden, 1993; Litowitz, 1993; Serpell, 1993; Wertsch et al., 1993). Litowitz describes the increasing personal responsibility for problem solving and accomplishing tasks that develops in each encounter in the zone of proximal development. The developing individual experiences a shift toward equal responsibility via a reversibility in the learning process as the adult gradually withdraws support for the learned activity. Learners become independent and autonomous vis-à-vis the learned task (but as Packer, 1993, argues, not independent of the social origins of the learning and the social empowerment that it brings). Learners "take on cognitive authority," which helps develop their sense of confidence and sense of "ownership" (mastery) of the new material (Serpell, 1993). In this regard, Bakhtin spoke of "liberation" and "actively choosing" after struggle with alien voices in one's polyvoice (in Cazden, 1993).

Litowitz (1993) describes two processes that seem to promote internalization in learning, and they speak to the role of the self in the process. First, identification by the child with the adult plays a role, through "the desire to be the adult or to be the one the adult wants him to be," or to impress the adult. Identification is depicted as a reciprocal function, for adults believe the child is becoming or can become a person like themselves. Second, resistance is important in the internalization function. Identification does not mean self-suppression, for one of its primary functions is to permit resistance to the adult and independence and freedom from him or her through the learned skills it fosters. Resistance to learning via identification arises in the first place because of conflict with entrenched prior learning.

Affect in Internalization.   As we have seen, the role of affective processes in internalization has been underscored by Valsiner, Litowitz, and others. Dean (1994; Rosen, 1994) argues that the work of Loewald (e.g., 1980) illuminates the affective and self-constructive core of the internalization process. For Dean, Vygotsky acknowledged the interrelated, parallel nature of the development of higher-order thought processes and affective ones. For example, Vygotsky wrote that for intellectual processes "every advance is connected with a marked change in motives, inclinations, and incentives" (Vygotsky, 1978, p. 92). However, for Dean, Vygotsky did not really consider the subjective feelings of the developing individual in the transition mechanisms that he described in cognitive development. In contrast, according to Dean, Loewald argued that internalization is a function which is used to "restore or promote a sense of well-being, security, safety, intimacy, individuality, self-confidence, competence, and psychological stability" (Dean, 1994, p. 45). The internalization process especially helps in this regard by serving to separate the developing individual from the object of internalization. The latter takes place because internalization acts to reduce or abolish the feeling of deprivation or loss of the object through the integrated unification with the object that is the result of internalization's activity.

Loewald applied these notions to the early mother–infant relationship, where a primary conflict is seen to reside in the desire to individuate or become independent of the mother and the desire for primary narcissistic reunion with her. In terms of internalization, this opposition between desire for separation and reunion with the mother is played out in the increased individuation that eventuates with each act of internalization. That is, each act of internalization, and consequent cognitive growth and potentially better adaptation and independence from the environment, brings with it a concomitant sense of loss of the mother as possessed narcissistic object. Consequently, each act of internalization engenders the desire to acquire even better means to deal with the environment (keep the mother within scope) in further acts of internalization in order to achieve ultimate symbolic reunion with the mother. In this manner, a lifelong cycle of internalizing acts accompanied by cognitive advance and the need for further internalizing acts is instituted.

Ideally, the parent is sensitive to the infant, and as he or she develops the parent presents to the child a positive self-image. However, the parent carries to varying degrees "libinized/aggressive" ties to the infant as an object. Thus, the parent can influence profoundly the developing child's self-image. "The child begins to experience himself as a centered unit by being centered upon" (Loewald, 1980, p.23), and the quality of that centering determines, in part, the quality of self-perception in the developing child.

Loewald's hypothesis is powerful, and although I doubt whether internalization serves such a narrow psychoanalytic end, I do not doubt that the parent or caregiver influences the process early in life and beyond. In Chapter 7, my particular model of the manner in which this may happen is presented.

Practice Participation

The Concept.   According to Saxe (1991, 1994; also reviewed in Biddell, 1992), the appropriate unit of analysis of cognitive development corresponds to Vygotsky's conception; that is, it lies in the interfunctional field conjoining all participants, both human and contextual, in sociohistorocultural activity. Thus, Saxe studied the way Brazilian children working as street candy sellers developed mathematical skills through "practice participation." First, the children developed practice-linked goals, such as context-sensitive price-setting. Through their activities, and in concert with their culture (e.g., more proficient peers), more advanced context-specific cognitive levels gradually were acquired (called form-function shifts).

For Saxe, like Rogoff, appropriation is the primary mechanism by which cognitive transformation is acquired. As the children repeatedly practiced and solidified candy-selling mathematical skills in their sales transactions, they came to appropriate the transactions as a cognitive tool of anticipatory analysis of future transactions. That is, through the juxtaposition of existing counting skills and anticipated candy selling patterns, novel mathematical skills emerged (e.g., ratios).

Yet these were not logical cross-situational generalizations, for they were specialized for a particular setting and fed by particular sociocultural realities. Nevertheless, inherent in each act of meaning construction is not only the process of specialization but also a simultaneous generalization, or transfer of learning across contexts. Thus, cross-contextual interplay takes place both within and between practices. For example, as the children acquired and appropriated a new skill at school, such as multiplication, they came to integrate it into their existing repertoires, reconstructing their mental functioning, and gaining increased control of their practice. Ultimately, it is the latter self-control in context to which cognitive development is oriented, so that there is no preordained ladder of developmental (sub)stages that all developing individuals must follow in a general antiseptic way.

Comment. In conclusion, it seems that Saxe is addressing one of my concerns about the way appropriation is treated in the vygotskian literature. Its central tenet is a powerful one, in that cognitive change is seen to derive from immersion in the sociocultural bath. However, specification of its products and processes is needed for its complete understanding. In this sense, Saxe has helped us understand that in practice participation an appropriated skill radiates through specialization and generalization within and across particular contexts. In a certain sense, with this terminology Saxe seems to be returning to the kind of language of developmental cognitive theories, such as the information processing and neopiagetian approaches. Yet, the paradigms, assumptions, and nature of the concepts that these terms call forth, as well as their meaning in context, differ radically in the vygotskian and nonvygotskian traditions. Nevertheless, it would be instructive to examine the way the latter theories treat the issue of transition mechanisms in development in order to determine if there are other concepts that can be imported and appropriated into the current examination of the concept of appropriation. This is done in the next section.

PROCESSING INFORMATION PROCESSING

Information Processing

Introduction. The information processing and neopiagetian approaches to the mechanisms of transition in cognitive development overlap so that for purposes of convenience they are combined to facilitate a rapid overview of the question. The major sources used for this section are Canfield and Ceci (1992), Kail and Bisanz (1992), Klahr (1992), and Kuhn (1992), as well as Case's and K. W. Fischer's neopiagetian models covered in Young (submitted). The reader is referred to Halford (1993), Pascual-Leone and Baillargeon (1994), and Siegler (1991) for excellent accounts of the topic. No attempt is made to describe the theories in depth.

Transition Mechanisms. Multiple mechanisms of cognitive change have been posited to play a role in cognitive growth by the approaches under discussion. The pool of mental processing resources may increase with age. Absolute processing capacity may be involved because digit span performance increases with age. Storage capacity, computational speed, or mental "power" also seem to play a role. Processing efficiency in the execution of fundamental activities such as encoding seems important, as well. The acquisition of new strategies (e.g., mnemonics) related to these basic operations may be at the source of increased processing efficiency with age. Fundamental operations such as encoding and representation may not only improve in execution efficiency, but also may improve in quality (e.g., selective attention in encoding). Mental effort may become more effortless and automatic with age (e.g., due to reorganization, better coordination). The standard developmental explanations such as practice effects, learning mechanisms, and neurological maturation also should be considered here.

The acquisition of more sophisticated rules and procedures has been mentioned. Siegler (1988) describes certain heuristics in mathematics skills acquisition. At a different level, Case referred to search, evaluation, retagging, and consolidation, in particular. Fischer mentions focusing, compounding, substitution, differentiation, and intercoordination, in particular. Another factor that increases with age is domain-specific knowledge, which may facilitate generalization across domains. Generalization also has been mentioned for rules and procedures, where it is thought that development witnesses increasingly general rule creation. Conversely, sometimes rules and procedures are too general and they are paired down in the process of specialization or discrimination.

The processes of generalization and specialization are part of a series of self-modification processes. Others include conflict resolution procedures, such as use of a fixed algorithm, and rule changing procedures, such as combining rules (composition) and constructing specific versions of them (proceduralization). Note that cognitive conflict is considered a relevant transition mechanism in cognitive development according to the approaches under discussion, just like it is in almost all other approaches. What differs from one approach to the other is whether the conflicts are internally generated (e.g., two different schemata; Lautrey [1993] adds an interesting neopiagetian twist here by suggesting that a symbolic-analogic information processing conflict may be involved), externally driven, e.g., by the environment pointing out or creating contradiction, or by an internal–external mismatch, e.g., an internal schema challenged by one formed in response to the environment. To this list of self-modification processes, one can add chunking, elimination of unnecessary rules and procedures, subgoal establishment, reordering, and replanning. Also, there are mental processes such as the use of analogy, induction, and anticipatory expectation.

Strategy selection, regulation, and execution, and metaknowledge about strategies also have been deemed relevant. These suggested mechanisms in cognitive development speak to executive self-regulation in the process. Self-modification and self-regulation in cognitive transitions are taking other guises such as redescription (Karmiloff-Smith, 1992) and self-scaffolding (Bickhart, 1992). For Siegler (1988), the self-regulation in information processing differs from that found in piagetian and vygotskian theory in that it "does not depend on reflection or on any other separate governmental process" (p. 272, in Klahr, 1992). Rather, it is part of the system.

Finally, there are internal and external constraints on the cognitive system related to affect, disposition, and wider group values and statuses (Case & Edelstein, 1993). For example, attachment style in infancy influences exploration and thus cognitive development.

Siegler and Ellis (1996) puts together many of these ideas in arguing that cognitive variability is crucial in cognitive development because it promotes conflict, the learning of new and integrative strategies in a variety of circumstances, the ability to anticipate the utility of untried innovative strategies, and ultimately cognitive change. Cognitive variability in children is found not only across related problems but also in the same problem tackled twice or even within the same trial. Most variability is found on trials just before or actually involving the discovery of solutions. For example, children were given instruction on the meaning of the equal sign in arithmetic. The children who learned most gave pretest explanations which suggested variability in ways of thinking rather than particular misunderstandings.

Conclusion

The basic goal of conducting this survey was to determine if there are transition mechanisms described in developmental cognitive theories such as information processing that could help better explain the way in which the process of appropriation specifically functions within the vygotskian paradigm. It seems that Saxe (1991, 1994) followed the same route in that he added to his description of the appropriation function processes like generalization, specialization, and anticipation. The only thing that I would add based on the current survey is that a metacognitive awareness by the child of the active, creative, and transformative role that he or she plays in the appropriation process may take place as an inherent part of the shared coconstructing cognitive system, and synergistically add to the process. This cognitive metaknowledge also may include appropriate strategy selection, regulation, execution, and autoevaluation relative to the appropriation process. Moreover, it should be constrained by both internal and external factors such as attachment history and cultural values. Demetriou, Efklides, and Platsidou (1993) developed a similar concept, calling it the hypercognitive-reflective system. It is considered a superordinate self-management and self-understanding system that functions before and during cognition.

The lessons learned in this section will be applied to the model of co-appropriation developed in Chapter 8. The next part of the chapter shifts gears from the information to the social arena, and its lessons will be applied to the model of the cognitive (mis)perception of the other developed in Chapter 7.

SOCIAL COGNITION

Intersubjectivity

The interface of developing mind and culture witnesses the growth of the cognizing social human. Cognition is exquisitely honed to serve social ends, and socioemotions are carried into the child's world on cognitive functions. How does the child's conception of aspects of the social milieu develop and influence her or his sociality? How does her or his emotivity and caring orientation influence this process?

For Kurtines, Azmitia, and Alvarez (1992), there are three distinct but interrelated spheres that comprise human existence, reality, and rationality—the objective, subjective, and intersubjective. Greenwood (1994) describes a similar notion in his concept of "identity projects" within "social collectives." Rogoff (1990) defines intersubjectivity as mutual understanding, cooperative intention, and/or joint attention that obtains between communicating people based on a common focus of attention and perhaps some shared presuppositions. For example, in a process termed social referencing, toddlers look to their mothers to help them disambiguate situations such as the way to react to an approaching stranger (Feinman, 1992).

Mundy, Kasari, and Sigman (1992) found that 20-month-olds displayed more positive affect during joint attention with their mothers than during acts of request directed to them, which helps to specify some of the parameters of intersubjectivity. Similarly, Yoder and Munson (1995) found a relationship between joint attention and maternal communicative responsiveness.

The concept of intersubjectivity raises the question of how much the adult or parent in cooperative relationships with children appropriates material from the encounter into their mental and affective functions and self-transform along with the children rather than simply supervising, instructing, mentoring, guiding, and modeling. The vygotskian perspective describes a mutual edification and participation in the cognitive joining of adult and child. According to Tappan and Brown (1992), in an authentic relationship the partners mutually share responsibility and authority for creating their experience and its meaning. Thus, when the child and caregiver are fully engaged both at the cognitive and affective levels, they participate in a mutual learning of the world and mind of the other in a dialogical, intersubjective communion, promoting both the child's and caregiver's cognitive and/or affective growth in a dynamic process. The caregiver provides more than a scaffold, for he or she engages the child in a guided, coconstructed, dialectical participation where there are no static, prefigured inputs but shared growth. Moreover, optimally the caregiver and child socially and affectively discover each other in their dance around the cognitive object. Ideally, each partner enters wholly into the encounter as if in an I–thou relationship (Buber, 1970). As I mentioned at the end of the presentation on distancing, learning about how a child learns may be the most significant learning.

It is in this crucible, of optimal mutual transcendence in the caregiver–child relationship, that the seeds of a caring intersubjectivity are planted. In general, a higher-order practical–moral, sensuous–moving socioethical knowledge-from-within emerges out of the subjective feelings that developing individuals experience as they negotiate their place with respect to the sociocultural entities around them (Shotter, 1993a, 1993b). In terms of vygotskian internalization, the developing individual especially incorporates standards of social and cultural relationship, which increasingly come under the control of their personal agency as embodied sensitivities and constraints.

Brown and Gilligan

The work of Brown and Gilligan (1992, 1993; Brown, 1994; Gilligan, 1982, 1994) and Clinchy and Belenky and colleagues (Belenky, Clinchy,

Goldberger, & Tartule, 1986; Clinchy, 1993, 1995; Handlin, 1993; Orr & Luszcz, 1994; Zimmerman, 1993), in particular, is important in highlighting the caring, intersubjective orientation of moral cognitive development. It shall be shown that their feminist perspective seems complementary to the general developmental theory that I have created.

Brown and Gilligan describe the way young preadolescent and adolescent girls may appear to be developing in a positive direction according to standardized tests, including ones on moral development, but show signs of conflict related to their "voice," which is the channel transmitting inner feelings and thoughts into the world of relationships. The primary voice is for open, connected, responsive, caring relationships involving codiscovery of knowledge. Generally, in early female adolescence and the transition period toward it, this voice becomes trained, dissociated, or silenced by the patriarchical culture, but even by the girls themselves in a self-supervised way if need be, in order to preserve a more superficial, but a more stable type of relationship with females and an unequal, traditional relationship with a male.

This process may lead to open disruption and political action in the girls, with concomitant stresses, in an effort to preserve authentic relations, or it may lead to second-order psychological reactions such as silent resistance if the genuine voice is repressed fully. Still another possibility is capitulation, complicity, and accommodation. To risk heartfelt expression is to risk loss of relationship and power. Another possibility is that the primary voice that animated childhood is lost, and experience, feelings, thought, and relationships do not remain genuine. If this happens, the self and not only the other is lost, for in disjoining from genuine meaning in relationships the self is disembodied from its culture. Disconnected, some girls even failed to recognize signs of emotional or physical abuse.

Belenky, Clinchy, and Colleagues

Introduction. Belenky, Clinchy, and colleagues interviewed women university undergraduates about the way they talk about themselves, or their ways of knowing and being, and analyzed their data from the perspective of Perry's theory of steps in adolescent and adult development (see Chapter 3). The authors' concept of voice is slightly different from that of Brown and Gilligan, because it refers to an epistemological core in understanding by whom and how "truth" comes to be known. Five steps in the development of growth in voice are described. With each step comes a more mature voice and more power, but not necessarily more happiness. The first one is related to Perry's initial phase of duality in thinking, but there is no real attempt to ground the full sequence in Perry's work, in general. The steps seem like eriksonian stages, where embryonic forms of each stage exist in stages prior to their full emergence, and for any replaced one, contextual factors can make it most salient once more.

The five conceptions of knowing that are described are termed *silent knowledge, received knowledge, subjective knowledge, procedural knowledge,* and *constructed knowledge.* These positions are described, in turn.

Silent Knowledge. In silence, a woman experiences herself as mindless, voiceless, incompetent, and powerless. There is an extreme denial of the self, and a numb, passive dependence on and unquestioned subordination to an all-powerful authority figure. Life is perceived in terms of polarities, e.g., bad-good.

The family of a woman who knows through silence uses violence (verbal, physical), abuse, despotism, and abandonment-neglect to achieve its goals. A woman exposed to this regime who wishes not to live it may attempt to withdraw, and may also manifest aggression or wrath.

Received Knowledge. A received knower perceives herself as capable of absorbing and reproducing knowledge from sources of truth, but not capable of creating knowledge by herself. Truth is considered absolute and concrete (e.g., dualistic, right or wrong). Because things in life are either right or wrong, there is no room for ambiguity. She listens, speaks without confidence, and speaks little in order to better hear others. The hearing is one-way, for the received knower does not think for herself or trust her experiences, which accounts for her relative silence. She is selfless and voiceless in her own way. She conforms, resists change, and denies differences, preferring old ways and sanitized uniformity.

The family of a received knower is tyrannical, belittling, squelches curiosity, and chastises when questions are posed. Yet there are reactions to this mode. For example, Zimmerman (1993) describes one client who complied with resignation to her interpersonal situation, but who manifested sarcasm, as well.

Subjective Knowledge. The subjective knower conceives of truth and knowledge as acquired through first-hand experience, as residing within the infallible gut based on one's own authority or inner voice, and as private, personal, fantasied, and intuited. Authority figures' answers and values are rejected. Logical analysis and abstraction are not trusted. The subjective knower refuses to make judgments, so that multiple truths are possible, but her openness really is an egocentric aloofness. Compared to events in the prior steps, there is more self-assertion, self-definition, self-protection, and the acquisition of a concept of the self, but the latter may be in flux. The reality of others is perceived only in part, is distorted, or is the product of projection. The world is fragile, insecure, unpredictable, and impermanent. The subjective knower may change her life-style in order to express herself better. But she would not adopt her own voice, for she believes that to do so might hurt others. Thus, instead she would be silent, withdrawn and conformist, and wish for freedom.

This mode can lead to rebellion, rage, fury, revolt, anger, and a breaking of past ties. Many subjective knowers had parents who were supportive of their attempts to become more independent, and so these women often succeeded in growing.

Procedural Knowledge.   The procedural knower ascribes importance to learning and to applying objective operations that enable alternate knowledge acquisition and communication. She uses either (1) detached, impersonal, objective, analytical, logical, planned, expertise-based, evaluative, reasoned, critical, judgmental ("separate") procedures (methods, skills, techniques, processes for constructing, comparing, discarding answers in order to arrive at solutions), or (2) empathic, caring, trusting, sharing, interdependent, perspective-sharing, accepting, nonjudgmental ("connected") procedures. The latter constitute an opening up to, passing into, and becoming part of another's experience in order to understand it better. In having one's personality participate in this way, it "stretches."

However, at this stage the two types of procedures are used separately without combining them. This runs the risk that the other is blanked out (in separate procedures) or the self is denied (in connected ones). Normally, a woman at this level prefers one of the two types of procedure.

The families of procedural women are intimate, connected, reciprocal, mutual, collegial, value equality, value their members on their own terms, and consider the self's needs without sacrificing family.

Constructivist Knowledge.   The constructivist knower sees truth as relative to context, mutable, or as an approximation. She tolerates contradiction, ambiguity, conflict, and complexity, and sees herself as the source of knowledge creation. She combines separate and connected knowledge procedures in an orchestrated amalgam of passionate knowing or intimate communion that leads to self and other. "Instead of suppressing self and ignoring her own experience, she uses her own experience to construct other people's realities" (Clinchy, 1993, p. 196). The knower is an intimate component of the known. The self is not lost in this active engagement or perspective taking of the other, but is included and edified or enriched (e.g., by new possibilities for the self). The self is used to rise to a new way of knowing. The constructivist knower is quite self-aware,

makes the unconscious conscious, and listens to the self. There is a resonance or integration of thought and feeling, objective and subjective, self
and other, one part of the self with another, specific and general, and
abstract theory and real life experience. (The constructivist knower seems
to show a balance of Bakan's (1966) paired concepts of human agency [self-
orientation] and communion [other-orientation] [Feingold, 1994; Helgeson, 1994].)

The constructivist knower who engages in conversation ends up cocreating emergent "new" perspectives. Disagreements reflect intermediate
positions involving mutual respect. The conversation becomes a mutual
confirmation of the other and her/his wholeness and full potential. It is
reciprocal, cooperative, intersubjective, shared, and communal.

The constructivist knower has an authentic voice. She opens her mind
and heart to embrace the world, create a union with that which is to be
known, and voices the unsaid. She moves beyond and outside systems to
use them for wider purposes. She acts from a constructed caring morality
"to help establish in the wider world the sort of community [she] ha[s]
helped to create in microcosm in [her] personal relationships" (Clinchy,
1993, p. 199). The constructivist knower works toward a more livable
world, committing herself to moral action in the larger community in order
to empower or improve the quality of life of others, just as her parents may
have done.

But there is one drawback to this mature way of being. If she is not
heard, the constructivist knower may slip into silence, withdrawal, and
anger.

Recently, Labouvie-Vief, Orwoll, and Manion (1995) described the
narratives of the mature mind in Clinchy-Belenkian terms. For example, in
this regard they refer to the reconnected, balanced, self-authorized, and
dynamically cooperative mind.

Conclusion

This kind of psychology is fully compatible with the model of the
cognitive (mis)perception of the other presented in the next chapter. In
particular, there is a clear parallel between the five positions on women's
ways of knowing presented by Belenky, Clinchy, and colleagues and the
current five stages of development, which were constructed independently
of them from a neopiagetian perspective.

In conclusion, although the general argument presented by Brown and
Gilligan, and also by Belenky, Clinchy, and colleagues, is sound, it seems
that the same process applies equally to adolescent boys and girls even if
some of the specifics may differ across the sexes. In this regard, research by

Silberman and Snarey (1993) shows that moral development does not differ in pace across the sexes when factors such as maturation rate are taken into account.

AN ONGOING STUDY
OF NARRATIVE IN CHILDREN
RELATED TO VYGOTSKIAN THEORY

Introduction

In this section, empirical data are presented from the ongoing study presented in Chapter 4 on storytelling in 5- to 6-year-olds and their mothers after a joint warm-up free play period. The mothers told a story from their imagination for 2 minutes based on the characters of a popular Quebec French children's television program, and then their child followed suit (see Young, submitted; Young & Young, in preparation). A scale was used to score the stories for level of cognitive complexity. This scale was derived directly from the current theory of 25 steps in cognitive development (see Table 6.1). Another scale that was used examined the degree of maternal interference-support-directives during the child's storytelling. It ranged from values involving the giving of a specific command or a specific direction to overt negative behavior by the mother. The mothers' instructions were to communicate with the child during her or his story only when it seemed necessary, so that the more they participated the more there was a presumed level of difficulty in the child's performance. The target measures of the study concerned the quality of the participants' linguistic performance in their narratives. Were cohesion and coherence evident in across-utterance connections? Were utterances syntactically sound and without much repair or pauses?

On the average, the mothers scored about one point higher on the scale of cognitive complexity in story compared to their children (3.6 vs. 2.7, respectively). As a group, then, the mothers seemed to adjust their story complexity to the anticipated level of performance of their child. However, were individual differences in the ability of the mothers to predict their child's performance related to her or his actual performance both at the cognitive and linguistic levels? The correlational relationship among the various measures was examined in this regard, and proved interesting.

Results

First, the mothers' cognitive complexity scores were correlated *negatively* with those of the child. This result seems counterintuitive, but the

Table 6.1 Synthetic Theory Derived Text Complexity Scale for Children

Score	Definition
0	Monologue given without any structure and/or sequentiality of events, descriptions. That is, no "true" story evident.
0.5	Structure and/or sequentiality in events, descriptions manifest(s) at times.
1	True story attempted; events, descriptions are sequential, temporally linked. But they are not necessarily subordinated to overall episodic theme. Impression is not one of unity at any point in story even if local connections between sentences are made. [Unity refers to clear presentation of a problem, or its resolution, an event, a situation, a person, etc.]
1.5	Isolated moment of unity evident. At one point in story, an attempt is made to describe a full situation/event, but this does not occupy the whole story.
2	Definite impression of overall subordination to unity in episode conveyed (e.g., stereotypic script with a setting, initiating event, response, and outcome). But there may be some unconnected utterances.
2.5	Episode manifests glimmer of phase distinctions having an organization. There appears to be a clear target end-point, with a preliminary contextual phase laying the groundwork. Usually this takes the form of problem and resolution described separately in a story plot. But it may also refer to subcomponent phases of events, situations, persons, etc., that manifest a working toward a concluding statement, comment, etc. The phases, however, are not yet joined, connected (e.g., a link between problem with plan to resolve it and problem resolution is not clear). For example, problem and resolution are in correct temporal sequence, but show an *ambiguous* and not an explicit causal relation between them. This may also occur when either phase is not fully developed in the narration. [Score 2.25 when target end-point/resolution is implicit.]
3	Groundwork and end-point phases clearly connected.
3.5	The story is comprised of two (or more) successive episodes, each with its own phases, with one major unit and (an)other secondary unit(s) such as a subplot, subepisode, intervening minor problem, or attempted solutions of the problem before resolution takes place. There are no longer units of somewhat equal complexity to the main unit. Secondary units may be embedded. The two elements composing the story lack an interweaving relatedness, for they are presented (and resolved, if this applies) in a sequential, associative manner. That is, there is no parallel nature to the story where the primary element can be left hanging several times and returned to each time while the remaining element is introduced and elaborated (resolved, etc.) in waves in its turn. [Score 3.25 when there are added utterances to story, but they do not constitute an episode or subplot.]
4	Two (or more) successive elements manifest clear links, with a parallel interwoven relationship.
4.5	The secondary element may include an embedded second plot (e.g., second problem to resolve), and not just be a subplot, so that both elements appear to be of somewhat equal complexity.
5	Interweaving of two somewhat equal story elements may take place in oscillatory manner, as described in scale score 3.5.
5.5	Abstract themes, issues, comments, etc., sometimes interpolated, interspersed (in haphazard way) in story.
6	The story is clearly abstract in nature (e.g., metaphorical, allegorical; about morals, values, personality).

Note. Quarter-point values are assigned when intermediate scale point values seem appropriate. The whole-number values refer to (sub)stages of the synthetic theory. The numbers 1 to 5 refer to the five perioperational substages (coordination, hierarchization, systematization, multiplication, integration). The numbers 0 and 6 refer to the prior sensorimotor and ensuing abstract stages, respectively.

context must be kept in mind; the mothers had to tell a story for several minutes knowing that their child would follow and so would be influenced by their story. Thus, it seems that their strategy was to adapt the level of complexity of their stories to the best interests of their child. Given this context, one possible interpretation of the result is that the more the mothers anticipated a poorer performance by the child, the more they augmented their own stories' cognitive complexity in compensation to serve as a better model. Another possibility is that the more the mothers poorly anticipated their child's performance, the less capable was the child in her or his performance. Finally, it could be that the more the mothers could restrain the tendency to tell complex stories, in keeping with the zone of inhibition development that normally they try to create with their children, the more their child's activation-inhibition or distancing skills were promoted and thus their stories were cognitively complex (see "Socio-affectivity"). More research is needed to disentangle the various interpretations of these data. For the moment, it can be argued that the format of the study has potential to elicit interesting results about the modeling process in storytelling and probably about the role of activation-inhibition coordination therein.

CONCLUSION

"[D]evelopment is the activity of creating the conditions for development, and the unit that engages in this activity is the collective" (Newman & Holtzman, 1993, p. 174). Personally, I find this conclusion on the implications of Vygotsky's theory most telling. It defines the communal social responsibility to develop continually and to assure continual development in all others. This theme is one that appears throughout the book.

Vygotskian theory has impregnated the narrative on developmental theory with profound foundational assumptions. It depicts the meeting ground of the developing individual and the sociocultural matrix as appropriated intermental cultural mediating devices that creatively transform in intramental functioning during participatory practice. However, as mentioned in the introduction to this presentation of vygotskian theory, there are several lacunae in the theory that need to be addressed.

First, the cultural values, ethics, styles of thinking, and ideologies that characterize different societies are pervasive, and the manner in which they come to be instilled in their members should be included in any sociocultural account of the developmental process. Different layers of the macrosystem in which the child is embedded socialize and orient her or him to particular cultural moralities, dogmas, and strategies of pragmatic thinking. The particular modality that I see in operation here is the cognitive (mis)perception of the other that individuals are encouraged to adopt by their home families and (sub)groups (discussed in the next chapter).

Second, vygotskians may have judged prematurely that theories of discontinuous stages in development cannot account for contextual sensitivity, developmental variation, and individual differences because of the universal sequence of steps that they prescribe. Current models do show the way piagetian and vygotskian accounts of development can be combined to allow for both universal and individual paths in development (e.g., Case, K. W. Fischer), and they are described in the next chapter.

Third, the products and processes of the appropriation process have to be specified in more detail, and a model of coappropriation that I have developed to this end is described in Chapter 8. It speaks to Vygotsky's use of the term *coknowledge*, Piaget's concept of equilibration, and the concept of adult-culture as social buffer in the child's development (Goodnow [1993] describes possible negative aspects in the zone of proximal development, and it is these that need to be buffered). Moreover, the suggested model of coappropriation incorporates several of the ideas described in the section on current elaborations of vygotskian theory, such as Granott's (1993) model of sociocultural interaction types, Moss's (1992) emphasis on the role of affect in cognitive development, Sigel's (1993) concept of distancing in cognitive development, and Saxe's (1991, 1994) refinement of the concept of appropriation to include, in particular, simultaneous specialization and generalization processes.

RE POSTMODERNISM

The vygotskian perspective on development that is described in the current chapter is built on the concept of constitutive mutuality in the development of higher mental function so that, as in the postmodern perspective, it is sociocultural, situated, contextual, coconstructed, synergistic, and thus not universal or liable to totalizing control. Development takes place in mutual growing zones where scaffolding, apprenticeship, guided participation, activation–inhibition coordination, and the like take place. The result is an evolving intersubjective corelational being of multiple voices with a coconstructed superordinate supervisory function that monitors and reflects on the self-other dynamic in which he or she is engaged. Connectedness characterizes being, and ontogenesis travels toward self–other (empathic) procedures where analytic strategies are used for the common good.

However, interpersonal interactions vary in their affective and supportive quality, and growth toward the mature postmodern, vygotskian individual-in-world is compromised in today's quasimodern sociocultural climate. The sociohistorical matrix out of which cobeings spring has regressive pulls and dominating pushes that are impacting on it. The long-term self, with its genuine sociality and caring morality, is sacrificed on the alter of short-term gratification as an appeasement to avoid annihilation by other policement. Postmoderns must meet moderns in the "zone of emancipated development" in order to infuse them by vygotskian processes with authentic constitutive sociocultural messages.

Burman (1994) has written an eye-opening book on the manner in which the science of developmental psychology is a mediating, colluding tool, apparatus, or technology of state practices that act to normalize, order, delineate, overdetermine, blame, castigate, scapegoat, penalize, and control its constituents while exonerating, legitimating, and perpetuating the state and its exploitative, oppressive practices. Through its tests and theories, developmental psychology deconstructs the individual in terms of race, class, and sex, in particular, so that dominant themes and individual (groups) can maintain regularizing hegemony without the necessity of fostering genuine opportunity and equality. "[D]evelopmental psychology (like the rest of psychology) imports ideogical understandings into its theories that are incorporated into 'science'" (p. 187). It "produces 'us' in its image ... and contributes to the maintenance of the social formation that gave rise to it" (p. 188).

Burman (1994) argues that the state and its agents, such as the discipline of developmental psychology, functions with these subjective, hidden, unconscious agendas and assumptions aimed toward homogenizing the understanding of human development, and consequently of societal development. Individuals and groups who fail to self-subjugate to psychology's privileged, normative, scrutinizing gaze, models, and prescriptions are pathologized as inferior. Moreover, in a pernicious manner, mothers, minorities, and the working class are subject to victim blaming, an inculcated constructed truth where they are treated as responsible for the problems that befall them in the failed environments they inhabit. In this regard, A. Harris (1987) provides the example of how cognitive developmental psychology emphasizes skill and problem-solving development in childhood, which can be seen as a sensitization of parents to prepare their children for later self-serving but low-paying work. "[W]ider structural relations enter into and are (re)produced within micro-social relations" (Burman, 1994, p. 44). Another example concerns the manner in which universal public school education was instituted in England in the last century in order to segregate, monitor, normalize, control, block, disenfranchise, and correct the potentially unruly, resistant poor. Finally, the description of developmental milestones that developmental psychology promulgates affords another example. "Development thus becomes an obstacle race ... with cultural kudos accorded to the most advanced, and the real or imagined penalties of professional intervention or stigmatization if progress is delayed" (p. 58).

Although I find the general message of the book attractive, it is presented in a polemical way without differentiation. The sociocultural and historicopolitical influences that control individual development and our science equally are not as monolithic and entirely evil as the author would have us imagine. Again, I am arguing that the degree of an individual or group's mistreatment of the other can be scaled according to the current theory's hypothesized steps in development of the cognitive (mis)perception of the other, as we shall see in the next chapter. (A scale to measure the oppressive nature of society's and psychology's scaling practices: Is there the rub? I hope not.)

PART IV

COCONSTRUCTED AMELIORATIONS OF VYGOTSKIAN THEORY

CHAPTER 7

The Cognitive (Mis)perception of the Other

INTRODUCTION

As mentioned at the end of the last chapter, there are three areas in the vygotskian literature that seem to need work and that are treated in this chapter and Chapter 8. In the current chapter, first, a model of the types of sociocultural pressures on the developing individual is presented. It concerns the cognitive (mis)perception of the other. In particular, it is based, on the current 25-step neopiagetian model of cognitive development. Second, I examine the question of whether a neopiagetian theory can coexist with a vygotskian one, especially at the level of the issue of universal stages versus individual differences in cognitive development. In the next chapter, an integrated model of the coappropriation process in cognitive development is presented. It also attempts to integrate the vygotskian and neopiagetian perspectives. Finally, at the end of that chapter, an empirical study is summarized that speaks to the issue of the influence of the level of cognitive (mis)perception of the other when dealing with the other.

SOCIOCULTURAL AND HISTORICOPOLITICAL PRESSURES

In the previous chapter it was shown that Vygotsky's concept of mediating devices that function in the individual's development of mental functions during her or his mutual, reciprocal relationship with the sociocultural context has been elaborated by Wertsch (1991) to include Bakhtin's concept of polyvocality, which includes cultural voices. Also, I had suggested that a broader notion of sociocultural mediating devices was needed to capture the full extent of societal factors that enculturate mental func-

tioning, i.e., its ideologies, dogmas, political pressures, historical tendencies, social conventions, and cultural messages; its fundamental morals,
values, and ethics; and its styles of perceiving, thinking, and behaving.

Psychology is taking note of the political pressures that shape attitudes toward the other, and how insidious those pressures can be. For
example, Fox (1993) dispels some of the myths that are harbored about our
"progressive" society, and argues for a psychology of action aimed at
promoting the most fundamental human values society acknowledges but
does not strive to implement fully. At a more concrete level, R.J. Smith
(1993) argues that some less enlightened ideas in capitalistic thought (ram-
pant profit-seeking and consumerism) infuse the media and have lead to
the explosion of eating disorders in our society (obesity in consumer-
goods-hungry lower social classes and anorexia in the savings/profit-
seeking-oriented middle class, respectively).

However, these general comments on the powerful influences of society on its members is in need of a more specific way of differentiating them.
Which influences are more crassly invasive and debilitating, which are
more manipulative and coercive? What particular reactions are engendered in developing individuals exposed to one type of societal pressure
compared to another? I have created a model that attempts to answer these
questions and related ones. It is based on the current 25-step neopiagetian
model of development. Presentation of the model, which deals with the
cognitive (mis)perception of the other, begins with a description of a
similar model by Sameroff. Then it moves to a discussion of the way
parents may be the linchpin in creating isomorphically similar patterns
leading from the world to the child's mind-brain. This sets the stage for a
detailed presentation of the levels in cognitive (mis)perception of the other
and the way they relate to society's (mis)perception of its members. After a
presentation of the model, I loop back to the issue at hand of the specific
nature of sociocultural influences on development seen from a vygotskian
perspective.

CONCEPTS OF DEVELOPMENT

Introduction

Sameroff and his colleagues (Sameroff & Feil, 1985; Sameroff, Seifer,
Baldwin, & Baldwin, 1993; Sameroff, Seifer, Barocas, Zax, & Greenspan,
1987) have developed a powerful model of the way parents' beliefs and
explanations of child development seem to reflect Piaget's stages of cognitive development. Different cognitive levels evident in parents' concepts
of the way development proceeds in children seem to be associated with

different lenses about children's behavior and needs and with different expectations about them. For example, a parent who views her infant from the sensorimotor perspective, Piaget's first major cognitive stage, may be more or less adequate as a caregiver in the first years of life, but will experience problems dealing with the child as he or she grows toward and into the next cognitive stage.

Given that Piaget described four major stages of cognitive development, at least in terms of the traditional manner of conceiving his work, Sameroff described four corresponding levels in parents' concepts of child development. Transitional levels also are posited between the levels. The first two of the four levels are the symbiotic and categorical levels, which parallel the sensorimotor and preoperational cognitive stages, respectively, in the early years of life. The compensating and perspectivist levels follow, and correspond to the concrete operational and formal operational cognitive stages, respectively, in older children and adolescents. The particular manner in which parents' concepts of development are measured involves a series of problematic family–child vignettes-stories. The parents are asked to try to explain the reason why the problematic situations have arisen.

The Levels

Parents thinking at the initial symbiotic level are concerned especially with the immediate relationship with their child, and manifest no differentiation between the child and themselves, so that the child's and the relationships' characteristics are seen as direct consequences of their own efforts. The danger of this level of conceptualization is that when parents perceive that their child is not manifesting the desired responses to their efforts (e.g., an infant fails to soothe), they can become quite distressed and reject the child. Also, as an infant develops a greater sense of autonomy and quasi-independent activity, parents may react negatively. Newberger (1980) describes the way child abuse may result from such parental attitudes. Thus, at this level of thought parents essentially are atheoretical and nonreflective when it comes to evaluating causes in child behavior. They find it impossible to reflect on the developmental process. Consequently, when tested for developmental concept level, these parents fail to see any causality in the problems in the vignettes and offer no explanation for them.

The categorical level is marked by differentiation between the self and the child so that the child's behaviors and attributes are viewed by parents at this level as intrinsic to her or him irrespective of their nature (positive or negative). Moreover, the child's behaviors and attitudes are considered products of unidimensional influencing factors (e.g., "He got it from me"). The danger of this level of perception of the child is that when a negative label is attributed to the child, parents may be dominated by the label and react to the child from its perspective even if (1) the child behaves only in a temporary way according to the label; (2) it only reflects a part of her/his repertoire; and (3) the child no longer behaves in the same way. Thus, when it comes to commenting upon the test vignettes, parents at this level offer an explanation of child/family problems in terms of a single cause (e.g., experience or genetic endowment).

Parents who function at the compensating level, which is the typical level found in parents according to Sameroff, understand that child development is a product of the interaction of two or more higher-order processes rather than one lower-order label. These processes are not defined in terms of inflexible attributes, as with labels, but they are more general (e.g., parents acknowledge that the environment influences development in interaction with the child's age, which allows for different behaviors at different developmental epochs). The limit of the parents' concept of child development is a lack of appreciation of the abstract nature of the influences on it. For example, the age dimension is conceived in terms of normative behavior at each age level so that developmental delays are seen as deviant. In summary, when it comes to analyzing the vignettes of problem child/family situations, compensating parents see two or more coordinated causes described at the level of processes.

Finally, at the perspectivist level explanations are multicausal, are general hypothetical constructs or processes (e.g., environmental-contextual, constitutional-congenital, psychological), and describe complex, dynamic transactions among them. For example, it is understood that if the context had been different or becomes different, the child may manifest a different developmental pathway. A danger at this level is that parents can spend too much time imagining all the disturbances that can go wrong with the development of the child.

Research

Sameroff depicts very well the way in which parents' belief about the process of development influences their behavior toward their offspring. He and his colleagues have performed a series of investigations examining the determinants and consequences of adhering to one belief or another. An important differentiating factor seemed to be the parents' socioeconomic and cultural background. The variables of lower SES, adherence to more traditional cultural systems, and lower intellectual level were associated with lower developmental concept scores (e.g., Gutierrez & Sameroff,

1990). It seems that a variety of constraints on the ability or need to think at higher levels about development impose restrictions on beliefs about it. The desire to conform, in particular, appears to be a potent inhibitor of thinking about development. However, all such factors together can account for only a limited portion of the variability in the data. There are important individual differences within any one social class or group, and there are cross-situation differences within any one individual. With respect to consequences of the different levels of concepts about development, Sameroff et al. (1987) found a positive association between mothers' reasoning level on the vignette test and their 4-year-olds' IQ. Future research should examine such results in more detail for possible partial cause-effect relations.

Pratt, Hunsberger, Pancer, Roth, and Santolupo (1993) performed three studies examining the development over age of levels of concepts about development and their consequences for parental tutoring, beliefs about authoritarianism, etc. In the first study, 7- to 59-year-olds showed an increase in vignette test score with respect to chronological age, formal operational level status, and degree of integrative complexity of reasoning in discourse. In the second study, developmental concept level in parents of fifth-graders was positively related to effective parental tutoring on a mathematics homework assignment and to parental responsiveness in an observational situation. In the third study, 18- to 85-year-olds showed an inverse correlation between age and their score on a right-wing authoritarian scale. Also, the older (60+) compared to younger adults obtained lower scores in reasoning about hypothetical but not real-life dilemmas. Overall, it appears that social factors in the life of individuals (e.g., even their political beliefs) are influenced heavily by level of reasoning about child development.

Conclusion

Cumulatively, the research with Sameroff's model suggests an important influence on child development of parents' level of belief about the developmental process, and validates a model of belief along these lines which is structured on Piaget's theory of the stages in cognitive development. In my own work on this issue, as I show in the next section, Sameroff's 4-step model has been extended in the following ways.

- First, the current neopiagetian theory of 25 substages in cognitive development across the lifespan served as the basis for elaborating a corresponding 25-step model of belief about the developmental level of the child.

- Second, the model is phrased in a manner which emphasizes the dangers of cognitively misperceiving the developmental level of the child, and consequently is labeled a model of the cognitive (mis)-perception of the other.
- Third, the model is formulated in order to apply to a variety of relationships, and thus seems applicable not only to the parent–child relationship but also to that of couples and the individual–society relationship.
- Fourth, the reaction that the misperceived individual should manifest at each of the 25 levels of the model also is described.
- Fifth, the relationship of the earlier levels of the model to different types of insecure attachment of the infant to the caregiver (avoidant, ambivalent-resistant, disorganized-disoriented) is specified along with corresponding types of caregiver quality with which they are posited to be associated in neobowlbian theory.
- Sixth, a particular empirical tool has been adopted to test the model. It concerns a 25-point scale of the type of supportive or interfering discourse in which participants engage in an interaction.
- Seventh, the model is not only neopiagetian and neobowlbian, for it also speaks to neovygotskian issues. That is, the sociocultural influences on the individual's developing concept of development and the resultant (mis)perception of the cognitive level of the other are emphasized in the current model, and shown to influence in turn the social and wider political values of the individual and the collective societies that individuals form.

Before the model of the cognitive (mis)perception of the other is presented, in the next section the manner in which societal pressures come to influence individual development is examined.

FRACTALS AND ACTIVATION–INHIBITION COORDINATION

World–Brain–Mind Isomorphism

The Concept. Vandervert (1991, 1992, 1995a, 1995b) tried to show the way that design properties of the environment are isomorphically represented in the brain and mind of humankind. An algorithm is a set of rules that perform operations in problem solving. According to Vandervert, the brain's algorithms are organized fractally, and self-refer (feedback) to similar designs as they try to understand the world, because, in general, the world itself is designed this way. Thus, Vandervert maintains that there is a homotopic isomorphism across world, brain (synapses), and mind (mental models) in terms of fractal design in algorithmic organization.

In their own way, Hermans, Kempen, and van Loon (1992) also have dealt with environment–mind homology. They argue that the self is spatially organized and "embodied." Through spatiotemporal displacement and interactions in the environment, humans come to know what is meaningful and the way it becomes meaningful. The mind is spatially analogous to behavior, which in turn is a spatial analogue of the environment. Thought is not purely abstract and propositional.

The Current Version.   I feel that the present work carries Vandervert's (1991, 1992, 1995a, 1995b) logic one step further by showing the similarity of brain organization, behavior, its development, therapy, etc., in terms of activation–inhibition coordination (Young, 1990a, 1990b, submitted). The world presents itself to the developing individual as an activation–inhibition flow of forward, backward, erratic, contained, and suppressed movement (and feeling). Thus, the algorithmic isomorphism which encapsulates world, brain, and mind in one dynamic should involve activation and inhibition balancing. In short, we can ask whether activation–inhibition coordination, which appears so ubiquitous in the world, brain, and mind, can be interpreted in terms of fractal design.

As Young (1990a) wrote:

> The aesthetic simplicity of the inhibition hypothesis ... should not escape our attention. The concept of inhibition applies fluidly across many levels of psychological analysis.... There are biochemical mediators of inhibition. Inhibition is a central characteristic of neuronal network and central nervous system function. Importance is attached to inhibition in overt behavior at multiple levels: motoric, cognitive, social, personality, etc. Even environmental influences ... can be conceived in these terms. (p. 119)

Thus, activation–inhibition coordination may be widespread across diverse psychological frames. Furthermore, in this regard, it may be asked what is the mechanism of interpolation from one frame (world, brain, mind) to the other. The brain and nervous system are honed in the world by natural selection to adapt to its exigencies, or to capture the particularities in it necessary for reproductive fitness. The social milieu and, in the early years, parents and caregivers, in particular, serve a Januslike function in this regard. That is, they are the crucial element in the niche of the world, yet buffer the developing child from it, acting within the parameters of the child's developing brain and behavior. The developing child attunes to their dynamic, incorporating it and modifying her or his own in light of it. Parents become "evoked companions" which the developing child carries, for their sense of security, moods, and vitality is superimposed on her or him (Stern, 1985).

Consequently, the question becomes the best way to characterize parents'/caregivers' behavior in terms of activation–inhibition coordination. What n-dimensional space is needed for this function? Can fractal geometry help in this regard? To what extend does the synaptic pathway and network organization of the brain homotopically reflect the activation–inhibition coordination evident in the larger world of the child, especially in terms of parental–caregiver patterns? Is the mind or submind nested hierarchy isomorphically structured in a self-similar, self-referenced way? How much do we grow toward our selves, toward the universe, and toward understanding the coexistential similarity of our self and the universe, or of our inner world, our parents' world, and the outer world through activation–inhibition interplay?

Parents as Activation–Inhibition Fractal Buffers

These kinds of questions imply that parents are the intermediaries in the transmission of activation–inhibition coordination from the world to the developing child. They help the growing individual to expand into the world, knowing the way to coordinate activation and inhibition in their behavior with the flux of activation–inhibition coordination in the world. Thus, the process of activation–inhibition coordination seems to allow the social dance, or the coexistential flow that is life. It helps regulate the appropriate outreach of the individual being, behavior, or psychological unit with the timely damping necessarily for its control in context. And fractals seems to possess similar properties, which permit them to function as an appropriate measure of activation–inhibition coordination. Thus, fractals can help represent activation–inhibition coordination because they seem especially sensitive to its essential properties.

Flam (1991) reports data supportive of this position in that fractals seem to involve inhibition. According to fractal researchers, nature loves fractals because they may provide shapes which better damp vibrations. Their repetitive irregularities repeated within nested levels may better contain resonances, as in the design of coastlines. In this regard, Thelen (1990a) argues that fractals have the ability to "tolerate and modulate perturbations." The same concept may apply to the buffering effect of parents and caregivers in the action of the world on the growing child. Parents may serve as activation–inhibition fractal buffering mechanisms. There may be a fractal topography in parental–caregiver activation–inhibition coordination. Parental fractals may be organized to provide a psychological containing effect on the onslaught of the environment's waves as they pound the shores of the child's developing mind. The potentially overpowering force of the world's activation–inhibition fractal may be modulated and channeled by and through the parents'–caregivers' activation–inhibition fractal, producing an increasingly competent activation–inhibition fractal in the growing child's brain and mind. It may be speculated that in different nonoptimal caregiving environments, there may be corresponding different nonoptimal activation–inhibition fractal patterns evident in caregiving behavior. The following model of the cognitive (mis)perception of the other gives psychological color to this mathematical approach to nonoptimal environments in development. I return to the question of fractalization in development in Chapter 12.

A MODEL OF THE COGNITIVE (MIS)PERCEPTION OF THE OTHER

Introduction

A model of different qualities and complexities in the adult's and society's perception of the other is presented (see Table 7.1, which is explained in the next section). It is derived from the 25-step model of development described in the current work. The model concerns the cognitive (mis)perception of the other, or the manner in which an individual is either appropriately evaluated or construed, or poorly, or inappropriately, evaluated or construed in terms of her/his current developmental level and potential to develop to her/his maximum or optimal developmental level. The (mis)construal or (mis)perception is considered to be an affectively influenced, developmentally based cognitive filter or lens of the construer that has repercussions for the manner in which the individual is treated (or mistreated, or otherwise not treated optimally), and the manner in which he/she responds to the construer. It can be applied to both perception of the self and perception of the other, to past, present, or future perceptions, and so on. It provides a bridge from personal developmental to sociocultural and historicopolitical analyses. Finally, its validity is indicated by its excellent match with the work of Clinchy, Belenky, and colleagues (e.g., Clinchy, 1993, 1995; Belenky et al., 1986; see Chapter 6) on five epistemological positions that developing individuals can adopt about truth or knowledge and the way it is acquired. Their model is incorporated into the current one as I proceed.

Reflexive Stage

Parents-caregivers who misperceive their child as reflexive at best, should have themselves personally experienced enormous trauma in the

Table 7.1 The Cognitive (Mis)perception of the Other: Adult–Society Working Schema and Individual/Group Response at Each (Mis)perceived Cognitive Stage of Other

(Mis)perceived stage[a]	Adult/society		Individual/group response
	Schema	Behavior	
Reflexive[b]	Their existence inconsequential	Negate/despotism (abuse, reject, deny)	Obliteration (silence)[d] vs. nihilism
Sensorimotor	They exist, so dominate	Subjugate/authoritarianism[e] (repress, oppose/compete, impose, manipulate)	Sterilization (to "receive" knowledge) vs. revolution
Perioperational	They think, so channel	Pacify/crude marketism—enlightened oligarchism (render docile body, tantalize)	Assimilation (and subjective knowing) vs. resistance
Abstract	They test, so partially disempower	Deglobalize/welfare marketism (limit consciousness, partially liberate)	Involution vs. evolution (use analytic or empathic procedures)
Collective intelligence	They're wise, so empower	Globalize/Market humanism (fractalize, symbiose, transmute)	Equalization vs. emancipation (construct knowledge; combine the analytic and empathic)

[a]Each stage is marked by five substages: coordination, hierarchization, systematization, multiplication, integration.

[b]For the first four stages, when target not realistically perceived, less than optimal pattern by perceiver obtains.

[c]When target's potential maximal stage is recognized, perceived style is optimal.

[d]Ways of epistemological knowing given in parentheses, as described by Belenky et al. (1986).

[e]An example of the manner in which the current scheme can be applied readily to the question of *the cognitive (mis)perception of the self* is supplied. The self can misperceive its (maximal developmental) level as a person who is a subjugator or an appropriate target of subjugation. Similarly, a partner in a relationship or even a society can so misperceive itself. Reactions of said individuals, partners, or societies to target actions may be based more on these misperceptions than on emitted behaviors. Thus, self-fulfilling, vicious cycles are induced (e.g., person functions as subjugator in light of image of self as such created by past environment, eliciting revolt, confirming need for subjugation).

past and also should be overwhelmed in their current life circumstance (e.g., without social support). The very existence of their child is inconsequential to them, so that physical or mental abuse of the child may be a chronic pattern provoked for idiosyncratic, irrational reasons. Patterns of rejection, denial, criticisms, insults, incoherence, and extreme neglect may characterize caregiving behavior, as well. Thus, this parental style is labeled *negation*.

In a couple, one adult partner may treat the other in the same violent way. Its equivalent at the sociopolitical level would concern despotic, tyrannic "absolutism," where a society's members are considered to function only for an elite, or ruling class or person. History is replete with such systems. Individuals conditioned to function at this level (whether child, adult partner, or member of an oppressed group) have their sense of self obliterated. They are silent, blindly obedient, with no mind, voice, or power.

If individuals do not succumb to this regime, at best their reaction is one of nihilism. That is, they function in an anarchic, chaotic fringe, orbiting around the perceiver's center. Wrath or withdrawal may be part of the individuals' reaction, but neither can lead long beyond the oppressor, because personal tools necessary for better adaptation have not been honed. If a child tries to escape her or his parents' misperception, or an adult tries to escape that of their partner (or a group in society tries to escape that of its oppressor), protracted (mental) anarchy or confusion likely will set in the individual before any equilibration or stabilization is achieved.

Sensorimotor Stage

Parents-caregivers misperceiving their child to be at the sensorimotor level at best acknowledge her or his existence, but have been too compromised by life experiences to do much more. They cannot accept that their child may be capable of independent thought. They are forever dominated by the forces controlling them, and so are controlling of their child in the sense of subjugating her or him to their own needs and desires. This leads the parents to manifest partial negation and neglect (scant attention), repression of any incipient indices of independence, imposition of personal agendas, and a general manipulatory shaping toward self-limiting goals. If any freedom in action is offered to the child by parents, it is either because they are overwhelmed themselves (and thus freedom obtains only through a lax supervision or an inadvertent loophole in control), or because they want to create a constrained space for refuge so that the child can refuel for the difficult submission ahead.

The equivalent of this style in adult relationships often would be accompanied by alcoholism or other resignations of control over the self. At the historicopolitical level, an example would be represented by a less absolute, self-serving form of rule as in an enlightened authoritarian or totalitarian system.

An individual or group exposed to this regimen becomes sterilized in mind and behavior. Some manner of external control insidiously invades all impulses toward autonomy. In this sanitized mental milieu, there is room only for passive acceptance, a receiving of given knowledge, and conformity. Normally, no personally derived thought would be possible.

However, if there is sufficient base for self-assertion, then full-scale revolution in behavior may be spawned. Rage may lead to breaking of chains to the subjugator, but the process of evolving toward more mature self-disciplined behavior would be an arduous one.

Perioperational Stage

A child misperceived by parents to be at the perioperational level at best is acknowledged to possess basic thinking capacities, but not more general, abstract logical ones. For these parents, a thinking child may be a menacing one, so that the child's cognitive effort must be channeled and neutralized before he/she explores issues personally sensitive to the parents (i.e., are the parents themselves cognitively controlled, channeled, neutralized). Thus, any threatening pathways in thought followed by the child would require that parents use either arguments that function to counter her/his logic, or more radical controlling strategies, like those used in the prior levels.

Normally, when a child or preadolescent is engaged in directed or cognitive activity, he or she functions at this thinking level being discussed, and uses it in a benign way. Thus, parents at this level will support and help elaborate their child's train of thought if the child desires help or if the parents are required to do so, as with homework. Otherwise, parents at this level may be too enmeshed in their daily tasks to bother with their child if the path in thought being followed is nonmenacing.

In general, parents at this level function according to an image of having their child become clones or copies of themselves. To accomplish this end, the optimal strategy used by the parents is to indoctrinate or impose rules of self-policing, self-control, or self-government in the child concordant with the ones championed by the parents themselves. Often, these rules inculcated in the child concern traditional values which enable the child to adopt limited roles in the wider collective (at school, and later at work), following the parental pattern. The parents may have been pacified in the same way by their own parents, in an intergenerational process of being rendered "docile bodies" (after Foucault, 1980; see Chapter 9).

A child may succumb to this process especially if it is accompanied by adequate parental warmth and appropriate reinforcements for compliance. Rewards tantalize the child, encouraging placated, co-opted ("bought"), assimilatory practices. The child ends up developing a subjective mode of knowing (immediate intuition without logical analysis), so that reality is only partially perceived, at best.

The spousal system may be marked by a similar relational style. Conformism to other- and self-imposed values may undermine both partners' growth. Also, a society may be organized according to similar principles (e.g., as in crude, consumptive, commodifying capitalism or marketism, or perhaps in an enlightened oligarchic regime).

Rejection of this mode of care normally would entail less revolution and more resistance and disappointment compared to the prior level, because the recipient of this mode of care would have developed enough thinking skills so that the person could be(come) self-oriented to obtain more advanced ends. In fact, parents may provide a good-enough environment when functioning at this level, especially when it is accompanied by much warmth and a (vague) hope for something better, promoting in their child an inevitable growth beyond this level. Yet movement toward less docility and/or growth beyond this level would be a long-term process for the developing individual.

Abstract Stage

Parents misperceiving their child or adolescent as an individual who will end up at most at the abstract level may attempt to inhibit her or his empathic feel for others and the planet. Adolescents can rationally evaluate their world, and be aware of (all) the variables impinging on it. They entertain notions of a wider consciousness, self-sacrifice, transcendence, etc., if they have not been subverted toward self-indulgent egotism. However, when parents have limited their own level of consciousness (e.g., to materialistic values, using the salve of governmental and charitable welfarism to assuage any guilt), optimal adolescent growth toward empathy becomes compromised. Parents unconsciously may place blinders on their offspring's attempts to be more holistic in world view. An emerging, nascent belief in universal altruism would be depreciated in the child through subtle (or even overt) means, if need be. The desire of an adolescent to "change the system" would be too threatening to the parents. Thus, any psychological weapon in the parents' regulatory arsenal would be wheeled out to disempower this concept and its carrier. Other developing conceptual domains which are less threatening to the parents would not be dismantled by them, so that partial freedom of mind would obtain in the adolescent. Because the parents would be undermining a global perspective in their adolescent when behaving in this manner, the behavior is labeled *deglobalization*.

An adult may behave similarly with a partner or a society with its members. Societies, in offering welfarism, hope to contain those who suffer, and not empower them. Yet only through full development of all parts of the self, especially our other-compassionate components, and of all selves, can self and society develop fully (Lévinas, 1985; see Chapter 2).

Without a working toward this philosophy, which can best occur if significant others do not counter it during childhood, the individual risks turning inward away from the other (in involution), with movement toward the self and away from the self–other communion as the center of being. However, an adolescent may not be exposed to the optimal model in her or his own home, but may come from a warm, caring family, nonetheless. This should facilitate an evolution of an encompassing movement of the self toward the other in the sense described. The adolescent in this context would use either self-focused, reasoned, analytic, judging, cold thought procedures or selfless, connected, nonjudgmental, feeling, empathic procedures to learn and communicate as he or she navigates the path toward full maturity. However, these two operations would not be combined into one amalgam, thus limiting their effectiveness in creating a full self and in feeling empathically the other without losing the self.

Collective Intelligence Stage

Parents who realize that their offspring is part of a global system (think at the collective intelligence level) will raise her or him with sensitivity toward sensitivity. They can be empathically wise, and encourage growth toward the same. They are many-faceted and find reverie and unity in their multiplicity (e.g., integration of different parts of the self, of emotion and cognition). They pursue personal and societal growth, cannot see the way the two can be separated, know that either self- or other-effacement or denial negates both self- and other-development, and support agent sources that actively lobby for or undertake constructive collective-oriented endeavor. These parents empower their child toward this attitude. They see their self in intimate communion with the universe and the universe in intimate communion with their self, in one enveloping, resonating system. They hope to transform their child into an even better collective-oriented being compared to themselves, which should materialize if all caregivers involved reciprocally support this attitude. Only at this level is genuine psychological emancipation possible. Full giving to the whole, leaving an absence of nontrivial choice, is full freedom (if performed in the context of this developmental level). Mature (creative, constructivist) thinkers are passionate knowers, integrating cold-analytic and warm-empathic learning procedures, self affirmation and other confirmation, present and future, reality and imagined possibility, personal and communal, and action and morality into one whole or macrocosm.

In their own evolving way, many couples and even our society are moving toward this philosophy. Without belaboring the point, it can be argued that economic growth should not only serve producers and enhance their growth, but also should be used to empower the deprived to become productive, empathic members of society in their own right. The market should serve humanistic ends.

Comment

A model is presented on how individuals perceive the other according to their own predominant developmental level. In reality, each individual simultaneously functions at all five levels of the model, either in terms of actual behavior, desired behavior, development toward mature behavior, or the hope to develop toward this end. However, the relative proportion of the five levels varies from one individual to the next. Moreover, any one individual varies in her or his ongoing developmental level according to situation, issue, person being related to, his or her own history, etc. For example, a parent in treating a teenager may mix rejection (in level 1), subjugation (in level 2), pacification (in level 3), partial limitation of consciousness (in level 4), and full empathic wisdom (in level 5). The same rule can also can be applied to development in couples and societies; they may also have one major way of being, but vary.

Substages

This completes presentation of the model of the cognitive (mis)perception of the other in terms of the five stages of the current developmental theory. In the following, the model is elaborated to deal with substages, which are seen to recur cyclically across the stages. It will be recalled that in the current theory, substages concern coordination, hierarchization, systematization, multiplication, and integration.

In the first substage of coordination, parents may adopt any one of the five styles just discussed in a relatively undifferentiated way. They would apply it in a similar way from one circumstance or domain to another. However, there would not be clear, articulated links across them. Essentially, the style would exist as a monolithic entity pervasive in all dealings with the child. Moreover, secondary (more advanced) beliefs may be coupled with the primary one at times, and applied in particular circumstances, but with no clear organization in the parents' rule structure.

Similarly, the child would be considered an undifferentiated entity, or only an individual that must exist as a reflection of the preponderant caregiving style. Thus, parents would be coordinating their all-encompassing attitude with secondary ones in a haphazard way, and with their child as a reflection of that attitude. In this sense, they would be acting from and perceiving their child from a coordination cognitive substage.

When parents refine their parental style, they are better able to link their behavior in various circumstances and situations to their predominant attitude, or rules may not be applied in equal ways across all contexts because the parents may realize the need for some situational flexibility. Or, they may allow a clearer space for alternatives concerning at least some areas in raising their child. Because a primary attitude dominates their behavior, even when a secondary (more advanced) attitude applies to part(s) of their style, it would be seen through the lens of the primary style. Thus, parents who adopt this style of behavior appear to be functioning according to a hierarchical structure. In a similar vein, parents may treat their child in a more differentiated way, perceiving her or him as having some independence or external existence beyond the predominant caregiving style. Thus, in this sense, as well, parental style evidences a hierarchical structure, and serves to open up more space for alternative reactions in the child.

When the primary caregiving attitude becomes more clearly differentiated in parents, and is applied with nuance across situations or domains, it creates a larger systemic framework with more room for secondary (more advanced) attitudes (systematization). For example, choices reflective of the predominant and alternative attitudes may be offered in relevant situations. This process would serve to open even more space in the child.

In the next substage, various system combinations of alternative parental styles may be created for different domains (multiplication). Here, parents would be accentuating the process of offering options to their child.

Finally, parental style may become so differentiated that its primary modality may be integrated into a complex pattern, facilitating its eventual transformation into a higher-order form. Here, parents behave with optimal flexibility and even reversibility with respect to the predominant attitude, and they perceive their child as having the right to the same characteristics in their behavior, within certain confines.

This description of substages in parental style based on comparable substages in the perceived cognitive stage of children illustrates that parents generally do not function in terms of one attitude, but display individually determined combinations. By considering that there may be at least four sublevels within any one substage (initiation, application, maturation, transition), then the range of possible combinations becomes even more elaborate. The same perspective applies to any decomposition of adult-partner relationships or historicopolitical systems; in both cases combined styles or substages should manifest.

Application to Adolescence

It is predicted that different types of adolescent–parent conflict should derive from the five types of reactions to the cognitive (mis)perceptions that have been presented. That is, (1) some adolescents in crisis manifest extreme anarchy; (2) others are fixated on revolt; and (3) still others show more subtle resistance; (4) less negative reactions involve voluble attempts at personal evolution; (5) while some may even struggle to engage in altruistic acts especially for the purpose of internal growth toward a mindframe for collective moral endeavor. Of course, there should be the usual substage (x 5) and sublevel (x 4) developmental steps evident in this model (e.g., are reactions coordinated, hierarchized, systematized?).

Current research on adolescent turmoil, turbulence, and stress is increasing (e.g., Eccles, Midgeley, Wigfield, Buchanan, Reuman, Flanagan, & Mac Iver, 1993; Hill, 1993; Larsen & Ham, 1993; Offer & Schonert-Reichl, 1992). However, it does not offer a differentiated perspective, such as the one advocated here, on types of adolescent problematic behavior that may be encountered.

In terms of attachment theory, very chaotic–abusive, dismissing, and preoccupied caregivers may misperceive their child at most as reflexive, sensorimotor, and peri(pre)operational in potential, respectively, leading to corresponding disorganized-disoriented, avoidant, and ambivalent-resistant attachment by the child (Main, 1991). That is, if a child is misperceived to be at a cognitive stage inferior to the one actually attained, or incapable or unworthy of following a normal developmental pathway to the most mature stages (e.g., abstract and collective intelligence), then this problematic assessment should engender consequent maladaptive caregiving and nonoptimal attachment, in turn. These ideas could be used in the study of adolescent attachment to arrive at a more differentiated perspective of their psychology.

Conclusion

The framework of the cognitive (mis)perception of the other that has been formulated speaks to us as psychologists. To what extent do we empower clients to have full other exploration, sensitivity, empathy, and altruism? The explicit goal is to *free* the client to pursue a regular path to full, optimal development (see Hatfield & Hatfield [1992], on cognitive development and wellness). However, to what extent is the implicit meta-goal to *freeze* the client at a less than optimal level, fitting the therapist's own "parental" style vis-à-vis her or his offspring and clients and fitting her or his wishes for society's treatment of its individual members (including the therapist) and its groups?

The schemata of (mis)perception of the other of any mental health professional serve as the lens through which all her or his past developmental processes pass when dealing with their clients' reconstruction of the past, the negotiated present, and the anticipated future. The preferred level of (mis)perception of the other for any one person, issue, etc., offers a comfort zone or escape pathway from incongruities and tension evoked by the glimmer of a superior level, whether it be in clients or therapists. Our task as therapists should be to work toward the propitious resolution of such tensions wherever they occur so that the development of more advanced levels of cognitively perceiving the other is facilitated.

A SCALE OF THE COGNITIVE (MIS)PERCEPTION OF THE OTHER

On the basis of the model of levels in the cognitive (mis)perception of the other, a 25-point scale was created for use in discourse situations (see Tables 7.2 to 7.6). The purpose of the scale is to permit the measurement of the quality of interference, directives, or support that participants provide each other in conversations, discussions, didactic sessions, etc. Thus, it is

**Table 7.2 Reflexive Substages of Discourse Quality
Based on the Cognitive (Mis)perception of the Other**

Substage	Discourse/quality
1.	The child is seen as an extension of the parent's self so that he or she can negate, abuse, reject, deny, and behave absolutely, with overt insults and rejection toward the child. The intonation is abrasive, negative, and rejecting.
2.	The child's reasoning or position is attacked, criticized, or rejected. The parent overtly denies the possibility of the child being correct.
3.	The child's reasoning or position is overtly dismissed with no effort to constructively redirect or guide understanding of the other's viewpoint. The child is told that he or she is "wrong," but there is no effort to explain why.
4.	Only part of the child's behavior or argument is treated as indicated in the previous substage.
5.	Despite such behavior, part of the child's behavior or argument is acknowledged or listened to by the parent. There is a differentiation and reversibility evident in the willingness to acknowledge/listen to the child.

**Table 7.3 Sensorimotor Substages of Discourse Quality
Based on the Cognitive (Mis)perception of the Other**

Substage	Discourse/quality
6.	There is a high degree of parental control, subjugation, repression, authoritarianism, opposition, imposition, manipulation, and dominance in the conversation. It is shaped directly by the parent's ideas or agenda. The child has no independent thought, but waits for the parent to provide direction. The parent uses language to control the child's physical actions and behaviors. An order is given that directs the path in the conversation (e.g., "You don't have to say that," or "You'd better ... You have to ... You must ...").
7.	The child's reasoning-position is competed with, contradicted, countered, or opposed in an effort to subvert, manipulate, control, or undermine it.
8.	The child clearly is directed to speak or act in a particular way with no constructive explanation given as to why (e.g., "No," "Tell me about ...," "Why don't you ...").
9.	Only part of the child's discourse is manipulated. Manipulative suggestions are made that flow from that part of the child's previous discourse that seems to have been judged possibly acceptable to the parent.
10.	Despite some signs of parental manipulation, etc., suggestions are made in a way that appears to give the child a chance to use them or not (e.g., "You know that you could get what you want if you did it this way.").

readily applicable to the typical vygotskian situations, as described in the previous chapter, in which parents and children engage. To this end, it was used in a study of adolescent–mother political dialogue (see Chapter 13).

The scale is divided into five sections, with each one corresponding to the five stages in the model of cognitive (mis)perception of the other. These are the now familiar reflexive to collective intelligence stages. Similarly, the five substages within each stage range from the familiar coordination to integration levels. As much as possible, these substages were translated in the following way in the elaboration of the scale.

Coordination refers to when adults treat the child in an undifferentiated, global manner across the cognitive and socioemotional arenas, and he or she must coordinate with their perspective. In hierarchization, adults especially deal with and critique the child's reasoning. In systematization, the child's reasoning is seen as part of a larger system with options. Multiplication is marked by a focus on only part of the child's train of reasoning. Finally, in integration at least part of the child's reasoning is openly listened to/acknowledged/encouraged, with the potential for overall coherence in it implied.

Note that instead of a substage model with a coordination of units, and

**Table 7.4 Perioperational Substages of Discourse Quality
Based on the Cognitive (Mis)perception of the Other**

Substage	Discourse/quality
11.	The parent channels/neutralizes/pacifies the child by disrupting/disorganizing/confusing the child (e.g., "You're not thinking right"). The parent gives "I don't know" answers to questions. The child directly attempts to keep the discussion going, but the parent does not participate or give an answer to allow the discussion to proceed. Indiscriminate rewards are used to foster a climate of compliance/assumption.
12.	With a younger child, passive listening without comments or encouragement is a type of pacification-channeling, because the child's thought cannot be advanced, coherent, etc., in and of itself. With an older child, a parent can pacify-channel in more indirect ways (e.g., ignore the child's thought, invalidate it; turn to own ideas after child's speaking turn without acknowledgement of listening). The parent is passive with no verbal or nonverbal expressions, direction, or guidance. The parent may acknowledge her or his listening role (e.g., "Hmm hmm"). The parent parrots or paraphrases the child's comments or requests minor restatements. Minor corrections are given by the parent (in vocabulary, pronunciation, grammar), but with no new information. The parent may make a direct request for information, or may ask a direct question (e.g., "Say that again," "What do you think about ...?"). The child is rewarded if he or she follows the parent's lead or suggestions, or if the (implicit) promise of such is possible. The result is that the same comments or ideas occur during the discussion. No advances in storytelling or thought are made. An intermediary value of 12.5 is assigned when the parent asks for clarification, e.g., "Is this what you mean?" or corrects constructively, (but still with the limit that channeling, neutralizing, or pacifying is taking place).
13.	The parent points out a position/option that is different from the child's own without constructive explanation (e.g., "Couldn't it be that ...", or "Yes, but another way is ..."). Or the parent enunciates own thought or position with some explanation.
14.	Despite some signs of channeling or pacification, a part of the child's discourse is acknowledged/accepted/praised on its own terms. The parent clearly acknowledges the child's answer or comment but without acccepting it (e.g., "Yes, I know what you mean," or "I was just going to ask you that."). The parent shows some evidence of warmth and active interest in the child's position, although the conversation is not completely interactive.
15.	A glimmer of possibility is left open for the child's position or argument to emerge as being correct, but in the context of others. The parent points out relationships between the child's position and (an)other(s), their own, etc., integrating the child's view as one differentiated member of a larger perspective (e.g., "You're right, but ...").

Table 7.5 Abstract Substages of Discourse Quality
Based on the Cognitive (Mis)perception of the Other

Substage	Discourse/quality
16.	The parent indirectly encourages partially independent, novel thought of other possible dimensions to the story/reasoning position, or the way given dimensions may interact (e.g., "Can you think of anything else"; "Why do you say that?"; "What else did he do or say?"; "How does *this* relate to *that*?"). The parent suggests that more may be possible or that there's something important missing (e.g., "Didn't you forget something?"). The parent does not provide information, but hints at a direction so the child can take the lead of the discussion. The parent listens to the child's response and continues the conversation by building on the child's responses or by asking indirect questions.
17.	Part of the child's reasoning is praised, reinforced by the parent directly with a constructive comment (e.g., "That's a really good idea because …"). The parent encourages the child to continue with her or his position/idea/comment. The parent allows the child to control the pace and direction of the discussion.
18.	The child's whole story/reasoning/position is shown to be valid in a constructive way.
19.	The child is prompted to expand on the immediate/proximate implications of her or his story/reason/position.
20.	The child is prompted to see how her or his story/reason/position fits into a larger picture and may be harmonious with it.

then their hierarchization, systematization, multiplication, and integration, the current substage model reveals the degree of inclusivity in the adult's/society's misperception of the other. Had we followed standard procedure, for the reflexive stage the fifth level would indicate a misperception of the other that would be fully reflexive. However, in the current approach, level 1 refers to a misperception of the other that is fully reflexive, and level 5 refers to one that is almost fully sensorimotor. The same logic was used in constructing levels 6 to 20. The only exception to this procedure was that for the stage of collective intelligence the standard model was followed. The logic guiding these decisions was that the scale had to begin with the worst possible misperception of the other (i.e., fully reflexive) and terminate with the most mature (i.e., fully collective).

Finally, in scanning the scale points, although it can be seen that they suggest an orderly progression in conversational support, it becomes clear that they do not conform uniquely to the current theory. In constructing the scale, the model of the cognitive (mis)perception of the other on which it is based was consulted. However, I also scrutinized similar scales in the literature; for example, the scale developed by Young and Young (in prepa-

Table 7.6 Collective Intelligence Substages of Discourse Quality Based on the Cognitive (Mis)perception of the Other

Substage	Discourse/quality
21.	The child is prompted to indirectly seek or explore alternative scenarios, stories, perspectives, even ones not espoused by the parent her or himself and which may be discrepant from the parent's own point of view. The parent should be encouraging a "collective" attitude/moral/value in this line of discouse as he or she proceeds (e.g., "Is there another way of seeing ...").
22.	The prompts above given to the child are given in a direct manner, but only for part of, not a full, perspective. The child is encouraged to see where trade-offs, negotiations, bargaining, or give-and-take may apply to certain collective-oriented positions. However, the parent instills in the child the idea that one of them is dominant over the other(s).
23.	The prompts above are direct, and are aimed at eliciting a whole new perspective. The parent encourages the child to consider alternative collective positions as being part of a larger system, and that all are considered equally valid, legitimate, and in a dynamic relationship with each other.
24.	The parent encourages the child to see the implications of adopting large systems and to compare them. The parent and child discuss together similarities and differences among them. The parent and child together realize that these sometimes conflicting systems can exist simultaneously.
25.	The parent encourages explicit attempts to put all previous systems into an overarching principle, tempered by contextual, pragmatic realities, e.g., living with and growing from conflict.

Note. Not used by the participants in our study.

ration) described in the previous chapter, Sigel's (1993) work on different levels of distancing in teaching strategies by parents, Pratt et al.'s (1992) research on parental behavior in the zone of proximal development (a homework assignment), Kruger's (1992) study on transactive dialogue in moral discussions between parents and adolescents, Berkowitz and Gibbs' (1983) coding manual of transactive dialogue behavior, and Kuhn's (1993) investigation of logical argumentation between parents and adolescents.

In the next section, we return to the vygotskian program and show the way in which the current model of the cognitive (mis)perception of the other informs it. In particular, it prescribes the diverse levels at which a society or its institutions may function in its reciprocal relationship with the developing individual. In this regard, the scale described in this section may be adapted for analysis of sociocultural pressures on development.

CONCLUSION

There is a lot that is positive about our society, and dichotomous judgments about its strengths and weaknesses cannot do it service. A more differentiated perspective is needed, one that captures the myriad possible relations between any one (sub)culture and its members. As has been stated, the model of the cognitive (mis)perception of the other based on the current 25-step model of the general substages in development (see Table 7.1) can help qualify the different ways that a larger group treats either smaller ones or its own members. A society can be described in general according to these labels, or its different components can be described separately.

Other scales have been constructed to measure the complexity of and belief about the function of political structure (e.g., Heath, Evans, & Martin, 1993; Suedfeld, Bluck, Loewen, & Elkins, 1994). However, they lack an inclusive theory and they lack differentiation compared to the current scale (e.g., its 25 points). There is much contemporary debate about the relationship of the individual and the polity, morality and the community, etc. (e.g., Burtt, 1993; Caney, 1992, 1993; Crittenden, 1993; Downing & Thigpen, 1993; Dupré, 1993; Fisk, 1993; Hill, 1993; Lund, 1993; Nordquest, 1994; Wilson, 1993). Perhaps the current model can give a developmental psychological perspective to the area. A recent application of Kohlberg's theory of the stages of moral development provides a good example for this enterprise.

Shapiro (1995) examined congressional debates for and against American involvement in the Gulf War. Some of the reasons offered pro and con included the following: Stage (1) our oil is threatened, vs. it would hurt our economy; (2) we can gain security of the oil supply, vs. we'll have more money for domestic issues; (3) we don't want the world to see us as weak, vs. we don't want to appear too militaristic; (4) the U.N. has laid down written resolutions which should be upheld, vs. war is killing and killing is against the law; (5) society's rights are threatened and need to be defended, vs. war is damaging to people and property and society agrees that is bad; (6) evil is on the march, and it would be morally wrong to allow it to continue, vs. although atrocities have been committed, it would be an even greater atrocity to wage war. This applied analysis of a public debate on a moral issue illustrates the manner in which the current theory of 25-steps in the cognitive (mis)perception of the other could be used to understand a society's collective thought processes.

The point is that we are all subject to the dynamic of the imperatives of culture. They are not amorphous, benign messages, but powerful, invasive, and often insidious ones. Our cultural heritage has its own history, and is moving toward the future that we are individually and collectively cocreating with it and for it in the balance of our passive and active stance before it. Cognitive development is often a question of social incubation of dominant discourses if not their inculcation. The individual and society engage in a reciprocal flow about the way they would like to be treated by the other, but the society's weight is the more powerful one. Societal ideologies impinge upon, channel, and transform the developmental process to their own ineluctable ends. We coconstruct meaning with a gargantuan, invisible, pervasive entity, as lilliputians in a brobdingnagian world, and the subsequent appropriation is relatively one-sided. To think otherwise is foolhardy. The developing individual may have a margin of resilience and active creativity before social pressure, but too often is swept up by its force.

The specific modality of transmission for the cardinal vygotskian issue of the way the sociocultural matrix and the individual conjoin in the individual's cognitive development consists of ourselves, our attitudes as parents. We are mediating devices, functioning in the dynamic of insemination and transformation of society's perceptions of their members into the developing mental functions of our children. Our cognitive (mis)perceptions of the other become the specific agents in this process, and they are posited to reflect in part not only our personal and parental but also our sociocultural past and present. Thus, my work on the cognitive (mis)perception of the other (e.g., by parents of the child) enables us to begin to understand and approach the question of the way in which societies' specific messages and values influence the psychological flow of society to children.

In short, I am expanding the concept described previously on the nature of world/caregiver/mind–brain isomorphism through activation–inhibition coordination fractal transmission to include the vygotskian perspective, in general, and the 25-step model of the cognitive (mis)perception of the other, in particular.

The model that I have described is not aimed at labeling one society or another as positive or negative. It is meant to apply especially to the evolution over time of the component parts of any one society, no matter what the general left or right wing label that one cares to give it. How does the society rate in its fostering of fundamental human values? This is the major concern of the model that I propose. In this sense, it can be applied to our own society in and of itself, and even if our society is relatively advanced in general in these regards, if a part or parts of it is or are characterized as lower than what we hope, this should not be interpreted as a potential advantage to any adversary, but as a signpost of the improvements that we would want to make.

CHAPTER 8

Individual Differences and Coappropriation

INDIVIDUAL WEBS IN UNIVERSAL SUBSTAGES IN COGNITIVE DEVELOPMENT

Introduction

In Chapter 5 it was shown that Vygotsky believed that there are higher mental functions that continue to develop in the individual. However, orthodox reading of his theory suggests that developmental movement marked by increasing complexity need not be the universal case, because the theory is especially contextualist and liable to different pathways (Rogoff, 1990). Also, we have seen the way K. W. Fischer et al.'s (1993) concept of developmental range permits neopiagetian stage theory, at least one that is applied to skill development in disparate domains, to coexist with vygotskian theory. That is, when environmental support is optimal, the individual will manifest a pattern of development that reveals discontinuous spurts in cognitive growth that are stagelike in appearance. In contrast, in less than optimal circumstances, due to contextual variability, large individual variations in continuous cognitive development accrue, so that universal stagelike sequences are not found.

Moreover, in the next sections it will be shown that Fischer describes individual nonlinear or partially ordered, webbed pathways in development which do not follow a universal, ladderlike sequential unfolding, even if he also describes a constant axis of one series of substages in cognitive development. Case has presented a similar theory which also is described. It will be concluded that one's stance in the debate on whether there are individual context-dependent or universal steps in cognitive development seems to depend on which side of a false dichotomy one happens to fall.

Fischer's Individual Developmental Webs

The Model. K. W. Fischer (K. W. Fischer & Granott, 1995; K. W. Fischer & Hencke, 1996; K. W. Fischer, Knight, et al., 1993) posits that particular developmental domains evidence multiple strands in developmental trajectory both within and between individuals and groups. Thus, each developing individual may manifest several developmental pathways across domains, and each developmentally relevant skill may show several patterns of growth across individuals. Factors such as environmental instruction and support, and affective meaning and cultural values, influence the strand followed in an individual's developmental progress.

Thus, for any one skill or domain, developing individuals manifest individual differences at several junctures. They may begin at any of several qualitatively equal starting points and finish at a variety of successful outcome points, again all equal qualitatively. However, they traverse individual strands through the manner in which they join the starting points and the outcome points. Also, many midpoints provide another source of individual variability. That is, if one considers a sequence of skills, a multitude of individual developmental strands should be possible. Also, when developing individuals are not advancing along one developmental strand (or domain), they may be moving upward on another.

In concert with this emphasis on individual differences in development, Fischer hypothesizes that once a particular skill such as reading is mastered, irrespective of the individual strand followed to arrive at this point, formulation of highly general conceptual structures is possible. These would be more universal and less individual in scope. K. W. Fischer and Hencke (1996) add that discontinuities in development group together over strands, producing stagelike patterning called a concurrent zone. Most strands show these stagelike changes by rapid growth and reorganization. The metaphor chosen to represent this developmental model is a web (also see de Ribaupierre [1993], and Hoppe-Graffe [1993] in this regard), because different developmental pathways are partially parallel or independent and partially intersecting or interweaving as they ascend from the initial to the end-point levels for a particular skill.

Research. To test the model, Fischer administered to good and poor readers of 6 to 8 years of age a series of six tasks for each of 16 words. The tasks involved word definition (saying or showing a word's meaning); letter identification (specifying a written word's letters); rhyme recognition (choosing from among verbally presented choices the word which matched a target word); reading recognition (choosing from among drawings the action or event referred to by a target word); rhyme production (of verbally presented words); and reading production (of the 16 words). Most good readers followed the developmental sequence hypothesized, as indicated by the order of the tasks just given, except that they had one branch where they passed the second or third tasks in parallel before moving on, and the link from one of these tasks (letter identification) to the fourth one was not clear. In contrast, poor readers showed three different parallel branches once they had mastered word definition.

In conclusion, it seems that Fischer has described a cognitive developmental model that emphasizes individual differences but that does not exclude more general sequences in the acquisition of skills, especially when environmental support is optimal and the level of analysis is global. When one avoids the piagetian assumption that there are only broad cognitive stages in development that synchronously cut across all developmental domains or unfold in a universal way in sequence over them (horizontal décalage), then there is room for an integrated theory with both individual difference and universality in ontogenesis.

Fischer couples this cognitive developmental model with the concept of developmental range, akin to Vygotsky's concept of the zone of proximal development, described in Chapter 5. It will be recalled that the developmental range refers to a range of performances that a developing individual may manifest for a particular cognitive skill, depending on the degree of environmental support involved. He concludes by stating that for each strand of the developmental web, individuals show a developmental range, thus acting to produce multiple levels of behavioral differences. The sociocultural world that the developing individual inhabits is not ignored in this theory, for it is seen to be at the very source of individual differences therein.

Case's Individually Branching Universal Trees

The Model. Case (Case, Okamoto, Henderson, & McKeogh, 1993) presents a very similar model of the interdigitation of individual differences and universal sequences in one theoretical fabric. Case has taken an intermediate position between a broad universal stage view of development and a view where there are numerous separate skills, which when analyzed in concert reveal innumerable individual developmental patterns. That is, he describes the developmental course as one where there are several (not one, not many) central conceptual structures (e.g., quantitative, spatial, social cognition) that encompass a series of correlated, component skills within them. Moreover, because they are systems of representational semantic nodes and relations, they are highly influenced by cultural factors, and liable to individual differences (e.g., not all cultures use the base-10 numerical system). Also, they do not deny the kind of individual webs in development that are found by lower-order analyses such as by Fischer.

Case represents this conceptualization of the developmental process by a superordinate metaphor of a tree with a trunk, branches, and webs. Depending on the focus, one may see major universal axes or delicate individual webs. The broader levels feed yet depend on the more differentiated ones in a reciprocal process.

Conclusion.   It seems to me that the dialectical tension between the search for individual and universal processes in development is beginning to produce viable superordinate models. Development appears as a quantumlike process which manifests simultaneously as a universal sequence and an individually navigated adaptation, or a universal scaffold of steps onto which individual differences are mapped (Young, submitted). However, the nature of the universal sequences and major influences that determine individual differences based on it remain open issues. Needless to say, I believe that the current synthetic theory deals best with these questions. It presents a differentiated 25-step model of the levels in development, one which is applied to a variety of developmental domains. Moreover, in the next section, I try to put together many of the theoretical strands in the book into one differentiated model representing the transition process in development and the individual differences that it permits.

A SYNTHETIC NEOVYGOTSKIAN MODEL
OF COAPPROPRIATION

Introduction

Rogoff (1990–1995) and Saxe (1991), in particular, have argued that Vygotsky's concept of internalization as a mechanism of development needs to be replaced by the concept of appropriation (see Chapter 6). Rogoff describes a shared cognitive movement from the intermental to the intramental plane, in a mutual joining of the individual and context where there is no hint of a separate role for the individual as he or she cognitively (re)organizes actively treated material from shared thinking and meaning. Saxe has expanded the description of the appropriation mechanism to include the functions of practice participation, generalization, specialization, and anticipation. However, it was argued that this elaboration of the appropriation mechanism should be considered a starting point, and that there are further modifications that can be instituted. Chang-Wells and Wells (1993) write that "a full understanding" of this function "has yet to be achieved."

In what follows, I describe a series of refinements of the vygotskian cognitive developmental transition mechanism of appropriation. Essentially, this neovygotskian model of the appropriation mechanism is a synthetic one that emerges from the confluence of the current model of development and the contemporary vygotskian and piagetian ones. First the product and then the process of appropriation is discussed. The latter is divided into the topics of equilibration, the environment, sociocultural buffers, individual differences, and mediating devices. The inclusion of the piagetian notion of equilibration in the current neovygotskian cognitive developmental process may seem surprising, but it has been tailored to the suggested model, and other vygotskians also have proposed this type of integration (Hatano, 1993; Valsiner & Leung, 1994). For the topics of equilibration, the environment, and sociocultural buffers, descriptions, and principles are presented, followed by basic dimensions pertaining to them. These dimensions include the most salient ones, but are not meant to be exhaustive. The reader may refer to Figure 8.1 below, presented in depth only after an exegesis of its major components, as a guide to the next few pages where these components are described. Given the integrative, emergent model that I developed of the appropriation function, and the fact that it refers to a shared, constitutive avenue to cognitive change, it is referred to as the *co*appropriation model of cognitive development.

The Product of Coappropriation

Description. It is hypothesized that at the level of the product of coappropriation, there are schemes or other cognitive control units whose coconstructed nature should be recognized by calling them *coschemes* or cognitive cocontrol units. Vygotsky entertained a similar notion when he spoke of "coknowledge" (Vygotsky, quoted in Leont'ev, 1981; in Rogoff, 1990, p. 197). Similarly, Hatano (1993) describes "collective" products in knowledge acquisition and Moll and Whitmore (1993) describe a "collective zone of development." For Vygotsky, the appropriate unit of analysis of mental function is shared mental construction, and he considered the mediating device of language as the epitome in this regard. If the semantic differentiation that is being suggested is applied to language, as well, then it should be called colanguage. In short, any co-constructed mental function control unit that behavioral scientists study should be given the prefix of "co-" in order to highlight its shared elaboration and significance (although for purposes of simplicity the generic term *coscheme* is used for the most part in the remainder of the present work).

Dimensions. The repertoire of cognitive coschemes available to the developing individual should vary along basic dimensions. For example, any one coscheme may vary in duration of existence, and also in stability (e.g., relatively short term unstable, long term stable). It should vary in its generality, scope, and complexity. Is it more reflexive or automatic or is it more complex and on-line? Is it more static, and concerned with objects, events, or people, or more dynamic, and concerned with relations, classes, and transformations (after Pascual-Leone & Irwin, 1994a, 1994b)? Is it broad-ranging or specific, part of a larger hierarchy or not, core to a hierarchy or peripheral, lower- or higher-order in it, and so on. It should vary in terms of its degree of isomorphism or similarity with the phenomenon that it is representing. It could be a passive, faithful representation of an action, event, person, or idea, or an active reworking or reorganization of it in a minor, local way or perhaps in a more creative, novel way; or it may even be a radical transformation. It can be either an expression of assimilation or accommodation, that is, either unchanged or changed relative to its prior status. Also, if changed, it could be at the same level of complexity as its predecessor, or it could constitute a qualitative shift to a higher-order level such as being part of a new cognitive substage. Moreover, it can vary as to whether it is an expression of the developing individual's maximum competence or some level of lesser performance.

It can vary in the degree to which it facilitates or hinders appropriate adaptation to the sociocultural milieu (dimensions involving to what degree it is internally consistent, well-formed, flexible, well-adapted, etc., or incoherent, poorly articulated, maladaptive, etc.). An important dimension related to this one is the nature of its linkage to affective correlates. Is it relatively well integrated and smoothly functioning with respect to its affective facilitators or are there problems at this level to varying degrees (there is more on affect as the section proceeds)? It can also vary in the degree to which it is coconstructed (ranging from a product of pure personal endeavor or imagination to passively absorbed in a learning situation to fully shared or negotiated).

Finally, at a more abstract level, coschemes can be qualified by the type of activation–inhibition coordination that both characterizes them and that they encourage in the sociocultural context. Different types of activation–inhibition coordination especially involve coordination over time, instantaneous coordination, or direct suppression (Young, submitted). Are coschemes of the first subtle kind, so important in fine motor or social coordination, or of the second, with its implicit concept of the gestalt and thus basic to more spatial functioning, or of the third, with its implied notion of (self- or other-)control? Presumably, other kinds of activation–inhibition coordination can be seen to underlie different varieties of coschemes.

Vygotskians perhaps would not accept the possibility that coschemes could vary to the point of being either passive copies or personally constructed. However, in a microgenetic sequence leading to a temporarily stable version of any one coscheme, the passive end of the dimension may apply for some of the steps. Even radical vygotskians could acknowledge this much.

The Process of Coappropriation: Equilibration

Description.   Equilibration and *equilibrium* need to be distinguished. The former refers to the process of dynamic movement of states, whereas the latter refers to the product states themselves. Piaget defined equilibration in terms of the twin processes of assimilation and accommodation, where active individuals try to assimilate (novel) external environmental objects, events, and activities into their internal cognitive structure, or failing this try to accommodate the latter structure to fit the former environment.

Equilibrium can exist in the individual or the environment, which concerns in effect the relation of the individual to the environment. For example, an individual's particular coscheme for a phenomenon may be more or less stable for a brief period of time. Or the configuration in the environment may be harmonious with the perceiver's coschemes, offering advantageous affordances.

The individual self participates in the equilibration process in an executive, active, autoregulative way, but also in a joint, sharing, mutual way with the sociocultural surround, if it is available. The latter especially refers to present parents-caregivers early in life, and then broader institutions such as schools, but with development it comes to refer increasingly to incorporated intermental tools integrated into the intramental plane.

When the sociocultural surround cannot or does not partake in the developing individual's equilibration process in a joint mutuality, especially early in life, negative ramifications result. The process will be disjointed, producing coschemes that may be too limited, inflexible, dissociated, etc.

In a process of environmental equilibration, the sociocultural surround may act indirectly in the equilibration process by attempting to place order in a disequilibrated environment in which a developing individual is behaving. Here, the sociocultural context is acting as a buffer. In a certain sense, for the very young, developing individual the environment is in constant disequilibrium, and the sociocultural buffering services of parents-caregivers are needed constantly. As mentioned, with development, other institutions increasingly become involved (e.g., day care centers, schools) in the same function, as do eventually incorporated, integrated sociocultural tools acting at the intramental level.

Disequilibration is the dialectical complement of equilibration. It is induced by either the individual or the environment. The developing individual is an active, seeking, coconstructing machine, and in her or his joint exploration with the sociocultural surround, static cognitive equilibrium is a temporary, evanescent state of affairs. Entropic disorder is sought so that a disentropic reordering toward increasing complexity can be gained. This process is almost continuous. The developing individual initiates the departure from homeostatic coscheme structure because, in general, the environmental cocontext is supportive of this self-opening, acts to encourage it, and puts in place buffers to facilitate and protect it.

However, the environment is not always so benign or supportive (for example, parents cannot or will not provide the appropriate buffers), and the world can be a foreboding, hostile place, even at the level of cognitive aliments. Through its disorganization, poverty, affective deficiencies, or even negative intentions, the cognitive cocontext joined with the developing individual may be detrimental. It becomes the source of personal disequilibrium in a process of environmental disequilibration. Goodnow (1990a, 1990b, 1993) came to a similar conclusion; for example, she states that adults may not wish to share their knowledge or encourage comprehension, or in one way or another they may promote an unwillingness to learn.

Dimensions. The dimensions along which equilibration can vary are the following. First, equilibration could apply to the level of local (re)organization or to more major (creative) and qualitatively different, emergent transformation, an issue that was dealt with in discussing coschemes. Also, the equilibration process may result in either novel coschemes or in conservation of prior coschemes after perturbation, but even then reinforcement and entrenchment of an existing coscheme modifies its character, so that equilibration could be conceived as a process that inevitably results in change in one way or another. In this regard, the dimensions of cognitive equilibration derived from my reading of Saxe (1991, 1994) and the information theorists fit at this point. That is, when equilibration produces evident change, it is accompanied by varying degrees of generalization and specialization, which refer to the contextual transfer and delimitation of the coschemes involved, respectively. There may be an anticipatory adaptation to the process, in a kind of feedforward mechanism, or there may be an autoregulative feedback process. Both of these mechanisms may be enhanced by a meta-awareness of their application, termed *hypercognitive reflection* by Demetriou, Efklides, and Platsidon (1993b).

Does the cognitive conflict that is involved in the disequilibrium concern an internal–internal, external–external, or internal–external mismatch? The first type of mismatch refers to two coschemes on the intramental plane that are in dialectical comparison and/or confrontation. A paired external mismatch refers to two contrasting externally present(ed) phenomena that elicit cognitive conflict. The last exemplar refers to an intramental coscheme mismatched with an externally present(ed) phenomenon. In a vygotskian sense, there is only conjoint construction of coschemes so that the distinction between the external and internal refers to intermental compared to intramental functions.

A dimension that needs special consideration in the cognitive equilibration process is the degree to which background affective factors permit it to unfold in an unfettered manner. It is safe to say that the cognitive–affective mutuality that swirls on the intramental plane as a reflection of the intermental one must affect the dynamics of both seeking growth-promoting disequilibration and resolving it in concert with the conjoint sociocultural milieu. Note that affective factors include not only volatile environmentally mediated ones, such as those related to attachment history, but also more intrinsic congenital ones such as temperament or other dispositional variables (not that these are divorced from the environment).

Another way that equilibration can vary is in terms of the type of activation–inhibition coordination involved. There is no contradiction in describing both the content and process of development in terms of activation–inhibition coordination.

The piagetian concept of equilibration has been placed at the heart of the level of process in the proposed model of coappropriation in cognitive development. Vygotskians may find this inclusion of the concept of equilibration in the coappropriation process anathema to their basis assumptions. It hearkens to a psychology of separate individual and context. However, Piaget's conceptualization of the mechanism of equilibration was quite contextual and coconstructivist, as pointed out by Biddell and Fischer (1992). Moreover, the equilibration process that is hypothesized to take place in the proposed model of coappropriation borrows from its piagetian host, but transmutes it to fit its context, as has been shown. Finally, Vygotsky (1985, cited in Schneuwly, 1993) himself acknowledged the importance of the individual, and individual-focused processes, in cognitive development. He wrote that "[t]here is in the mind of each learner *taken individually* a sort of internal network of processes which, although they are provoked and put in motion during teaching/learning, have their own proper logic of development" (p. 269).

The Process of Coappropriation: The Environment

Description. It is acknowledged that the environment can be negative or hostile and not only positive or alimentary. The traditional conception of the environmental input into the child's developing cognitive functions assumes that it is neutral (e.g., a nearby toy) or more positive and supportive (e.g., the mother holding out a nearby toy with affective reinforcement). However, the literature on the child's developing affective function makes no such assumption about the character of the environment, and in fact focuses on differences in secure and insecure attachment, nonabusive and abusive parents, regular and ambiguous, negative situations, facilitative and interfering attitudes, beliefs, and values, etc.

The child's developing cognition is colored by and even serves her or his developing affect. Any conception of the child's cognitive environment cannot dissociate it from the full affective medium in which it subsists. This environment is potentially amorphous or even hostile, and part of the sociocultural responsibility to the developing child is to assure that the cognitive environment, as he or she traverses the ontogenetic pathway, is as optimal as possible in light of its real and potential undermining dynamic.

Dimensions. The environment varies in level of immediacy and scope, object of focus, control and structure, activation and inhibition, expertise and collaborative intention, distancing, and affect or warmth. These dimensions are discussed, in turn.

The environment can be proximal in context such as in a dyadic setting or family situation at home. Then, there are more distal settings of influence such as the school or the parents' work environment. At a more removed level, the wider sociocultural milieu is important. This includes the values and ideologies of a society, as shall be seen below. The object of focus in the environment may be inanimate or animate.

In terms of control and structure, the environment varies at both the physical and psychological levels. For example, do the affordances (discussed in Chapter 5) in the child's playroom invite pleasurable play and cognitive stimulation? Does the wider society overtly oppress, subtly manipulate, proscribe, and prescribe? In Chapter 5, various conceptions of the environment and culture were reinterpreted as compatible with the concept of activation–inhibition coordination. Thus, the dimension of structure-control can be rephrased in terms of whether environments serve to facilitate-instigate and/or channel-suppress in a process of activation–inhibition coordination.

Granott (1993) presented a model of sociocultural environment in terms of variation along two dimensions—the degree of expertise of the participants relative to the child and the degree of collaboration in which they are involved with the child (see Table 6.1). Similarly, K. W. Fischer et al. (1993) presented the concept of developmental range, akin to Vygotsky's concept of the zone of proximal development, where the environment provides a range of cognitive supports from little to optimal.

Sigel (1993) described differences in teaching acts or strategies along the dimension of distancing. Through appropriate self-distancing organized to teach appropriate distancing controls in the child, the child comes to develop increasing cognitive distancing. Thus, the concept of distancing can be applied both to the caregiver's behavior and the child's developing cognition, so that a certain world–caregiver–child's mind–brain isomorphism seems to characterize cognitive development. (Moreover, this concept of distancing can be reworked readily in terms of activation–inhibition coordination.)

Finally, the environment can vary in its affective nature. It can be positive, neutral, or negative and even overtly hostile. This leads to a last dimension along which environments vary, the degree to which they serve as protective buffers before the negativity in the environment. The next section is devoted to this question.

The Process of Coappropriation: Sociocultural Buffers

In light of the potential dangers in the environment for the developing child, the equilibration process that takes place in cognitive development should be viewed as being subserved by sociocultural buffers. Others have described a similar concept, but without giving it central importance. For example, Valsiner (1987) wrote that "the developing psychological processes of the child are ... buffered against occasionally excessive fluctuations in the environmental conditions" (p. 229).

Early in life, the sociocultural buffers against environmental turbulence especially are parents/primary caregivers. But parents themselves are buffeted by the wider historicopolitical forces that envelop them, and become their conduits, in general. However, parents may resist, transform, or even buttress against, overcome, or replace the messages contained in sociocultural forces. They coconstruct lenses or mediating devices with the sociocultural context, and actively participate in their adjustment.

Of course, as the child ages, he or she is exposed increasingly in a direct fashion to historicopolitical forces that act to shape developing mental function. And these in turn are not monolithic, but variegated in means and messages. Often they oppose each other (e.g., think of pro and con advertisements for cigarette smoking). At the cognitive level, an example of an opposition such as this would concern the push for formal regional or national matriculation or entrance examinations to permit entry into higher educational levels as opposed to the viewpoint that a more local, flexible process is needed. However, in one way or another, society attempts to provide its developing members with opportunities for schooling in order to educate and/or entrain. The institutions that it creates act as sociocultural buffers in the child's cognitive development as much as do parents beyond a certain point in life. Moreover, general values and attitudes prevalent in the society do the same (e.g., at a more enlightened level: schooling is important; all subgroups in the society have equal access to the educational system).

Thus, coappropriation is a recursive dialectic where the sociocultural context engages developing parents in a constitutive construction of their parenting approach, and this in turn serves as the mediating device in the parents' and children's constitutive coconstruction of the children's developing sociomental function. Gradually, in the developmental process, children's mental function increasingly becomes influenced by the general cultural context as opposed to the parental one, a process which is counterbalanced by an increasing self—as opposed to interregulated sociomental function. Thus, when children become parents, in their turn, it is their own voices, along with those of their parents and culture, that are speaking to their own children. It is in this sense that previously I have referred to an isomorphism across world, caregiver, and developing mind-brain.

The Process of Coappropriation: Individual Differences

The proposed revision of the appropriation process in cognitive development engenders a view of individual differences in cognitive development that argues that no two cognitive developmental trajectories can be alike. Systems theory emphasizes the continuous peripheral, contextual adaptations that developing individuals must make, because there are no prefigured central templates but only preferred central guides in development (Young, submitted). In the context of the current book, preferred cognitive guides refer to the 25-step neopiagetian model of cognitive substage progression that is hypothesized to unfold universally. But this sequence is considered only a scaffold, an axis on which delicate tapestries of individual realities are interwoven in the mutuality in which developing individuals interlive with their particular contextual catalysts.

The Process of Coappropriation: Mediation and (Mis)perception

Much of the individual differences in cognitive development are seen to be mediated by the level of cognitive (mis)perception of the other at which the developing individual is perceived to function or at which he or she should function in her or his specific sociocultural world. The particular level of cognitive (mis)perception of the other that the developing individual carries is seen as a product of the synergistic influence of sociocultural ideologies, other particularities in context, the intracouple dynamic of the developing individual's parents, the voices that the developing individual hears in her or his dialogue with them, and her or his own active transformation of all such parameters. It has been shown that there are five possible levels, with five sublevels in each level, in the way parents can (mis)perceive their child, couples can (mis)perceive each other, and the wider cultural group can (mis)perceive its member individuals and subgroups.

These cognitive misperceptions in their turn lead to different affective experiences and attachment qualities with parents. It is from these intrinsic socioaffective wellsprings that the developing individual funnels her or his treatment of others and expectations of the way others should treat her or him, including at the level of cognitive development. Thus, for example, parental physical or psychological abuse is also cognitive abuse for the child target. Behavioral dissociation in "good" and "bad" parenting is also cognitive dissociation induction in the child target.

Also, depreciating comments and the like by parents deplete self confidence or a sense of banduran self-efficacy and inhibit eriksonian initiative, adding to the risk of fixating affectively the developing individual at lower neopiagetian substages of cognitive functioning. For example, an adult can use formal abstract reasoning to institute a nefarious, reflexive goal.

The Process of Coappropriation: Conclusion

The last examples reveal the synthetic nature of the proposed model of coappropriation in cognitive development. It suggests that coschemes are formed in the constitutive reciprocity of developing individual–cocontext mutuality, and that the sociocultural context varies in affective quality and degree of protective buffering. The equilibration process that takes place in coscheme formation can be either more individually or jointly instigated, depending on the degree of buffering. Individuals bring into their participation in the environment a host of individual differences in mental function related to their past and present contextual circumstances and socioaffective baggage. They cocreate mediating lenses which function as two-way filters in their behavior toward and expectations of their sociocultural surround.

These lenses have been qualified especially as different levels in the cognitive (mis)perception of the other. I have shown the way they reflect underlying neopiagetian substages, as described by the current 25-step model of cognitive development. To me, they appear to be the epitome of mediational tools that are constructed in the encounter of developing individual and surround. They inform the way any one individual treats another, whether child or adult (e.g., spouse), and expects to be treated by them, and the way society treats its individual and subgroup members. Other important mediational devices such as language or socially constructed practices are funneled through their primary reality. Invisible but omnipresent, they are hidden keys for understanding human behavior.

I have developed a 25-point scale that helps determine the level of cognitive (mis)perception of the other that is manifested in discourse situations, e.g., involving parent and child (see Tables 7.2–7.6). With instruments such as these, researchers will be able to reach the hidden keys and relate them to the systemic factors contributing to their emergence. They should vary with bowlbian attachment-related experiences and, in a process of intergenerational transmission, lead to the use of parental patterns personally experienced in childhood. In turn, they should affect the child's sociocultural participation in the cognitive environment through their effects on her or his socioemotional–cognitive complexes such as one's sense of banduran self-efficacy and eriksonian initiative.

Comparison with Pascual-Leone

To date, Pascual-Leone has developed the most integrated neopiagetian model on cognitive transitions (e.g., Pascual-Leone & Baillargeon, 1994; Stewart & Pascual-Leone, 1992). A brief, incomplete outline of it is offered in order to help point out some similarities between it and the current model.

For Pascual-Leone, mental attentional energy is an endogenous mental resource that refers to the number of distinct schemes (elemental information-bearing modules) that the individual can boost simultaneously into activation beyond those boosted by her or his context, per se. With development the mental attentional capacity increases in size in a scalar fashion, and with each of these steps the development of a new piagetian substage is potentiated (e.g., low and high pre-, concrete, and formal operations). Mental attentional energy works in tandem with an inhibitory interrupt mechanism to produce mental effort. Silent cerebral hardware operators are independent constraints that dynamically influence schemes and other aspects of behavior. For example, the executive operator is a dominant collection of executive or planning schemes which are activated initially by directing affective goals or affective schemes. The field operator serves to integrate the various activated schemes into an integrated behavioral whole by working through a principle of schematic "overdetermination," or sensitivity to dominantly activated schemes.

This capsule summary of Pascual-Leone's theory of schemes and operators in cognitive development highlights several similarities between it and the current model of coappropriation in cognitive development. For example, both models give importance to the central role of schemes that develop according to piagetian (sub)stages, that are contextually determined and activated, that are subject to inhibitory constraints, that merge into wholes through system dynamics, and that are affectively guided. In this sense, I feel more confident about the piagetian turn that I have given to the vygotskian appropriation process in the current model.

GRAPHIC REPRESENTATION
OF THE NEOVYGOTSKIAN MODEL
OF COAPPROPRIATION

Figure 8.1 depicts the cyclical process that constitutes the proposed neovygotskian coappropriation mechanism in cognitive development. It shows the way the developing individual, through coschemes, actively seeks catalytical disequilibration in her or his entry into the sociocultural world. This world is not necessarily supportive or may even be hostile. Two pathways in development bifurcate at this juncture. If the context is negative, or if the developing individual is very young and supportive adults are not around, then the only option is that self-equilibration must take place. More than likely, it will be disjointed in one way or another. However, if sociocultural buffers mediate the developing individual's commerce with the entourage, they will modulate the environmental disequilibration induced by the world, especially if it is negative or hostile. Environmental equilibration results, presenting the developing individual with a cognitively protected, optimal world. In this sanctuary, equilibration can take place in a joint, constitutive process. The products of this cycle are more or better developed cognitive coschemes, ready for the next recursive dialectic.

To summarize, the proposed coappropriation cycle in cognitive development seems to make a significant contribution to the field by (1) its base concept of mutual, constitutively created, vygotskian coschemes; (2) its incorporation of a modified model of piagetian equilibration; (3) its awareness of the potentially negative, hostile environment at the cognitive and not only affective level; (4) its provision for sociocultural buffers that can moderate poor structure or negativity in context; and (5) the way it sees individual differences in sociocultural buffers and thus in developing sociomental function. Consequently, individual differences in mediating devices such as the level of an individual's cognitive (mis)perception of other(s), her or his emotional (e.g., attachment) history and temperament, and the broader sociocultural and even historicopolitical context, help determine the efficacy and nature of social buffers in mental development.

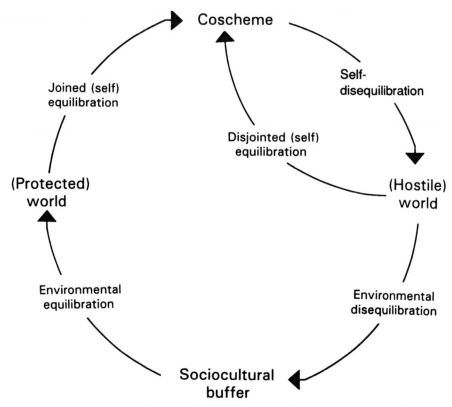

Figure 8.1 A Neovygotskian Model of Coappropriation in Cognitive Development

A NEOVYGOTSKIAN STUDY OF POLITICAL DIALOGUE IN ADOLESCENTS

Santolupo and Pratt (1994) studied the nature of mother–adolescent dialogue about political issues. Santolupo (now Macdonald) and Young (see Chapter 13) have reexamined the original data for the cognitive complexity in the adolescents' text using the scale presented in Table 8.1, which was extrapolated from the cognitive complexity scale for discourse in children presented in Chapter 6. Aside from looking at the issue of whether an experimental situation could affect the complexity of the discourse, we also examined whether individual differences in the nature of the mothers' supports-interventions-directives affected the adolescents' discourse performance. To this end, we used the scale based on the 25-step model of the cognitive (mis)perception of the other (see Tables 7.2 to 7.6).

Table 8.1 Text Complexity Scale For Adolescents and Adults

Score and stage	Description
6. Abstract coordination	The text, narrative, or story is abstract (e.g., metaphorical, allegorical; concerns values, morals, personality).
	A duality (e.g., right vs. wrong) is explicit or implied.
	There is only one "appropriate" and/or correct way of interpreting the story, or there is only one legitimate path, theme, plot, or idea referred to.
7. Abstract hierarchization	There is some tolerance for accepting that the way in which a theme or plot is interpreted or recounted may be incorrect or incomplete, but there is not complete acceptance of this idea.
	Certainty that one theme or idea is more important than the others.
	The other themes and ideas are devalued by attempts at logical reasoning.
8. Abstract systematization	Recognition and acceptance that there are several complementary, related perspectives-views-themes-elements of narrative events.
	Absolutes are preferred, even though uncertainty, exceptions, or conditional acceptance of different perspectives are allowed.
9. Abstract multiplication	Recognition that new perspectives-views-themes grow out of old ones and can be embedded within them.
	Acknowledges that all viewpoints are legitimate and relevant.
10. Abstract integration	There is a weighing, evaluation, and comparison of viewpoints-plots-themes.
	There is evidence of simultaneous deduction and induction (reversibility) in find-tuned, subtle logic (differentiation).
	Examination of relations, combinations of relevant viewpoints-plots-themes toward creation of overarching totality or morale (integration).
	However, there is no comparison or synthesis of different overarching principles.
11. Collective intelligence	Synthesis of different overaching viewpoints, principles is beginning to be evident.
	Recognition that different overarching viewpoints, principles can occur simultaneously and also can be interactive with each other.
	Nevertheless, (incipient) commitment to one overarching viewpoint, principle may be evident.
	This viewpoint, principle should concern elements of self-abnegating symbiosis with communal future. It is intended to encapsulate the interaction between the individual and the community.

Note. In the current scale, there is only one level pertaining to the collective stage of intelligence. If necessary, five substages readily can be elaborated by following the prior pattern.

The results of the study support the face validity of the current synthetic theory from which the scales were derived. For example, the adolescents' cognitive complexity scores for their discourse on the political issues discussed with their mothers correlated positively with their (1) age and level of education and (2) scores on another scale of cognitive complexity in discourse, that of integrative complexity (Baker-Brown, Ballard, Bluck, deVries, Suedfeld, & Tetlock, 1992). (3) The adolescents' cognitive complexity showed stability across the two situations involved. (4) Also, the mothers' scores for discourse support and for cognitive complexity (both for the current and original scales) were positively correlated. This result is noteworthy, for it suggests that the cognitive level that mothers are willing to see in their adolescent (misperceive in them) determines the complexity of discourse that they permit in their dialogue with them. (5) Another result found in the study was that the mothers' discourse support was positively correlated with their own perception of the degree of their authoritative parenting style (Baumrind, 1991), which speaks to the validity of the discourse support scale.

(6) Finally, the scores on the discourse support scale for the mother were *negatively* correlated with the adolescents' cognitive complexity scores (only for the original measure, not for the new text complexity measure). This result shows that mothers' attitude may impact on the discourse complexity of their adolescents as they engage in political dialogue. It seems that the mothers behave in ways that create a zone of inhibition development (Moss, 1992) or zone of activation–inhibition coordination, as discussed in Chapter 7. The more they are restrained or hold back in their comments and give the adolescents free rein, the better the adolescents do.

In conclusion, the current study supports the validity of the 25-step model of development through the nature of the results obtained with the two scales derived from it. Moreover, the study supports the notion that the vygotskian approach to sociocultural influences on cognitive development includes not only an activation component but also an inhibition one, as captured in the phrase "the zone of activation–inhibition coordination."

RE POSTMODERNISM

Disney as a Film of Society

Introduction. Postmodernism parses culture for its hidden edicts. An example of the manner in which culture propagates different levels of value can be seen in the recent series of Disney animated films (C. Young, 1995). These films describe five different types of hero–heroine relationships, and they fit the model of the cognitive (mis)perception of the other of the present theory. That is, as shall be demonstrated, the films show an evolution of relationship from one where women, compared to men, are expected to be passive, reflexive, and silent to one where they are expected to be more powerful, mature, and equal. In short, in an unlikely manner the media giant Disney seems to have provided a way of examining a culture freeing itself from its modern entrapments toward postmodern liberation.

In the classic films of Disney (*Snow White, Cinderella*), the young female protagonist passively lives a life of abuse or oppression by evil forces, awaiting her hero. The message to women is baldly chauvinistic, for they are treated as passive, "silent" (to use the language of Belenky and Clinchy), objects.

Recent Disney Animated Films. Ariel, the undersea princess of the film *The Little Mermaid*, the first in the contemporary film series, is dominated by the life structure set up by her powerful father king. But she shows initiative, and desires to meet a male. However, the constraint of her father's power forces her to fantasize meeting one outside her world, that is, a human of the land. Women are conceptualized as receptacles to be filled by the wisdom of powerful males (in this film women are "received knowers"), so that they must turn to a most primitive mechanism, that of fantasy, to escape patriarchical oppression.

The heroine of the next film that was released, Belle of *Beauty and the Beast*, has an easygoing father, but male authority figures still embroil the scene through their courting, via the controlling, evil Gaston and the awesome, needy Beast. Belle follows her heart to the Beast, engaging the world of men in a "subjective" fashion.

Jasmine of the film *Aladdin*, who has a passive but concerned father like Belle, is more strong willed than the other female protagonists to date, and is attracted to a young man of her own age and of her emotional and intellectual standing. However, external evil forces, represented by Jaffar, are against their union, and external benevolent forces are enlisted to help them (the genie, in particular). Jasmine participates in her own struggle, acting bravely and logically when needed. But in the end, the nature of her love for Aladdin is based on the simplest emotions rather than the maturity that can mark attraction in a couple. In Belenky and Clinchy's terms, connected and separate knowing processes are not conjoined in one procedure.

Finally, Pocahontas lives a more equitable relationship with the male protagonist than does the heroine in any of the previous films. She saves his life, rather than the reverse, and she returns to her people rather than follow him at the film's end. Throughout the film, it is evident that both good and evil reside in the self or the people themselves, and not in external forces. For example, Pocahontas possesses many admirable attributes, and manifests a power in her presence and behavior. God or godlike powers do not intervene in the human drama, for the leading characters write their own futures through their actions. Also, the collectivity or unity matters most, whether it be in terms of respect for peoples' origins, the spirituality felt in the kinship with nature, or the respect for departed family members (in this case, Pocahontas's mother). In short, it appears that Pocahontas is a constructed knower who functions from the level of collective intelligence, and has had that attitude fostered by her father and people.

Conclusion.   In this analysis, even though we have smoothed out the scenarios to some extent, one can see that in their films Disney portrays the five major types of relationships in which one can engage from the perspective of the current theory. Depending on the way one is treated by authority figures, whether they be parental, godlike, or societal, specific relational affinities are facilitated. The Disney films show an evolution toward the most mature style, and it is hoped that society will grow in general to this level. The lens that we place on the visions we have for our children in their future relationships is influenced by the cognitive (mis)perception that we have of the other, in general. Their transformation is our transformation, as with any aspect of postmodernism.

Coappropriation and Postmodernism

The model of the cognitive (mis)perception of the other fits into a larger mechanism that has been posited to serve in the transition process in development, that of coappropriation. It is an extension of the vygotskian concept of internalization or appropriation, where socially negotiated intermental acquisitions come to rest on the intramental plane. Coappropriation has been expanded to include especially the concept of coscheme in order to underscore the socially constitutive nature of cognitive control units, the piagetian concept of equilibration because of the internal motivating force for cognitive development that it brings, and the concept of sociocultural buffers to speak to the needed damping of the environment when it is less than optimal for cognitive development. The damping quality of sociocultural buffers vary according to the level of cognitive (mis)perception of the other involved. Postmodern or highest level buffers can spring only from postmodern minds in the parental milieu and in the containing culture. When parents and society are optimally mature, the probability that their charges will develop toward and into the same is optimally potentiated. Again the message is that the responsibility for the developing other lies in ourselves. The postmodern mind and society would have it no other way.

PART V

THERAPY AND EPISTEMOLOGY

CHAPTER 9

Postmodern Adult Therapy

INTRODUCTION

Outline

The next three chapters examine practical therapeutic applications of the synthetic theory and the epistemological basis that undergirds the therapy suggested. Chapter 9 treats therapeutic issues, Chapter 10 presents my particular therapeutic model of transition therapy, and Chapter 11 moves on to epistemological considerations.

This chapter is concerned especially with brief therapeutic familial approaches, and involves presentation of techniques which should be compatible with others in the field (de Shazer, 1991; O'Hanlon and Hudson, 1994; Walter and Peller, 1994). It does not attempt to deal with the concept of mental disorder, per se (see Lillienfeld & Marino, 1995). Family therapy is still being criticized by those not up-to-date on its recent formulations (e.g., Pam, 1993). Henggeler, Borduin, and Mann (1993) and Pinsof (1995) show that outcome research reveals family therapy is as successful as other therapies, although there have not been enough investigations to differentiate the efficacy of different approaches within the field. There are two major streams in family therapy—the more orthodox one that orients to empirical investigation and the more radical one that rejects this outlook. In this chapter, it is shown that both are fruitful approaches.

At the chapter's outset, the postmodern therapy movement is described. Then, research based on Greenberg's process model is presented, after which the more discursive perspective of Tomm is described. Attachment therapy is investigated, as well. Next, the postmodern, coconstructivist, narrative approach of Michael White on agency internalization/ problem externalization is given in detail. Parry and Doan (1994) have systematized White's work. They describe 16 authoring and 12 revisioning tools for use in narrative therapy, and their book is summarized. Other

narrative approaches to therapy also are presented. The chapter includes
the presentation of a model of the classification of therapies in terms of two
axes, where one involves the contrast between constructivism and empiricism and the other is related to the dimension of activation–inhibition coordination. It is suggested that all these perspectives may profit by including in their approach a developmental theory such as the current one.

I have been using a variant of the narrative approach in my clinical
work, and it is presented in Chapter 10. In particular in this transition
therapy model, client problems are graphed as vicious circles surrounding
a core of positive characteristics. Moreover, the problems themselves are
perceived as the result of external stresses (e.g., familial, societal), in a
process called second-order externalization. That is, stories are coconstructed with the client where client presenting problems are considered
second-order externalizations originating in exterior influences, such as past
or present difficulties, and thus capable of being controlled by personal
strengths and abilities which have been overwhelmed but not eliminated.

In proceeding this way, I may attempt to show which of the 25 steps of
the current synthetic model of development are implicated in the clients'
problems by referring to story themes which reflect these steps. That is, I
have created story themes for each of the 25 levels which highlight their
positive and negative poles (see Table 10.1). Thus, appropriate agency-
internalizing and problem-externalizing story titles are employed for each
of the developmental steps that may be at the base of clients' issues. This
recent innovation in my therapeutic work should constitute its most significant therapeutic contribution.

In Chapter 11 on epistemology, it is shown that constructivism is not a
monolithic approach but one with diverse points of view. A synthetic
epistemological model is described, where six different constructivist
schools are considered equally valid and coexistential.

Postmodern Therapy

Introduction. Postmodern therapy is a movement as opposed to a
theory, and speaks with multiple voices (Gergen, 1994b; Gergen & Kaye,
1992; Mills & Sprenkle, 1995; Niemeyer, 1995; Niemeyer & Mahoney, 1995).
Therapies that are considered modernist aim to elucidate client essences
by an imperious theory and its agent, the therapist. The narrative that is
imposed on the client is doctrinaire, fixed in its formulations, closed to
alterations, truncated in life options, insensitive to client differences, decontextualized and abstract, and a privileged authority on "cause and
cure."

However, in the postmodern perspective, narratives are not replicas of
the client's reality but interpretive tools for its (re)construction or (re)con-

figuration. Thus, the therapist's reality is not superior but different to that of the client, and new client–therapist dialogic narratives are cocreated collaboratively in encounter. The therapist achieves this end by acting sensitively in her or his deconstruction of the client's modernistic, totalizing misconceptions about the "problem," and avoids any modernistic pretensions about her or his own "expertise." Such an approach opens space in the crucible of communion where alternate possible realities can be elaborated or socialized. Egendorf (1995) captures well the live, resonating hearing attunement that promotes this outcome in therapy. By hearing people through their pain, a partnered therapeutic relatedness forms that can be an oracle of knowledge and fount of healing.

Lone individuals cannot "mean," for meaning emerges and is reconstituted out of joint action or in a relational nucleus of lived, shared understanding, and joint actions themselves extend into the multiple laminations of interdependent dyadic, familial, and cultural relationships in the past and present. Narratives are at once outcomes of extended relationships in culture and local creations which can have repercussions even across culture. In this sense, they are manifold mulitrelational intelligibilities, and the therapist helps add but one more voice to the panoply.

Unfolding local ontologies develop in particular niches, and not all of these are adaptive in clients. In the therapeutic relationship, the client's mental world is reconstructed along a different path in a process of polysemous recontextualization. Problems, causes, and cures are relativized. Marginalized voices are discovered and amplified. New stories are oriented to the pragmatic relational context in which they must fit, and to their role as potential change agents. Moreover, a new story is recognized as historically and culturally situated, contingent, indeterminate, and capable of transformation. It is proactive and anticipatory, shaping the course of its social reality through its planning processes. This aspect indicates its self-organizing function. Also, it is considered plural (or heteroglossic, after Bakhtin), or one that can become plural in a horizon of narrative multiplicity, yet without losing an emergent, amalgamated, unitary status. Despite its coherence, a new story is not necessarily consciously known. It may function as a whole, but only parts of it may be verbally articulated, even in therapy. Thus, it is an implicit, tacit entity for the most part. Although it gains its voice as it revises the client's living, it does not function in its turn as a hegemonic, modern absolute truth, inflexible to change, and exclusionary of alternatives, in place of the tale it replaces.

A new story is dynamic and responsive to the "shifting tides" of social relations. Yet, this does not render the client-narrator a deceitful manipulator, for contextually sensitive narrations reflect an honoring of the differing relationships into which one can enter, or the multiplicity of human connections that comprise life. Eventually, clients learn to consider the implications of the narratives that have been authored for them in the past and the new ones that are coauthored in therapy, and they can weigh the balance of the competing scenarios appropriately and live the roles prescribed in the new script. Ultimately, the hope is that clients learn not only to write a new story or stories about the self but to be aware of and value the ongoing process of self-story writing in a social context, or of continuous incubational participation in creating and transforming meaning in relationship.

Note that postmodern therapy need not exclude the construct of self, for postmodernism's other can exist only in contradistinction to the self (Mascolo & Dalto, 1995). Socially constructed realities are adjusted to the constraints (and data) of context, and postmodernism has to adjust to this theory-building contingency. Similarly, selves are defined in relations, but bring personal agency with them and organizational coherence (structure, prioritization) to their multiple status. Postmodernism must be more than monstrous reality- and self-relativism.

Similarly, Neimeyer (1995b) maintains that our constructions must adapt to the insistent realities of the world (e.g., the loss of a loved one is painful) within a theoretical framework that respects communality and individuality. Thus, not only is perceived reality constructed but grounded in the empirical world, it is also social but unique. O'Hara (1995) also adopts a dual constructivist position in this regard, but advocates a theory where one or the other perspective may dominate at any one time. As for the tension between the personal and social nature of constructivism, Held (1995, following Neimeyer, 1993) also adopts a dualist position when she describes knowledge as "(inter)personal." In a similar vein, Friedman (1995) talks of a dialogue between experienced presentness and social otherness, Bohart (1995) of the personal interpretation of configured patterns from experience, and Polkinghorne (1995) of hearing silences in and around exchanged words. In all these cases, the personal, experiential nature of constructions are emphasized, but without excluding the social.

Note that I concur that there are undercurrents of inclusive opposition in our constructions, and try to integrate objectivist and constructivist perspectives on reality, on the one hand, and personal agency and social construction in reality processing, on the other hand, as we shall see.

FAMILY THERAPY

Process Therapy

Introduction. In the next sections, two important family therapy techniques are described, and it is suggested that they should be complemented by more developmental perspectives. Greenberg's process-oriented therapy is presented first, and then Tomm's interventive interviewing procedure is described.

Heatherington and Friedlander (1990) analyzed two demonstration interviews by the structural family therapist Minuchin in terms of Greenberg's task analysis. Greenberg's procedure is an intensive "discovery-oriented" one (Greenberg, 1986). It seeks internal representations governing a "problem space" or "psychotherapy event." Clients may recall a problematic incident, and the astute therapist realizes through the client's nonverbal behavior (e.g., intonation in voice), in particular, that a "problematic reaction point" or "marker" has been arrived at. Through a process of "systematic evocative unfolding," or therapist intervention, the therapist helps the client reexperience the incident.

The "task environment" is to have clients systematically focus on their problematic reactions. The clients must (1) describe the incident; (2) recognize the self's emotional reactions; (3) recognize any new aspects of prior construals about the incident; (4) then they will experience resolution and relief via a map of alternative pathways.

Heatherington and Friedlander (1990) found that task analysis can help explicate the interviews analyzed. Using a measurement of relational control patterns (assuming, giving up, neutral), they showed the way intrafamily patterns changed once the therapist Minuchin had realized that a "marker" had been manifested, and the moment was right to lead them through a process analogous to the one described by task analysis.

Greenberg et al.'s Emotional Processes

Greenberg (Greenberg, Rice, & Elliot, 1993; Greenberg and Pascual-Leone, 1995) has elaborated upon this process perspective of moment-by-moment facilitation of change in psychotherapy. The therapist trained in this perspective aims to facilitate the construction of emergent emotional meaning in clients by having them monitor, pay attention to, focus upon, or process ongoing experiential information (encouraging bottom-up awareness, not top-down thinking). Reality is constructed by a tacit, unconscious representation to oneself of one's activated functions. Clients participating in this therapeutic reality reconstruction reconfigure their sense of self and modify their emotion schemes which are combined cognitive–affective structures relevant to the self. They are internal but action-facilitating synthesizing models, modules, or processors that preconsciously or tacitly process a variety of context-specific information sources (cognitive, motivational, affective, actional), generating experienced emotional response. Thus, they provide complex but automatic guides to the construction of personal meaning is emotionally toned.

One's experience of these reactions engender one's sense of self. That is, emotion schemes produce an embodied feeling or sense of oneself in the world, informative of one's emotional reactions in current and similar past situations, giving feedback about automatic appraisal of the meaning of events. They combine synergistically to form "superordinate emotional meaning/action structures." That is, they cohere to form integrated, dynamic higher-level cognitive–affective modules, or consciously symbolized syntheses. These form subjective reality, underlying one's holistic experience of locus in the world and evaluation of the significance of life events, or one's lived awareness of internal, contextualized mental life. Once experienced, attended to, and symbolized into reflective awareness, internalized meaning constructs of emotional experiences contribute in their turn to the generation of new tacit distinctions in experiences that can be included into explanatory conceptualizations in a feedback process. Constraints in the encountered world also offer feedback to reality construction, for encoded, subjective, ideal reality dialectically engages raw, objective, empirical reality. Finally, coherent explanations are generated for symbolized experiences, producing narrative identities. Identity thus springs from immediate experience and cognitive processes. Representations of identity are examined, evaluated, revised, and replaced by alternatives. Multilevel, multiple selves are constructed continuously in consciousness. Language is used in this process of narrative formation, and brings with it linguistic distinctions that constitutively sharpen the meaning-making process. Thus, a continual interchange of thought and emotion serves an integration toward psychological growth.

Yet emotion schemes do not achieve all this through the automatic generation of emotion, per se. First, they work with a lower level of emotional experience, that of immediate sensory experience and expressive–motoric response. Then, they create the complex felt meanings that derive from this level. However, although lower-level emotional phenomena are available for moment-to-moment conscious symbolization and incorporation into awareness and synthetic meaning construction, this process occurs only if the affective responses that they induce, due to appraisals of the individual's context in relation to a concern or a need, are attended to internally. That is, lower-level emotional phenomena are not always amenable to processing, for they may be weak, attenuated signals to which attention is not paid. The manner in which this attenuation may take place speaks to therapeutic issues.

The "conscious synthesizing constructive process" in which emotion schemes are engaged is oriented to ongoing problem resolution and general contextual adaptation. Thus, inevitably, it is influenced by learned familial and cultural messages (e.g., others' views of one's self-worth). These may not always be positive (e.g., others acting to depreciate one's sense of self-worth), leading to interference in the process. Consequently, when attention to subjective experience is disturbed, affecting cognitive–emotional interplay, then negative psychological sequelae are potentiated. That is, with this particular lack of interior attention, individuals' conscious evaluation of themselves does not include their automatic emotional responses, which may lead to maladaptive perceptions and behavior. Therapy may be called for when the conflicts engendered by this process become difficult to deal with.

Therapy. In Greenberg's therapy, clients' emotional structures and meaning configurations are reorganized and even created de novo. This takes place through the therapist's empathic attunement to and process diagnosis of clients' ongoing emotional experiences so that the meaning constructs controlling clients' emotional experiences are activated in therapy, attended to, and deliberately and automatically controlled, facilitating online work with them. The therapist refrains from directing the creation of new emotional meanings, being content to stimulate the process of their construction by facilitating change in conscious experiential processing, including to what attention is directed (in terms of automatically generated emotional states, in particular), and how attentional foci are symbolized and reflected upon. For example, instead of talking about a problem or the way to solve it, the therapist directs focus to the full expression of the feeling in a client's wavering voice, an understanding of the problem (e.g., the sense of failure) that underlies it, and an acknowledgement of unmet needs. In so doing, current emotional experience self-organizes at a more integrated level. Modes of engagement or therapist tasks, such as the two-chair task, are used in a directive manner, but always with the goal of eliciting the self-creation of emergent meaning.

In this perspective, when considered at the conscious level, emotions are reconstructed from potentials. Thus, by definition, therapy is not concerned with unconscious, repressed, blocked, or disavowed emotions. Rather, it concerns the accessing of appropriate emotion schemes right in therapy sessions so that they can be integrated into more equilibrated structures of meaning. The underlying postulate is that emotions associated with painful experiences are not stored or maintained in memory. Instead, they are resynthesized in the present as memories associated with the emotion scheme that is evoked into awareness during the recall of painful experiences. Thus, "[a]n important therapeutic focus becomes one of activating emotion schemes and helping people attend to the emotional experiences generated and their emotional meanings" (Greenberg et al., 1993, p. 70). Additionally, therapy works because of the human organism's inherent growth tendency to continually reorganize coherently at higher levels of complexity.

Pascual-Leone's Dialectical Constructivism.   The epistemology underlying this concept of client change is dialectical constructivism, developed by Pascual-Leone (e.g., 1991, 1995). In this model, client consciousness, or the lived, vital, reflective experience of oneself in one's world,
develops in the interactive transformation of two polar opposites in the
stream of consciousness: (1) automatic, direct, immediate, subjective, embodied, felt experience and (2) active, reflective, reasoned, objective, delib-
erate cognitive mediating concepts or representations of meaning of what
that experience should be. "Consciousness is the final arbiter of meaning,
both by selecting what source of information to attend to and what interpretation to generate" (Greenberg et al., 1993, p. 60). Consciousness includes willful executive processes and the possibility of options. It is
dynamically multidetermined and multiple in outcome. "Consciousness
is thus the arena for the dialectical synthesis of the different sources of
information about the self as the person encounters and resolves felt contradictions between aspects of self, and between self and the world"
(Greenberg et al., 1993, p. 60).

Client distress arises in the contradiction between actual experienced
reality and conceptions formed in consciousness of what it is or ought to
be. In therapy, exploration and synthesis of contradictions such as this are
facilitated, because once they enter the linguistic life of the client the
words used help transform experience through their feedback influence on
it. Simultaneously, experience is discovered and created, differentiated
and integrated, in this dialectical manner, producing "symbolization of
experience in awareness" and new meaning. Thus, experience, and one's
multilevel, modular, multiple sense of agentic self-in-the-world, reside in
neither of the poles of thought or of emotion but in the emergence promulgated by their dialogical mutuality.

Conclusion.   Greenberg and Pascual-Leone's conceptualization of
cognition–emotion interaction remind me of Falck's (1994) assertion that
there was an original unity of descriptive and emotional meaning sustained by a primitive mythic awareness, a unity that has been lost and can
be regained through metaphorical reconstruction, in part. Similarly, Shotter (1995a) speaks of engaged, involved, lived, practical–moral reason (and
common sense) in the quotidian contacts of ongoing life. For both the
micro- and macrodevelopmental levels, Lewis (1995) describes a positive
feedback in cognition–emotion interaction. It is seen to involve a cycle
of self-organized emotion-guided or highlighted attention-boosting to, cognitive interpretation-appraisal of, and adjustment to emotion-eliciting
events.

Guidano (1995) describes the ontological condition as a cycle of immediate experiencing and explaining, which includes a cycle where the

acting, experiencing *I* immediately experiences oneself, leading the observing, appraising *me* to self-reference ongoing experience. Thus, the me is derived from an emotional etching out of the experienced I, and it can produce experience-manipulating strategies if exposed to maladaptive contexts. Consequently, therapy often involves changing the me's evaluation of the experiencing I.

Similarly, Gonçalves (1995) conceives of humans as neither subjects nor objects, but projects who simultaneously and endlessly understand through existence and exist through understanding as embodied, constructed, thrown forth metaphors whose movement cannot be predicted. Humans are their socially constructed theories, which in turn are analogical equivalences of their motor and emotional activities in relationship. Life becomes a transcendent, constant creation process, for "[a]s we create, we create ourselves through the creation" (p. 201). The I implements projects which the me appraises. In authoring characters in self, a sense of authorship is created.

Guidano's, Gonçalves's, and Greenberg and Pascual-Leone's concepts of self-appraisal, constructed projection, or conscious arbitration are typical adolescent–adult acquisitions, but the development pathway toward these higher levels of thought is not addressed in depth in their work. That is, the current work can be seen as a complement to theirs because it explores the link between cognition and affect, like them, but also is explicitly developmental.

Note that Pascual-Leone's notion of dialectical constructivism speaks to the constitutive constructionist approach emphasized in the current work, as shall be shown later on.

Tomm's Systemic Therapy

Interventive Interviewing. Tomm (1987a, 1987b, 1988) is a systemic therapist who has elaborated guidelines for interventive interviewing. Therapists' conceptual postures are particular stances that they adopt, or enduring attitudes that maintain "a stable point of reference" in clients' thoughts and actions while implicitly inhibiting others. Postures include hypothesizing, neutrality, circularity, and strategizing. Hypotheses are conjectures about the family that are presented to it. Neutrality is a noncommitted stance. Circularity refers to the interrelationship between therapist and family (second-order cybernetics, distinct from the circularity within the family system, first-order cybernetics). The therapist probes, paraphrases, draws distinctions, or moves in relation to the family movement. Strategizing is a posture with the explicit goal of achieving therapeutic change (e.g., involving new plans of action).

Tomm (1987b) adds to his depiction of interventive interviewing by describing reflexive questions. They are aimed at triggering self-healing by altering the connectedness of preexisting structure in cognition in a constructive way through the family's own activity once the process has been set in motion by the questions. Types of reflexive questions include future orientation (e.g., "What is your collective goal for this period and how will you know that it has been accomplished?"); observer–perspective questions ("Just how did you feel?"; "What do you think she felt?"); triadic questions ("When your parents argue, what does your sister do?"); unexpected context-change questions (e.g., with positive connotation, paradoxical); and embedded questions (e.g., reframes) (see Table 9.1).

In the next of the series of articles, Tomm (1988) places the four major

Table 9.1 Hypothetical Example of Condensed Interventive Family Interviewing

Context	Questions
Recalling their child's past, parents remember that instead of inducing nesting, discovery of pregnancy brought on turmoil. The parents seem dismissing or disengaged in style, and their child avoidant in attachment. The child seems aloof, distant, calm, and bordering on the asocial. His social skills do not appear deep, nor his self-esteem high. He shows no interest in excelling at school, but readily seeks out friends. This appears to be a consistent, third-generation pattern of behavior. The child, apparently being at the substage of perioperational hierarchization, has working models involving expectations of dominant–subordinate self–other, other–self relations. But signs indicate that the models are detached or split, at times, especially concerning "bad" parts of his parents. Various indices point to the mother and father being mostly at the level of the young adolescent, abstractly aware conscious self despite their age of 25 and 27, respectively. The danger signs for this period are prevalent, including that of overconformity so that the normal identity seeking of the next phase appears to have had been aborted in regression. In examining the family history of	How does T. react when you come home from work? Is it the same way that you greet each other?[a] What does T. feel inside when you come home and greet him? And how do you feel? Do you think that there are other hidden feelings? Are there other ones that should be there? T., tell me about your best friends, the ones you mentioned before. What do you feel when you play with them at home? At day care? What do you do with them? How do they act when they see you for the first time in the day? How do you act? What do they (you) feel inside? How does that make you (them) feel inside? What do mommy and daddy do when they see you the first time in the morning? What do you do? How do you feel inside? What does she (he) feel inside? What should she or he do to make you feel the happiest? How do you think that T. would react if your typical way of greeting him or being with him involved these kinds of feelings? How would you feel about such feelings in T.? How would each of you feel in seeing the other feel this way and cause such pleasant feelings in T.? Which of you is more happy that this does not happen? Why? Imagine that you are T. and try to feel

types of questions in his family therapy approach within a framework which varies on two axes—whether the questions are orienting or influencing and whether they are circular (holistic) or lineal (reductionist) in underlying assumption. Strategic (corrective, constraining) questions fall in the lineal-influencing quadrant, lineal (what is the problem, investigative) questions in the lineal-orienting one, circular (exploratory, liberating) questions in the circular-orienting one, and reflexive (facilitative, generative) questions in the circular-influencing one.

Comment. In a more recent work, Tomm (1991) argues that therapists should strive as much as possible to encourage empowerment in clients. For example, a resistant client may just mean a resistant therapist, i.e.,

Table 9.1 (*Continued*)

Context	Questions
stances adopted, the optimal one has always been subverted, with the stance instead having been consistently negative. The parents, when trying to prune their child's new initiative, show punishing zeal but more often an uncontrolled neglect. A combination of circular and reflexive questions are asked about feelings. The goal is to explore parenting attitude, inner sentiments, their effects on the child, and new possibilities. In keeping with the line of the interventive questioning, an on–off ritual prescription is set up for alternate days of the week, with Sundays free. The goal is to encourage inhibition of dysfunctional parental patterns and appropriate deployment of adaptive ones (activation–inhibition coordination), leading to the maintaining of control of the child in a balance of concerned delimiting and affectionate motivating.	how he would feel in more pleasant circumstances. What does this tell you? What is there that may have led you to behave in other ways? What do you think that others do and feel in similar situations? When you feel the way you do and behave with T. that way, what does the other do? feel? When you yourself experience this type of behavior coming from someone else, what does this make you want to do? What do you think that you are trying to tell each other? Did you ever realize that what you do makes the other behave (feel) like that? Is (s)he so sensitive or vulnerable that the hurt from the past is masked in this way? What do you have to do with each other to help change the pattern? How does what we are learning today relate to the turmoil in the pregnancy? Yes, I agree that that rough period may have been forgotten about prematurely and that it comes back in other ways; for example, being its opposite, being uncaring. Good, you want to undo that attitude. How might you proceed? Yes, being the opposite should help. How can we do this?

[a]Questions about the client's actions or feelings should be presented as bifurcations (e.g., "Does T react with joy or sadness [or in some other way"?]) as much as possible. This type of question should accompany the more general one or even replace it. To have done this throughout the table would have made it excessively long so that only the shorter general version of each question is presented. An alternate way of approaching questions about internal feelings is to ask about "experiences," "what happened to you," etc., in order to get at underlying cognitions and beliefs as well (Safran & Segal, 1990).

manipulation may not be required where it seems necessary at first glance. Empowering questions are branching in nature, for they include information enabling the client to become aware of choices and become active agents in decision making. They bifurcate to include both problem-oriented questions and solution-oriented questions in one global question. For example, if related to past turning points, they may include not only past failures but also past successes. Or, if oriented to present choices, they may focus on present weaknesses or passivity, but also include present strengths and initiatives. Finally, if concerned with future alternative behavior, they would include both limitations and new possibilities.

Tomm's family therapy approach has clear cognitive components of a constructivist nature. His interviewing procedure is very meaning oriented and often attempts to restructure a family's self-construal. However, it is not diachronic in nature, or adapted to the different developmental levels of family members. The types of questions asked should fit the client's cognitive level and consequent socioemotional capacities. For example, reflexive questions in Tomm's approach should be very different when addressed to a 10- as opposed to a 45-year-old.

ATTACHMENT THERAPY

The First Work

Even attachment theory, as applied to family therapy, is not fully cognizant of the different developmental levels of children, although it is quite diachronic in nature (e.g., Stevenson-Hinde, 1990; Stevenson-Hinde & Shouldice, 1995). The concept of family scripts has been an important mediator in integrating attachment theory and family therapy (Byng-Hall, 1991, 1995). Families create mutually held, dynamic, working models or representational schemata about typical attachment situations (e.g., separation, reunion) and the way the multiple persons in the family mentally represent and operate in response to them. When difficulties within the family manifest, its members may invoke either mutually protective scripts which inhibit violence (safety scripts) or scripts which "reduce intolerable emotions, or memories, from being evoked" (defensive scripts). The nature and intensity of these scripts may impede conflict resolution or add other problems. Families also create secure–insecure family bases, concerned with the type of care available to family members.

Because much of the attachment relation between caregiver and infant is concerned with proximity–contact regulation, families can be seen to develop approach–avoidance conflict mechanisms, in a too far/too close system. Each family member tries to maintain the other(s) at an emotional equilibrium point, but conflict may escalate rapidly at each approach, or as withdrawal is resisted, in a positive feedback loop. Children can become ensnared as distance regulators of parental conflict. Thus, the ambivalence across the innate push to grow psychologically and the pull of the family to assume a static, childlike role becomes marked in children when this happens, producing symptoms symbolic of conflict.

Aside from distance regulation dysfunctions, insecurity in familial attachment can serve to facilitate several other maladaptive behavior patterns (Byng-Hall & Stevenson Hinde, 1991). One family member may be actively pursued or "captured" at the expense of others. An inappropriate attachment figure may be pursued (e.g., a parent turns to a child). Parents may replicate intergenerational patterns, which may not be adaptive if they are insecurity promoting. Or they may overreact in the opposite direction to those patterns, especially if they are negative, e.g., compulsive instead of absent caregiving. Finally, families may try to avoid repetition of unresolved traumas, but unwittingly lead to their reemergence (e.g., fear of divorce leads to emotional independence facilitating its occurrence).

More Recent Work

Erickson, Korfmacher, and Egeland (1992), Lieberman (1992), and Marvin (1992) contend that therapeutic intervention in an attachment relationship that is maladaptive must orient to the internal working model of both the child and the parent(s). By promoting a positive working alliance and facilitating insight, a corrective attachment experience with therapist as secure base or trusted companion is created. The focus of insight is the manner in which assumptions and conceptions based on childhood experiences come to influence parenting practices. Blocked, uncomfortable ideas, memories, and emotions are explored without fear of criticism and rejection. Ineffective, entrenched means of coping are examined and shown to have been adaptive in the circumstances of their origin. Defensive mechanisms and their repercussions are exposed. In particular, the mechanism of projection is underscored, because it is accompanied by a pressure to comply with the content of the projection via a rigid interaction process. The child is used as a trigger in therapy, e.g., to link the parent's own early memories to their child's apparent experience, to see things from the perspective of the child, to interact with her or him and then dissect the interaction, and to have the therapist model appropriate caregiving behaviors with her or him. Also, a range of family therapy techniques are used with the parent.

Crittenden (1992) offers an intricate account of attachment therapy, because she differentiates it to include the two major types of insecure attachment (ambivalent, avoidant), works a lot with the child her or himself, focuses on the memory system underlying the internal working models of the child and parent, and uses a range of behavioral, cognitive, and psychodynamic techniques. Finally, West and Sheldon-Keller (1994) in their counseling, for all styles of insecure attachment act to facilitate the mourning of a desired but never lived loving, fully authentic relationship with the primary attachment figure.

As a therapist, Byng-Hall (1995) serves as a temporary secure base where he can offer protection to help analyze core familial anxieties and conflicts and help parents regain safe control of their children. He achieves this goal partly by helping them understand their distance conflicts, e.g., withdrawing may act to maintain a relationship, indifference may reduce tension, demanding behavior may be a sign of insecurity, and pushing away or threats of abandonment may be strategies to elicit clinging.

Conclusion

This marriage of attachment and family therapy is fascinating. However, it can be expanded to include the cognitive (mis)perceptions of the other that may underlie different attachment problems. Consequently, the points of view described should be seen as a beginning, which the current 25-step developmental model may help elaborate. This position is considered in Chapter 10.

ACTIVATION–INHIBITION THERAPY

Introduction

In this section, a novel perspective on therapy is examined. First, it is suggested that because much of behavior is concerned with activation–inhibition processes, then therapies should be oriented in this direction. Second, the question of constructivism versus objectivism in behavior is examined (see Chapter 11 for an in-depth presentation), and I argue that both views are necessary to capture human reality. It seems that therapies would profit by respecting both poles of this dichotomy. The ramifications of combining the two issues in therapy, i.e., inhibition-related therapies and constructivism–objectivism, are discussed in conclusion.

It may be worthwhile to examine all intervention procedures in terms of the inhibition-related processes in the client that they tap. Inhibition processes in behavior especially include chained activation–inhibition coordination in complex behavior. Also, other inhibition processes (e.g., complete stopping; momentary coordination to allow figure–ground, spatial, contextual, or gestalt perceptions) may be involved in this process (see Chapter 7).

Thus, it may be possible to differentiate therapeutic interventions by the type of inhibition-related activity that it fosters in the client. Does it better enable or teach outright efficient sequential activation–inhibition coordination? Or perhaps it is aimed at modifying or disrupting dysfunctional, maladaptive coordinations. Also, many techniques may be oriented to full behavioral suppression, while others hope to broaden or alter contextual, gestalt, figure–ground perceptions. An inhibition-based classification of therapeutic activities may help orient workers in the helping professions by pointing directly to the basic nature of clients' problems and the most effective means of assisting them. In fact, novel therapeutic approaches may be derived from an attempt such as this, because optimal strategies may need to be created to facilitate the inhibition processes called for in therapy.

Traditional therapies are considered objectivist, mechanical, or empirical. In these schools, reality is seen as an external given that the therapist attempts to discern and order onto the client. More organic approaches such as Tomm's questioning format are decidedly constructivist, with therapist and client seen as coconstruing reality in reciprocal dialogue.

It is argued in Chapter 11 that a moderate position on the issue of constructivism versus objectivism in the philosophy of humankind would acknowledge the heuristic validity of both views. In this regard, schools of therapy that adhere to one perspective or the other should not be considered adversarial but complementary. Duncan and Parks (1988) advocate a similar approach when they contend that behavioral techniques can complement family system procedures in an integrated therapy, for each set contributes different ingredients to the optimal therapeutic equation.

The Model

Table 9.2 organizes this discussion of inhibition in therapy and constructivist–objectivist approaches to therapy in a two-dimensional framework. (For another way of using epistemic stance as one dimension in a classification matrix of different therapies, see Held [1992]).

Therapies can be qualified as inhibition-based in the following ways. They may be adding to (facilitating, refining) sequential activation–inhibition coordinations or subtracting from them (overtly modifying, disrupting). Or rather than managing complex sequences, therapies may serve to fully suppress or excise them (subtraction) or work on contextual,

Table 9.2 Classification of Therapeutic Approaches

Epistemological stance	Activation–inhibition process	Mathematical process	Therapeutic approach
Objectivism	Sequential coordination	Add	Behavior modification
		Subtract	Cognitive
	Context/suppression	Add	Psychodynamic
		Subtract	Medical, manipulation
Constructivism	Sequential coordination	Add	Reflexive, empowerment
		Subtract	Strategic
	Context/suppression	Add	Circular
		Subtract	Lineal

figure–ground, gestalt factors (reciprocally activating–inhibiting salient features–background in a process of addition).

In light of this classificatory structure, selected examples of contemporary therapy can be chosen for each type of therapy, while recognizing that this process is both approximate and tentative. First, traditional objectivist approaches are considered.

Behavior modification attempts to induce the learning-shaping of more adaptive actions, while trying to extinguish dysfunctional behavior patterns, in particular. Thus, it can be seen as sequential and coordinative in activation–inhibition. Cognitive therapy shows the irrationality of ongoing thought patterns, in particular, leading to the acquisition of more adaptive ones. This makes it concerned with subtraction of activation–inhibition sequential coordinations as much as anything else. Psychodynamic models work especially at underlying, background unconscious influences, skirting behavior as given, thus rendering it contextual and additive for the purposes of the current classificatory scheme. Finally, drug regimens or other manipulations (e.g., punishment) are meant to suppress maladaptive behavior.

Constructivist therapies also deal with these four avenues in therapy. For example, Tomm's reflexive questions are facilitative and generative, provoking "spontaneous" reorganization in clients' core construals. As such, they can reorganize or replace by addition the complex sequences of activation–inhibition coordination which are governed by such thought patterns. Strategic therapies aim to correct and constrain, suggesting that they subtract (overtly modify, disrupt) complex activation–inhibition sequences. Circular questions also are called "contextualizing" ones (Real, 1990), for they are exploratory and liberating. In this vein, they correspond to the additive context/figure–ground inhibition type of therapy. Finally, lineal questions often are investigative, conservative probes aimed at discerning problems that need excision (i.e., suppression).

Comment

An optimally integrative therapy will be cognizant of all these possible approaches to therapy, and apply them in the correct combination for each client. It is hoped that a more inclusive model of psychological therapy can be elucidated by considering (1) this classificatory system of therapeutic procedures; (2) the developing individual's substage in the cognitive, socioemotional, self, and family arenas of development (as presented by the current synthetic theory); and (3) classificatory systems of attachment and caregiver quality.

Note that all these various therapeutic modes cannot be applied equally to all developmental phases. Crittenden (1990, 1992) points out that (1) behavioral techniques orient to sensorimotor procedural memories; (2) cognitive interventions target representational (semantic) ones; and (3) psychodynamic approaches speak to the older child's episodic memories. In this regard, there may be a developmental progression of appropriate therapies corresponding to the reflexive, sensorimotor, preoperational, and concrete operational (i.e., together perioperational), formal operational, and postformal (collective intelligence) levels in neopiagetian psychology. Roughly speaking, respectively, these therapies would be the simplest manipulations (e.g., involving simple classical conditioning, punishment, drug regimens); behavioral (e.g., behavior modification); cognitive, psychodynamic, constructivist (e.g., familial); and activist (empowerment of the individual in the communal milieu) approaches.

In the following section, an important contemporary therapeutic approach is described, and I indicate the way I have refined it in terms of activation–inhibition coordination.

INTERNALIZATION/EXTERNALIZATION COORDINATION THERAPY

Michael White's Systemic Therapy

Externalization. The common dictum that parents should address discipline uniquely to the child's annoying act, and not to the child as a whole, is a powerful procedure. It protects the self-esteem and sense of attachment of the child, while aiming to extinguish the presenting misbehavior. White (1984, 1986, 1991, 1993a, 1993b, 1993c, 1994; White & Epston, 1990; Epston & White, 1995; Epston, White, & Murray, 1992) and those influenced by him have adapted a therapeutic technique related to this procedure that they claim can be effective even with the most severe dysfunctional behavior (see Adams-Westcott, Dafforn, & Sterne, 1993; Brecher & Friedman, 1993; Chang & Phillips, 1993; Combs & Freedman,

1994; Dickerson & Zimmerman, 1993; Durrant & Kowalski, 1993; Epston, 1993a, 1993b, 1993c, 1994; Freedman & Combs, 1993; Freeman & Lobowitz, 1993; Friedman, 1993, 1994; Furman & Ahola, 1994; Griffith & Griffith, 1993; Hoyt, 1994; Madigan, 1993, 1994; Mittelmeier & Friedman, 1993; Nyland & Thomas, 1994; Prest & Carruthers, 1991; Price, 1993; Tomm, 1989, 1993; Tomm, Suzuki, & Suzuki, 1990; Wylie, 1994a, 1994b; Zimmerman & Dickerson, 1993, 1994a, 1994b).

White's technique concerns *externalizing the problem* while internalizing personal agency. For example, in 1984, White described the way he personified a child's encopresis, or lack of bowel control, as "Sneaky Poo," an externalizing procedure which helped lead to the child freeing himself from his problem. This example illustrates that people can become "decisive agents in their own change" because the credo of the approach is that, "[t]he person is never the problem; the problem is the problem" (O'Hanlon, 1994, p. 24). Or as Parry and Doan (1994) put it, "[p]roblem externalization involves talking about *problems* as problems rather than *people* as problems" (p. 52). According to Tomm (1989), the therapist "linguistically separates" or distinguishes the client's problem from her or his self identity.

Normally, the problem masks problem-free experiences within an individual's memory and self-perception, filtering out hope and a sense of self-empowerment. Internalized conversations restrain self-description to narrow bands with little choice. However, when the therapist can lead the client toward dissociation or separation from the problem, he or she can determine when the client had mastered in the past the problem or had not fallen victim to it, and the way personal skills or significant others had facilitated such control. Unique outcomes, or exceptions to the rule, are sought. Space is opened for a sense of personal resourcefulness, options, and alternative modes in the relationship of the client to the externalized problem. Not only is the problem protested, but an injunction is imposed on the self, inhibiting it from submitting to the problem (Tomm, 1994). Clients can view the problem with distance, detachment, and curiosity (Parry & Doan, 1994). They come to view themselves as uncontaminated by the problem, nondetermined by it, free to take responsibility for their behavior, and accountable for the option chosen among the choices which could be made in relation to the problem (O'Hanlon, 1994). Ultimately, an externalization alters the title of client stories from "Influenceable Me" to "Me in All my Multiplicity" (after Parry & Doan, 1994).

Parry and Doan (1994) offer the following general rules for externalizing in therapy. First, externalizations should be offered at a nonspecific level before becoming specific. Thus, terms such as *trouble* should be used before "The 'I've Got to Move' Bug." However, for certain clients the specific level may not be effective. I would add that for other clients the general level works less effectively. Second, externalizations work best when they incorporate the clients' own terminology (e.g., depression is like an attack of "an army of Blue Meanies"). Third, the best externalizations personify the meaning which supports key symptomatic behavior (e.g., perfectionism in the case of depression). Fourth, externalizations may be linked to childhood–adolescent experiences in order to provide a developmental and external context, thus acting to free clients from thinking that their problems are inherent to them. Fifth, interactional behavioral patterns may be externalized where appropriate. For example, a predator–prey relationship in a couple may take the form of pursue–withdraw patterns that hide fear-of-rejection/fear-of-attachment motivations.

White's Narrative Therapy. In more recent works, White (e.g., 1993a, 1993b, 1993c) has rephrased his therapeutic technique in terms of the narrative discourse in which client and therapist engage. According to him, the dominant narrative of the client, internalized from conversations with others, disqualifies her or his own experiences and limits access to alternative discourses through the discounting inner dialogues that they engender. However, through coconstructive conversational exploration and bifurcation of the client's dynamic struggle, the balance is tipped in favor of enhancing a reconstructed story, antiplot, or counterdiscourse at the expense of the previously dominant one. The client comes to deconstruct, unmask, alienate from, and restory or reauthor her or his problem-saturated discourse, and its controlling practices of understanding self and relationship, with a liberating, authentic, reappropriating, reclaiming discourse that invites rather than imposes.

Meaning making (Bruner, 1990) is coconstructed through "archaeologizing" for unique outcomes, or gaps, inconsistencies, and contradictions in prior private, transfixing stories, and through externalizing the previously dominant discourse in therapeutic conversation. Both the "landscape of action," or story sequences, and the "landscape of consciousness," or thoughts, feelings, etc. (Bruner, 1990), are explored through questions in the new coauthored story. If it helps to situate the problem in dominant, oppressive cultural knowledges, narratives, and practices, this is done. In authentic therapeutic encounter, positive unforeseen, unintended histories that shape perceptions of the past, present, and future can emerge and come to have performed meaning or claims for the client. A preferred vista on the self is constructed collaboratively with the client. "[S]tories provide the structure of life" (White, 1993a, p. 36) in the narrative genealogy that is coconstructed with them in emancipatory handiwork. Narrative scaffolds memory, and with the constitution of alternative, transformative stories, prior experiences that have been effaced by dominant stories reverberate or resonate in memory and are written into the new dialogue in constructive ways. Recruitment of the appropriate mobilizing audience for the performance of the new discourse is worked out in order to ensure its continued presence on the stage of the client's life.

All this takes place without the denial of objective reality, only with the alteration of experiential reality. In this sense, White's philosophy is one of constitutionalism. There are no foundational or essential verities, only constructed truth statuses that physical realities may affect but not template. There are no expert therapists, only consultants to the client's authoring process and knowledge-making skills, for imported knowledges stultify and stupefy a client into patienthood, bonding them to their problemhood.

Wylie (1994a) describes in a most elegant manner the power of White's narrative therapy. She uses his archaeology metaphor to describe his conjoint meaning making. "White sifts through the undifferentiated debris of experience for minuscule traces of meaning—the tiny precious shards of struggle, defeat and victory that reveal a life" (p. 42). Clients express "subtle, half-forgotten, almost unrecognized dissent" from or "little pockets of noncooperation" with their oppressive iron stories of "lived misery and assigned pathology" through a momentary "spiritual valor," "autonomy, self-respect and emotional vitality" that helps recall "tiny saving fragments of formerly lost experience" (p. 43). "[T]he 'trance' imposed on people by the powerful forces of history and culture" are broken," making visible the invisible pattern of ordinary ... acts of violence that comprise much of civilized life" (p. 43). Together, the client and White transform "a hopeless story with a foreordained ending into a dramatic epic" (p. 44). Clients, who have "become nonpersons to themselves," are transfigured and step "into new ways of being and thinking that bring new options and possibilities for action" (p. 47). In summary, White "carefully nurtures the small triumphs in the lives of people he sees, honors the transient moments of competence, initiative, resoluteness" so that neglected stories "become the seeds and the soil of human transformation" (p. 48).

Others' Narrative Therapy.   Others have described similar narrative therapies, many basing their approach on White's work. Parry (1993) describes a "democracy" of stories in therapy.

> [N]either of us can go forward until we both realize that the stories are connected, each of us having entered the world of the other. Such a sense of story calls for each of us to improvise constantly like jazz musicians each playing off what the other introduces. (p. 458)

For Parry and Doan (1994), clients never have been or are no longer authors of their own stories. For example, they might recount one totalizing story or stories told by others, or they may not be aware of masked stories ("hidden texts"). Thus, therapists must facilitate clients to give legitimacy to their own stories about their own experiences in their own voice or words. Old stories, in both clients and significant others, are viewed as adaptive survival mechanisms and the just object of compassion. We participate in each others' lives, and "[a]s each person expands that sense of participation to embrace all life—that is to say, every being capable of suffering—each can develop her or his own metanarrative" (p. 30). The other should be loved because and not in spite of differences from oneself. The major procedure used to reorient clients concerns the intertwined processes of story deconstruction and story reconstruction (which appears comparable to inhibition and activation, respectively). The former concerns old story identification. They are considered childhood survival stories which merit admiration for the manner in which they had been constructed in order to help clients survive difficult circumstances. They live clients or inhabit them, but are interpretations, meanings, or views that are amenable to change. The latter concerns story revisions, which replace the now unworkable old stories. They are cocreated with clients through stopper mechanisms such as the question, "What story is this?" The primary mechanism, however, involves the externalization procedure, as described above. At therapy's end, clients go forth "to join with others in the universal human action of multiple authorship" (p. 43).

Zimmerman and Dickerson (1994b) act to bring forth marginalized, multiple, unvoiced stories masked by normative, expert ones in a reciprocal, dialogic construction of meaning. Penn and Francfort (1994) convert unresponsive, negative, fixed, single-voiced inner monologues to multiple voice and self dialogues which inaugurate different connections and ripples in the person's narrative multiplicity. O'Hanlon (1994) speaks of the enhancement of reinvented, reidentifying, life-enhancing narratives within the adult-within at the expense of colonizing stories so that gateways to parallel universes are elaborated. Efran (1994) refers to mystery, Vogel (1994) to incongruity, Angus and Hardtke (1994) to reflexive analysis of past, current, and future events, and Widdershoven (1994) to radical openness in narrative therapy. Terrell and Lyddon (1996) describe a hermeneutic, reciprocal, and recursive scaffolding, bridging, or connecting of stories, leading to a "broader multiplex of realities and possibilities" (p. 39). Neimeyer (1994) refers to coherence and the speaking into being of new worlds of possibility, and S. Friedman (1993) speaks of "possibility" therapy. (In this regard, Pynchon wrote that "[t]here is the moment, and its possibilities"; cited in Parry [1993], p. 453.)

De Shazer, in his solution-focused work, has a similar perspective on the importance of "exceptions," or different stories, to the client (de Shazer, 1991, 1993a, 1993b; Berg & de Shazer, 1993). "The more they talk about exceptions, miracles, and so forth, the more 'real' what they are talking about becomes" (Berg & de Shazer, 1993, p. 21). (I disagree with de Shazer [1993b] that *exceptions* is a better term than *unique outcomes*, because only the former implies a new rule that has potential for change; however, his points are well taken that in externalizing the problem as an antiproblem to be vanquished, and in using his own rather than the clients' language, White focuses less on the client's personal solutions. See below for elaborations of these points.)

Derrida (in Lax, 1992) described the "différance," or tension between what is said and what is not said, which creates the potential for the emergence of new words said in therapy. Similarly, for Galooshian and Anderson (Anderson, 1993; Anderson & Galooshian, 1990; Galooshian & Anderson, 1992; Hoffman, 1990; Penn, 1992), client and therapist create together new histories from the not-yet-said, not-yet-told, or unexpressed narrative that clients can language or story about themselves. Through dynamic conversations, presenting problems are meaningfully coconstructed, or linguistically reshaped or distinguished, leading to shifts in behavior and belief (Griffith, Griffith, & Slovik, 1990): "We talk. Therefore we are." Client and therapist conversations "fold over" each other, like "kneaded dough," creating a new conversation in consequence (Lax, 1992). Reified stories coconstructively are replaced by or are reorganized into different habitations in which lives are lived more meaningfully (Becvar & Becvar, 1993). A "deliberative" discourse engaging all participants in the couple or family unit is used to promote respect for all of them and have them feel that new solutions are advantageous to each of them (Goldner, 1993). Narrative therapy is more creative, exploratory, reflective, elaborative, and intensely personal than corrective, directive, persuasive, analytical, and technically instructive (Neimeyer, 1993). Mair (1989) described the conversational or poetic approach to therapy as one which "involves speaking together and telling what we know. In this it is of importance that we try to speak the 'full word' from a position of imaginative participation, as well as speaking of more distant positions of reflective afterthought" (p. 197).

Questions.   Tomm (1989) described the typical sequence of circular and reflexive questions used by White to externalize a client's problem (e.g., acknowledgement questions). He also presented questions which point out alternative responses to the problematic situation, and what they reveal about personal agency (relative influence questions), and terminated with questions that act to maintain or stabilize any progress the client may have made (e.g., with respect to self-perception, views of the future). When I use this procedure with clients, I add a series of introductory questions to help prepare the context for the client (see Table 9.3; O'Hanlon [1994] for a slightly different model of the appropriate question sequence in the externalization process.)

Introductory questions are necessary to set the stage by naming and personifying the externalized problem. For younger clients, it may be useful for the therapist to use the analogy of a virus or "bug" invading the body when introducing the concept of externalization. For older clients, the language of bad habits or vicious circles is best. The strengths of the self and its potential for personal agency must be pointed out clearly to the client at this juncture. Each client should have her or his own individualized and realistic pattern of attributes used to underscore these strengths.

Acknowledgement questions are aimed at having the client assimilate the reframing of her or his problem in terms of externalization. The client then has less reason to blame her or himself for the problem, because the bad habit becomes the culprit and not the self. The extent of the ramifications of the problem are delineated, as well, but without ascribing blame to significant others, where applicable, for they are depicted as having their own bad habits. Acknowledgement questions also can be used to have significant others blame less the client or themselves. Finally, an indirect effect is that therapists become less likely to assign blame to clients or significant others.

Relative influence questions have been described by White (1986). According to him, cognitive restraints (e.g., presuppositions) channel human behavior. Adaptive options (news, differences; Bateson, 1979) can take hold (are differences which make a difference) if the client is ready for change or has cognitive restraints "relaxed" (e.g., by a therapist joining the system). As options emerge in therapy, the influence of the bad habit on the life of the optional system is mapped, and contrasted with the inverse influence of the optional system on the bad habit. With the use of attention-catching language, parallel or double descriptions are elicited and pose dilemmas for the client, for he or she can see the self as either competent or not, as having options or not, and as a fully responsible active agent in her or his own life or not. This leads to ways of pushing back the problem (the radical option), which contrast to the traditional ways the problem dominates the client (the conservative option). Experiments are constructed in concert with the therapist not only to push back the bad habit and keep it at bay when it invites regression, but also to replace the behaviors it prescribes by more adaptive ones. For example, I asked a troubled student, "How could you tell irrational fear that you have learned enough from it and now it must learn from and listen to you?" She answered, "Exactly that way!"

Maintenance questions act to solidify gains made in pushing back the

Table 9.3 Internalization/Externalization Interventive Questioning

Topic	Questions
Introduction	Do you realize that you are a strong[a] person who has endured so much in a resilient (incredible) way? Do you realize that just as our body tries to fight off viruses which come from the outside, we are all trying to fight off[b] behavior bugs?[c] They try to attack us. Bad habits invite us into their traps. Does this make sense? In response to that bad habit, we surrender.[d] The survival[e] of the bad habit takes place only because we encourage[f] it.
Acknowledgment	Do you realize that you are a person who has a bad habit that attacks you? That creates problems for the strong you? That may affect other parts of your life like _____? And other parts of your self? That invites or brings out the bad habits of other people around you? [To child] When does the _____ bug attack you? [To significant other] When he or she has been attacked, do you realize that there may be a bad habit that attacks you? [Repeat cycle]. [On a scale of 1 to 10], do you recognize when it attacks you? How frequently it does so? How intensely it does so? How difficult it is to control? The first time it began attacking you?
Relative influence	How would you be different if the bad habit didn't take over? If you could change your relationship to it? If your strong self could push it back? If your bad habit would let your strong self lead you? [Questions adapted from M. P. Nichols and Schwartz, 1991]. Do you recognize that when the bad habit doesn't attack you that you are more your strong self? Do more of what you want? That he or she [the significant other] may do more of or give you more of what you want? And let you do more of what you want? Would you like to push it back? When have you done so, and in what circumstances? What have you done to do it? What did you tell yourself that helped? How did you get ready to take this step? How did you resist turning back? In what other ways have you pushed back the bad habit? What developments occurred in other areas of your life that helped? What in your past helps understand how you took this step? [To child] How can you push back the bug? What does he or she do that lets you push it back? What can he or she do to help you push it back? [To significant other] Have there been times when you resisted or escaped the bad habit [and its invitation to react by screaming, hitting, crying, etc.], [and offered support or kindness instead]? How did you do it? What in her or his past enabled this step to take place? [Repeat cycle].

Table 9.3 *(Continued)*

Topic	Questions
Maintenance	By successfully pushing it back, what does this tell you about your abilities [that you may not have otherwise noticed], about your real self, about what you want from life? Why were you able to take a further step against it? How did you prefer to be a strong person with a weak bad habit rather than a weak person with a strong one? What did you do that helped push back the bad habit? How did you avoid the mistakes of others in the same situation? How did you manage to take this step forward? Do you realize that by doing so you have demonstrated your strengths and that you have cast a vote for yourself and not for the bad habit? Can you see how important your pushing back has been? That you have reached a turning point? Are growing? That by taking such action you have made a choice for yourself? That you have taught the bad habit a lesson by refusing to let it attack you? How does this new life story of your defeat of the bad habit contribute to a new direction in your life? Affect other parts of your life? Affect your attitude toward yourself? Your relationships? Your future? How will your new future differ from your old future? Had you known all this before, what difference would it have made in your old past? What difference will these steps make on a day-to-day basis? How will your family (friends) think (feel) if they become aware of these new steps that you have taken? Who would be least surprised by them and why? What have these steps told them about who you are? How could you let them know what has happened? [To significant others] How surprised are you at these changes? When did you realize that there is a new direction? How does this change your perspective of her/him? Remind you of better times? Do you realize that there may be "hiccups" where the bad habit temporarily comes back to attack you [contingency plans discussed]?

[a]Competent, skilled, resourceful, efficient, courageous, strong-willed, determined, caring, kind, sensitive, loving, warm, etc.

[b]Chase away, be boss of, control, push away, attack back, resist, contain, fight back, put in place, defy, limit the influence of, fight off, not hang out with, turn the tables on, declare independence from, become expert against, shrug off, gain the upper hand over, reduce to silliness or absurdity, defeat, revise the relationship with, turn back, separate from, escape from, be innocent against, direct, confine, dismiss, strike against, reauthor our story with, restory about, outrun, undermine, challenge, write a new account about, counterattack, counter, trick, make progress against, loosen grip of, win a victory against, extend influence over, improve 50% or _____ % against, salvage self against, deprive, outsmart, protest against, teach a lesson to, break through against, comeback against, overthrow, not cooperate or comply with, take the offense against, suspend, take further steps against, take life back from, be hopeful against, have own mind against, resurrect ourself against, pull rug from under, be effective against, walk away from, get the better of, trade, no longer accept invitations from, repossess self from, deny, oppress, influence, overwhelm, overcome, grip, trick, dominate, intrude, overpower, invade, infect, coach, sneak up on, suffocate, ambush, terrorize, haunt, catch unawares, take advantage of, subjugate.

[c]Habits, frustrations, attitudes, angers, fears, devious–cunning tricksters, Sneaky Poo, etc.

[d]Submit, succumb, give up, cave in, comply, resign, become docile, live under its rule, are made a fool of, sit in the corner, are tricked.

[e]Career, life-style, life support.

[f]Fuel, finance, watch, are an instrument of, are trained to be vulnerable to, are caught in the web of.

problem and in valuing the self. They encourage constructive interaction patterns, means of resisting relapse, and help to widen the net of social support (the audience).

Roots. Bateson and Foucault, in particular, have inspired White in the elaboration of his therapeutic approach. Bateson (1972, 1979) took a constructivist approach to therapy, affirming that objective reality cannot be known so that it can only be "interpreted." Meaning and understanding derive from receiving contexts or networked maps of premises and suppositions. Thus, a crisis can be positively connoted as progress without denying its distressing aspects, especially where some evidence for this can be culled. The narrative framework that we have discussed is similar to this approach for it views dominant life stories as limiting lenses which must be reauthored to incorporate the fertile, vital lived experience or unique outcomes that it excludes or neglects. By externalizing dominant stories, the therapist interrupts their "habitual reading and performance" and encourages their reauthoring.

Similarly, Foucault (in Bracken, 1995; Flaskas & Humphrey, 1993; Fairlamb, 1994; Madigan, 1992; Matthews, 1995; Morss, 1992; Redekop, 1995; Robinow, 1984; White, 1991, 1993a; White & Epston, 1990; Wylie, 1994a, 1994b) describes dominant discourses (cultural practices) that function as oppressive "gazing eyes," power vehicles, technologies of self, of power, of social control, specifications of being, normalizing truths, regimes of truth, invisible and isolating judgments, or subjugating unitary knowledges. Discourses can be positive (e.g., promoting certain myths, constitutive) or negative (repress, restrict, prohibit, control, hold back); and dominant cultural discourses are especially of the former ilk, and so are more insidious. They "thingify" or objectify persons into "docile bodies" or souls through controlling "dressage" operations or techniques that recruit individuals to discipline themselves. A person's own "normalizing judgment," "internalized gaze," or proactive positive (linguistic) power constitutively controls self-perception and presentation along externally defined lines. These "desired" ways of living are illusory truths that disguise the molding operations they entail, so that individuals happily collaborate and continuously collude to suppress their lives and relationships, their self and other selves, to the ruse. Dominant discourse practices come to mask the historical struggles that led to their entrenchment so that questions about their ascendancy are subverted. Railing is the most defiant action possible because alternative discourse potentials are limited by the omnipresent, invisible powers that are in control.

However, according to White, in the foucauldian world as it applies to therapy, subjugated, disqualified, secondary, local, (or anti-)knowledges can be resurrected or insurrect against primary knowledges, leading to critical work. Again, externalization techniques can help the author-client reconstruct and expand her or his history and future to encompass previously disqualified knowledges, once dominant discourses are deconstructed and juxtaposed, by bipolar questions, to preferred versions. Foucault expressed this juxtaposition of options in the following way.

> We must open our eyes ... to what enables people ... to resist the Gulag, what makes it intolerable for them, and what can give the people of the anti-Gulag the courage to stand up and die in order to be able to utter a word or a poem ... There is ... something which is by no means a more or less docile or reactive primal matter, but rather a centrifugal movement, an inverse energy, a discharge. (Foucault, 1980, pp. 136, 138)

White (1993a) differentiates Foucault's concept of technologies of control into two related forms. First, technologies of the self are self-governing instruments that shape the individual to external standards or specified ways of being. Second, technologies of power subjugate the other through policing procedures such as isolation, surveillance, and comparison to normative standards. Here White is building directly on Foucault's claim that "power produces knowledge" by stipulating the means people use to obtain power or be limited by it.

Variations of the Model

The Kan-No-Mushi. In applying the model of self-internalization and problem externalization in my clinical work, I encountered a difficulty in the way the problems are conceptualized. The implicit assumption is that problems must be vanquished, eradicated, and are negative or dangerous. However, even the most intensely negative emotions and moods (e.g., anger, jealousy) can be adaptive in appropriate circumstances, especially if they do not become chronic (Nesse, 1991). Moreover, the concept of the need to vanquish problematic behavior values power and confrontation. This may serve to accentuate inadvertently in the client the dimension of control as the primary personal resource in interpersonal problem resolution relative to more socioaffective dimensions such as sensitivity to self and others.

This point is driven home by Tomm et al. (1990) who explore a widespread concept in Japanese child rearing. Japanese parents often refer to the Kan-No-Mushi, which is a mythical bug or worm that causes children to have temper tantrums when agitated. In this sense is resembles an "inner" externalization. The bug is accused when children misbehave. No attempt is made to destroy the bug, but compromise or a modus vivendi with it is sought. There is no language indicative of defeating, mastering, or escaping the worm, for cooperation and peaceful coexistence are highlighted. The metaphor of the Kan-No-Mushi may assist developing Japanese children to better deal with frustration and anger, because they are being reared with an effective strategy for teaching social collaboration and personal control.

Freeman and Lobovits (1993) also eschew the confrontational approach inherent in White's approach to externalization, for it fits our culture's violent-prone morality and may lessen the client's sense of responsibility for her or his actions. Rather than setting up an opposition between the client and the externalized problem, Freeman and Lobovits use metaphors of relationship, relatedness, and coexistence. For example, instead of asking how the client was able to resist the tyranny of the problem, they ask about "dealing with," "communicating with," "turning away from," "seeking other options to," "aligning with," "making friends with," "liberating from," "freeing oneself from," "growing from," "embracing the transition from," "rising above," "climbing above," "letting go of," and "balancing in relation to" the problem.

Partial Selves.   Schwartz has developed a therapeutic model which readily lends itself to incorporation into White's externalization procedure (M.P. Nichols & Schwartz, 1991; Schwartz, 1994; Schwartz, Barrett, & Saba, 1985). He noticed that his clients engaged in internal sequential dialogues or relationships among internal voices, partial selves, or subpersonalities (autonomous internal personalities more complex than habitual feeling states or patterns of thought; also see Lester, 1993–1994, who reviews several workers who describe a pluralized community or panoply of selves, and Glass, 1993, who presents a fascinating case of multiple personality disorder, and relates it to the question of multiplicity in self). Schwartz also noticed that relationships among the parts of the self could even include protective alliances or conflictual power struggles that had repercussions for other partial selves. For example, the fearful and self-denial selves of one client aligned to block the disliked assertive self, just as her parents blocked this self in the past, producing rare but intense explosions of assertive anger. This reactive behavior only served to reinforce the entente by the first two part selves against the "dangerous" assertive part. In another example, a client avoided his sad self because it had "overtaken him" in past interactions, producing a fragile, helpless feeling. Other part selves united to "keep him away" from this self.

By asking clients to imagine their different part selves and have them interact, clients would experience the part selves' interference patterns. Schwartz asks clients to imagine themselves intervening to have the disputes stop by putting the part selves in "separate" rooms. When clients followed this advice, and separated from problematic part selves, they would experience a liberating calm, a differentiated entity Schwartz called the Self. The interfering parts "suddenly" were viewed more positively, and then negotiations would follow about a new relationship with these parts. For example, the assertive self described above was perceived in a compassionate way by the client to have been abandoned and isolated by her, and subsequent negotiations involved allowing it expression so that it would not try to usurp the floor.

Normally, the self is a trusted, respected, active leader or conductor of the internal family orchestra of potential selves, and engages in communication, nurturance, mediation, etc. Once this process is activated in clients, it continues between sessions and beyond. When applied to families, the goal is for the Self of each member to lead in turn in familial interaction. For example, in one dysfunctional cycle that was turned around, a child's rebellious part activated his father's furious part which in turn triggered his mother's protective part.

Clients are empowered because they realize that the only thing that has to change is a "small part" of the self or of the self of a family member. Family members may unite against problematic part selves. In the example above, the family viewed the rebellious child as relatively normal with one troublesome part and a Self that wanted to negotiate with it.

In therapy, aside from the imagining techniques described above, appropriate questions are asked; for example: "How difficult is it to control the part(s)?"; "How would the problem be affected if the part(s) didn't take over? If you could stay yourself instead?"; "How could you change your relationship with the problematic part(s) [and all the part's interrelations]?"; "Ask the part to let your Self lead the discussion about the problem this time and see how it goes."

Implications. Schwartz's model of therapy speaks to several issues raised about the internalization–externalization model of White. First, like White, Schwartz has the client focus on internalized strengths and minimize problematic behavior. However, instead of considering the problem external to the primary self, it is considered one of its own subcomponent partial selves. Moreover, rather them being a static entity, for the most part the problem manifests as an interaction among several partial selves. Also, the problem may involve more than one individual, for partial selves of several family members may be involved. Most striking is that Schwartz does not consider the partial selves as adversaries to be defeated or excised, but as integral units of the self which must be listened to, modified, transformed, etc. Destructive alliances between problematic part selves are disbanded by deft questions which open space for the maestro self to orchestrate relevant negotiations. In short, part selves form system wholes that seek equilibrium and may need therapeutic intervention to facilitate this process. The message here resonates with the one from the previous section on the Kan-No-Mushi. Problematic behavior has adaptive constituents that must be oriented and contained rather than eliminated. Part selves cannot fully suppress each other; and so therapists should not be expected to suppress them with finality, but only help the client integrate them into healthy relations. Another recently developed therapeutic technique offers conclusions consonant with the ones emerging in this section, as shall be shown below.

The Dialogical Self.   According to Bakhtin (1973), Feodor Dostoevsky created an innovative literary form, the polyphonic novel. Dostoevsky's heroes/thinkers voice independent, mutually opposing views so that his vision does not predominate in his work. His protagonists could even disagree-rebel against him. Their multiple perspectives were not unified under the author's voice, but existed in dialectical relation as a plurality of consciousnesses or worlds which created a coherence in the story. Kozulin (1991) described Bakhtin's literary theory as one that saw life as "authoring" or "becoming." Consciousness is open-ended, unfinalized, and indeterminate. It is a decidedly constructivist view, where the self seems discourse-immersed or "dialogical" (Hermans, 1995a, 1995b; Hermans, 1996a, 1996b; Hermans & Kempen, 1993; Hermans, Kempen, & van Loon, 1992; also see Shotter, 1992).

Hermans and colleagues use Bakhtin's ideas to help present their model of the self as a dialogical narrator. Through stories heard and told to different selves, the self builds models of the self, the world, and their relation, including ones that may be entirely novel, or emergent from the diversity of dialogues. The multiple *I* components of the self imaginatively narrate discourses with the multiple *me*'s in the actor role. The stories of each me is relatively independent of the others, but they can interact at times, just as in Dostoevsky's polyphonic script. Thus, a multiplicity of fairly autonomous, imaginal dialogical selves can interact dynamically and exchange information among themselves and with the actual self and others. There is a "dynamic multiplicity of relatively autonomous I positions in an imaginal landscape" (Hermans, 1996a, p. 33). They need not be subsumed to a master I, and in fact in some cultures clearly they are not, but in our culture the self does not fragment because the same master I is involved with the different selves. In summary, an individual's understanding of the world is imaginatively constructed, complex, multiple, polyphonic, relative, decentralized, dialogical, interpersonal, and compared with lived experience.

Nevertheless, the multiple selves may move toward yet never attain a final coherence or unification. A metaself akin to Schwartz's self may act centripetally to juxtapose, interrelate, integrate, and synthesize different I positions, but there may be resistance toward achieving this end. The dialogical self is like a composer (and not Schwartz's conductor) who combines different decentralized styles of being to produce new and unexpected self structures. It engages in synthesizing activities rather than in end-point synthesis as it makes meaning in movement. Self-construction is dynamic, endless positioning.

This polyphonic perception of the self has been applied to the therapeutic context by Hermans and colleagues. Clients actively explore their multiple selves in terms of their content and organization. Often these dialogic entities are incorporated images and narrations of significant others in the clients' past. The voice and messages of the therapist becomes one more self which clients carry with them and use to guide their behavior. Another help in therapy is that selves that have been suppressed may become liberated.

The approach of Hermans et al. is quite similar to that of Schwartz. Relatively positive and negative components of the supraself exist and engage in interaction. In this sense, the conception that they espouse fits with my own work, where self strengths are valued and its negative constituents are contained by internal dialogue, as shall be shown later on.

Authoring Tools in Narrative Therapy. Parry and Doan (1994) have applied White's concepts on externalization and narrative therapy to their therapeutic practice. They have excelled in turning a very new and abstract perspective into a series of systematized and powerful techniques. Their techniques of narrative therapy are summarized in order to provide the reader with a synopsis of their work, and to prepare the way for a description of my own applications along these lines.

Sixteen tools for inviting clients to become authors are identified. (1) The therapist should monitor any theme that could help in story reconstruction. Therapists could tell clients, "So it seems you have always tried to be a good (caring, competent, etc.) person. That part of your old story seems successful and liberating to you." (2) The old story-problem should be externalized, as discussed previously. Clients could be asked the many questions outlined previously in Table 9.3. Other examples include, "Does Anger visit you only 25 or 50% of the time? Could it not be Hurt In Disguise convincing you that you have no control over Rage? What did this habit protect you from in childhood? How can you get the result that you desire in your life today with it under control?"

(3) The strategies that old stories-problems use to resist change should be clarified. They automatically act to isolate clients, disqualify their personal experience, and impose impossible rules to live by, or standards of specification. For example, feelings that restrain include fear, guilt, self-depreciation, and anger. By active exploration or "going on spy missions" against these old stories and their strategies, space is opened up for counterstrategies without letting go the lessons to be learned from the original stories. Therapists could ask, "If you did research or go on a scouting

mission to discover how the old story stays strong, what would you find? In order to stay in control, is it that Hurt as Rage uses the strategy to convince you that others must respect and appreciate what you do, and if they do not, then your only choice is to cooperate with Rage?" (4) Deleterious specifications of personhood should be analyzed. These are particular expectations imposed by others and old stories on persons which act to constrain the expression of their selfdom. (5) Similarly, more general rules or agendas that delimit personhood should be enumerated. About points 4 and 5, clients could be asked, "Who authored that list of rules and roles by which you were expected to live? They do not play fair, and thrive when you pretend that they do not exist. But they are allergic to small changes, and cooperate with people who undertake them. Where did you get the strength to make these changes, to develop your own rules?"

(6) Clients should learn to tell multiple alternate stories. They should practice recounting different interpretations for the same sequence of life events and include in their new stories overlooked or censored elements. To foster this attitude, clients are asked the difference between living life as a sentence ending with a period or with a question mark. The former invites "givens, facts, and unchanging certainties, whereas question marks invite a language of wonderings, ponderings, and multiple possibilities" (p. 61). One could ask clients, "Which story has been most useful and which fits with the person that you would like to be? Which is an opportunity for growth and which is an invitation to trouble?" (7) Rituals should be used to mark and guide progress. Symptoms should be seen as "wake-up calls" or invitations to needed change, and rituals such as burning a list of personhood specifications could accentuate this frame of thought, or indicate that its construction has been consolidated or even completed. Therapists could ask their clients, "Do you think that it's time to consider a ceremony or a rite of passage to your new story, such as happens when young teenagers go through a communion or a bar-mitzvah? What would this ritual that you have chosen mean for your future?"

(8) Clients can be given imagined "as if" assignments. For example, they can role-play their new character in the reauthored, revised story that they are writing. They could be asked, "Imagine filming yourself in your new role, and then project what the camera might capture in your behavior. What if your old story is also a pretense? Which story would you rather 'pretend at', the old or new one?" (9) Therapists should be continually alert to client revisioning that has already taken place. Here Parry and Doan are referring to White's concept of unique outcome, as discussed previously. The goal is to elicit noticeable exceptions to the dictates of their old stories and create unique or new redescriptions and possibilities. Clients could be asked when they last did not cooperate with the old story, how they accomplished this feat, and what this means about them for themselves, for

others, and for their future. (10) Clients can be asked the miracle question (de Shazer, 1991), which asks them to describe how things will be different in their behavior right from the moment a miracle happens and their problems are solved. Once clients acknowledge that the miraculous changes would be wonderful, therapists could present a bifurcation which potentiates the miracle's concretization. For example, they could request that clients, "Flip a coin when you get up. If it comes up heads, pretend that the miracle occurred while you slept. If it's tails, try to pretend that nothing has changed."

(11) Clients are led to evaluate the colliding stories told by themselves and their significant others or family. Each person involved is asked the following questions: What is my story, where did it come from, who wrote it, and what role is important for me to play in it? What other roles do I need from the other(s) involved to play in the story? What supporting roles am I willing to play in any story told by the other(s)? For example, a client could be asked, "How did my story develop, and how does it impinge on her story and let conflict run our relationship?" (12) The clients and others are encouraged to gather round to listen to each other's stories by passing around a "talking stick" which confers the floor to whomever is in its possession. After the technique had been used, therapists could ask clients, "What was different in the stories that you heard? How could you continue to keep conflict at bay so that each of your stories could be heard on a regular basis?" (13) Clients should understand the intergenerational stories that run in families, and determine whether they control or allow personal control. In this regard, one could ask clients, "Which of those stories invited you to conform, and which ones asked you to be an individual (in the good sense of the word)?"

(14) Clients also should evaluate whether they are parenting their children to prepare them for life or parenting through (over)protection. They should determine which of these patterns they experienced in their upbringing. Appropriate questions here would include, "Should the title of your story be 'Protecting my adolescent with the risk that either he never leaves or rebels' or 'Preparing my adolescent for life with as few risks as possible'? Which title would your adolescent(s) prefer? Why?" (15) In a process of externalization, therapists should emphasize that there are conflicting stories, not conflicting people. For example, clients could be asked, "How does her anger childhood survival story, which we can see as the means she chose to protect herself from pain, explain her noncooperation and apparent dislike of you? How does conflict rely on the differences in your stories to remain in control of your relationship?" (16) Therapists should help clients examine the intentions in their stories, thus facilitating that they take responsibility for their behavior. For example, they could ask, "When did this intention start? Which of his intentions are most

surprising? What is stopping you from making a larger percentage of your intentions action rather than reaction?"

Revisioning Tools in Narrative Therapy. The therapist as editor serves as catalyst, guide, and consultant, and, if need be, second author of clients' stories. In their book, Parry and Doan (1994) describe 12 therapeutic techniques ("editorial guidelines") which help clients edit their stories so that therapists optimize therapeutic effectiveness. (1) Therapists should maintain a neutral stance. All stories are worthy of validation. Questions to clients that reflect and promote this attitude include, "Who would react most if each person's story was treated as equal invalid? Who would find it more difficult to believe that she could become more responsible?" (2) Therapists should be constantly curious as if they want to know everything. This entails that they do not present as persons who know everything, that they have a stance of questioning, and that they consider that their job is "not to know." (3) Clients merit compassion (e.g., they should be encouraged to believe that they can reauthor their stories). Compassion is facilitated by knowing all the parameters in a case, and should not be confused with approval. (4) Everything is potentially informative about clients (e.g., their manner of dress). Symptoms communicate information that cannot be communicated in other ways. (5) Therapists should "go with" resistance, because it is imperative to let clients reauthor their own lives. A resisted assignment must be an inappropriate one to begin with, especially given that not all may be known of relevant childhood survival stories, or it may reflect an inadequate rapport between therapist and client. (6) Therapists should be constantly vigilant for client strengths.

(7) When clients' stories are not making sense, the focus should be expanded (e.g., from marital disputes to patriarchy). (8) Therapists should give themselves the right not to know, to be confused, etc. This guideline also refers to the salutatory effect of not presenting as an expert so that clients are free to reauthor their own stories. (9) Therapists should not work harder than clients. They should stimulate and discover stories; and not dictate them. (10) Therapists should focus on underlying meanings of symptoms. (11) They should ask questions in the form of "What would it mean" (e.g., "if you let him try himself"?). (12) They should be gender sensitive.

CONCLUSION

Mills and Sprenkle (1995) list other developments in postmodern therapy that speak to its innovation, such as the use of reflecting teams, self-disclosure, and sensitivity to the feminist critique. The excitement being generated in the field of postmodern therapy is contagious, and I hope that I have conveyed my infection. To some it may appear more intuition and art than logic and science. However, Parry and Doan's work illustrates that the approach can be systematized, and White's work, in particular, forms the basis for a coherent therapy. However, the postmodern movement in therapy is missing a diachronic, developmental component, and in the following chapter, I show that part of my application of it to my clients includes this element.

CHAPTER 10

Transition Therapy

THE CURRENT THERAPEUTIC MODEL

Introduction

The affirmative face of postmodern psychology and therapy describes more than dissolution of personal and cultural totalizing myths, for it has a deep faith that personal growth is an inherently continual process. It envisages a profound respect and sensitivity for the other, for it maintains that if truth is contextual and nonunitary, then the truths of others merit a voice as much as the subjugated stories of the self. Thus, development and therapy both concern ongoing transformation toward higher-order integration and the discovery of factors that arrest, inhibit, or otherwise block rather than facilitate or promote it. But growth can take place on the horizontal as well as the vertical plane. Movement can follow the path to an alternate, better adapted state at the same level of complexity of a maladaptive one. Here, there is adaptive change, but without a qualitative leap to a superior level of functioning. In this sense human growth can be characterized as continual transition rather than continual transformation, per se, although it is granted that adaptive horizontal moves are facilitative of transformational ones.

Consequently, the most appropriate qualifier of the current postmodern therapy should be one that captures its change potential, whether the change be horizontal or vertical in nature. In this regard, I have chosen to label it a therapy of transition. At other points, I refer to it as multiplicity therapy, in keeping with another of its fundamental characteristics.

Despite postmodern therapy's insistence on the transformative nature of human nature, it is not genuinely developmental or diachronic. It has yet to well incorporate developmental theory into its field. In this regard, I have taken tentative steps to intertwine the current synthetic theory of development with postmodern therapy. Thus, I was tempted to call my therapeutic approach "synthetic therapy" or the like. However, I believe such a label would be premature without further integration of the synthetic developmental approach into the therapy.

Transition Therapy

Graphic Representation. In working with the internalization–externalization coordination model of therapy developed by White, I have instituted a range of adjustments in order to attempt to improve its efficacy. The main focus has been to use a graph that the client helps me elaborate and which serves as a schematic summary of the dialogue about her or his issues (see Figure 10.1). At times by the end of the first hour I have succeeded in visually capturing the presenting pattern of the client. Of course, not all clients appreciate or understand the visual models that are constructed, and not all cases are amenable to schematization such as this, but the procedure seems to fit many clients.

A major proviso to consider is that each client presents a unique constellation of developmental, familial, and behavioral features so that visual sketches of their dynamics must be individual and made from scratch. It is especially important to capture and amplify the particular strengths of each client (e.g., caring, competent, determined, courageous). Moreover, the actual words of the client are used as much as possible.

Dynamic Considerations. A client's problem is conceived as a second-order externalization in that an inner core self is seen as buffeted or surrounded by a problem (e.g., anger), which itself is seen as the product of external stresses. The client is made aware (through reflective questions initiating their own awareness, if possible) that the problematic entity can serve adaptive functions and needs channeling not elimination. Most often, an individual is not controlled by a static difficulty such as a negative emotion, for behavior such as this is founded in a social matrix. Consequently, the central self is mapped at the center of a vortex or vicious cycle of interpersonal patterns. Similarly, Safran and Segal (1990) have described dysfunctional interpersonal cycles. Arrows chart repetitive social exchanges, which I take pains not to consider lineal or causal but rather circular and bidirectional. These graphs of inner strengths and external problems usually are applied to an individual, but may also concern two individual diagrams which are juxtaposed, showing complementary or oppositional behavior cycles. A diagram could also concern a central *we* (couple, family) rather than a central *I*.

The depictions can be modified or refined with increasing knowledge of clients over sessions. Usually clients help unravel more complex stories

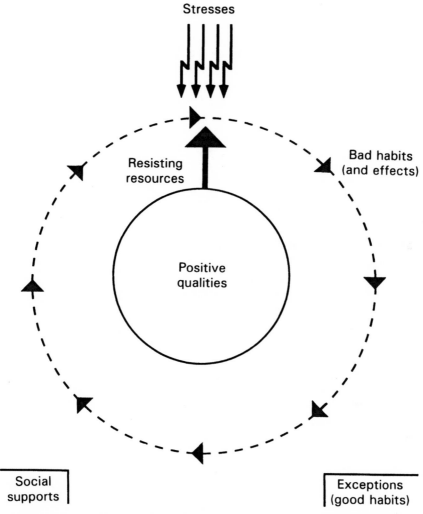

Figure 10.1. Self-Internalization/Second-Order Problem Externalization

as behavioral, developmental, and familial dynamics are elucidated. For example, personal and familial transitions over time may show parallel structures, inversions, etc. Clients can be shown to manifest patterns like or opposite to patterns in a significant other, to be seeking them out or avoiding them, to be actively reversing or resisting them, to be projecting them on others when not called for, or to be creating other negative patterns out of them.

Reflexive circular questions are used to have clients call forth more adaptive visions of themselves in the future (e.g., in one year). These questions are also used to have clients recall when and how they have successfully resisted their problem's invitation to behave in its image, and the positive consequences which resulted. In the end, an alternative story of the client's narrative is constructed where their positive behavioral exceptions in courage are noted and mapped for their effects on their surround. They are seen as transformative steps back to their central core because of the quality of that core, their inherent coping mechanisms, and the social support that they have.

After the graph is drawn, clients understand that the particular bad habit that had been the central character in their dominant story essentially is an externalized problem facing an array of personal and social resources with which it must deal. It is seen to have emanated from a set of stresses, so that it is not inherent to the clients. It is viewed as a behavior that is confronted by a series of strengths and coping mechanisms that have succeeded in the past in controlling it at times and allowing alternate options to emerge that tackled the issues to which the bad habit had been addressed, but in a more constructive manner. Finally, the support offered in the social milieu is documented, cementing solidarities that will continue beyond therapy.

Developmentally Appropriate Internalization/Externalization Stories. One way that I introduce the developmental dimension with my clients is to reframe their presenting problems as signs that they are in transition to a higher level of development. This procedure works well with teenagers, for example, because their age period by definition is considered one of transition. Thus, they are asked how their personal issue reflects a desire to grow, a well-intended but inappropriate solution toward growth, a possible learning experience for growth, etc. But this approach is a general one that does not consider the different stages of development.

In this regard, it has been possible to marry the synthetic developmental theory of 25 steps in development with the internalization–externalization coordination therapy being advocated. For example, by referring to Chapters 3 and 4 on optimal self and family behavior at each of the 25 steps of the current theory, to Chapter 7 on the model of the levels of the cognitive (mis)perception of the other, as well as to the prologue listing dangers in development, I try to place the primary difficulties to be externalized in my clients and their families roughly at the developmental level implicit in their functioning. Then, as part of the internalization–externalization process, the client and I examine inappropriate thoughts, feelings, and behaviors in the self and significant other(s) that comprise her or his dominant, problematic "old" story and that represent-encourage maladaptive functioning at the indicated level, and identify alternate more appropriate options that can foster movement away from that story. Table 10.1 lists story themes that can be used in the internalization–externalization process in this way.

Any one theme cannot capture the complexity of a developmental level. Thus, in this sense the ones chosen are inadequate. Also, they were chosen from the perspective of asking what developmental issues adults would face if they were troubled by a particular level. That is, the developmental steps involved were not considered from their original perspective in ontogenesis but from the viewpoint of what each developmental step means when transposed into the psychology of the adult. For example, the first level in the model concerns reflex coordinations, but from the point of view of adult psychology is best referred to as the issue of a continued will to live. Nevertheless, the story themes should serve as adequate markers in understanding development and the way it can go awry in clients.

It is essential to consider individual differences in this process, because the 25-step progression may seem like a universal model when in fact it is only a guide. The externalization story themes that are listed seem the primary ones for the 25 developmental steps, but they are not the only ones possible. Each client will manifest a pattern of problematic levels individual to him or her (perhaps necessitating an inclusive story theme, and one that is particular to her or him). Moreover, any one developmental level will be compromised in different ways in different clients according to developmental history, contextual factors, etc. Also, the slant that a story has at one level for a client will differ according her or his modal developmental level and the degree to which the story has been carried forward into more advanced levels. Finally, for the fifth level, problematic emotions may come in so many different guises that the example given, if used, should be employed only in a general way as a prelude to more specific externalizations.

In effect, the model presents a 25-step pathway in development that clients can grasp intuitively. Thus, when appropriate, it is recommended that clients be shown Table 10.1 to help them understand the developmental pathway. The first five steps concern the reflexive stage of development, and seem to describe a developmental path from self to other. It begins with the will to live, and follows with self- and then other-oriented behaviors (self-caring and other awareness and acceptance). The stage terminates with the onset of emotional activity. Then, in the five sensorimotor substages, an increasingly complex series of other-oriented social behaviors is seen to emerge (from conversational to sharing acquisitions). Next, in the perioperational series, self skills are emphasized primarily, from getting the self together to trying out different roles. In the fourth stage of abstractions, the developmental trajectory turns from refined cognitive acts to refined affective ones (from consciousness-identity to nurturing-love-empathy). Finally, the fifth collective intelligence stage seems marked by a

Table 10.1 Positive and Negative Themes in Stories about Development

Positive theme	Negative theme
1. Want to live, not hurt self	Want to die, hurt self
2. Take care of self	Not care for, ignore self
3. Be aware of, acknowledge other	Disregard, ignore other
4. Accept (care from) other	Reject care from other
5. Appropriate emotion (e.g., directed, adaptive)	Inappropriate emotion (e.g., rage, fear)
6. Active dialogue, involved conversation	Monologue, one-way conversation
7. Trust, confidence in other	Mistrust, no faith in other
8. Sociability makes other secure	Not securing other
9. Independence, autonomy	Dependence, self-doubt
10. Share, give and take with other	Not share, give or take with other
11. Self as together, coherent	Self as not together, fragmented
12. Initiative, energy, perseverence	No initiative, inertia, guilt
13. Accept/identify with parents	Reject/Not be like parents
14. Like to try best/know (e.g., at school)	Not try best/Feel inferior (e.g., rebellious/lazy)
15. Personality/Role try out	Personality/Role confusion
16. Open conscious (e.g., see past, change future)	Close, confine conscious
17. Search for identity, inner essence	Identity cut-off
18. Nurture, take care of other	Not nurture, not care for other
19. Feel mature in adult role	Feel isolated, alone
20. Empathy/genuine concern for any other, any community	Nonempathy
21. Feel integrated in society, e.g., act for community	Feel disillusioned with society, not being for community
22. Role model, demonstrate way to others	Self-absorbed, stagnate
23. Reevaluate/Redefine life-course/path	Crisis/confusion in life-course/path
24. Examine/Find joy in life's meaning	Despair at life's emptiness
25. Feel oneness with life, universe	Feel abandoned by life, universe

Note. Our lives are a series of stories that we tell to other people and to ourselves. This questionnaire lists common themes within these stories. They go from the developmentally simple to complex. In our development, we need both the positive and negative poles to some extent; for example, learning to become *independent* can only take place because of the importance of *dependence* in our development. Moreover, each developing individual tries to balance the positive and negative stories of each level. Also, each developing individual simultaneously lives at all levels, but with different relative proportions across them depending on developmental history, experience, situational context, hopes, etc. Individuals may feel that they are at one developmental level for one aspect of their lives, but at another level for another aspect. Also, for any one level, individuals may feel more positive than negative for one aspect of their lives but more negative than positive for another. Each person's pattern will be different, and there is no one pattern that is optimal. What is important is the person's will, acting in concert with social supports such as family and friends, to balance any dominant negative stories with positive alternate ones, and to maintain and strengthen positive ones. On a scale of *0 to 10* (e.g., 0 = not applicable, 5 = somewhat applicable, 10 = very applicable), indicate the degree to which each of these themes is applicable to the *last few months* of your life by writing beside each one the appropriate number. The total score for the two scores of any one line does not have to be 10. If you are not yet concerned by later particular levels, enter very low scores for them (e.g., 1 and 1, 0 and 0). For the remaining relevant levels, enter the values that are right for you (e.g., if more negative than positive, 2 and 10, 3 and 7, 0 and 5; if more positive than negative, 9 and 2, 7 and 3, 5 and 0). Feel free to ask questions. If the questionnaire applies to other than the last few months (e.g., to your hopes for next year), this will be indicated below.

movement from societal to interior focus (i.e., society-modeling functions to queries-meanings-spirituality).

Table 10.1 is accompanied by a note which permits its use as a scoring instrument of client progress. It emphasizes that there is not one normative or optimal developmental sequence, and that each developing person has a unique, valued developmental trajectory and that change is possible. Then, the client is asked to score separately on a scale of 0 to 10 the positive and negative story themes which encapsulate each developmental level. Once the instrument is administered, the therapist obtains an overview of the client's developmental status, and further questioning can pinpoint and clarify more specific information. The instrument can be administered across sessions to monitor changes in therapy, or its use can be altered in order to approach other issues. For example, it would be interesting to compare perceptions of the past, present, and future, so that specific developmental targets become enunciated as part of the client's multiple potential. Or each member in a couple or family can be compared for their own and significant other(s)' perception of themselves. In fact, the process of filling in the questionnaire may be therapeutic in and of itself, or the therapist may orient toward this end with appropriate intervention (e.g., going one down even for low score responses).

At the outset of the chapter, I decried the lack of a genuine diachronic or developmental perspective in family therapy. The current developmental perspective on the internalization–externalization process may, however, constitute one adequate rectification of this lack. In a certain sense, this developmental elaboration of the internalization–externalization process in therapy may represent the penultimate therapeutic contribution of the current work, at least once it has been applied across the lifespan with many cases so that its validity can be demonstrated effectively.

Terrell and Lyddon (1996) described the psychotherapeutic encounter as one where clients retell and eventually come to reauthor their lived stories. They equate the process to the changes in developing individuals' life narrative as they pass through Erikson's eight developmental stages. I hope that you concur that I have expanded their notion in the current 25-step developmental therapeutic model of story in therapy.

Case Presentation. I will describe the case of a client where graphic representations were important in both diagnosis and treatment. He experienced unjust paternal criticism and control as a child, which led him to feel like a boy and belittled. He learned what could be called a critical–control life-style. He would project and see others as critical-controlling, including his wife. Her neutral statements would get misinterpreted as critical or controlling. He did (or sought to) criticize and control others. This included his wife, his friends, and confreres in sports and music. In the same vein, he would criticize himself, for example, at work and in the previously mentioned recreational activities. When he felt that he had erred with his wife, he could break down and sob. Yet he tried to avoid these vicious cycles. He would apologize before any mistake was made in order to avoid potential criticism. Once he made the mistakes and was criticized, he would agree with the comments made without conviction in order to avoid being labeled controlling, but this submission could lead him to call his wife controlling. He manifested clear reversals in his behavior. For example, he would give excess praise and leave an impression of insincerity (e.g., praising his wife excessively with friends, not alone with her). Also, he would seek excess praise (e.g., asking for many "Thank you's" from whomever he went out of his way to help).

A secondary trap that he created involved amplifying the difficulty of projects in order to avoid criticism in case they did not work out. This also led to self-deprecation and criticism from his wife. Another trap emerged as a key focus in his improvement. He would not carry through in discussions of his feelings, but engaged in angry spirals with his wife, cutoffs, etc. Spontaneously, he had been trying at times to self-correct his maladaptive cycles (e.g., confronting his father in a quiet way, holding back unjust criticism of his wife). Thus, he had experienced an alternative behavioral pattern by bringing to bear appropriate coping mechanisms to help him resist learned reactions. A suggested intervention was that the couple engage in an on–off procedure of sincere communication of deepest feelings on alternate days for a week. One member of the couple had the freedom to speak and the other was to listen empathically, and vice versa. In combination with other therapeutic suggestions, and insight gained over the weeks, the client was able to recognize "the trap of being like Dad." He would feel his neck tighten, treat it as an early warning signal, and calm himself by repeating, "Stop to think. Think to stop," and other sayings. The tension would vanish and he would feel "elated almost." He said, "It's like a 'Pacman' chewing up the stress." This process enabled him to communicate increasingly in a more sensitive manner with his wife. Maintenance of gain techniques included the visualization of problematic emotions and their active transformation into related but more adaptive ones. For example, anger would slowly become determination or assertiveness, sadness metamorphosed into sensitivity, and a critical attitude became a desire to make constructive suggestions.

ADVANTAGES AND DISADVANTAGES OF THE CURRENT APPROACH

Pantheoretical Inclusion

Combs and Freedman (1990) present several graphs of client difficulties in which sequences of internal thought processes rather than behavioral actions are mapped. Sluzki (1992) describes multiple levels in which change in clients' narratives can take place. White and Epston (1990) speak of externalizing a series of levels in schizophrenia, from the problematic illness in the body to the particular symptoms and habits through to the "pathologizing assumptions and presuppositions." It will be recalled that Schwartz and Hermans et al. speak of part selves in this regard. In short, it should be recognized that in qualifying the core self or the externalizing problem(s) of a client (including any entrapping cycles), behavioral, cognitive, feeling, and part self components may be involved.

This underscores a main advantage of the current therapeutic technique. It is quite encompassing; almost any other theoretical model can interface with it, synergistically compounding their different strengths with it. For example, I integrate into this approach other brief therapeutic approaches. To be specific, de Shazer's (1991, 1993a, 1993b) solution-focused "miracle" question fits in nicely with it ("Suppose that a miracle happens during your sleep tonight and your problem is solved. What will be changed so that we will know that a miracle has happened?"). I actively recruit cognitive therapy in determining the constructs, values, and beliefs freezing the client's system, and attachment theory is used to schematize transgenerational interaction patterns. I have even found myself having recourse to more psychodynamic concepts such as identification, super-ego, etc., in graphing client narratives. Behavioral concepts have also come into play. For example, when I use systematic desensitization with driving-phobic clients who have experienced posttraumatic stress disorder after a motor vehicle accident, I constantly coconstruct with them self-enhancing narratives that they use to talk down incipient stress and externalize the problem (e.g., "Fear will listen to me when I speak to it because within Fear is Ear" [and we had a good laugh, too]).

Working with Clients

Another advantage of the current procedure is that clients readily can understand the concepts underlying the language used, e.g., bad-habit attacks from outside self. There is no hidden agenda, for the diagrams are mutually constructed with the clients and directly represent the concepts connoted (e.g., vicious cycle). Thus, clients can use the same language that I use with them in their languaging to themselves or to significant others in their surround. Mothers can use problem externalization almost immediately with their children once they grasp the concept. For example, one client had her child stamp out the "Not listen" bug immediately after some relative influence questions. In this vein, the concept of pushing back the bug readily lends itself to gesturally pushing out, which can be an important aid with children and even older clients.

There is a particularly salient advantage of these diagrams of self strengths in opposition to external problems. In order to trigger clients' own healing potential, it is necessary for them to control the damaging sequences that govern their lives. The therapist must guide them to actively explore alternative responses or narratives of interpersonal relatedness to replace maladaptive ones. When diagrams illustrate the latter in the client's own language, then the former can jump out of them or at least be coaxed readily from them. At times I will cut the arrows in a diagram's cycle with transverse lines, symbolically breaking the chains that the clients must break. Metaphor is not far removed from reality with this procedure.

Together, we work out plans that may involve doing the opposite prescribed by a vicious cycle, backing off from it, etc. For example, one overzealous disciplinarian was asked to let her child determine her own discipline when needed, and to her surprise there was no abuse of this privilege. One husband was asked to role-play his wife's tension in her interactions with her mother, and she was to be relaxed, knowing that she had his support. The relaxation she experienced when with her mother gradually grew.

Dangers

There are dangers inherent in this approach of graphically depicting vicious cycles and the like, and they stem from their careless use. Not everyone understands or appreciates visual representations, as mentioned. Some diagrams may be too complex to share with clients, and only parts of them may be needed in this sense. The diagrams may be reified or become real for the clients or therapist. They may become fixed and not flexible to change as new information is acquired. A vicious cycle involving significant others is not meant to blame them, for these others should be shown to have their own bad habits, but this message may not be heard readily. Finally, the therapist may be tempted to suggest direct ways of breaking vicious cycles instead of patiently prompting such strategies from clients in a collaborative dialogue. Clients should teach clinicians, not vice versa.

Cocreated Explorations

Introduction. Once the internalization–externalization process with clients has been initiated, I may also use the following therapeutic measure. I may ask the client what the set of the sayings listed in Table 10.2

brings to mind. The most recent one that I developed (in session with a posttraumatic stress client) was in response to the difficulty of dealing with chronic pain. ("Chronic pain. Chronic courage.") Clients to whom the table is given choose the sayings which are most appropriate for them. The goal is to cocreate in a reflexive manner partially revised feelings for and meaning narratives of the clients' past, their self and its development, their current context, and their future.

Another innovation that I can use in this regard is to ask the clients to examine the drawings of families pictured in various states of disharmony. The goal is to have them realize that all families, even those that seem to be better off, have their strengths and weaknesses, and that all families, even those that are in momentary difficulty, possess the means for self-healing.

Finally, I may read to and then give to clients a poem written by myself that captures the internalization–externalization process. I introduce this poetic therapy gambit by saying that the poem had been written to a couple-family-child-adolescent-individual adult, as the case may be. At least a part of the poem usually inspires any one client (group) to which it has been given. The poem reads as follows.

A Healing Poem

When did your Self and selves know
that It, the Bother,
should hear different ways
should speak the not-yet-spoken
should join the chorus
of your song to the world
that it could no longer be the maestro
among the array of voices
with which you compose to the world?

When did you come to know
that it would not live serfdom
and you would live selfdom
that you had always resisted
and exceptions had always persisted
that it was learned and external
and your strengths are innate and internal
that it could not know
the shadows of your future
in the dark of its past?

How did you escape from its furies
to put its demon fires at bay
and return to its metamorphosis?
How did you placate its fearing voices
have your wise selves resource for you

undo the hidden plans of subjugation that it had for you
convert its wasted energy to directed synergy?

How did you decide to climb your mountain
to become guides who grow in guidance
When did you know that interior victories
could mark your mind
like the words of a holy book mark its pages?

Who can attest to your valor
who knows the majesty of your strengths?
To whom shall we narrate this tale of liberation
this story of vanquish and reconstruction
this discovery of the path that leads
to other paths where all paths are possible
this new history of your self and its multiplicities
this new scenario of hope and ardor
this new play where you are writing
the dialogues of being and sharing
the discourses of giving and caring
the actions of competence and daring
the feelings of tenderness and loving?

How did you create
to whom should we relate
this desire for growth and spirituality
this quest for learning and mutuality
where you fuse with the eternal
become the maternal and paternal
and
know and understand
by warm logic
and
by paintings from the soul?

You have been your witness
and I have been your scribe
You have mined the buried script of your life
and I have heard you restory it
You have chosen not to ignore
the sages among your selves
that were always there
and I am listening to their parables
When one wing decides to glide free
the other follows
When one feather is cupped in the hands of the wind
the others share in the journey away from destination
And when all is revisioned,
when your emancipatory handiwork
has fashioned from the clay of yourself
a growing sculpture,
what will your archeological self
tell the Bother as it lies part of the sand?

Table 10.2 Circular Reflexive Savings
for Use in Counseling

Construct	Complement
Know the past	Allow the future
Bad habits are learned	Unlearn bad habits
Think to stop	Stop to think
Small victories	No defeats
Lose vicious circles	Win virtuous cycles
Love seeds	Seed love
Wealth buys goods	Good buys wealth
Free pain	Free gain
Open feelings	Feel openings
Givers receive	Receivers give
Sharing needs friends	Friends need sharing
Talk honestly	Honesty talks
Trust communication	Communicate trust
Hurting hurts hurters	Domineering dominates dominators
When fear freezes	Freeze fear
Laugh a little	Live alot
Family binds	Bind family
Caring rewards	Reward caring
Magic words	Work magic
Fair discipline	Fair response
Teach learning	Learn teaching
Respect stops excess	Excess stops respect
Do your best	Can't be better
Face death	Face life

EDUCATING PROFESSIONALS

Introduction

The following excerpts of a report (a combination of two similar cases, with the background reduced in scope) illustrates in depth both the nature of brief systemic therapy as I practice it and the difficulty that this approach entails when writing reports. I believe that proponents of this perspective must not shirk from their responsibilities to their ethic, and can emerge with effective reports when guided by it.

A Report on a Client

Background.   Our office received a phone call from lawyer X about one of his clients. He asked us to contact his client Mr. Y in order to set up 12 to 14 hours of therapy for anger management and alcohol drinking prior to an upcoming court date.

On the positive side, Mr. Y stated that he was sorry for what had happened, and that he was looking forward to reconciliation with his family. My therapeutic style is to ask a lot of questions so that clients bring forth the solutions to their problems in dialogue rather than to lecture, teach, or deliver instructions or sermons where solutions are spoonfed to them. Mr. Y consistently gave answers reflective of an understanding of how in the past at times he had gained self-control of his behavior even in the most difficult of circumstances, and how he could continue to do so in the future.

On the negative side, Mr. Y foresees the future as one where there are more home activities, control, and listening in the family, but I sensed that this may be a control and listening from his perspective, in particular. Thus, a good part of our therapy involved techniques which not only fostered the acquisition of self-control but also fostered better ways of heading off disputes through appropriate communicatory strategies. The legal system has acted as a brake on his behavior, and now it is up to Mr. Y to internalize increasingly the lessons learned so that he becomes his own manager.

Treatment.   Primarily, befitting the brief systemic therapeutic approach, we engaged in conversations where I would listen empathically, ask therapeutic questions, seek solutions to the issues confronting Mr. Y within his own behavioral repertoire even if the solutions or their precursors occurred infrequently, emphasize personal resources and strengths, and create with him emergent constructive meanings of the actions of both he and the other family members.

One theme was to explore the past and try to elucidate intergenerational transmission patterns in attachment and in discipline. My approach here is to ask questions like, "How is that behavior by your parent(s) in your childhood not only similar but also different from your behavior with your son?" In this manner, Mr. Y came to understand in part both the chaining of the past to the present and his actual and potential escape from its negative aspects.

Another theme was to examine the context of the drinking and physical actions against his son. We constructed a step-by-step videopicture of the manner in which family disputes arise and drinking takes place. Typically, in Mr. Y's case there were external stresses which precipitated a lack of control, whether it was verbal, behavioral, or drinking-related, and according to me a simultaneous desire to control family members. At this point in therapy, when the vicious circles are clear, I underscore that the bad habits that develop in clients are not inherent in them, but are consequences of exterior factors such as financial pressures, work pressures, parental pressures, and so on. And with their personal resources and social supports, that we list together, I emphasize that clients are fully capable of resisting the bad habits that stresses engender. Bad habits are learned and not prescribed by innate factors, and so can be unlearned or controlled.

One of the first things that we did was have him role-play his son so that he could try to experience the emotions felt by his son as a result of his physical actions. I felt that this exercise was less successful than it could have been. Also, when asked to list the positive attributes of family members, the list for his son was difficult to get out, simple, and short. However, I feel that Mr. Y will come to perceive his son in a better light as new family patterns of being are established through the processes that have begun already and that I helped solidify.

A major topic that we covered was techniques of self-control. This began with the notion that in dialogues there is active listening, appropriate questioning, validation of the other's point of view even if it is not accepted, negotiation, communication, reasonable reaction when reaction is called for, and the search for compromise and especially win-win outcomes in disputes.

I introduced an externalization of his bad habit by calling it a virus and asked him how he could resist its infection of his mind. He invoked his willpower and his "thinking power." I also called his bad habit a "Fighting Story" (or "Anger"), and asked him how he could resist its influence on his mind ["When it wants to visit you, what could you tell it?"], so that he and his family could write a "Loving Story" instead. Again, he spoke of the control that he had in general of his behavior and the knowledge of the consequences when he did not.

The language of offering options rather than dictates was introduced. Instead of saying things to his son like, "You have to listen," I asked him if it might be better if he stated that there is a choice to listen or not, with an explanation of the consequences involved with each option, so that his son ends up making the choice about which pathway to follow rather than having but one pathway imposed on her or him.

Some of the other procedures used in therapy were: (1) to examine his miscognitions about the value of the bad habits under question, and (2) to explore means of reinforcing in a constructive way some of the behaviors that he was seeking in his family, and how he derived certain constructive reinforcements (e.g., happiness) when he did not engage in his bad habits. All these techniques are complementary, and act to reinforce a sense of personal agency and a sense of internal control of issues, making them more manageable.

Conclusion. It should be clear at this point, in terms of the result of therapy, that Mr. Y seems to have learned much during our week together:

He brought a lot of desire and will into the sessions, and I acted to bring forth, solidify, and expand upon his self-knowledge. However, he still clings to some ideas and expectations that may lead him into conflict with his family. Nevertheless, in terms of a prognosis, I trust that his solidified, expanded, and newfound habits and hopes are ingrained sufficiently in his behavioral repertoire and coping mechanisms so that vicious circles in behavior that lead to physical actions will be avoided.

To conclude, Mr. Y is part of a sociocultural matrix that, on the one hand, promotes either implicitly or explicitly (and even condones: see recent Canadian legal decisions on men, drinking, and criminal behavior) stereotypic, patriarchical, and sometimes abusive/violent images of contemporary men. Yet, on the other hand, our society decries the effects of this model. The individual and her or his culture are fused in a spiralling interdefinitional dance, and until we as a society as a whole become more just partners in the exchange, the confusing signals sent to Mr. Y and others like him should be held responsible in part for their behavior.

CONCLUSION ON THERAPY

White's internalization–externalization coordination therapy appears to be conceptually similar to activation–inhibition coordination in clinical work. The former seems to be one exemplar of the latter, for in helping the client to internalize an alternative narrative replete with a competent, strong sense of self, the therapist is cultivating the appropriate field of activation, and in helping the client to externalize the problem and its vicious cycles, the therapist is targeting the appropriate field of inhibition. White (1986) speaks of the client's need for restraint in his internalization–externalization therapy, fitting the current emphasis on inhibition in this regard.

Usually the components in a client's bad habit can be functional if deployed appropriately (e.g., anger). They may need more appropriate contextual expression, removal of maladaptive intruding exaggeration in a normal sequence, additions to the sequence which refine it, etc. Thus, more often than not, the therapeutic endeavor is not aimed at full suppression of a pattern. Nor could it be construed as a directed, unidirectional activity, for coconstruction with the client takes place both in terms of understanding the issues and finding ways to use them to alter behavior.

Consequently, in terms of Table 9.2, the current technique both balances activation (internalization) with inhibition (externalization) and is constructivist in doing so. Moreover, it adds to the empowerment of the client and promotes self-healing, for example, by using Tomm's interventive interviewing technique when engaging the client in therapeutic conversation. In examining transgenerational patterns, attachment theory has proved invaluable.

Finally, the current approach can include a developmental perspective. It is called transition therapy for this reason, for in being genuinely developmental it maintains the view that clients wish to follow an inherent growth to higher orders of psychological integration, but they may be stuck in maladaptive behavioral patterns impeding their progress. Consequently, the therapy aims at horizontal movement outside these vicious circles in order to foster vertical movement to more advanced developmental levels. For both cases, horizontal and vertical change, activation–inhibition coordination would seem essential. Emerging adaptive habits inevitably grow on the back of controlled, transforming maladaptive ones.

Process researchers in psychotherapy (e.g., Eckert, 1993; Greenberg, 1991; Persons, 1993) focus on the particular events, functions, transactions, and so on, in the therapeutic encounter that best foster client progress (e.g., therapist empathy, client nonverbal markers indicative of crucial experiences and/or readiness to change, the encouragement and effect of empowerment, the fostering of compensatory skills and alternate schemata of central beliefs). In this regard, the concept of activation–inhibition coordination may offer a guide to the way therapeutic advance is enhanced. That is, Rosen (1991) maintains that all therapies work in one way or another by inducing knowledge revision and reorganization. Thus, any form of therapy, including activation–inhibition coordination in therapy (e.g., internalization–externalization balancing), may succeed when it promotes the perception of contradiction or incongruities. Disequilibrium sets in, through an inherent confrontation of incompatible polarities in thought, accentuating conflict. This leads to "work" toward disconfirming the more maladaptive conceptualization. Resolution and equilibration follow by an integration of the more adaptive conceptualization into primary behavioral processes. This transformative journey on the part of the client seems to involve activation–inhibition coordination of adaptive–maladaptive schematic representations and behavior. Thus, activation–inhibition coordination, functioning as controlling parameters guiding state shifts toward increasing complexity (to use the language of dynamical systems theory), may serve as an important underlying variable in the experience of therapeutic progress.

The next chapter deals with the theme of epistemology. Basic notions on constructivism and empiricism were introduced in this chapter, and the former approach, in particular, is differentiated in the chapter.

CHAPTER 11

Epistemology

CONSTRUCTIVISM VS. OBJECTIVISM

Description

Constructivism (organicism, idealism) is diametrically opposed to objectivism (mechanism, empiricism, positivism, realism, rationalism, determinism). Their epistemological stances are compared in Neimeyer (1993, 1995; Neimeyer & Feixas, 1990). Constructivism argues that reality is actively construed as meaning (ordered, invented, constituted, created; Held, 1990) in the knowledge-generating organs of the observer, and so does not exist in one particular fashion but is multiple (also Feixas, 1990b; Keating, 1991; Real, 1990). The construals are generated actively in that they are constantly sought, self-organized, and revised and are proactive and anticipatory. Meaning of the experienced world is coconstituted or negotiated in self–world interaction, and so is adaptive, contextual, and historic. It is not inherent in the external world nor the internal state but is the product of the conjoint interaction and relation of the two (Buckley, 1967; in Duncan, Parks, & Rusk, 1990). Thus, reality is a product of mind.

Similarly, hermeneutics concerns reflection on the meaning or "interpretative character" of psychology and related disciplines (Tappan & Brown, 1992; Terwee, 1990). Through examining larger contexts, history, internal relations, etc., meaning becomes evident in phenomena. Meaning must be explained from more than initial conditions and laws, for it even can be implicitly (re)constructed from context, for example. Thus, knowledge can be derived from other than objective empirical means. In short, according to hermeneutics, there seems to be a dialogue between subject and object in reality construction.

For objectivism, humankind is reactive, and knowledge is a gradually acquired, direct copy or representation of absolute truth and not subjectively constructed through successive interpretations. There are immanent facts to be discovered; the invention of knowledge is a false process. There is only one true reality and it can be verified by the senses. The notion of multiple possible realities is anathema to objectivists. This school also rejects the concepts of (1) validating interpretations through consensual processes and fit with existing knowledge structure, and (2) hierarchical, self-organized systems. Objectivists believe that human interaction is instructive, involving the transmission of information. They reject the notion that interaction such as this consists of structural coupling or systems coordination (and that instruction is imposition; Held, 1990).

Comment

Constructivism is garnering some unexpected adherents. Ellis (1990) disavows any link to objectivism in ratioemotive therapy, long considered a bastion of epistemological realism in therapy. Learning theorists such as Bandura (1989) emphasize that there is mediation by expectations, beliefs, etc., in determining the effects of stimuli on behavioral responses. Sperry (1991), whose neurological work on split-brain patients is classic, argues that free will influences brain function. Nevertheless, objectivism is not limited to a vestigial bevy of radical behaviorists. This viewpoint dominates much of contemporary psychology, and is boosted by some research on neural networking, artificial intelligence, etc., which equates mind with machine.

Moreover, there are contemporary theoretical positions that emphasize the way humans are adapted to the ecological niche which they inhabit. Darwinian natural selection assures us that sensory, perceptual, and cognitive faculties are primed to detect and analyze salient features in the milieu, because there are external realities to which the organism must accommodate. Similarly, in the gibsonian perspective the environment offers "affordances" which fit preexisting, adapted information-processing mechanisms (Gibson, 1982; Reed 1993). Although I have emphasized constructivism throughout this work, sometimes stimuli do have a direct effect on behavior, outcomes are entirely predictable by examining factors extraneous to construals, reality is certain (e.g., a recent violent rape of a saleswoman was taped by a security camera; child abuse is immoral), etc. In terms of therapy, sometimes we do have to edify by instruction, seek out unconscious influences, modify reinforcement contingencies, extinguish maladaptive responses, replace them by coping mechanisms previously unlearned, and train cognitive self-inhibitions. It is best to be theoretically and practically polyvalent, eclectic, and pragmatic without being dilettante, haphazard, and inscrutable.

I maintain an intermediate, integrated, emergent position on which of the two epistemological schools under discussion seemed adequate, by arguing that at least six constructivist epistemological positions may co-exist in one overall model called coexistentialism, and that among them is one where objectivism is central. Lyddon (1995; Lyddon & McLaughlin, 1992) has come to a similar conclusion at the end of a presentation of four of these schools. Similarly, Mahrer (1995) argues that individuals construct their worlds in a variety of ways, and reality informs only some of them. In the following, the six schools are described, leading to their integration.

Radical, Material Constructivism

Maturana (1991) is an example of a radical constructivist, for he proposes that reality is only a conjecture, a hypothetical proposition exclusively a function of the workings of a species' cognitive structure and thus experience. The underlying assumption is formist, i.e., the intrinsic, stable attributes of phenomena (e.g., categories, distinctions) explain their functioning. The constructing organ of the knower is much more important than the triggering stimulus or information in the environment in understanding how realities or distinctions are "brought forth" (Maturana's structure determinism [1991]; Israelstam, 1989). Thus, the knower is organizationally closed and self-organizing, with neither input from nor output to an independent reality. One can never know what exists in reality, for there is no way of comparing one's conjectures about it with its properties, or perceive it independent of these conjectures. This is not to say that "nothing exists," for truths of situations grow within and are revealed within the discourse that produced them (Stenner & Eccleston, 1994).

Efficient, Objective Constructivism

In contrast to this position, efficient, objective constructivists view the process of construction of knowledge as dependent on information inflow (Lyddon). This form of constructivism endorses the mechanistic postulate that knowing is an active process of receiving and storing meaningful environmental input, and that phenomena may be understood by analyzing linear cause–effect relations, or their efficient cause. That is, although knowledge acquisition is active and interpretive, it is largely derived from and linearly directed by the environment. Cognitive models (e.g., schemata) essentially reconstruct (identify, transform) preformed information contained in the external environment, although self-mediated influences obtain. These models are rule-governed, interpretive, yet environmentally determined structures. In short, this view is the one which has most incorporated objectivism within its framework.

Social, Formal Constructivism

Social, formal contextual constructivism assumes that meanings are actively and continuously constituted in a social context, in particular, and thus constrained by the social milieu (Lyddon). It is based on the assumption that meaning emerges from the form or organized pattern of phenomena within context over time, or from a contextual, situated, continually changing synthesis. Thus, symbolic social interaction and exchange, such as conversational language and negotiation, delimit personal concepts. Individual understanding is built on social experience, where socially constituted knowledge forms are imposed on the interpretation of and action in experience. This position has taken a narrative turn. Conversation is seen as reality (Anderson, 1993; Anderson & Galooshian, 1990; Galooshian & Anderson, 1992; Hoffman, 1990; Penn, 1992). "Human beings who live in language, live in a *multiverse* rather than a universe" (Dell, 1985, p. 16). White and Epston (1990) have a somewhat similar position in their notion that the individual textually authors the meaning of her or his life history. Mair (1988) writes:

> Stories are habitations. We live in and through stories. They conjure worlds. We do not know the world other than as story world. Stories inform life. They hold us together and keep us apart.
> We inhabit the great stories of our culture. We live through stories. We are lived by the stories of our race and place. It is this enveloping and constituting function of stories that is especially important to sense more fully. (p. 127)

Existentialism

Vandenberg (1991, 1993) contrasts the "epistemic constructivism" of Piaget with an existentialist view of development (e.g., Buber 1923/1970; May, 1983). According to this latter view, the primary focus of living derives from the uncertainty of the meaning of life and death. Reality is not knowable. Thus, humans adapt to the futility of life by commitment to belief in shared meanings and social customs. We are social from birth and moulded to relate to "cobeings" with a willed sense of morality.

Critical, Final Constructivism

This constructivist approach is based on the organismic postulate that knowledge is constructed as a dialectical synthesis of the inherent contradictions that emanate from individual–environment interaction (Lyddon). The concept of final causation undergirds the position, in that it conceives of phenomena undergoing a directed, teleological unfolding toward greater although unspecifiable complexity of organization and abstraction [Lyddon, 1995; according to Mahoney's [1995] definitions of teleology and teleonomy, *teleonomical* may be the more appropriate root word here because it refers to a less explicit developmental destination than the former.)

Piaget's epistemological position is an example of critical constructivism. Lyddon describes Piaget as a formal constructivist who sees humankind as actively self-organizing, open, and emergent, or transformational. His approach has been called constructive interactionism or scientific realism by Chapman (1988). That is, the understanding of reality is acquired in an indissociable interaction between epistemic subject and external object across time. It is developmental and constructive in that schemes or relational totalities are used to interact with the world, and they evolve through (pro)active emergent accommodative (re)construction or self-(re)organization over time in response to discrepancies between assimilating cognitive schemas and unassimilable encountered realities. It is convergent or scientific realist in that object properties become known only through their study in interaction. Developing humans move away from an initial state of ignorance by coordinating a broader range of perspectives (decentering) and developing a better approximation of reality. But there are asymptotic limits to knowledge acquisition, for it can be endlessly approached but never reached. Knowledge of reality is dependent on the knower, who is also part of reality. Thus, as the knower acquires knowledge, "reality, in effect, comes to know itself."

Piaget's stance can be summarized as arguing that reality informs its gradual construction. Through successive approximations developing humans approach better but never reach absolute reality construction. Other theorists have maintained positions similar to Piaget's. Pascual-Leone's dialectical constructivism is similar to its parental counterpart, that of Piaget, but adds the element that part of the constructive process includes a dialectic between emotions and cognitions (see Chapter 9). According to Feixas (1990b), Kelly (1955) is an example of a critical constructivist, in that he affirms that external reality is the signpost that constructivist humankind aspires to understand. There is a true universe which gradually is apprehended.

Coconstructivism

Speed (1991, 1994) gravitated to a compromise position on the question of constructivism versus objectivism. Constructivism views thoughts as determined by what we know, objectivism contends that reality determines what we know, while coconstructivism maintains that knowledge is grounded in the relationship between the knower and the known. That is, objective reality exists, but it cannot be known with certainty; it is constructed or mediated by social intercourse, "generated within the social groups in which we participate." Here, there is a similarity with social constructivism. Following Elias (1971), for Speed (1991, 1994) knowledge acquisition is a gradual accumulation of advances in relation to prior levels of knowing. It does not concern truth validation but the realization of more adequate versions of what truth must be. Here, the similarity lies with critical constructivism. Also for Speed, reality contributes to what the observer observes and cannot be discounted in the construction process. "Just because reality is filtered through our perceptions does not mean it does not exist and does not affect those perceptions" (Speed, 1991, p. 407). Here, Speed maintains a position comparable to objective constructivism.

Pocock (1995) elaborated Speed's (1991, 1994) model of coconstructivism by placing it in the narrative tradition. Humans are perceived as developing increasingly better stories in their interpretation of reality. Constructions survive only if they fit the constraints of external reality, even if the full truth of reality can never be known. Constraints concern pragmatic adaptation, others needs-wishes-feelings-beliefs, justice, emotions, etc. Thus, the better story position ignores neither the modernist, objectivist nor the postmodern, relativist perspectives on reality, while protecting against their extremes. Larner (1995) calls Speed's intermediate stance between the modern and postmodern the paramodern, e.g., the known power differentials in society are to be acknowledged even as a therapist adopts a nonknowing stance facilitative of client story reconstruction.

Coconstructivism is an epistemological stance with many appealing characteristics. It emphasizes gradual knowledge acquisition and there is room for absolute realism in reality comprehension. Objective truth can impose on apperceptive faculties at times (see the examples above). Knowledge acquisition is not always only uncertainty reduction.

THE RELATIONSHIP OF THE SCHOOLS

Table 11.1 provides a summary of the six schools of thought about constructivist epistemology. They can be classified according to their perspective on two major issues. (1) Does objective reality influence knowledge acquisition? (2) Is knowledge acquisition always a process of social construction or not?

There are three epistemological stances which do not adhere to the view that objective reality can influence very directly knowledge acquisition. First, radical constructivism argues that reality does not influence the

**Table 11.1 Epistemological Stances about Constructed
Knowledge Acquisition of Reality**

Is knowledge acquisition of reality social?	Does objective reality influence its acquisition?	
	No	Yes
Not relevant	Radical, material constructivism (reality is constructed)	Critical, final constructivism (reality informs its gradual construction)
Not necessarily	Existentialism (constructing is reality)	Efficient, objective constructivism (reality dictates its construction)
Yes	Social, formal constructivism (shared constructing is reality)	Coconstructivism (reality informs its social construction)

knowledge acquisition process and is apprehended through mental approximations; it is invented. Because reality is constructed within organs of the constructor one can read implicitly in it that social processes are not necessarily inherently important in knowledge comprehension. Second, existentialism attributes fundamental importance to the social process in knowledge acquisition, in that it argues that participatory cobeings share cultural meanings in the quest for stability in their uncertain, truth-unknowable lives. Given existentialism's emphasis on the angst of void, it seems that in existentialism constructing, per se, becomes crucial in the acquisition of knowledge. Third, social constructivism's approach of reality construction through conversation echoes the previous one, but adds that only through social dialogue can constructs of reality emerge and change.

Three epistemological positions contrast with the ones just enunciated by advocating that objective reality can directly affect the process of knowledge acquisition. First, critical or alternative constructivism (e.g., Piaget) maintains that humans gradually acquire an increasing accuracy in their representation of reality through the adaptive accommodation of schematic constructs of interactions with reality. But in his writing, Piaget clarifies that reality construction is not necessarily a social act, for his primary examples concerned tasks with inanimate objects rather than animate, social human ones. Second, efficient constructivism perceives reality's role as more direct and immediate in fostering its own understanding. In this epistemological approach social objects may be involved in the process of knowledge acquisition, but it does not obtain that they are necessary to it. Third, in coconstructivism, objective reality always coparticipates in or informs the social dialogue in which conceptions of reality are formulated.

CONCLUSION ON EPISTEMOLOGY

Coexistential Constructivism

Given that it is impossible to establish which viewpoint of reality presented here is the "true" one, I believe that each harbors a certain validity. The most integrative approach to epistemology is the developmental, final or epistemic, critical constructivism of Piaget. However, one's perspective of reality is grounded in what objective reality informs, what is cocreated in social dialogue, both verbal and nonverbal, and the way cognitive skills change with successive qualitative steps in growth. And not all objective reality involves constructivism, for realism has its role in any polyvalent model of epistemology. Also, not all constructions are social, although most must be so rooted. Finally, not all reality comprehension is influenced by objective reality. Thus, I advocate a flexible epistemological posture, one that can be called coexistential.

The diverse approaches documented here seem mutually exclusive on first glance, especially in terms of what an individual may believe at any one instant of time. However, a lifespan perspective would acknowledge that any one individual may come to believe more than one of these models of reality if not all of them. They are not only relative to each other, but also they are dialectically symbiotic, permitting their holistic synthesis into one coexistential unity where each is subsumed into a fuller vision of knowledge acquisition of reality.

Mahrer (1995) suggests a similar model, where constructions are considered multiple in origin. The world acts on the person with its reality constraints, but the person is active before it even to the point of deciding to be either passive before its impingements, oblivious to them, or coconstructive with it in creating lived reality.

Lyddon (1995) offers a similar conclusion. According to him, different epistemological positions seem viable, each with a unique window for understanding reality. Moreover, the various constructivist epistemologies are coevolving toward "a more integrating and encompassing model" of human knowing involving "continual becoming" (e.g., being agentic, purposeful, generative). In this regard, Mahoney (1995) speaks of traversing eternally the unknown of arriving moments, and in a poem describes the pilgrim in process who is given the secret that one should be ever in quest.

Being-Becoming-World/World-Becoming-Being

Lyddon's conclusion on continual becoming as the pinnacle of being human, brings us to a more elaborate way of examining the manner in which the six constructivist schools coexist. It relates to Heidegger's concept of being-in-the-world or Dasein, which concerns an opening to being and meaning (Dallmeyer, 1993; C.U.M. Smith, 1994). According to Heidegger, Dasein is not a separate state, but "the unity of living-through" and part of it is being aware of itself. But in everyday inauthenticity, Dasein is hidden from itself. Being-in-the-world also involves relating in a caring manner to fellow "cobeings" in concernfulness, gathered together and in relation among themselves. Also, it involves a bringing-forth self-unfolding of its origins as well as its fruits ("as is shown by the blossoming-forth of blossoms"). Thus, it is dynamic potential. "It is a mode of being ... which is never static, always moving forward towards new potentialities ... 'Dasein is in every case what it can be, and in the way it is its possibility'" (Heidegger, 1927/1962, p. 143).

Heidegger insisted that the concept of being-in-the-world underscored as arbitrary the cartesian duality of mind and body. Objectivists maintain that the mind, the will, the self, the soul, and similar phenomena can be reduced to the body, the brain, the physical, and physiological processes. Humanists and others contend that these phenomena exist as irreducible wholes, akin to the systems theory argument that there are emergent properties that can form from system element ensembles.

Moreover, Oyama (1993) and Packer (1993) both maintain that the separation of body and mind does not take place when one partakes in genuine mutuality with the surround, so that the problem of cartesian duality is obviated in this type of encounter. For them, being-in-the-world is quintessentially human. Similarly, we have seen that Fogel speaks of "being-in-relation," Bakhtin of human becoming, and Buber of I-thou authentic relatedness. Vygotsky (1981) expressed something similar when he wrote that "humans' psychological nature represents the aggregate of internalized social relations that have become functions for the individual" (p. 164). Conceptions of maturity discussed in Chapter 5 and elsewhere raise similar issues, e.g., intersubjectivity, a genuine communion with the cosmos, a fusion of self and surround leading to both self- and other-enhancement, etc. However, it was Levinas who carried these conceptualizations to the point of defining the essence of human nature as a responsibility for the other.

By combining these perspectives, mind and related concepts may be characterized, in particular, as "becoming being-in-world/world-in-being," or more simply "being-becoming-world/world-becoming-being." When defined at this level, the separate-in-the-individual animal body and machine mind do not seem to exist. Nor do the separate self-defined-as-distinct-from-other and other-defined-as-distinct-from-self.

A coexistential perspective on epistemology should include other combinations of the terms *being, becoming,* and *world.* Becoming-world-being/being-world-becoming and becoming-being-world/world-being-becoming also belong in a full model on these lines (see Figure 11.1). Thus, the ethic described by Levinas seems embodied in these terms. They mirror all possibilities of self–other relating, but their mutuality dialectic especially speaks to the interrelatedness or community of all selves and all others. Moreover, the becoming component of the terms reflect the eternal growth and transition toward other-responsibility that take place in development which we have seen in Chapter 2, is an element that Levinas missed in his model.

Implicated in this concept of mind as a shared relation is that it must be *activity* in the vygotskian sense of the word. Its ethos is ethics; its action is moral practice; its agency is communal; its communion is agentic. If Freud described mature life as work and love, I would qualify it as *world work* and *world love*. The meaning of life is the life of meaning, especially as constituted in togetherness. At this level, work and love become orders of magnitude more vibrant, more authentic, and more enduring. Bradley (1993) called for a new moral poetic in developmental psychology. I would hope that in this sense our ideas rhyme.

Comment

The current 25-step model of development may provide a framework to describe the way that shared mind develops. For example, it may be that

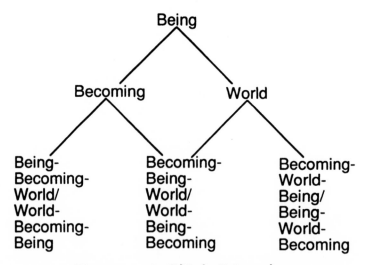

Figure 11.1. An Ethic for Epistemology

the current model of the cognitive (mis)perception of the other speaks to this issue. Heidegger expressed a similar notion; he maintained that the imitating child shares the mother's being-in-the-world (Warren, 1993).

The practical implication of the current, relativist conception of epistemological stances is that therapists need not be guided by one epistemological vision. Reality is not always coconstructed in dialogue, empirical "truths" may be valid for a client, with minimal obfuscation possible by reauthoring, and so on. The sensitive therapist should accept this dialectic, and adopt the epistemological moves necessary to facilitate client progress.

According to Birch (1991), ontology is the study of "What there is," or the nature of humankind. For example, ancient Chinese ontology considered that discrimination brings forth thousands of things out of the unknowable eternal matrix. The current volume is especially about the human ontological "what," and probes its "how," as well. I have labelled the book's philosophical underpinning as coexistential to underscore the integrative nature of the theory and to underscore the social nature of our species. We are immersed since birth in a social field that interexists with each of us, defining and molding us in a reciprocal, coevolutionary process. Now the label coexistential takes on a broader meaning through the effort to show the relation between various epistemological stances. Thus, in the synthetic theory described in current book the qualification "coexistential" seems to apply to both its ontological and epistemic inquiry into humankind.

REVIEW

The current chapter examines in depth the issue of epistemology. Traditionally, the field is marked by a simple dichotomy between constructivist and empiricist points of view. In the current approach, an integrated perspective across six different constructivist schools of thought is sought. Thus, the current quest for a synthetic theory of developmental psychology is completed at the epistemological level, complementing the emphasis on the ontological one in the remainder of the book.

RE POSTMODERNISM

The previous chapters on therapy and the current one on epistemology are directly postmodern. They highlight important postmodern themes such as the socially constituted nature of reality, the power of dominant stories to oppress, the possibility of alternate narratives of life, and the developmental growth course toward the postmodern collective mind that is everyone's birthright. Moreover, they underscore that therapy, in freeing the individual toward her or his potential, can accentuate the locus of agency within the person, the essential need for respect of and authenticity with the other, the multiplicity of self and other and of mind and voice, the eternal coconstructed becomingness of being-in-world, and the relativism of epistemological perspectives on the nature of reality. The means by which these messages are portrayed with the client in my personal transition approach to therapy involves co-constructed graphs of internalized strengths and externalized problems. Thus, my own solutions never become a frame of unitary restriction or sabotage in the narrative construction of future possibilities by the client.

It is worth emphasizing that the chapters do not pretend to offer pervasive panaceas for the postmodern person in her or his efforts to be soothed when development goes awry and counseling is called for, or when epistemological or existential questions are pondered. For both the former and latter cases, only related perspectives in progress can be offered; but the postmodern practitioner and mind will gladly accept the challenge of contributing collectively to the postmodern search for contextual but overarching truths in these areas.

PART VI

CONCLUSIONS

CHAPTER 12

Elaborations, Conclusions, Contributions

INTRODUCTION

In the first part of this chapter, elaborations and extrapolations based on the current model of five stages in development are presented. Issues as different as personality development, censorship, the biology of mate selection, parenting, and the nature of reproductive strategies are discussed. The section terminates with speculation about the nature of the most mature cognitive stage in the current theory, that of postformal collective intelligence, and the nature of the stage of intelligence that may develop in the future when medical technology permits a much longer lifespan than that of today. The second part of the chapter comprises a summary of the contributions of the book to the movement of postmodernism.

ELABORATIONS BASED ON THE STAGE MODEL

The Big Five Personality Factors as Stages

Introduction.   In the field of personality development, there are two major approaches, and one has already been examined in some detail. That is, one dominant perspective is the stage approach as represented by the work of Loevinger, in particular, theories that were explored in Chapter 3. Another perspective is the trait approach (e.g., Pervin, 1994a, 1994b, and commentaries), and it differs from the stage approach mainly in its emphasis on the stability of five factors (or some similar number of factors) in personality across the adult years (Costa & McCrae, 1994, 1995; Goldberg, 1994; Goldberg & Rosolack, 1994; Goldberg & Saucier, 1995; McCrae &

261

Costa, 1994), if not before (John, Caspi, Robins, Moffitt, & Stouthamer-Loeber, 1994; Robins, John, & Caspi, 1994), and on the importance of individual differences in personality.

Trait theory is not without its critics (e.g., Block, 1995a, 1995b), and the two criticisms that I deal with here concern its relative neglect of development (Halverson, Kohnstamm, & Martin, 1994) and its antimonious relationship to stage theory (Loevinger, 1994). In what follows, I build an integrated five factor-stage theory of personality development around the current model of five stages in development by showing that the five major factors in personality are related to the stages. Thus, I circumvent the two major criticisms of the trait approach, and accommodate to the critics of stage theory that it is universalist and insensitive to the general stability evident in the factor research.

Factor analysis of personality data of various types consistently yield a five-factor solution. However, there is no unanimity on the nature of the factors, the terms that best represent them, whether there are five or two more or less, and whether they are unipolar or bipolar. Costa, McCrae, and Goldberg have developed the dominant model in trait theory and they maintain that their factor solutions consistently reveal a personality structure of five dimensions on which individual differences in personality can vary. Costa and McCrae label these factors *extraversion*, *neuroticism*, *agreeableness*, *conscientiousness*, and *openness to experience*.

Development.   Hagekull (1994) worked with Digman's (1994) variation of the classic model in her developmental elaboration of trait theory. She considered the basic dimensions of personality as bipolar in form, and the first three factors become extraversion-introversion, neuroticism-emotional stability, and friendliness-hostility. Hagekull's data show significant correlations in 4- to 10-month infant temperament and 4-year personality structure. Ahadi and Rothbart (1994), Angleitner and Ostendorf (1994), and Martin, Wisenbaker, and Huttunen (1994) also have either suggested or found similarities in infant temperament and later personality development. Thus, it is conceivable that precursors in infant temperament mark the development of the five personality traits, and their stability is due to the impact of their early developmental origins.

Given that there are five major stages in the current stage theory of development, it could be that for each individual the key traits in personality pass through the five stages and are transformed from the first stage onward. An alternative model which combines the trait and stage theories would argue that each of the five traits corresponds or develops maximally in a corresponding stage, so that for each of the five stages one of the traits has the potential to be prominent.

In this regard, the order of trait development that seems most appropriate in terms of establishing a correspondence to the developmental stages of the current theory (reflexive, sensorimotor, perioperational, formal operational, and collective intelligence) is the following: Extraversion (because of its activity, it seems central to the neonate); agreeableness (because of its pleasantness and adaptability is cardinal for the infant); conscientiousness (because of its will and persistence is critical to the preschooler); emotional stability (because of its manageability and attention is important to the adolescent); and openness to experience (because of its intellect is a key to the adult).

Conclusion.   The implication of this model is that the potential for all five major traits of personality are present in each of us from an early age onward, although they develop sequentially in terms of only one being represented as a major developmental issue at any one time. Note that any other nonstage view of personality could be subject to the same type of logic applied to trait theory. For example, Maslow's need hierarchy could be reworked to fit a five-stage model as has been undertaken for trait theory. Also, note that the question of substages and levels within stages has not been treated in this section because it is too early in the theorizing process in this area to be more differentiated than I have been up to this point.

Because the study of the lifespan development of the traits of personality is in its infancy, these various conjectures must be considered preliminary. Nevertheless, they point to the importance of examining developing traits in terms of a stage model of development, whether it be that of myself or someone else.

The Development of the Unconscious

Introduction.   It is suggested that the unconscious develops in terms of the 25 steps (5 stages × 5 substages) of the current synthetic theory, like other parts of the developing individual. Moreover, in this work the broadest perspective of the unconscious is adopted. That is, it is seen to include not only individually determined repressed ideas but also certain collective mythic figures, representations of evil, communal fantasies, godlike beings, and so on, which appear to be cultural manifestations of the phenomena. In the following, these unconscious expressions are modeled briefly in terms of the five stages of the current theory. This applies whether they are considered constructive or destructive entities (see Table 12.1, left-hand column).

The Model.   When unconscious psychic motivating factors are formed in, deal with, treated from, or spring from a reflexive framework, the initial stage of the current theory of development, they are considered omnipotent, centered on the self, and insensitive or ignorant of the other (equiva-

**Table 12.1 Stages in the Development of the Individual Unconscious
and of Societal Institutions**

Stage	Unconscious entities	Societal institutions
Reflexive	Omnipotent, self-centered	Cater to base instincts such as sexual pleasure
Sensorimotor	Fiery, controlling	Are more physical, like in competitive sports
Perioperational	Calculating, aware of the individual	Function in terms of control, e.g., police/judicial system
Abstract	Knowledgeable, engages in dialogue	Are more contemplative, e.g., universities, libraries
Collective intelligence	Encompassing, inclusive of self and other	Concern the discovery, creation, immersion in, and dispersion of communal wisdom, e.g., some religious communities, sexual pleasure in mature, loving, trascendentally moral beings

lent to the id). Next, they may be more sensorimotor and thus more fiery
and controlling, yet in the service of basic contextual analyses (informing
the ego). If perioperational, they are more calculating and aware of the
other (like the superego). If abstract, they appear more knowledgeable and
willing to engage the other in dialogue. Finally, if communal in orientation, they are more encompassing and self-inclusive.

On Censorship and Political Correctness

The Debate.   Currently, the debate between those for and against zero
tolerance in the liberty of expression, or censorship of potentially offensive
material, is anchored in a view of both the individual and society that is not
as evolved as it could be. Undoubtedly, those on both sides of the debate
would censure clearly illegal (e.g., hate-inducing) material and would not
censure material that includes mention of difference in an individual or
group that is clearly benign in nature. The gray area between these extremes is the subject of debate on whether "nonpolitically correct" ideas
have the right to be voiced. Is material that is offensive but not overtly hate-
inducing acceptable, for example?

One school of thought would argue that even if a large portion of
society disagrees with material such as this, the person holding the opinion has the right to express it, since it is better to voice publicly potentially
dangerous material. That is, individuals have the right of freedom of expression no matter how distasteful their ideas may be, and when material

such as this is out in the open it can be countered better and the public can be educated against it. Moreover, the costs of censorship outweigh its benefits in that it could be misapplied and lead to abuses such as the suppression of valid criticism, e.g., of entrenched oppressive authority.

The other school of thought would argue that the fundamental right of freedom of expression must be tempered by the superordinate right of the other or others to have their fundamental rights respected. Anything that would violate or endanger their sense of security, freedom, or dignity should be suppressed.

A Metaperspective. If we adopt a metaperspective one step beyond this ongoing debate, we see that it serves as a barometer of the level of development of contemporary society. The fact that the debate is allowed to take place in our society speaks to its relatively advanced status relative to many others. However, a society more advanced than ours would not artificially separate individual and society, but would facilitate and live their inherent interdependent unity. The self and society are mutually grounded, situated, or embedded. The dualistic opposition of the two camps described above on freedom of expression would not obtain in such a society, or at least it would be considered as part of a larger debate on the nature of society as a whole.

The individual is not an isolated island and society is not solely a sea. Islands are defined by their communion with the surrounding sea and are evanescent configurations when seen across the expanse of geological time. At the same time, a sea's boundaries and patterns of flow are crafted in part by the earthen entities which surround and populate it. This metaphor informs us that false oppositions such as the cartesian duality between mind and body, or the ones between thought and emotion or individual and society cloud the inherent fusion that inevitably defines, contains, and constrains the components involved.

A Mature Society. In a mature society, each individual should be accorded the inalienable right to evolve toward full psychological and moral maturity. In a mature society, each individual is treasured for that potential and has it actively fostered by society, and because of this societal attitude each individual grows to treasure that society, and actively contribute to its betterment. Individuals growing toward maturity in a mature society are imbued with a sense of we-ness, not (only) I-ness. They are constantly "becoming"; they are constantly "being"; and they are constantly "in" the world, while hoping and acting to see others constantly becoming, constantly being, and constantly in the world.

In what way does this vision of a mature society relate to the current debate on freedom of expression and censorship? Individuals in our hypothesized mature state would be developing an exquisite sensitivity both to their developing sense of self and the social environment in which they are embedded. Thoughts and acts would reflect movement toward an individual-in-the-collective or self-in-relatedness integrity. The individual's sense of self would be a coself, or an expanded, contextually situated, other-sensitive, socially enriched, and socially constitutive one. In this regard, mature members of a mature society would partake in, receive from, contribute to, and symbiotically share in a forever emerging, dynamically evolving society. Neither individual nor society would be conceived as separate, and it would be understood that it is logically impossible that it could be any other way, for the individual is defined by the relationship network in which her or his development takes place and society is a concatenation of the massive, webbed, individual-in-relationship contributions in it.

Thus, there would be both minimal individual egotism and societal imposition. Any individual thought or act that could clearly hurt the collective, or part of it, at the expense of apparent (and false) personal satisfaction would be reworked, channeled, and transformed by the individual toward mutually self- and other-enhancing thoughts or acts (e.g., a racist idea reworked into a constructive inner or public dialogue about attendant fears, stereotypes, past education, etc.). For hurting the communal is hurting the self just as polluting a flowing river potentially poisons the circulating blood. Similarly, any societal behavior that could hurt the individual, or part of her or him, at the expense of apparent (and false) collective aggrandizement would be reworked, channeled, and transformed by society toward mutually society and individual enhancing behavior. For hurting the individual is hurting society, just as harming the child potentially poisons the abusing parent.

Conclusion. In short, in the human village of the future, the debate about freedom of expression and censorship would be obviated or minimized and put in the context of a larger debate on how best to foster a mature society which acts to promote the optimal development of all its members. The extent to which a debate in a society is fixated on simple dichotomies and is separated from larger issues speaks to the psychological level of the society from which the debate originates, the manner in which this society perceives and treats its members, and how far the society must evolve. If history has ended, it is only in the sense of an end for grand external events serving a role in defining a society's course. Now history can move on to have society better foster the development of grand internal events so that, in turn, they can serve a role in defining a society's course, and thus create a never-ending process of reciprocal influence, feedback, and growth between the individual and society in their fused dance. In this sphere, individuals or social institutions prone to an idea that obviously may offend would have the education, sensitivity, and courage to self-censor, and then rework, channel, and constructively transform the idea in the wider world of people and ideas, and in so doing facilitate (psychological) growth and autotransformation. This vision of the constitutive relationship between individual and society certainly is utopian, but without an attempt to define the ideal parameters of a society's development, we risk that its progress regresses, flounders, or is slowed.

Warren (1993) describes Habermas's vision of a moral, mature society, and it is quite consonant with the current conception. For Habermas, developing individuals are socialized in context and develop according to piagetian and kohlbergian stages of cognitive and moral development. If they are to participate truly in a democratic society, they must develop into a stage beyond the traditional six that Kohlberg described for moral development. That is, they must engage others in a dialogical, transformative discourse ethics where "discourse is both aligned with reason and attentive to the particularity of conflicts" (p. 239). Barber (1984, in Bader, 1995) also analyzes different forms of democracy and citizenship according to a progression. Representative democracy concerns a contract that is vertical in structure where the citizen is passive. Unitary democracy concerns a horizontal fraternity where the citizen is self-sacrificial. Finally, in strong democracy citizens are dialectically cooperative and active. Such theoretical progressions would profit from operationalized equivalents, and in the following section a scale is presented in this regard in terms of censorship.

A Scale.   An explicit five-point scale is described on which different individuals, groups, and societies can be compared for the complexity of their attitude toward censorship (see Table 12.2; I do not review the table in the text). It has been extrapolated from the previously presented concept of the cognitive (mis)perception of the other. The ideal attitude that has been outlined above constitutes the fifth level to which we all should aspire. Where do relevant governing bodies stand on the scale? In fact, one can ask to what extent the scale is applicable to the way that any authority figure treats others either in terms of overt censorship or the process underlying it, that of interpersonal control. Keep in mind that the reality for any one issue usually reflects a mixture of varying proportions of different levels of complexity related to the issue, that scale values will vary across issues, and that transition values between levels readily could be added to the scale.

As mentioned, the level of censorship that a particular group or individual adopts or champions should be conditioned by their cognitive (mis)perception of the other. Because these in turn reflect other influences (e.g., economic, sociocultural, historicopolitical, parental), then no simple answer obtains in understanding the dynamics of preferred censorship modality.

Table 12.2 Stages in the Complexity of Censorship

Stage	Type	Description
Reflexive	Omnipotent censorship	Because the state deserves full power over its citizens, it has the right to censure without justification
Sensorimotor	Constraining censorship	Because the state knows best, it has the right to censure in the best interests of its citizens
Perioperational	Enlightened censorship	State censorship should be used to contain only the worst excesses of its citizens
Abstract	Liberalistic censorship	State censorship should be used only when any one citizen's fundamental rights are endangered
Collective intelligence	Mutualistic censorship	The state and its citizens self-censor and constructively rework ideas when any one citizen's fundamental rights are endangered

Note. This progression in societal censorship can be applied to other groupings such as censorship in the family or in the couple.

The Development of Societal Institutions

Introduction. Coté (1993) described social institutions in terms of the psychodynamic conception of the id, ego, and superego, which has prompted me to examine them in terms of the current model (see Table 12.1, right-hand column). Thus, reflexive institutions would cater to base instincts, like sexual pleasures. Sensorimotor ones would concern those that are more physical, like competitive sports. Perioperational institutions would be framed in terms of control, such as with nonbenevolent police and judicial systems. Abstract institutions would be aimed at activities more contemplative in nature, e.g., university courses and public libraries. Finally, collective intelligence institutions would concern the best that academic, cultural, and spiritual communities have to offer, e.g., the discovery, creation, immersion in, and dispersion of communal wisdom.

Elaboration. Note that different examples of institutions are given for each of the stages of the current theory, but each of the examples could be treated at any of the other stages with modification. For example, sexual pleasure in the context of a loving relationship between two beings living at the moral level implied by the level of collective intelligence is a pleasure that exists at the plane of that stage and not the reflexive one. Similarly, the physical exertion in the ballet dancer's craft is more than sensorimotor skill, for a host of associated cognitive and emotional accompaniments elevate it to a communal cultural activity. As for the third example, the policing and judicial systems (and governmental institutions, in general) need not exist only at the level of control. They may range in attitude from being absolutist with no recognition of human rights to being quite sensitive to the human condition and the power that they have in alleviating suffering and improving society. Finally, institutions that typically are concerned about humanity and its future, such as universities and religious or charitable institutions, may not always live in the light of their mission statements, and instead lapse, for example, into crude profit-seeking fervor or secret military research, acts characteristic of lower stages of consciousness.

Fractalization

Introduction.   In Chapter 7 the concept of fractals in behavior or what may be termed *fractalization* was introduced. It concerns the generation-construction and replication-propagation of self-similar patterns in psychological processes either within or across individuals. The former reference to within individuals refers to fractal organization across different levels of the same system within an individual; for example, different levels of a conceptual hierarchy or different phases of a sequential unfolding (e.g., a horizontal décalage). The latter reference to across individuals refers to fractal transmission or coconstitution across individuals. Examples that have been treated include Vandervert's construct of a world-parent-child isomorphism and its translation into the concept of activation–inhibition coordination transmission (in Chapter 7; also see Globus, 1995; Vandervert, 1996). These are codevelopmental processes, where individuals emerge in coconstitution.

The passage from one qualitatively distinct stage in development to another also should reflect fractalization. For example, the current model of 25 steps in neopiagetian cognitive substage development seems to reflect a cycle of coordination, hierarchization, systematization, multiplication, and integration in terms of stages, substages, and sublevels (see Young, submitted). That is, descriptions of the stages of reflexive, sensorimotor, perioperational, abstract, and collective intelligences seem to reflect and can be reworked into the language of the five corresponding substage labels, and the same logic applies to the five sublevels of the substages. Moreover, there are self-similarities in pattern organization from one (sub)stage to the next. Given that they are based on the construct that each stage incorporates the prior ones, this is inevitable. The obvious examples lay in coordination and multiplication, but the other three also show an inclusion of prior gains within them, partial replication, and the like. Finally, the concept of substage (and sublevel) replication itself speaks to fractalization patterns in cognitive development.

As a concluding comment, I would add that the irreducible unit that appears to propagate within and across fractal patterns in development appears to be an activation–inhibition structure. In the prior paragraph, fractalization in transmission across the society-parent-child's mind-brain was presented from the perspective of this construct. It could be that the basic psychological unit in any domain can be translated into this metric, and its dynamic characterizes the fractalization process in development, in general.

In short, psychology may be redefined as the study (1) of system fractalization in behavior and its organization both within and across (developing) individuals, and (2) of the dynamical processes that subserve its change (including those involving fractals). The social mutuality in human ontology leads me to consider designating the fractalization process in psychology as cofractalization, just as I labeled the particular developmental process codevelopment. At the developmental level, perhaps one should refer to *codevelopmental fractalization*.

Grand Designs.   Salthe (1993) has shown that a wide variety of natural (living and nonliving) phenomena conform to a five-cycle path, and his conception seems similar to the current one. For example, for the cell cycle he shows that the molecular events correspond to the phases of nascence, choice, growth, metastability of senescence (defined as the final stage of growth, and not as aging), and transcendence. These phases appear to be somewhat parallel to the current progression of coordination, hierarchization, systematization, multiplication, and integration. For example, nascence allows coordination, choice implicitly is hierarchical, growth is systemic, metastability of senescence may be like multiplication, and transcendence concerns integration. According to Salthe, the pattern in the cycle drives the particular events where it is found in nature rather than the reverse reductionist case.

At another point in his book he describes the steps in the dialectic process, and, independent of the first model, also emerges with a five-step sequence. The traditional thesis–antithesis–synthesis series is viewed as one involving subjectivity (e.g., deconstruction of complexity; taking a subjective view because subjects change), diachronicity (becoming; discovering complexity diachronically), interpenetration into change (entering into change itself; with commitment), contradictory interpenetration (also with commitment), and emergence (unity of opposites; negation of negation). Again, a possible parallel with the current five-step cycle is evident. For example, deconstruction permits coordination, diachronicity can be hierarchical, interpenetration is systemic, contradictory penetration becomes multiplication, and emergence concerns integration. Thus, both of Salthe's series may be reflections of a dynamic that is even more general than the ones that he describes. It could be that the manner in which I describe the five-step growth cycle represents a major dialectical pattern of change in living and nonliving systems, in general. It may be the ultimate fractal pattern in this regard, one that characterizes and emerges out of any system in dissipation of disorder. Alvarez de Lorenzana's (1993) appendix to Salthe's book also implicates the inevitabity of a five-step repetitive cycle in system growth (However, the mathematics here are beyond the scope of the current work).

Study of client change in psychotherapy supports the concept that a five-step progression often characterizes the change process. Prochaska, Norcross, and DiClemente (1994; Maddox, 1995) believe that clients pass through five stages of change once they emerge from the precontemplation stage. First, they contemplate change without commitment. In current terms, they coordinate conception of their current state with the possibility of change. In the next step, clients prepare for change with appropriate plans, or hierarchize a current state with commitment to change, to use the current terminology. Then clients deliberately engage in action to change their behavior and context, which I would characterize as systematization. Next, clients enter the maintenance stage, where gains are consolidated and preventive steps instituted. Here, the focus seems to be on a diffusion or distribution of progress made, or a multiplication effect as I would predict. Finally, clients terminate with problem resolution, confidence, and control, or with integration in current terminology.

As a last comment on fractalization in change, I add that the partial disintegration or even full dissolution of systems may be characterized by a constant developmental progression akin to or even in reversal compared to the process described for constructive evolutions. Is dissipative unfolding orderly, and if so how? I leave this question in the rhetorical domain.

The Biology of Love

Introduction. The biological perspective on mate selection (e.g., Buss, 1994, 1995; Buss & Schmitt, 1993) appears too simplistic. This position speaks to a shaping by natural selection of behaviors limited to the most basic couple and parenting behavior and ignores the more refined ones that seem to be involved in the process. (I am not disputing a role for biological influence in parenting, only the depth of the analysis. See Burgess [1994] for a defense of the evolutionary position as it applies to the family through cost–benefit analysis, and see Pérusse [1994] and Scheib [1994] for research on Buss's model.) Essentially, the biological argument is that reproductive females potentially can have fewer offspring than reproductive males so that compared to males they are more interested in caring for offspring and nurturing them in their development. Thus, they seek mates who can provide resources for facilitating this task (e.g., food, protection, power, parenting, opportunities for learning by the offspring, including at the social level), or at least show signs of their potential to do so (e.g., higher social status, ambition, industriousness, intelligence). In contrast, males seek mates who show signs of fertility, such as facial and bodily attributes indicative of health, youth, etc. Both sexes also seek mates who show signs of superior genes, commitment, cooperative and division-of-labor abilities, and good parenting skills.

However, according to Buss and Schmitt, it is not clear which signs mate-seekers can use to predict potential skillful parenting. Possible signs include intelligence, nurturance, kindness, affectionate behavior, understanding, loyalty, responsibility, and stability in personality. They call for more research. In the following I argue that the signs of good parenting must relate to five parental strategies that are derived from the current synthetic theory of five stages of development.

In order for humans to produce quality offspring (in the sense of psychological maturity) who continue to produce quality offspring, and so on, which I presume is the optimal way to assure propagation of resource-rich gene-carriers, parenting must be optimal. It appears to me that there are five major degrees of quality in parenting behavior, and that they relate to the five developmental stages of the current synthetic theory (newborn reflexive, infant sensorimotor, childhood perioperational, adolescent abstract, adult collective intelligence). There must be parental behavior oriented not only to basic physical (reflexive) and nurturing (sensorimotor) care, but also facilitation of wider educational experiences to foster intellectual (perioperational) growth and the appropriate preparation for complex (abstract) functioning in the immediate adult community in which mate selection and child rearing will take place. Moreover, any parenting that instills an ability (and humanitarian concern) in offspring to deal with wider society (collective intelligence) can only help them in their fitness journey. The ability to parent should develop in five stages according to the order indicated, and moreover, in keeping with the general nature of the current theory, each stage should pass through five substages (coordination to integration).

I hypothesize that the genetic potential of each human is to parent simultaneously at all five of these levels, but that in practice this is done to varying degrees of success based on personal and contextual factors. In this regard, the key mediator should be the level of the cognitive (mis)perception of the other that is experienced by developing individuals in their own home and society as they grow up.

The implication of the model being described is that from an evolutionary point of view both sexes should be interested equally in giving the best quality parenting behavior to their offspring (consisting of all of the five levels just described) if they aim to promote optimal reproductive behavior in them. Thus, the ideal mate for either sex should be someone who possesses these parenting characteristics, or at least signs of them. The more the higher-order parenting attributes are in evidence or will clearly develop in the mate and come to be used in parenting, maximizing reproductive success, the less likely alternative reproductive strategies will be employed, such as high quantity sperm dispersion (e.g., adultery and disinterest in and abuse of offspring by males). In this regard, both sexes should seek optimally mature partners, but the system in which this biological impetus is embedded is environmentally sensitive, so that it does not always develop in full.

Reproductive Strategies.   In Young (submitted), it was shown that the five stages of development in the current theory appear to be related to different types of evolutionary pressure (see Table 12.3). The reflexive, sensorimotor, perioperational, abstract, and collective intelligence stages were associated with individual fitness, kin selection, using group for individual structures, reciprocal altruism, and group selection, respectively. At the most basic level, there is classical darwinian natural selection for reproductive success. However, beyond this level other more differenti-

Table 12.3 Contextual Pressures, Alternate Evolutionary, Reproductive, and Parental Strategies

Contextual pressure: (Mis)perceived stage of other	Evolutionary strategy promoted by pressure	Reproductive strategy facilitated	Parental strategy facilitated
Reflexive	Individual fitness	Quantitative: many gene carriers	Physical, corporal care at best
Sensorimotor	Kin selection	Qualitative: secure base in carriers	Emotional attachment encouraged
Perioperational	Group for individual	Qualitative: knowledge base also	Education encouraged
Abstract	Reciprocal altruism	Qualitative: resource access also	Immediate social–economic community opened to offspring
Collective intelligence	Individual for group	Qualitative: resource replenishment also	Wider community integration and humanitarian thought both encouraged

ated evolutionary pressures have selected more refined means of adaptation. These pressures concern, in turn, (1) inclusive fitness or kin selection; (2) prestructured group for individual activity; (3) reciprocal altruism, or mutually beneficial processes; and (4) group selection, e.g., as in a communal giving to set up group for individual activity (and kin if not immediate offspring benefits). Parenting can be analyzed in terms of these five reproductive strategies in the following way.

Specifically, reproductive success can be promoted at the most basic level of individual fitness by adequate physically based, reflexive caregiving right from birth, which should lead to offspring survival into sexual maturity. But because of lacks in parental behavior, there should be poor offspring ability for optimal mate attraction and selection and for high quality parenting. Thus, parenting at best in offspring should be the same as received, i.e., with a focus on basic needs and physical care, in particular.

Next, reproductive success can be promoted by parents giving offspring not only individual selection-based physical care but also kin selection-based nurturant care and opportunities for attachment to a secure (emotional) base. With appropriate nurturance by parents of each of their offspring, the family forms a superordinate system with a good balance of positive to negative sibling play, imitation and learning, and affection and support. That is, through nurturant parental behavior family solidarity and extended family networking is promoted so that what eventually develops is self-giving to kin by kin (= reflection of kin selection), i.e., among offspring, as well as from parent to offspring. All these behaviors should lead to better offspring ability in mate selection and parenting (again in terms of the replication of patterns experienced). That is, if a parent receives an adequate emotional base, he or she can be capable of at least providing for offspring a secure environment from which exploration and basic learning can take place in the short term and sibling cooperation in child-rearing in the long term.

At the next level, reproductive success can be enhanced by adding to the parenting repertoire behaviors aimed at older offspring at the representational–concrete operational (perioperational) stage of development. That is, parenting should come to include the arrangement of optimal educational experiences in the group-structured educational settings available in the immediate community. In this third level of parenting, offspring continue to take advantage of developmental environments prestructured for them. They develop intellectual and knowledge-based skills that enhance the potential for better quality resource acquisition, mate attraction, and parenting, and come to repeat these parenting styles that were experienced.

In the next level, reproductive success of parents is magnified by the use of parental strategies that involve in their own behavior and encourage in their teenaged and young adult offspring an exchange of social and resource give-and-take (reciprocal altruism). This behavior is manifested because at this point all have, and apply, the formal, abstract intelligence which underlies these social skills. In order for offspring of this age to set up optimal reproductive shop in the immediate community, access to resources is a promise as much as a reality, and part of that promise is the web of social and economic connections that the individual can establish due to the presence of appropriately developed alliance- and pact-creating skills, and so on. On the one hand, offspring may profit from already established connections in the parental social network, and on the other hand the skills are available for the creation of new connections. Finally, these skills can be incorporated into and transmitted by the eventual parenting behavior of the offspring themselves.

In the final level of parenting strategies that contribute to reproductive success, parents develop the ability to use on their own and also foster in their adult offspring collective intelligence, which permits a symbiotic sharing with wider society. This process enables those involved to gain personal advantage through a greater network of resource acquisition and replenishment channels while also contributing to the common good. Thus, the previously mentioned group for individual level or levels in reproductive success can be sustained to some extent by such behavior, leading to better structures for all of the society's individuals, including the offspring of the parents involved in fostering this behavior. (Yes, group selection can, but need not, lead to the direct reproductive profit of each individual involved.) When humankind will be especially involved in the intergenerational transmission of collective-oriented actions such as these, the phenotypic potential of the species' genotype will have been realized.

Conclusion.   Experience and context determine to what extent each reproductive strategy is turned off and on in any one individual and in a certain sense in a group of individuals. Generally, parents act at more than one reproductive level at the same time in their behavior; they do not wait for the child to reach the age corresponding normatively to a particular strategy before employing it or its precursors. Thus, for example, in one sense a parent who has a collective-oriented psychology will manifest the appropriate behaviors necessary to promote the same attitude in their offspring right from the early years of the offspring. The collective-oriented intelligence and behavior that has been described throughout this book, including those that are related to parenting, represent the extension of the last-described individual for group level of selection. Consequently, they are not utopian, maladaptive aspirations but biologically rooted, potentially universal adaptations.

In short, the viewpoint presented here is that parents through their behavior use and promote up to five different strategies of reproductive success in their offspring. Aside from fostering behavior indicative of classical darwinian natural selection oriented to individual fitness, parents may activate in the manner indicated behavior associated with kin selection, group for individual behavior, reciprocal altruism, and group selection. Thus, the modalities to fitness normally should be varied, but the higher-order ones, in particular, may be curtailed by experiential inputs. The intergenerational isomorphic transmission of parental style may limit not only the psychology of parents' offspring but also the fitness strategies of their offspring and consequently themselves. If parents are incapable of adopting the superior parental strategies, it should be understood that they may have been limited from doing so by the society in which they are embedded. That is, they parent from the perspective of their cognitive (mis)perception of the other, and this in turn is sensitive to sociocultural pressures and impositions, as has been shown in Chapter 7. To summarize, society tailors parents' biological reproductive strategies to its psychological level.

How does this model of optimal parenting strategies in terms of reproduction concord with the model of optimal family development presented in Chapter 4? The two models are quite complementary, and map onto each other. One deals with strategies that parents follow (as presented in this chapter), whereas the other deals with behaviors that are manifested to implement those strategies (Chapter 4). Both are related to the same underlying synthetic model of five stages in development, so that this conclusion should not be surprising.

Self-Organization and Natural Selection. Kauffman (1993) has argued that species self-organize on a fitness landscape, optimizing the process of filling niches by balancing as a system on the cusp of disorder and order. In this perspective, no recourse to natural selection is needed to explain species radiation. In the model above on reproductive strategies, natural selection and related processes were considered fundamental in the evolution of mate selection and parenting strategies. Nevertheless, in my own way, like Kauffman, I suggest that darwinian processes are secondary in evolution compared to systems theory, although the domain of their application was to an ontogenetic and not a phylogenetic phenomenon.

In the current model of reproductive strategies as applied to parenting, the five suggested reproductive strategies can be reinterpreted into the language of the substages of the developmental model presented previously (coordination to integration). Thus, the first level of individual fitness permits a basic *coordination* between parents and offspring, but not much more. Second, kin selection allows a *hierarchical* arrangement between secure-base parents and attached offspring and to a certain extent across offspring. Next, at the group for individual level, which involves local community, larger *systems* in which offspring are implicated are created. Then, with reciprocally altruistic behavior, the range of social networks involved is more widespread or *multiplied*. Last, group selection brings with it *integrated* behavior.

This book on the developmental system suggests a ubiquity for a five-step ontogenetic model, and this model may reflect a sequence that helps explain the self-organizing properties of the evolutionary system. Species may radiate phylogenetically across a fitness landscape, but it is conceivable that the pattern involved in this progression fits the five-step ontogenetic one of the current model. No matter what their content domain, systems may share in the five-step sequence because it represents the most economical, graceful, or less turbulent, resisting pathway in autoequilibration, as discussed in a prior section of the chapter. If I may engage in metasystemic conjecture on the metasystem involved, the five-step pathway may be the ultimate fractal because its design properties are the most adaptive contextual dynamic. In the system pattern wars, it may win the local battles because of *dynamic darwinism*, to coin a term. As Stewart (1995) argues, evolutionary mechanisms evolve themselves. But if diverse systems cooperate in a wider collectivity, then dynamic darwinism may be an insufficient metaphor.

Relational Meaning Worlds

Introduction. I will now integrate or relate into a partially coherent perspective several of the major themes or meanings of the current work. Its postmodern aspect emphasizes the metasystemic, collective, relational, mutualistic, fused emotional–cognitive, empathic, self-creating, forever questioning, nonessentialist, nontotalizing, relativistic, pluralistic, and transformational attributes of adult thought. Collectives such as parents, families, or culture are considered a conjoint crucible of powerful mediating devices and artifacts that influence the developing cognition of its members, especially through cognitive (mis)perceptions of the other, which reflect the underlying developmental level of the system involved as it passes through the 25-step progression described in the current series, or as it becomes fixated or regresses to or otherwise has difficulties with certain of its levels. These levels of (mis)perception also characterize the developing individual, who can influence collectives in her or his turn. Therapy is described as a process of coconstruction with clients of alternate liberating narratives where agency is internalized and problems are externalized, so that the natural transitional course of development toward postmodern thought is potentiated while preserving individual differences. As with all living systems, the systems that are being examined here (in particular, adult mentation, culture, and therapy), are subject to self-organizational tendencies where the whole is bigger than the sum of the parts and novel patterns can emerge from their confluence.

The Concept.   All this suggests that a human world larger than the individual exists separately from all individuals, although it is emergent from them. I call this world *Relational Meaning Worlds* in order to capture

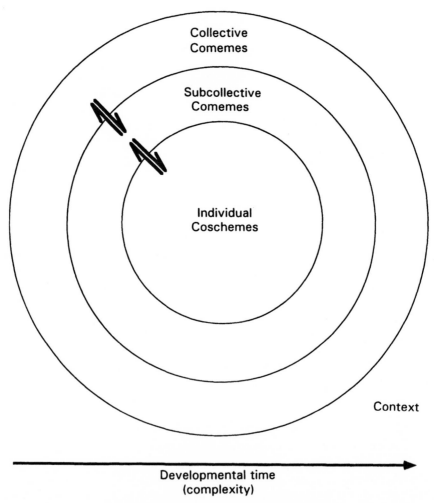

Figure 12.1.   Relational Meaning Worlds

its socioemotional, multiple, living, quasi-independent, and transformable status (see Figure 12.1). Such worlds are characterized by the following:

- Relational Meaning Worlds, or cominds, are individual and (sub)-collective emergent emotional–cognitive integrations of socially constructed realities.
- Emotions (and the related processes of feelings and moods), through emotional meaning structures, impregnate Relational Meaning Worlds and are socially constructed in the course of development.
- These emotional meaning structures are hierarchical in organization, with multiple, reciprocal layers ranging from immediate lived feelings to meta-aware, conscious integrations (after Greenberg & Pascual-Leone, 1995; see Chapter 9).
- They are represented in the form of *co*schemes, which are dynamic, contextually sensitive, socially (re)constituted cognitive–emotional structures (see Chapter 8).
- The cognitive and emotional qualities of coschemes are born undifferentiated in the palpable encounters of developing life. They may become dissociated with developmental context.
- Biological processes underlie emotions; corporal processes embody them; social processes ground them; cognitive processes channel them; the emergence in these and related processes constitute them.
- The primary social constructions (and coschemes) formulated in emotional development revolve around the four dimensions (and 48 dimensional intersections) of the current model of emotional development, with its 48 basic emotions in the first two years of life (see Young, submitted).
- Superordinate lamellae in the hierarchic organization of meaning development include individual and (sub)collective (family, group, subculture, society) higher-order integrations. These are the essence of Relational Meaning Worlds.
- If coschemes refer to lower-level individual repository structures of emotional meaning, then *comemes* (after Dawkins [1989], but with Vygotsky [1987,1993], see Chapter 5) refer to equivalent (sub)collective units (e.g., individual metameaning; supra-individual family myths, gang norms, cultural beliefs, scientific hypotheses, ideological hegemonies). They are emotional–cognitive units of collective relational meaning which influence but also are influenced by individuals. According to Dawkins, memes are units of cultural transmission which replicate or are living structures that form complexes.
- Individual and social Relational Meaning Worlds are continually

evolving and transforming. Wisdom is continual participation in praxic meaning transformation.

- Transformation of Relational Meaning Worlds may be positive or negative (regressive, repressive, maladaptive), depending on context, experience, and biology.
- A major factor which underlies this transformation is the sequence of steps which marks development. According to the current theory, there may be up to 100 cognitive shifts in ontogeny. Each new level acts like a chaotic attractor (in systems theory), penetrating all regions of the developmental state space and thus inevitably reorganizing the cognitive–emotional coschemes within it.
- Parenting, socialization, and therapy comprise coconstruction of transforming coschemes partly through facilitated internalization or coappropriation of comemes.
- Ideally, this process involves the creation of new emotional flow in the banks of meaning of Relational Meaning Worlds, optimizing ongoing meaning metamorphosis to higher orders of complexity rather than capture by eddies of stagnation.
- Therapy thus becomes alteration of Relational Meaning Worlds through the coconstruction of altered, postmodern(-directed) comeme narratives in client metameaning.
- Relational Meaning Worlds and their constituent comemes carry cognitive (mis)perceptions of the other from individual and collective to individual and collective.
- Given that the level of the cognitive (mis)perception of the other varies in complexity and sensitivity to the other with the manifest developmental level of the system involved (individual, family, society), we are called on as individuals and collectives to optimize comeme development.
- At the level of philosophy, I believe that I am defining Levinas's lost preoriginal for-the-other, Heidegger's Dasein, or being-in-the-world, and Buber's I-Thou, and showing how they can be (re)constructed via societal and parental responsivity and maturity (via comeme coappropriation).
- At the poetic level, at its optimal each Relational Meaning World is an ongoing state of being. It is a cooperativity into which we are growing, a heart which shares us, a conscious which invigorates us, a diversity which gathers us. It is a hope that infuses our vision, that pulls us as we form or push it. It values a growth that values growth through and for the other at the multiple levels of existence, encouraging our passion and compassion, our separation and union, our senses and sensitivity, our immediacy and mediation, our vitality in

birth and in death, and whatever it and we grow into in its open living with us.

Conclusion.   Shweder (1995) developed a concept very similar to the present one, when he argued that Mind subsumes or encompasses individual mental functioning and culture. Humans have mental access to a multiplicity of concepts and mental processes. However, they activate only a subset of them, either as individuals or groups. Shweder's Mind is analogous to the collected ideas in the current concept of Relational Meaning Worlds, and its components are comparable to my notion of comemes.

Similarly, Ilyenkov (in Bakhurst, 1995) believes that ideal, nonmaterial phenomena exist as supraindividual "objectifications" of meaning in human activity. Humanity's activity "idealizes" objects and even all of nature into its spiritual culture. Humanized nature exists parallel to nature and both constitute the "surrounding world." Thus, a transcendent, objective independent world of thought exists beyond individual minds.

Gergen (interviewed in Gülerce, 1995b) seems to support a concept similar to the present one when he writes that "When we move to a relational perspective, we speak not in terms of 'knowing minds' but of ... discursive communities ... which come to rely on various texts ... which they come to treat as 'real' " (p. 300). Gergen's concept of discursive communities resembles the current Relational Meaning Worlds, whereas his "real" texts seem an example of the current concept of comemes.

Similarly, Hutchins (1996) argues that culture does more than affect the cognition of individuals. That is, systems of cultural activities have cognitive properties independent of individuals. Paré (1995) developed a similar idea in his notion of families as interpretive communities or storying cultures. That is, knowledge is textual interpretation located in a community of persons, or is intersubjective/consensual articulations of performed meanings. Valsiner and Gupta (1995) present a related concept in their description of collective as opposed to personal culture and Cole (1995a) considers that wider culture is a fertile garden for other less inclusive levels of individual and subcultural organization. He writes of "collaborative sense-making" (Cole & Engström, 1995). Shotter (1995a) refers to collective or joint activity, intentionality, and behavior, arguing that these situations are ethically active, living entities. For Hermans and Kempen (1995), society is an extended self with a collective voice, and for C.U.M. Smith (1994) language reflects the activity of numerous generations of speakers. Wertsch's (1995a, 1995b, 1995c) concept of culturally mediated actions, means, or tools (e.g., language genres), and Cole's of mediating artifacts (e.g., texts) creating an open system of change between the child and world also are somewhat similar to the present one, for they are

socially engaged cultural devices serving as the minimal unit of psychological analysis. Similarly, Jankowicz (1995) describes a community of
enquiry, Kreiglstein (1995) a partnership thinking, and C. U. M. Smith
(1994) a supraindividual cognition.

Nevertheless, despite some similarity of these concepts to the current
one, they manifest important lacunae relative to it. That is, they do not
include mention of the emotional core in the meaning-making enterprise,
although this must be implicit in the relational foundation they take as its
crucible, and they are not developmental, unlike in the current case.

It should be noted that the concept of Relational Meaning Worlds is
congruent with recent arguments that individual humans may not be the
smallest unit of human life, and that, in fact, the smallest unit in this regard
may be as big as the largest. For example, there is the well-known concept
that the earth is a living entity called Gaia. The concept that humankind is
forming a vast single superorganism, called metaman (Stock, 1993) is
congruent with the Gaia hypothesis, and adds that the living entity involved recruits technological, cultural, and biological support in its mission. Jung's mystical concepts of Uroboros, Creatura, and Pleroma are
somewhat similar, for in this latter irreal place all is union and foreverness
(Freedman & Gorman, 1993). Also, Lonergan (in Nordquest, 1994) describes Cosmopolis, implicating a self-transcendent community of being.
Sachs (1993) sees a philosophical chain from Maimonides to Spinoza and
Liebniz to Einstein, all arguing for the unity of the universe (and inevitably
of humans in the universe). Recent cosmological theory is arguing that the
universe may be alive, and only one of multiple evolving universes (Gribbon, 1994). The growing influence of the philosophical position of (moderate) communitarianism, with its collective orientation, may be a sign of a
collective operation (e.g., Caney, 1992; Daly, 1994; Downing & Thigpen,
1993).

Epilogue

Emergenesis. There may be novel behavioral properties springing
from an individual's genetic complement, ones that are not specified by or
predictable from any particular gene or combination of genes. These behaviors may arise dynamically out of the gene matrix pattern of any one
individual as wholes which are more than the sum of any parts. Through
this particular genetic process, called emergenesis, complex qualities,
such as leadership, may arise at different levels of skill across individuals
(Lykken, McGue, Tellegen, & Bouchard, 1992; but see Miller, 1993). Even
if genes underlie the process, the resultant emergent behavioral potentials
are not inherited or passed down from one generation to the next. Because

they are dependent on gene patterns, and these are shuffled in the sex cell creation and fertilization processes, they are not subject to the typical inheritance pathways.

One can ask to what extent the hypothesized stage of collective intelligence of the current theory is a product of the same mechanism. Is it possible that an intelligence which can be accompanied by a consciousness and socioemotional behaviors involving self-abnegation for the common good, and which leads to the creation of supraindividual, cultural entities such as comemes in Relational Meaning Worlds, is an emergent property of patterns in parts of the human gene pool, and not specified by any one particular gene or set of genes? If so, then its quality should vary from one individual to the next partly due to the genetic pattern involved.

Complexity Theory. These ideas are congruent with complexity theory, which emphasizes that systems gravitate to the intermediate state between complete randomness and complete order in order to facilitate their adaptation toward more complex emergent forms (Kauffman, 1993; Lewin, 1992). Complexity theory has been applied to the Gaia theory by reinterpreting it to mean that life (the planet) exhibits an inherent emergent homeostatic survival mechanism. One could speculate that Gaia-related behavior by collective living organisms is an emergent property through emergenesis from the collective genome of all species involved. If life, larger universes, or the universe(s) are living entities, to what extent is the property an emergent one not specified by any one part (e.g., species)? In this sense, how much are humans collective agents of Gaia or mini-Gaias (Lewin, 1992). If the quality of the human minisystem is not collectively adaptive, it reduces life's adaptive collectivity, and life may "choose" to extirpate us.

Complexity theory has been applied to theological issues. Even if the origins of the universe can never be known with certainty, perhaps it can be speculated that a vital force is emergent from the supersystem called the universe. Perhaps God did not create the universe, but it could be that the universe created God, as an emergent property of its inherent organization.

Summary. The collective behaviors that adults organize are examined for their possible genetic and evolutionary bases. These behaviors are comprised of collective intelligence and associated consciousness and empathic, self-abnegating behaviors. The concepts of emergenesis, complexity, and group selection are analyzed, laying the foundation for a hypothesis of emergence of these behavioral phenomena. That is, these behaviors are considered emergent from our gene set, and not specified by particular genetic codes. The question is asked to what extent Gaia-like behaviors emanate from our communal genome. Are we constantly developing to assure constant development?

Future Expansions

There are many domains of study in development which could be examined from the perspective of the current 25-step synthetic model of development. Other domains that have been approached by developmental stage theorists, but have hardly been touched upon in the current work, include the development of morality, values, spirituality, and so on. These topics cover much of what makes us human, and deserve treatment in future work emanating from the synthetic model.

One example of the way the current theory may be applied to other areas would be to ask what the development of cognition would look like in the future when medical technology will permit a much longer lifespan than the one found today. In this scenario it could be that the wise elderly will spearhead genuine *communal collective intelligences*, where different species collectively contribute to and share in a symbiotically elaborated group intelligence. In the coordination and hierarchical substages, this would concern the relationship between pairs of species, in particular, either between our own and others one at a time or between two others that humans would facilitate. The systemic level would concern wider communal interspecies collective intelligences, ones that could be incorporated into multiplicative combinations, leading to a superior integrative substage. Will interspecies communication across planets be incorporated into this stage or be the basis of the one to follow?

Overall Conclusion

Trans. Development is about the morning's eve, the potential which unfolds in each of us. The frame of 25 developmental levels postulated in the current book suggests that human growth is not a haphazard, reinforcement-shaped pattern, but a constructive, structured, freeing toward integrity and synthesis. Ontogenesis is a renewal, a transformation not only for the growing individual but also for the contextual human surround in which it takes place. The crucible of development is in the meeting of child and parent, in their intersubjective mutuality, and the mediating devices that they share. Thus, it is contextually sensitive and individually patterned.

Nevertheless, the process of development is stage-governed, and so constrained in direction, with all humankind hopefully growing toward the final most mature level. Moreover, the current systems conception of development is deterministic, for crucial parameters are thought to guide stage advances. Yet the last stage of growth in the current theory where postmodern thought is seen to develop specifies ultimate freedom through a union with the social envelope. We determine to follow only one path, to become universal, to be impregnated by shared moral thought and to act from this perspective. Gradually we accrue a free will in shared moral action and social maturity. In this regard, therapy is more than a freeing of an individual's stuckness. It is also a (re)sticking of the individual to a normative transitional path to freedom.

Form. Development is characterized by a series of intertwined twin-nings. Self and surround are bound. Developing individuals engage in a mutualistic interexistence with the contextual matrix. Universal stages punctuate the developmental trajectory; individual differences are built delicately on their axis. Cognition is affectively charged; affects are prod-ucts of appraisal. Cognitions are internal maps of external experiences and events; coschemes develop for both the other and the self. Relational Meaning Worlds grow beyond the individual into the collective; responsi-bility for the other goes beyond the collective toward each individual. Quality of attachment in the growing child varies; it is mediated by quality of caregiving by caregivers. Self is inherently empty without the fuel of others, especially caregivers and family; others exist only as vessels of our construction of them. The self's developing internal mind [and brain] are constituted by fractally organized activation–inhibition coordination programs which are mirrored in the external world; and the buffer between the two consists of similar programs in parents/caregivers. Transition mechanisms in development include both socially shared coappropriation and internally experienced (dis)equilibration. Both ontology and episte-mology in the current theory can be characterized as synthetic; humans grow toward and within integration, and acquire knowledge using inte-grated multiple models based on empirical and constructivist stances.

The mind exists as being-becoming-world/world-becoming-being. Humans form a collective unity or superorganism in the universe created in a fractal propagation that speaks to the nature of the unity that may have begun (been at the singular basin in) the unfolding process. Humankind is both propagating a fractal with the inherent potential for living unity and fracturing that fractal. Therapists act to promote self-healing in clients. Humankind needs to work toward universe self-healing.

Ing. The human life field is considered the universe. Adults are considered to grow into the universe through the development of their collective mode of thought. Levinas's philosophy of a preoriginal responsi-bility for the other speaks to this notion. It argues that we are born to face and give to the other as other and as part of all others without concern for self. If living entities conform to system dynamics, and systems form suprasystems which include their surround, then ultimately the self belongs to the universe and the universe to the self. Fractals are self-similar patterns propagated across different layers of organizational systems, permitting isomorphic similarities from their simplest to their most complex levels. Fractal dispersion within and across developing individuals, through the flow of activation–inhibition rhythms, solders cohesion in the interstices of our social architecture. Relational mutuality reigns in the human realm (Gergen, Vygotsky), and defines us. Our planet is a living system called Gaia with self-correcting life-preserving mechanisms. The quantum nature of matter allows correlative effects where particles moving in opposite directions at the speed of light still can mutually influence each other. In this birthing place, Relational Meaning Worlds which exist beyond the individual at the (sub)collective level emerge in transforming interactions. They are comprised of constituent comemes, or cognitive–emotional meaning carriers, which influence but also are influenced by individual minds. Comemes vary in complexity and maturity, and possess enormous intermediational power in our weaving of action. Mind and body, self and other, subject and object, cognition and emotion, idea and idea, dualism and dualism, all meld back into the source which imagined them apart. Forever unfolding, forever becoming, forever being, forever interexisting, forever in reverence, being-becoming-world/world-becoming-being, living in world work and world love, all this begins to define the state of mature adulthood, those growing there, and those coconstructing in therapy. Mature human development is defined by transformation toward the facilitation of universal developing transformation.

CONTRIBUTIONS TO POSTMODERNISM

Re Postmodernism

This chapter deals with the concept of fractalization, which is relevant for the postmodern perspective in psychology. It is related to the concept of activation–inhibition coordination, which may address the manner in which very different levels of behavior and its developmental mechanisms may be similar or translatable from one to the other, and thus are centripetal and not centrifugal, due to their common root in this dynamic. In this regard, in fractalization there is a cyclic recursion of developmental substages that may be a repetition of the same pattern in the stage cycle. Both of these behavioral isomorphisms, that of activation–inhibition coordination across disparate levels in behavior and that of fractals across substage and stage progressions in development, suggest that there may be wider generalities in the postmodern mind than postmodernism would allow, albeit generalities that need contextualization.

In brief, the postmodern mind is a developmental one that possesses an economic architecture where each part flows into the other (through an activation–inhibition coordination process or the like) and each developmental acquisition is incorporated into successive developmental layers (by a fractalization process or the like). In this sense, it is a mind exquisitely honed to find the unitary contextual truths that has been suggested is its focus.

The developing postmodern mind of the adult is in a constant process of transformation or preparation for transformation. It is becoming, being, evolution. It is nonfoundational, relativist, pluralistic, heterogenous, interpretive, recognizant of possibility, alternatives, ambiguity, and conflict, and decries totalizing modern "truths." It is ultimate fusion, of cognition and emotion, of self and other, of idea and idea (metasystemic, second-order abstractions), of process and metaprocess (e.g., of abstract second-order thought and ultimately the awareness of who created it and how it was created), of dualisms in dialectics. It is self-authorizing, and narrational.

Because it is reflexively aware of its self-construction and the constructed nature of realities, it also understands that the other's realities are constructed. This lays the conceptual foundation for genuine other-sensitivity and empathy. The relational, coconstructive mutuality in which thought and emotion are constituted, their local, situated social contextuality, lays the socioemotional foundations for such other-sensitivity. It symbiotically partakes and contributes to the collective (supraindividual) Relational Meaning Worlds within which it lives, sharing in comeme (collective, constructed emotional–cognitive meaning carrier) cocreation and co-appropriation. Open to all others and, in effect, to the universe, realities are bathed in passion, reverence, and awe. Communally birthed and oriented, the postmodern mind is activist and bears a levinasian responsibility for the other. World work and world love define its ultimate constructed reality. Thus, it avoids cognitively misperceiving the other, whether defined individually or collectively (e.g., a family, a culture, others' environment), as lower in potential than their optimal developmental level.

Synopsis

The synthetic theory of development that has been described in this work has been given a certain coherence through the manner in which it has been related to postmodernism. The two perspectives bear a reciprocal relationship to each other, in that the current theory contains implications for postmodernism, and vice versa.

Postmodernism is conceived as a multiple perspective on the multiple nature of truths. Its several forms could be ordered in terms of complexity; for example, its constructive side seems more advanced than its deconstructive one. The mature postmodern mind, parent, or couple develop in favorable contextual circumstances, and their responsibility to live in constituted authenticity with others marks their situated, negotiated practices with them.

Postmodernism has gained in its contact with the current theory by living a genuinely developmental theory. The postmodern adult can be conceived as one who has entered into the stage of collective intelligence as defined in the current work, where a symbiotic engagement with others leads to contextualized, second-order overarching abstract truths which embody genuine emotional–cognitive fusion. Also, postmodernism has learned that the postmodern adult mind authors narratives about perceived truths that are scaffolded on emotional experiences. It lives on the edge of chaos, or in the region between order and disorder because that is where developmental change best takes place. It is multilayered and relational in its representational coschemes, which develop and interrelate through coappropriation, activation–inhibition coordinations, and other transition mechanisms.

There are other cognitive stages that precede the collective postmodern one in development in the current theory, and optimal attachment histories and other experiences facilitate passage through them to it. About the former cognitive stages, fractal projections render them isomorphic. And for the latter attachments, different qualities create different intergenerational transmission patterns. In particular, different levels in the quality of the cognitive (mis)perception of the other, as defined by the current theory, are the cardinal mediating lenses in the development toward the postmodern mind, or even couple and society, for when cognitive (mis)perceptions of the other are not optimal, developmental potentials are undercut, and reactions in behavior are provoked.

Postmodern therapy should be an attempt to free developmental potentials toward their mature postmodernistic attributes. The therapeutic approach described in the current work is a brief familial one that is based on activation–inhibition coordination processes, and is aimed at this self-healing. It promotes internal agency while externalizing the problem through liberating conjoint discourses or coconstructed narratives and graphic representations. It is labeled transition therapy because of its developmental and liberational themes. It expresses an epistemological position that is a pluralistic, heterological, intermediating postmodern synthesis of six constructivist stances. Finally, one hopes that postmodernism has grown by its encounter with the synthetic theory. Throughout, I have emphasized the 25-step developmental progression proposed by the theory. It gives a universal scaffold onto which contextualized individual differences in development map as the developing individual grows continually toward the individualized continual growth of the postmodern adult level.

Multiplicity Man

Recently, consulted on the case of a young man. It involved in part his struggle in the transition to the postmodern collective stage of intelligence. He had been sent by his mother since childhood to see 10 different psychologists in order to find out "what was wrong with him," had been diagnosed at one point in the past as clinically depressed, and the current presenting problem was his sense that he was an imposter or shallow in his college and other intellectual work despite clear signs to the contrary such as his ability in learning English to a superior level by self-study, very high marks, and entry into a prestigious university. His family had had to leave a third world country when he was school age, had immigrated to Canada after having lived for 10 years in a western European country, and professed to be fully integrated in the western mentality. Psychological testing revealed an exaggerated split in verbal and performance–motor coordination skills, with superior verbal skills paired with below normal standing on the latter skills. Results on some of these latter skills improved when conscious efforts were made to use verbal mediation strategies.

It seemed possible to me that at several levels in his psychology the client was experiencing and had experienced much separation or dissociation among the multiple modules or domains comprising them. His background involved the loss of the parent culture and nuclear family in which he had grown up. His mother had tried to foster his best interests in some ways (e.g., education), but also had sought to determine the nature of his "problem." His emotional level had varied in the past to the point of being labeled depressed. His intellectual skills profile revealed a variability in score. His academic performance was high achieving yet disqualified as counterfeit. His self showed both determination and self-deprecation.

The manner in which he seemed to use his superior verbal skills to bootstrap performance in other areas seemed an appropriate starting point for reframing his issue as one of struggling to have his disparate parts integrate in contextually meaningful ways. It was suggested that his apparent assimilation in the western world be used as an anchor to explore any masked pains in the loss of his original culture and other related losses, that the odyssey of diagnosis on which his mother had sent him be used as a linchpin to understand her concern for him, and that his determined, successful side be presented as counterevidence against the case that he had constructed about himself. Finally, his doubts concerning his intellectual argumentation skills were cast as inevitable outcomes in his quest for higher levels of cognitive development, that is, toward postmodern post-formal thought. In moving out of the abstract stage of intelligence toward the multimodal, postformal, postmodern one, his intellectual foundations were uprooted before they could be reconstructed on firmer ground. That is, all transitions bring variability, and given the other foci of doubt in the client's life, the cognitive conflict between the certainty of one-dimensional abstract systems and the postmodern uncertainty as to whether any uni-dimensional system can be adequate was unduly excaberated.

In short, this client's problems seemed an excellent representation of the postmodern dilemma; in acknowledging one's multiplicity in order to obtain better contextual and psychological adjustment, coherence is endangered. The postmodern personal issue is how to accommodate to our multiplicities at the level of the self, culture, skills, etc., and thus the postmodern therapeutic issue is how to have the client acknowledge the need for an accommodation such as this. In this sense, the postmodern therapeutic approach adhered to in the current work is a therapy of multiplicities or can be called *multiplicity therapy*, to complement the current emphasis on its transitional nature. That is, by externalizing the problem through discourse practices and coauthoring alternative narratives of client lives, the current activation–inhibition coordination therapy seems to be opening up the space for multiple possibilities at each level of psyche. As a therapist, I become the multiplicative mirror in which the client can see the reflection of her or his adaptive future.

CONCLUSION

The synthetic nature of the current theory, both at the ontological and epistemological levels, should be evident. In terms of ontology, the postmodern integration of the neopiagetian, neovygotskian, neobowlbian, neoeriksonian, neobanduran, and neosystemic perspectives on development is considered a major theoretical advance. Also, particular models are considered pertinent, such as the ones on the 25 steps in the development of the cognitive (mis)perception of the other and the one on the nature of coappropriation in cognitive reorganization (with its emphasis on coschemes, (dis)equilibration, potential negativity in the environment, and social buffers). At the level of epistemology, the synthetic nature of the current theory is revealed by its coexistential, heterological, moderate foundational model integrating six different constructivist schools.

The current synthetic theory of development appears to be making a relevant contribution to the field. Perceptions of its lacunae should be balanced by ones of its expanse and its future improvement, whether by me or others. A postmodern theory would have it no other way.

CHAPTER 13

Appendix: Political Discourse in Adolescents with Their Mothers

ABSTRACT

The synthetic theory of development was used as a basis to develop discourse coding systems (i.e., a text complexity measure which examines the cognitive complexity of narrative texts and a conversational support scale designed to investigate the quality of social discourse). The scales were applied to an empirical study of 48 mother–adolescent dyads who participated in individual interviews and a discussion on two sociopolitical topics. This study had been analyzed previously (Santolupo & Pratt, 1994) with other scales, and the general result was that older adolescents showed more complexity of political reasoning on a pretest than did younger adolescents. However, there was no evidence in support of several of the predictions, and inspection of the coding systems used suggested that their limitations may have played in this result. The new coding schemes were applied to the transcripts of the adolescent–mother discourse with the goal of supporting the predictions that were not substantiated previously.

Both the text complexity measure and the conversation support scale gave significant results where none were found in the original analysis. For example, text complexity was found to correlate positively with increasing age and with increasing education level of the adolescents. Also, a positive correlation between the conversational support measure and an authoritative parenting style was found. In addition, the two scales were correlated positively between them for mothers. The two new coding systems appear to be useful measures because they are based on an internally consistent developmental framework and produce hypothesis-consistent data.

INTRODUCTION

The Synthetic Model

The synthetic model of development integrates several neopiagetian perspectives into one 25-level model (consisting of 5 stages × 5 recursive substages; see Table P.1). Also, in this theory, socioaffective growth is seen to parallel cognitive growth in terms of an equivalent 25-level progression through which individuals can advance. However, the theory does not provide enough concrete or everyday examples of the way thinking or emotions are qualitatively different in one substage compared to another.

In the next section, it is shown that Perry (1970) is much more detailed in his provision of practical illustrations of how "forms" of moral and ethical development proceed from being fairly simple to being complex. However, his work lacks an underlying theoretical structure, unlike the case for the current work.

Perry's Model

Perry's (1970) work related to postformal reasoning attempts to trace the "forms" or structures of the way students in college interpret the nature and origins of their own knowledge, values, and responsibility (see Table 13.1). He describes the development of nine stages or positions, beginning with "Basic Duality" and ending with "Developing Commitments." This sequence of positions reflects an orderly progression where complex forms of thinking or values are created by the differentiation and reintegration of earlier, simpler forms.

More specifically, Perry's first three positions are rooted in simple origins where the world is interpreted in unqualified polar terms of absolutes (right vs. wrong, good vs. bad). Gradually, individuals are believed to develop from a dualistic absolute view of the world toward a more generalized relativistic perspective where different viewpoints can be compared and evaluated. The major milestones that Perry describes in the middle positions are the steps that individuals go through when attempting to make sense of a world full of diversity. Perry's fifth position, relativism, reflects a major developmental transition because it is believed that at this point human knowledge and values are recognized as being relative, contingent, and contextual. In Perry's last three positions, individuals orient themselves in a relativistic world through the activity of personal commitments. Thus, they come to affirm commitments in a world of contingent knowledge and relative values.

As we shall see in the next section, Kuhn also describes three main categories within which an individual's reasoning may be grouped. Although neither Perry nor Kuhn explicitly describe any theoretical rationale for how reasoning shifts from simple to complex forms, both provide rich descriptive information of "types" or "forms" of reasoning.

Kuhn's Model

Kuhn (1991, 1993) interviewed male and female individuals in their teens, twenties, forties, and sixties who were either college educated or noncollege educated. She asked her participants to discuss their personal theories regarding causes on three topics, to justify their theories by providing supporting evidence, to generate possible alternative views, to supply rebuttals, and finally, to describe the epistemological origins of their own thinking.

Kuhn depicts three epistemological theories which capture the participants' implicit theories of knowledge. She reports that 50% of the subjects were classified as absolutists. These participants regard knowledge as being certain and accumulative. Kuhn's second category, which consisted of 35% of her subjects, were classified as multiplists, or relativists. Multiplists take note that even experts disagree about certain causes, and therefore maintain that nothing is certain and that all opinions are equally correct because everyone has a right to his or her own opinion. The final category outlined by Kuhn is comprised of evaluatists (15% of the population). Here, subjects consider knowing as a continuous, open-ended process that involves thinking, evaluation, and judgment. It should be noted that Kuhn's three epistemological types (absolutist, multiplist, and evaluatist) correspond to Perry's "Basic Duality," "Multiplicity Correlate," and "Initial Commitment" forms of thinking, respectively.

Comment

A review of Perry's (1970) book confirms that, indeed, there is no mention of a theoretical guiding framework. Similarly, Kuhn's work lacks clear, well-defined theoretical explanations for the manner in which argumentative reasoning progresses from an absolutist to an evaluatist stance. Her work, as is Perry's, is largely descriptive of the "types" of evidence, counterevidence, or rebuttals, generated by participants.

Thus, in the current research the synthetic model seemed the most appropriate axis on which an effective measure of cognitive complexity could be built in order to reexamine the data gathered in Santolupo and Pratt (1994). Consequently, the current coding system of discourse com-

**Table 13.1 Comparison of Three Developmental Models
of Reasoning for Adolescents and Adults**

Perry (1970)	Young	Baker-Brown et al. (1992)
Basic duality (right vs. wrong)	Abstract coordination (11–13 years)	Linear reasoning: One simple unidimensional rule; Only one way of looking at the world is legitimate
Multiplicity prelegitimate (people with other viewpoints lack enlightenment)	Abstract hierarchization (13–16 years)	Still not tolerant of others' viewpoints: Uncertainty is not accepted
Multiplicity subordinate (different views acknowledged but still adherence to absolutes)	Abstract systematization (16–19 years)	Some tolerance or uncertainty in judging events: Exceptions to the rule; Potential or conditional acceptance of different perspectives or views
Multiplicity correlate ("Everyone has the right to his or her own opinion.")	Abstract multiplication (19–22 years)	Differentiation: Different viewpoints are acknowledged and there is acceptance that these viewpoints are legitimate, relevant, or valid
Relativism correlate, competing, or diffuse (viewpoints now compared and/or evaluated)	Abstract integration (22–25 years)	Tension in the weighing or evaluation of all the multiple viewpoints: There is a relationship among viewpoints or alternatives; There is a need for further information before judgments can be made
Commitment foreseen (all views are relativistic)	Collective coordination (25–28 years)	Integration: Integration of viewpoints is clearly evident; Mutual influence; Different views can occur simultaneously and are also interactive; Synthesis of viewpoints
Initial commitment	Collective hierarchization (28–39 years)	Give and take trade-offs

(*continued*)

Table 13.1 (*Continued*)

Perry (1970)	Young	Baker-Brown et al. (1992)
Orientation in implications of commitment	Collective systematization (39–50 years)	Hypothesis-testing or reality-testing Alternatives are plans/processes/actions that are made up of several moving parts All parts affect each other in the system Aware of two alternative courses of action and is able to compare their outcomes with regard to long-term implications
Developing commitment (restructuring or expanding commitments)	Collective multiplication (50–61 years)	Several commitments accepted and all are viewed as legitimate These commitments are viewed as occurring simultaneously even though some of them may be contradictory to each other
Commitments consolidated (various commitments made over the lifetime solidified and integrated)	Collective integration (61+ years)	Overarching principle pertains to the nature of the relationship between alternatives This principle has developed as a result of the person's simultaneous consideration of these levels Realizes that one's view depends on combinations of legal, moral, and scientific judgments

Note. The last stage in Perry's model and the second-to-last one in Baker-Brown et al.'s model have been extrapolated.

plexity is based on that model, but borrows from the other sources as required. In the next section, the new scale is compared to the original one used in the analysis reported in Santolupo and Pratt (1994), the scale of integrative complexity (IC) developed by Baker-Brown et al. (1992).

Baker-Brown et al.'s Model

Baker-Brown et al.'s scale of cognitive complexity, called integrative complexity (see Table 13.1), was constructed in light of an underlying premise on the nature of the developmental process. That is, it is defined primarily by two cognitive stylistic variables, differentiation and integration, characteristics which are seen to define the developmental process. Differentiation refers to the number of different perspectives or dimensions of a problem, whereas integration refers to the degree to which differentiated concepts are interrelated in a tightly consistent system.

Baker-Brown et al. have written a manual that has been developed to effect the application of the model. However, despite a general theoretical structure in terms of differentiation and integration, there seems to be little theoretical justification for particular scale points.

Comparison of the Models

The similarities among Perry, Baker-Brown et al., and the current model may be gleaned from observation of Table 13.1. At a general level, this table delineates a parallel progression in the three models from "simple" to "complex" thought. Closer scrutiny reveals further parallels across them. For example, if one considers the first row of the abstract coordination substage, all three approaches describe a coordination in abstract thought (e.g., a unitary type of thinking chosen from a formal understanding of an opposition between right versus wrong). In the next substage, all suggest that a hierarchy of views or opinions occur because several views/opinions are explicitly recognized, but only one or some are accepted while others are not. In the next level, similarities among the three models occur in the belief that there is conditional acceptance and/or acknowledgement of others' or secondary viewpoints or opinions. This constitutes a system in the current model, for there is an expansion and simplification of hierarchized viewpoints. At the next level of abstract multiplication, different viewpoints are readily accepted and acknowledged. Thus, the previous systematization of opinions has been replaced by a combination of multiple, equally legitimate systems. Finally, the current abstract integration substage parallels Perry's relativism correlate, competing, or diffuse stage, and Baker-Brown et al.'s corresponding stage in that all three consider the way an individual would compare, evaluate, weigh, and relate multiple viewpoints.

In the next level, Perry, Baker-Brown et al., and the current model all consider reasoning to have reached a new plateau. There is a foreseen commitment, a synthesis, and a collective element in thought, respectively. This level can be described as a type of coordination, for different viewpoints are relative, mutual, and can occur simultaneously. In the next level, where the current model describes collective hierarchization, Perry speaks of one commitment or opinion becoming more dominant over the others. Similarly, Baker-Brown et al. describe this level as one where there is a give and take or a trade-off when considering commitments or opinions. Then in the next level, the current model describes collective systematization, and Baker-Brown et al. adopt a corresponding language and describe alternative commitments, viewpoints, hypotheses, plans, processes, or actions as being part of a larger overall system in which components affect each other. Similarly, Perry's mention of implications of commitments also speaks to a systems construct. Next, the current model refers to collective multiplication, for example, the presence of several systems and expanding commitments occurring simultaneously. Similarly, Perry talks of restructuring or expanding commitments. However, Baker-Brown et al. do not really address this level, so we have added an entry to the table on how they might have dealt with it had they followed the current theoretical model. Lastly, Baker-Brown et al. and the current model view the integration substage as a time where an overarching principle, which encapsulates all previous systems or viewpoints, is considered as being more precisely differentiated and as being dependent on combinations of legal, moral, and scientific judgments or evaluations. We have added an entry to the table in order to fill in Perry's model, for he has no comparable level at this juncture.

Now that this first scale of text complexity and the theoretical model on which it is built has been discussed, a second coding system that attempts to examine the nature of the discourse in our data is addressed. It deals with the support or its lack provided by the mothers in their dialogues with their adolescents. It was developed in order to replace the coding scheme developed by Berkowitz and Gibbs (1983, 1985) on transactive dialogue which had been used in the original data analysis in Santolupo and Pratt (1994).

CONVERSATIONAL SUPPORT

Transactive Dialogue

Berkowitz and Gibbs (1983, 1985; also see Berkowitz & Keller, 1994) have shown that new moral stage acquisition is promoted by discussions in which each member directly engages the reasoning of her or his discussion partner with her or his own reasoning. The underlying assumption is that moral reasoning is most likely to ensue from discussions that produce cognitive conflict or disequilibrium. More specifically, transactive discussion, or transactive dialogue behavior (TDB), comprise statements which involve cognitive operations upon another's reasoning in the context of an attempt to resolve, explain, or comprehend differences in reasoning about issues. Berkowitz and Gibbs examined this process in transcriptions of moral reasoning discussions collected from college undergraduates, where they coded higher-order (operational transacts, e.g., extend, refine, complete, critique) or lower-order transacts (representational transacts).

One problem with Berkowitz and Gibbs' coding system for transactive dialogue behavior, however, is that it fails to capture the emotional aspect of dialogues between two discussants. When applied to a normal discussion, many statements cannot be categorized by it because it does not allow for supportive or interfering emotional assertions. For example, in the original analysis of the transcripts in the Santolupo and Pratt (1994) study, up to 70% of the conversational turns were uncodable in terms of the Berkowitz and Gibb's coding scheme. It is strongly suspected that the "unscorable" statements could reveal valuable information concerning the type of interaction occurring between mothers and their adolescents. Variations in warm and less positive maternal support in discussions with adolescents should result in important differences in the nature and complexity of the discussions.

The Current Scale

Young and Young (in preparation) developed a conversation support scale that helps account for the emotional component of discussions between parents and their children. They investigated the degree to which mothers facilitated their children's recounting of narratives in a positive, supportive or negative, interfering fashion.

In Chapter 7, this approach is carried one step further by describing a scale of discourse participation that is based on how individuals' (mis)perceptions of the cognitive level of others influences behavior toward them (in a 25-step model). In this (mis)perception model, Young suggests that the extent to which a family is seen to control or guide their child's cognitive development is linked to the specific cognitive substage at which the child is (mis)perceived emotionally to have actually developed or is capable of optimally attaining.

That is, Young implies that most parents project the cognitive level to which they have limited themselves onto their children, so that an intergenerational transmission of socioaffective limitations on cognitive development is realized. Thus, the different perceptions that parents have of their children's developmental cognitive level have a profound effect on the manner in which parents interact with and care for them.

Conclusion

In conclusion, the text complexity scale and the conversation support scale should have many applications. For example, it should be possible to apply both scales to any age range and ascertain the degree of complexity in and conversational support for an individual's narrative or dialogue. Second, it should be possible to forecast future development in cognitive complexity. Knowledge of an individual's current level of cognitive development in conjunction with the typical support that he or she receives can allow prediction of the level of further cognitive progression. Also, the conversation support scale can be used to elucidate the relationship between different patterns of complexity and different patterns in caregiving style. In addition, knowledge of a parent's (mis)perception of her or his child's cognitive level, as ascertained by the conversation support scale, perhaps can be used to trace and circumvent abusive interactions.

In what follows, we will show that the text complexity scale and the conversation support scale are useful and valid measures for investigating sociopolitical discussions. The data on adolescent–mother dialogues that were analyzed in Santolupo and Pratt (1994) are reanalyzed with these two synthetic-theory derived scales because certain hypotheses were not confirmed with the scales used in the original analyses, and these two new scales seemed better suited for the investigation.

EMPIRICAL SUPPORT
FOR THE SYNTHETIC MODEL

Predictions

Originally, the transcripts of the 48 mother–adolescent dyads that were gathered had been analyzed using Baker-Brown et al.'s measure of integrative complexity and Berkowitz and Gibbs' coding system of transactive dialogue behavior (Santolupo & Pratt, 1994). For the current reanalysis of the data, we predicted that as children progress into adolescence, they would show a positive age-related and education-related increase in the complexity of their thought, as assessed by the text complexity scale. This latter prediction was not confirmed in the previous analysis when the integrative complexity measure was used.

Second, we predicted that a positive relationship would be found between text complexity scores and conversational support scores. That is, adolescents who showed high text complexity scores also should have received a higher degree of conversational support in the discussions with their mothers. This prediction also was not confirmed in the previous analysis.

Third, we expected a positive relationship between conversational support offered by mothers and an authoritative or more supportive parenting style (Baumrind, 1991). This prediction was somewhat supported in the previous analysis where it was reported that an authoritarian parenting

style was related to a higher proportion of challenging or critical statements made by mothers.

Finally, it was hypothesized that only adolescents who experienced a
discussion with their mothers on the political topics of interest would
show gains in posttest reinterview text complexity scores relative to their
pretest scores. This hypothesis was not confirmed in the previous analysis.

Method

Participants.   Forty-eight children (24 adolescents, ranging in age
from 12 to 15 years; and 24 adolescents, ranging in age from 16 to 19 years),
as well as their mothers, served as participants in the study. From each of
these two age categories, 12 children and their mothers were randomly
assigned to either the experimental (discussion) or control conditions,
with the restriction that the adolescent participants in each group in each
age category were equally divided according to sex. All participants were
recruited from advertisements which appeared in local newspapers in a
medium-sized Canadian city. All were living at home with their mothers.

Mean ages of the younger experimental and control group adolescents
(collapsed across gender) were 13.9 years (s.d. = 0.9) and 13.7 years (s.d. =
1.16), respectively. The mean age of the older experimental and control
group adolescents was 17.6 years in both cases (s.d. = 1.08 and 1.16, respectively). Mothers' ages were similar across experimental and control groups,
as well (M = 38.5 to 43.8 years). All of them had obtained at least a high
school education. Their occupational backgrounds varied widely, from
unemployed to elementary school principal. Most of the participants were
Caucasian.

Materials, Coding, Procedures.   In order to measure complexity of
reasoning for both adolescents and mothers in the experimental and control groups, a series of five questions was developed pertaining to the
political issues of unemployment and public servants' right to strike (see
Santolupo & Pratt, 1994, for a full presentation of the procedure). The
unemployment topic and probe questions were adapted from the work of
Kuhn (1991) on adults' everyday reasoning. An example probe item was,
"If you were trying to convince someone else that your view is right, what
evidence would you give to try to show this?" A parallel series of probes
was used for the right to strike issue.

Complexity of thought was scored according to the text complexity
scale described earlier. The open-ended responses to the pretest and posttest interviews were scored using this scale. For each participant, an average score for level of sophistication of reasoning was obtained across the

five interview questions. Two independent raters scored a sample of 200 specific responses. Interrater reliability for items from this subsample was high, $r(94) = .89$, $p < .001$.

Mothers and adolescents in the experimental group were asked to participate in a dyadic discussion on specific exemplars of either one issue or the other. All discussions took place in the first session and followed the pretest interviews. Each dyad's goal was to read the presented paragraph about a specific issue, discuss it, and come to some type of agreement, if possible, on the manner in which the presented conflict could be resolved. The discussions were transcribed subsequently, and scored for the amount of conversational support provided by mothers according to the scale described earlier. A reliability check for scoring of the discussions was conducted by two independent raters on a sample of six discussions. From this subset of 342 turns of dialogue, Cohen's kappa across the major categories was determined to be .85.

A seven-item questionnaire which measured parenting styles through family decision-making, adapted from Dornbusch et al. (1985), was completed by the mothers. An example question from this index was, "Who decides when you have to be home on the weekend?" These questions addressed the child's view of the decision-making patterns used in the home environment. Dornbusch et al. (1985) reported reliability assessments using Cronbach's alpha of .69 for Parent Alone decisions (authoritarian), .63 for Youth Alone (permissive), and .69 for joint decision-making (authoritative). To control for possible general developmental trends in these decision-making styles (e.g., more "youth alone" patterns for older teens), partial correlations of the parenting styles with the dependent measures, controlling for adolescent age, were calculated.

RESULTS

Age-Education and Complexity

The Pearson product-moment correlations for the pretest and posttest IC measures and the text complexity measures are reported in Table 13.2. Like in the Santolupo and Pratt study, age of the adolescent was partialled out in these calculations. As can be seen in the table, the text complexity measures for both the pretest and posttest scores were found to be positively correlated with the integrative complexity of reasoning pretest and posttest measures. This relationship was found for adolescent text complexity scores as well as for mothers' text complexity scores. For adolescent age, we found a significantly positive correlation with the posttest text complexity measure, $r(46) = .46$, $p < .01$, but not for the pretest measure,

**Table 13.2 Pearson Product–Moment Correlations
between Integrative and Text Complexity**

	AIC2	TXT1	TXT2	MIC1	MIC2	MTXT1	MTXT2
AIC1	.57**	.49**	.32*	.03	−.15	−.13	.001
AIC2		.45*	.63**	.14	.17	−.12	.10
TXT1			.57**	−.05	−.08	.02	.08
TXT2				.03	.22	.08	.20
MIC1					.56**	.36*	.18
MIC2						.19	.18
MTXT1							.34*

Note. $N = 48$ *$p < .05$ **$p < .01$
AIC1 = Adolescents' Integrative Complexity Pretest Scores; AIC2 = Adolescents' Integra-
tive Complexity Posttest Scores; TXT1 = Adolescents' Text Complexity Pretest Scores;
TXT2 = Adolescents' Text Complexity Posttest Scores; MIC1 = Mothers' Integrative
Complexity Pretest Scores; MIC2 = Mothers' Integative Complexity Posttest Scores;
MTXT1 = Mothers' Text Complexity Pretest Scores; MTXT2 = Mothers' Text Complexity
Posttest Scores.

$r(46) = .26$. However, positive relationships were found for both the pretest
and posttest complexity measure with adolescent education, $r(46) = .30$, p
$< .05$, and $r(46) = .44$, $p < .01$, respectively.

Complexity and Support

A second set of analyses concerned the predicted relationship between the conversational support measure and the text complexity measure. In order to investigate this relationship, Pearson product–moment
correlations were computed, again controlling for age. Table 13.3 reveals
the significant findings. Contrary to predictions, the maternal conversation
support measure was not found to be significantly correlated with the
adolescent text complexity score. Indeed, when looking at adolescents'
complexity posttest scores, a negative relationship was found, $r(22) = −.51$,
$p < .01$. However, a positive relationship was found between mothers'
pretest text complexity scores and their conversational support score,
$r(22) = .51$, $p < .01$.

Last, as predicted, the conversational support measure was found to
be related to an authoritative parenting style as perceived by mothers,
$r(22) = .41$, $p < .05$. Thus, mothers who provided more conversational
support during conversations with their adolescent also rated their parenting style as being more authoritative. No other significant result for the
conversational support measure was found.

**Table 13.3 Pearson Product-Moment Correlations
for the Maternal Conversational Support Measure
in Relation to Text Complexity and Parenting Style**

Support correlated with	Particular variables involved			
Adolescent	AIC1	AIC2	TXT1	TXT2
Complexity	$-.24$	$-.51^b$	$-.13$	$-.32$
Mother	MIC1	MIC2	TXT1	TXT2
Complexity	$.43^a$	$.23$	$.51^b$	$.25$
Parenting	Permissive	Authoritarian		Authoritative
Style	$-.14$	$-.39$		$.41^a$

Note. $N = 24$
$^a p < .05$
$^b p < .01$

Group Results

Unreported analyses (Macdonald, 1994) revealed that adolescents in the experimental group when compared to control group adolescents did not exhibit a significant gain in complexity regarding political issues due to participating in discussions with their mothers. Overall, means on the complexity scale for adolescents varied only modestly across groups from pretest to posttest.

Mothers' text complexity scores ($M = 4.95$) were significantly greater than were adolescents' text complexity scores ($M = 4.08$). In the experimental group, both mothers and adolescents had significantly lower posttest text complexity scores when compared to their pretest text complexity scores. However, the control group mothers and adolescents did not show any significant differences between pretest and posttest text complexity scores (see Table 13.4 for means). Thus, as was predicted, the control group mothers and adolescents did not change in their text complexity scores, for they did not participate in the discussion intervention. However, contrary to our predictions, the experimental group showed lower rather than higher text complexity scores.

DISCUSSION AND CONCLUSION

Discussion

Two scales derived from the synthetic theory of development, a text complexity scale and a conversation support scale, were applied to adolescent–mother discussions regarding political issues. The purpose of this study

Table 13.4 Means of Text Complexity
and Posttest Scores for Mothers vs. Adolescents

Participant	Group	Pretest score	Posttest score
Mothers	Experimental	5.29 (0.85)	4.80 (0.56)
	Control	5.02 (0.40)	4.69 (0.60)
Adolescents	Experimental	4.15 (0.99)	4.12 (0.72)
	Control	4.03 (0.71)	4.00 (0.66)

Note. Standard deviations are shown in brackets. $N = 96$ $n = 24$ per row.

was to evaluate the validity and usefulness of these new measures and to determine whether predictions not confirmed in the original analysis of the data in Santolupo and Pratt (1994) could be confirmed with reanalysis of the data using the new scales.

In the current analysis, the text complexity measure derived from the synthetic theory did show strong developmental trends, as was predicted, for both the adolescent age measure and the education variable were positively correlated with the adolescents' text complexity scores. It is interesting to note that, in contrast to the current results, when the integrative complexity of reasoning measure (IC) was used in the original analysis, no significant correlations were found for adolescent age or education (Santolupo & Pratt, 1994). This finding suggests that the text complexity scale may be a valuable measure for investigating developmental advances in complexity of thought.

Furthermore, the validity of the current scale of text complexity is suggested by the correlation between it and the original integrative complexity measure. The results also show that the text complexity scores evidenced stability (and thus reliability) from pretest to posttest for both adolescents and mothers. In addition, as one would predict, it was found that mothers score about one substage higher in cognitive level during discourse when compared to their adolescents (i.e., approximately "5" versus "4" on the scale, or at the levels of perioperational integration versus perioperational multiplication, respectively). Note that the level of complexity elicited in the participants during their dialogues in the current study does not seem to be very high on the average; generally, the abstract level was not attained even though the topics of discussion seemed current and interesting.

The validity of the conversational support scale also is revealed by the current analysis, specifically by the positive correlation between scores on this scale for mothers and their perceptions of their level of authoritative parenting behavior. Apparently, the more mothers felt that they were authoritative, or limit-setting, yet stimulative and supportive in their parental style with their adolescents, the more they gave positive support to their adolescents' ideas during political dialogues.

Also, we predicted a positive relationship between the text complexity measure and the conversational support scale, a result which would speak to the validity of both the scales. This prediction was confirmed for mothers, and thus points to the validity of both of the scales. It seems that mothers engage in a cognitive level in their political discourse consonant with the degree of social support that they offer their adolescent offspring. The exact nature of the relationship between these variables needs to be determined, but it could be that the mothers limit their cognitive and social manifestations when with their children to the developmental level at which they (mis)perceive themselves as functioning.

A negative relationship between the mothers' conversational support scores and the adolescents' posttest text complexity scores also was reported. This suggests that in certain circumstances parental support facilitates child cognitive development, but in others, such as the current one, parental withdrawal does the same. A parent may wish to encourage independent thought or personal problem solving in adolescents, especially for sensitive topics, and thus offer less and not more support in discussion. That is, parents may set up a "zone of inhibition development" (Moss, 1992) or "zone of activation/inhibition coordination" (see Chapter 6), which would lead to the type of result that was obtained.

There was little support for the final hypothesis of the current reanalysis of the Santolupo and Pratt data, which stated that adolescents exposed to a brief discussion with their mothers would show significant gains in text complexity posttest scores when compared to pretest scores. It seems likely that a single discussion such as the one used is not sufficient to have much effect on adolescents' complexity of thinking. Or, perhaps an intervention such as this cannot work with adolescents given their "independent" phase of development.

The last finding that we discuss concerns the decline in cognitive complexity scores from the pretest to the posttest in the experimental group for both mothers and adolescents. Although no similar decline in IC scores was reported in the original analysis from pretest to posttest, it has already been suggested that the text complexity scale used here is a more sensitive index of developmental progression than the one used originally. A possible explanation for this noted decrease in scores could concern the adolescents' and mothers' boredom when having to discuss the same topics that they had already discussed only one week earlier. The relatively low level of complexity that was obtained for the participants during their discourse (see above) speaks to this interpretation. Research with more extended interventions and different more interesting formats seems warranted.

Conclusion

In conclusion, the text complexity scale and the conversational support scale that have been derived from the synthetic theory appear to be reliable measures derived from a valid theory and seem useful measures for studying political dialogue between mothers and adolescents. These scales allow relevant information to emerge in terms of how adolescents progress through levels of thinking about political organizations, and how the content and structure of adolescent thinking can be influenced by maternal styles of interaction.

CHAPTER 14

Postscript:
From Adult Development
to Communitarian Politics

POSTMODERNISM

A last survey of the recent literature helps both to confirm the basic tenets of the book and to nuance some of them. This chapter does not attempt to recapitulate or integrate in full previous material. It deals with the issues of postmodernism, adult development, culture, philosophy, and therapy, and describes some personal contributions.

The term *postmodernism* is presented in the book as if it represents a coherent, readily definable approach. However, Bertens (1995) makes it clear that in some senses postmodernism stands for diametrically opposite concepts in different disciplines. For example, it may involve a turning away from or turning to narrative and representation, depending on the discipline. Given this definitional uncertainty of the term postmodernism, one may ask whether there is an external objective reality or essentialist foundation, whether it can be represented; and if narratives are superordinate representations in this process, whether they are relative with respect to or reflective of that external reality. It will be recalled in Chapter 2, I described that there have been two phases in the development of postmodernism as it relates to psychology, with a deconstructive period preceding a more affirmative one (Gergen, 1994a). Both phases reject representation and universal metanarrative as source and arbiter of truth, but the second phase adds that individuals and cultures in dialogue require an extreme sensitivity to the particular local, situated narratives of the other. Also, I emphasized that realism–representationalism and its opposites are blending in the current phase in the intellectual evolution of postmodernism, in what Larner (1995) calls the paramodern turn, or what Wittgenstein calls moderate foundationalism (Falck, 1994).

Similarly, Held (1995) argues that postmodernists are not necessarily anti-realist in their writings despite their affirmations. Any postmodernist accepts that battering of women has a "patent reality status." There are not only indirect, mediated (e.g., by theory, narrative, discourse) components of knowledge of independent reality but also direct, spatiotemporal, non-linguistic unmediated knowledge of other aspects. Thus, the most appropriate epistemology is one based on a modest, limited realism. As well, Bertens (1995) claims that in practice, thinkers in the field dialectically oscillate between universalism and particularism. Decenterment, difference, dissensus, fragmentation, and centrifugal forces need to be balanced by their opposites, such as consensus and homogenization, and these may be "less clearly visible" but still present. In this dialectic, he contends that we need to accept a balance and "negotiate a permanent crisis in the name of precarious stabilities."

Echoing Held (1995), Globus (1995) argues that "postmodernists are staunch realists." Individuals know by direct resonance with reality through attunement rather than through intermediary emblematic representation. Resonant attunement obtains by the principle of least action, continual self-organization, and so on. Because we are *thrown* into the world (dwell in it, are amidst it, settled into it; Dreyfus, 1991), we live an ongoing personal eruption of ungroundedness in situated groundedness and text (or other) eruption. Again, a moderate foundationalism is implied.

Finally, Billig (1996) confirms that postmodernism is about the other. Because the universe is a multivocal pastiche, there is always lost, suppressed, silenced, inhibited, censored, disdained communal- or self-denied voices of otherness that require questioning, recovery, reinstatement, assertion, or "rhetorical reminding," which is, "above all, a freeing of collective memory from its ghetto." In this regard, Gergen (interviewed in Hoyt, 1996a) maintains that otherness, relatedness, or dance is the essential matrix, and that in looking to relationships instead of to distant abstract principles morality develops in a "relational responsibility." We are constituted by relationship, "acting out of and into relatedness" as we "generate practices of relationship." Relationship precedes individuals and meaning. The appropriate metaphor is the "relational sublime," in which a "sensibility of pure relatedness" develops out of immersion in relationship.

ADULT DEVELOPMENT

The current theory builds heavily on the stage theories of Piaget and Erikson, in particular. Neopiagetians and neoeriksonians argue for the validity of these theories (e.g., Lourenço & Machado, 1996; de St. Aubin & McAdams, 1996, respectively). For example, the former show that in Piaget's later writings he thought that the age of onset of the adolescent formal operational period began later than he had proposed originally, that it was context-dependent, and that development occurred throughout the life-span in a never-ending process. The latter studied the relationship across generativity (in terms of concern and action) and other variables such as personality traits and ego development.

Piaget's contributions to developmental psychology are highlighted in a recent series of articles (Brainerd, 1996). For Flavell (1996), Piaget founded the field of cognitive development in its present form. Siegler and Ellis (1996) organize his contributions around the constructs of constructivism (an important concept throughout this book), essentialism (with respect to his universal stages), and dynamism (on change processes), while Elkind (1996) speaks of progress, universality, and regularity. He notices that for Piaget, context can help impede the development of the last stage in development, yet the organism is "forever attempting to transcend itself" (Piaget, 1978, p. 139). Gopnik (1996) describes Piaget's future in developmental psychology, and to her analysis I add that in this quote Piaget showed the possibility of a constant adult development, which begs the question as to why he never envisaged a postformal period, per se.

Commons, Demick, and Goldberg (1996) have edited an important book that examines the interface between adult development and clinical psychology. Its chapters deal with both stage and nonstage theories. For example, Llave and Commons (1996) compare psychological boundaries from the perspective of three nonstage theories—psychodynamic, cognitive, behavioral. Commons (1996) describes three approaches to adult development in which stage theory has been influential—the points of view of "whole life" theory, classic stage theory, and "period of life" theory. He argues that the three theories form a synergy. Demick's (1996a) life-transition perspective provides an example of the first type of theory, which is the only one not intuitively obvious. It emphasizes person-in-environment transitions throughout the lifespan, where transitions are considered to be distinct and more than amorphous periods between plateaus of development. Similarly, the approach of evolving systems (Tahir, 1996) perceives the development of creativity in thought as a constructive series of restructurings. The process takes time, and so is considered a process of "protracted epigenesis." (Fischer and Biddell, 1996, eloquently describe epigenesis. "Between nature and nurture stands the human agent whose activities and integrative capacities drive ... organize individual and environmental contributions to development" [p. 209].)

The contributors to the book by Commons et al. (1996) cover a broad range of stage theorists. Shaughnessy and Carey (1996) adopt the classic piagetian model, Cleave-Hogg (1996) bases herself on the model of Perry

(1970), often considered a neopiagetian; and Broderick (1996) and Popp (1996) work with Kegan's (1982) neopiagetian stage theory, the one described in depth in Chapter 2 of the current volume. Noam (1996) performs his research using Loevinger's (1976) stage theory of ego development, which is related to Erikson's stage theory (see the Prologue).

Goldberg (1996) criticizes the manner in which eriksonian and related theories are formulated as a series of developmental challenges with negative and positive options (e.g., trust vs. mistrust), considering this approach too "black and white." He maintains that the Commons et al. (1996) book is a step toward the creation of a theory of an "organic whole" in adult development. Similarly, Demick (1996b) refers to the terms organismic and synergistic when speaking of the relationship between adult developmental and clinical psychology. In this regard, work by both Kegan (e.g., Kegan, 1986, in Demick, 1996b) and Noam (Noam and Dill, 1996) indicate that for the most part psychopathology is not distributed differentially across different "sociocognitive" stages of development in the adolescent and adult age periods. However, with more mature stage acquisition, symptoms become less intense and more cognitive than behavioral, and requests for modality of therapy fit this pattern (e.g., it becomes more insight-oriented).

Levenson and Crumpler (1996) describe three models of adult development, and in so doing contrast different approaches to stage theory with nonstage theory. They argue that ontogenetic or stage theories seek universal, age-linked, intrinsic changes in adult development, such as in Erikson's theory, but that they are too biological, fixed, or deterministic relative to the flow of human development. The sociogenic or nonstage perspective is socially contextualist, thus allowing unlimited different developmental paths in the adult, and reducing in importance the determinative role of biology in adult development. A third viewpoint, called, liberative is preferred by the authors. It is based on Loevinger's (1976) stage theory, where stages are described in terms of an increasing freeing from deterministic biological and social forces. According to this approach, later stages in development may weakly determine or influence development, but personal consciousness, individual choice, commitment to change, receptivity and openness to experience, etc., become important influences, as well.

Dannefer (1996) clarifies that in the sociogenetic perspective social forces are considered not mere influences but constitutive matrices in adult development. Self (e.g., through creativity, imagination) and society and its institutions interpenetrate continually in this process. In a similar vein, Noam and Fischer (1996a) contend that relationships have a foundational role in adult development. They are not simply "internal influences" on relationship members, for members "participate in each other's minds." I agree with this notion about the importance of the constitutive construction of the person in the communal crucible, and at the end of this chapter further speculate on this developmental process. As we shall see, it seems to me that a moderate synthetic perspective may be taken on the issue, one that leaves room for each of stage and nonstage, individual and culture, biology and environment, influence and constitutive pressure, etc., in one adult developmental model.

In a pair of fascinating articles, Strayer (1996) and Labouvie-Vief (1996) examine the midlife adult development of the queen in the folktale *Snow White*. The queen is seen not as the evil stepmother, which the story portrays, but as the victim of her self-image. In support of this argument, Strayer (1996) introduces James's (1890) distinction between the subjective I self and the objective me self (see Chapter 3). The queen appears trapped in the mirror that she summons for an opinion of whom is the fairest in the land. She overly seeks approval from others, aggrandizing the me self at the expense of the I self so that it becomes a false self. According to Strayer, with appropriate cognitive–emotional reformulation the queen comes to see, acknowledge, and create each of herself, others, relations, and the images involved from multiple, relativistic perspectives. Thus, I-persons will develop instead of false selves, producing more of a being in the world through appropriate agency, relationships, and the like. Labouvie-Vief (1996) adds that adult development involves successive transformations of a balance between the inner personal and the outer cultural, through a mutual, reciprocal, relational, dialectical mirroring. Through this "suprapersonal" process, development becomes whole and redemptive of early psychological tragedies and resultant trapped energies, so that deepened empathy and generativity may emerge in adult development. Labouvie-Vief's view contains within it the social constitutive emphasis of Dannefer (1996), but she is a noted neopiagetian who has developed an excellent model of the nature of the postformal adult period of development (see the Prologue). In this regard, I believe that she would support the model I developed that is presented below and alluded to in the prior paragraph.

Themes similar to the ones encountered in the prior debates appear in the one among the articles on moral development by Day and Tappan (1996), Lourenço (1996), Lapsley (1996), and Puka (1996). Day and Tappan (1996) espouse the narrative approach to moral development and not the traditional cognitive one (Kohlberg, 1981, 1984). In the latter perspective, a disembodied, disengaged, personal subject develops internally through stages of moral thought and justification, whereas in the former perspective moral development is perceived as a dialogical, relational, shared, intersubjective discourse among the many selves of the self and other. Bakhtin's view is important for Day and Tappan, and he maintains that the self has many voices that engage in relationships demanding of "answerability" (responsibility, accountability; e.g., Bakhtin, 1980; see Chapter 6). One enters into the process of "ideologically becoming" the other, or at least the words of one of her or his voices, by selective assimilation or appropriation. Similarly, Niebuhr (1978) speaks of dialogue within a community of moral agents. Thus, for Day and Tappan (1996) moral development is promoted, in particular, by contextual conflict, struggle, collision, collusion, contest, combination, and shaping of relationships. Also, there are no universal invariant stages of moral thinking that permeate this process, for it is individual, situated, and grounded in action rather than thought.

Lourenço (1996) defends the stage approach to moral development on several grounds. He maintains that it is only through universal principles that valid criteria for moral action are constructed. Later moral stages, for example, are based on principles of universal respect and dignified treatment of all humanity. Unlike the cognitive approach, the narrative approach to moral development may lead to nihilism, opportunism, or relativism. Lapsley (1996) appreciates the communitarian and relational fount given to the development of moral selfhood in the narrative approach. According to him, it fits with Taylor's (1989) emphasis on the "web of interlocution" in identity development. However, Lapsley argues that the narrative approach to moral development "absorbs" the individual. Even if the meanings of words are relational and embedded in the network of shared language, as Wittgenstein argued, it does not follow that individuals do not live nonlinguistic realities, and that these realities are unrelated to language. For example, Wittgenstein wrote that meaning "comes through use and forms of life, presumed to be ... the local property of individuals" (Murdoch, 1992, p. 187, cited in Lapsley, 1996). Finally, Puka (1996) argues that cognitive theory and narrative theory can learn from each other about moral development. For example, the cognitive view can help narrativism with its relativism and the narrative view can help cognitivism with its absence of multiplicity in moral discourse.

Culture

The model toward which I am building profits from the following discussion of recent research on culture and adult development. It deals with some of the same issues as in the prior section, for example, the nature of reality and meaning, the role of the individual and community in identity development, and the validity of stages in development.

Miles (1996) combines the individual psychological and the collective social points of view in his account of the development of cultural identity. He contrasts the need for fixed roles and of a "real" self in the modern period to the fragmentation of society, development of a consumer mentality ("the cultural capital of consumption" Bourdieu), and diversity in identity construction in the postmodern period (Baudrillard, 1983; Bourdieu, 1984; Derrida, 1986; Foucault, 1980; Lyotard, 1984). Contemporary youth develop stable consumer identities that bind them because power centers in society that seek to submit them to their imperatives permit this to unfold. Class distinctions are learned through the "habitus," or group-specific social and cognitive frames that embody cultural dispositions (Bourdieu, 1984).

Similarly, Gergen (1994c) argues that meaning is created and constrained communally through recursive action-supplement relationships that extend to society as a whole. The *I* and its ability to mean develop only through our interdependent interlinkages. Communities develop meanings, and through misunderstandings and the like they develop counter-meanings as well. In Gadamer's (1960/1975, in Phillips, 1996) hermeneutical approach, object and interpretive subject are entwined in encounter. The past and present overlap into one grand horizon in a "fusion of horizons." Text invites dialogue about itself and to the "implicit question" to which it had been addressed when created. But for Ricoeur (1981, in Phillips, 1996), this does not mean that a client's text in therapy is solely hermeneutic or interpretation, for there are causal mechanistic forces at play also. One is reminded of Wittgenstein's moderate foundationalism.

McNaughton (1996) deals with the construction of parenting practices in the developing adult and argues that they are constituted both at the collective and personal levels. Cultural frames of reference provide guidelines and boundaries for the development of situated individual personal frames. Together personal frames and their institutionalizations comprise the collective frames. As the latter are used by parents, they are personally reconstructed and revised, thus contributing to individual participation in the reformulation of collective frames. These may also change through collective historical and contextual contingencies. Thus, culture and cultural identity are continually coconstructed by individual and collective processes.

Etzioni (1996) proposes a most interesting concept to resolve the communitarian–liberal debate on the basic unit of human organization. His "moderate" communitarian proposal is that neither the community nor the individual are the central social unit, but that the "I&We" (presented as one word) is the primary "supreme social necessity." "The self is congenitally contextuated within a community" (p. 157). Individuals and society form a bond marked by an underlying "productive," "creative" tension that is subject to societal adjustment. Both parties profit from the exchange, for community creativity and change is galvanized by "uncom-munitized personhood" on the one hand, whereas service and support to the community is derived from communitized personhood. (Personal fulfillment is seen to derive from the first of these parts of the person, in particular, but I imagine that a more equilibrated perspective would allow for both parts to have substantial influence in this regard.) Similarly, communities should seek to integrate the development of subcommunity pluralism to community unity. In this perspective, individual rights and social responsibilities are not considered to be in opposition but are complementary. Bauman (1996) arrives at a similar conclusion when he argues that each of communitarianism and liberalism are one-sided. The individual must navigate between the points of view "community without freedom" and "freedom without community."

Developmentally, the process of identity formation may involve a reconstitution of a lost original *we*. Wallon (1942) and Zazzo (1993; Zazzo & Zazzo, 1968; in del Río, 1996) proposed that humans inherently develop first a symbiotic dyadic we, which splits to form the I and the other or *socius*. Del Río (1996) adds that the phase of dyads in development lead to the phases of group structuring and then cultural communities. He states that the individual develops in these sociocultural *we*'s, and that they have "banks of consciousness" that facilitate growth.

Fernyhough (1996) examines the dialogical interpersonal processes that promote the development of higher mental functions, such as mediated memory. Vygotsky (1978) contrasted these functions with elementary ones, and referred to their developmental paths as the cultural and natural line, respectively. Fernyhough (1996) relies on Bakhtin's (1981) concept of ideology within voice, referred to above, to underscore that higher mental functions develop dialogically and reflect a dialogical mind. Thus, "mature functioning involves the simultaneous coming-into-conflict of differing internalized perspectives." For example, autistic children seem to be monological in thought, and thus will never develop the dialogical, openended thought processes of the normal adult.

Hendriks-Jansen (1996) refers to the interactive emergence of thought. Cultural plans develop through situated activity in cultural scaffolds, which include explicit cultural artifacts such as pedagogical language, parental concepts, and role models that act to shape deliberately in situ the developing person. Cultural plans are negotiated public meanings that act as shared but flexible guides in meaning development. They may help in the teaching of thinking and meaning, but when learned they do not automatically think and mean for us.

Philosophy

Up to this point in the chapter, various aspects of postmodernism as it relates to psychology have been reviewed in terms of the most recent literature. In the first section, some basic tenets of postmodernism were examined, such as the issue of the construction of reality. The previous section on culture emphasizes the communal, scaffolded generation of dialogical meaning in the fusion of horizons of self and collective so that an I&We develops. The section before the last one on adult development speaks in part to the issue of moral responsibility as an individual and societal project. In this section, I return to the philosophical underpinnings of postmodernism in order to shed more light on the nature of moral development in the adult. In particular, I dissect two articles that deal with Emmanuel Lévinas, the French philosopher whose work is considered to have provided the cardinal philosophical underpinning to the progressive, affirmative side of postmodernism that animates this book (see Chapter 2).

We have seen that for Lévinas, truth lies in an unconditional responsibility for the other. The *I* can be selfish but also "singular" facing infinity. But according to Lash (1996), Lévinas's ethics is "world-denying," or not as grounded in a plurality of particular forms of living such as participation in less structured groupings compared to institutional and individual contact. Lash continues that for Lévinas the "event" or moment of the interpersonal relationship is the primary ethics ground. Also, he adds that in Lévinas's work the face of the encountered stranger is featureless, without singularity, for, according to Lévinas singularity lies not in the world but in the infinite. Lash maintains that all this indicates that Lévinas is missing the notion that recognition of the other's singularity is derived from an ethics of practice or sociality in which there is open dialogue, long-term being-in-the-world, sharing of extenuated social rhythms, and respectful responsivity to the individuality (radical difference) of the other. Lash concludes by saying that a postmodern ethics must manifest both ground and groundlessness, or a "groundless ground," an idea similar to the one of Globus (1995) presented above.

Gardiner (1996) has a very different reading of Lévinas with respect to the issue of his stance on how the responsible individual is seen to relate to the other. According to Gardiner, Lévinas's ethics valorizes the sociality of everyday life, the spontaneity of quotidian social interactions, the direct living of experience, affective and meaningful dialogue with concrete others, situated intersubjective social embeddedness, and the like.

Gardiner first describes the philosophy of Buber (1970) and his concept of "I-Thou" relatedness. Although it differs somewhat from Lévinas's concept of the I's responsibility for the other, especially because Buber considers the other to be one person for the most part, there are important similarities between the two perspectives. Similar to Lévinas, Buber speaks of responsibility, real responding, dialogue, encounter, living relation, copresence, the interhuman, and the communal. He rejects the possibility of total fusion between the I and other, obviously without arguing for their separation. Rather than fusion, Buber perceives a daily responsivity to the demands of social living, a full attentive participation and receptivity to the other.

Gardiner (1996) then describes Bakhtin (1990), for whom self and other almost merge in dialogue but do not fuse. The radical difference of self and other is maintained in encounter. Ethical relations occur on the "boundary" between self and other when self relates through and for her or him. The self is "answerable," so that responsibility cannot be delegated. Bakhtin wrote that "[t]here is no 'alibi' in being."

As for Lévinas himself, according to Gardiner (1996), the self is plural, lives in the alterity of the other, is nondominative and nonintentional, and is deeply receptive and open to the other. The self's relation to the other is proximate, immediate, and an "epiphany." There is a mixture of distance and communion without fusion, for fusion would "erase" the self. The sense of responsibility to the other is asymmetrical, so that Buber's I-Thou reciprocity does not obtain.

How to conclude this section when the same worker is read in so radically different ways? Future scholarship may dispel the confusion, but the different versions of Lévinas that have been presented on whether or not he emphasizes the importance of practiced everyday sociality in moral behavior may not have an uncontested, noncontextualized answer. For present purposes, he remains a powerful postmodern figure who guides my approach. I believe that if he were alive he would rejoice in this responsibility, and the everyday interactions that he and I have in our Relational Meaning World.

Therapy

Recently postmodern therapy has reached both its apogee and perigee with the special section of the *Journal of Marital and Family Therapy* devoted to it (Bailey, 1996) and the review of Neimeyer and Mahoney's (1995) tome on constructivism in therapy (Snyder, 1996). The former journal series reveals the range of topics to which the postmodern perspective has been applied in family therapy; yet despite some positive comments, the latter review calls it "old wine in a new bottle," wonders whether it can attract clients, and suggests that it needs to document its efficacy.

One aspect of postmodern therapy that augurs well for the challenges outlined by Snyder is that it continues to be self-critical and innovative (e.g., Bischoff, McKeel, Moon, and Sprenkle, 1996; Fish, 1996; Flemons, Green, and Rambo, 1996; Fowers & Richardson, 1996; Paré, 1996; Spellman & Harper, 1996). In this regard, Fowers and Richardson (1996) are an example.

According to these authors, family therapy implicitly accepts the normative model of the modern nuclear family, thus promoting individualism at the expense of collectivism. The nuclear family lives a relatively isolated self-protective life that denies open connection to community and tradition. If society would adopt a communitarian position, families would engage in dialectical moral conversations with collectives, which have legitimate interest in their well-being. Family therapy in this perspective would facilitate dialogues 'etween families and culture about morality, values, ideals, ideas, mores, traditions, social trends, meanings, purpose, commitments, and so on.

Hoyt (1996a) has edited an important volume on constructive therapy. In Hoyt (1996b) he reviews the fundamentals of constructive therapies, and then engages several leading practitioners in conversations about their work (e.g., Hoyt, 1996c, with Gergen on postmodernism and relationship in therapy; Hoyt & Combs, 1996, with White on his approach to therapy, as described in depth in Chapter 9). In his interview Gergen argues that it is inappropriate to define therapy, although its process is to reconstruct multiple meanings and actions in both local and cultural contexts. The therapist should facilitate a more fluid movement by the client in the world, with better ability "for coordinating the disparate as opposed to eradicating the opposition." (Similarly, Gergen, Hoffman, and Anderson [1996] decry the diagnostic imperative in the mental health professions, and Gergen writes in the article that "[t]his view of therapy and diagnosis entail uncertainty.... I question the ethics of certainty.") The White interview serves as an update to his approach on externalizing or separating the problem from the person by giving the problem labels, such as Mr. Trouble, to which therapeutic collaboration is addressed. Alternative stories or intelligibilities are coconstructed with the therapist to fill the transparent cultural vacuum with modes of living that extend to include ethics, responsibility, accountability, partnership, collaboration, possibility, spiritualities, reverence, and awe in daily living. Similarly, Andersen (1996) describes constructivist therapy as a *both/and* collaboration instead of an *either/or* hierarchical unpleasantness.

Certainly, I listen to and attempt to live these suggested ways of being in the therapeutic world. I try to do the same with all ideas encountered, whether in the written or oral mode, and whether presented by professionals, clients, or others. Therapy has become for me a tapestry of innovation continually rewoven on a background of constant sensitivity to the client and increasing personal competence. (Note that here I deleted the term professional expertise for the one in its place. Kindly excuse the other locations in the book where terminology could be edited this way to reflect postmodern sensitivities. Old totalizing attractors or habits leave fossilized interfering trajectories which capture new more flexible yet vulnerable counterattractors, to use the language derived from dynamical systems theory. This applies not only to my writing but also to the lives of clients. The psychotherapeutic task is to promote the self-organization of more resilient, adaptive counterattractors, buttressed by altered controlling parameters or facilitative agents. But that is another story [see Young, submitted, which is partly on dynamical systems theory and psychotherapy].)

The IWEMEUS

Etzioni's (1996) concept of the I&We has provided the bridge permitting a moderate integration of the major themes dealt with in this chapter. To give background, in Chapter 3 a model of the development of the subjective I self was presented, and the development of the objective me self in terms of self-efficacy was treated briefly. In Chapter 11, in particular, I tried to navigate the stormy issue of the cartesian separation of mind and body, self and other, etc. It will be recalled that I included in my suggestions the concepts of coexistential, heterological constructivism in epistemology, which elaborated the viewpoint of moderate foundationalism, the ethic of being-becoming-world/world-becoming-being, and the notion of world work and world love, which spoke to the question of situated, practiced activity in daily living and morality. Similarly, in Chapters 7 and 12, I have amplified the nature of cultural scaffolds through the concepts of the cognitive (mis)perception of the other and Relational Meaning Worlds, respectively. Thus, in many senses I feel that I have addressed the recent concerns discerned in the literature. However, at the same time Etzioni's (1996) concept of the I&WE is one answer to the question on the development of cultural identity to which I dialogically answer, integrating the above contributions.

According to me, the minimum unit of identity in social organization, which the concept of I&WE addresses, must include both the subjective existential and objective evaluative side of social identity. James's (1890) I-me distinction is aimed at the individual, and extrapolation to the collective suggests that there is an equivalent we-us differentiation in communal identity. Cultures both experience identity and reflect upon it. There are numerous part selves that develop in the individual, as we have seen in Chapter 10, so that the basic dichotomy discussed here is only a beginning. Nevertheless, it is sufficient for the current purposes, that is, to show how different individual and collective identities may juxtapose and coexist in one coherent suprasystemic model of cultural identity.

The cultural identity that develops in both individuals and collectives may be called the IWEMEUS. Not only does it refer to the four pronouns involved; it is also an acronym for the concept of "individual–world epigenetic, mutualistic, emergent, universal (identity) stages." I will examine each of the components of this term in turn.

The construct of *individual–world* is consistent with the concept given above by various workers that self and world do not fuse but are symbiotic in their dialogue. However, it appears logical to add that adults can engage in moments of sheer union, that horizons integrate into wholes revealing new skies, that superior morality hinges on such empathic mutual abandonment cum enrichment. Thus, I would argue that in the range of situated social encounters comprising the practice of daily sociality there are four types of encounter—positive self-focused, other-focused, additive, and multiplicative or fused relationships (of course, neutral and negative interactions may take place at all these levels, as well). To conclude, implicit in the "individual–world" term of the IWEMEUS is the full pronominal repertoire of the concept, that is, the subjective and objective personal and plural components of identity development.

The *epigenesis* referred to in the IWEMEUS concept implies, as explained previously, that identity development unfolds without any deterministic biological or environmental template, but is channeled by the multiplicative conjoining of all the parameters that impinge on the developing organism as well as by the characteristics of the developing organism itself. There is never any separate or minor influence of one variable compared to another, for all together form an indissoluble system which acts on the developing person. The individual is ontogenetically altered in a constitutive fashion in each of its encounters with the system in which it is embedded, whether the components of the system be more biological, social, or personal. If universal stages mark the developmental passage, it is not because they are preprogrammed icons but because they are the best fit solutions for all developing persons to the particular situations they live. Furthermore, each particular stage only serves as a scaffold on which individual differences are constructed in vivo. Also, they do not condemn developing persons to mindless, choiceless, deterministic thought. For example, the last stage in the current 25-step theory propose that adult development is about postmodern thought, where one seeks nontotalizing but grounded truths. Finally, the concept of epigenesis does not imply that all development is guided by stages. There is room for a multitude of developmental models and pathways.

On the positive side, the term *mutualistic* refers to the dialogical, dialectical, shared, reciprocal, interminably entangled communitarian relationship in which individuals and the social surround engage. Although situated, contextualized, scaffolded, and conflicted, it is consultative. It is practiced activity in daily living, harbored in the sensitivities of lived experiences. Because no totalizing truths intervene between self and world, contact is genuine. The embeddedness of the other's embeddedness is grasped, and actions are undertaken that create a more harmonic field in the relationship of the other components of surround such as school, work, family, social life, culture, and ideological grounding are undertaken. The other becomes the singular infinity in the actions of responsibility. The other is given to without the prospect of personal profit, but often profit obtains reciprocally. The cultural identity of the other and the self usually both develop in and through encounter of the self and other. The other may be partner, child, friend, subcommunity, or even community. Gain by the community may be laborious, but happens. Thus, community has its own IWEMEUS, which then is a comeme, or reciprocally constructed emotional–cognitive structure carried by a collective (as defined in Chapter 12; also see Lave, 1996, on learning as a social collective and Baltes and Staudinger, 1966, on interactive, reciprocally influencing minds). That is, the cultural concept that a community has of itself enters its Relational Meaning Worlds as part of the comeme complex of which it is constituted. Of course, these concepts can be negative, or worse yet the collective can perceive any one subcollective or individual as negative, or it can act negatively as a result of a negative collective identity. This idea is explored further in Chapter 7 on the cognitive (mis)perception of the other.

The term *emergent* in the concept of the IWEMEUS refers to the dynamic, systemic, self-organizational, and self-regulative nature of identity formation. Out of the confluence of individual and world may emerge de novo a whole contained in neither constituent, a pattern that cannot be predicted before the subtle complexities of interactive union takes place. Each constituent may catalytically aliment the other in a runaway feedback process that can burst identity beyond its bounds toward hidden or unimagined possibilities.

The term *universal* does not refer to a common preprogrammed structure or stage sequence that governs identity development, as we have seen. Rather, it refers to a path of steps that I believe are taken because of the principal of least action as it applies to the repetitive, situated interactions in the contextualized world. To simplify the material on fractals presented in Chapters 7 and 12, we have seen that the 25-step developmental theory that I describe (and probably the sublevels contained within the steps) appear to be self-similar patterns at different levels of the same system, or fractals. Moreover, they are bred by fractal transmission processes in world to parent to child transmission. Fractal patterns in development recur because of the economy of their algorithms. In Chapter 3, the 25-step substage sequence in development that I describe in the book has been applied to self-development. It can be expanded readily to include a sense of cultural identity. Thus, just as with self development, the sequence in cultural identity development should develop universally.

The term *identity stage* in the concept under discussion focuses on the reflexive evaluation that takes place as individual and culture grow through their interaction. I have mentioned that there are four kinds of positive relations in their encounter—self-focused, other-focused, additive, and fused. Identity development is not fixed at one of these types for any one individual. Rather, a fluidity in social encounter marks the developmental parade, and different styles may conflict at any one time, coexist, combine, alternate, follow each other sequentially, juxtapose, and so on. There may be strategic planning of relational type, or relational moves adopted by participants in the social dance as they navigate the complexity of daily living. Even though the fused type may appear the most mature, developmental history and current context may call for other types at any one social time. The consequent scenario of relational types that mark individual–world interaction form a superordinate structure that coheres each developing individual in a identity development system.

In conclusion, again I hope that the book will be of interest to more than just developmental psychologists. For the first time, the book does not simply develop concepts from the base of developmental psychology toward the sociopolitical arena but takes a concept developed in sociopolitical theory (Etzioni's, 1996, moderate communitarian concept of I&WE) and expands it through developmental psychology toward a common usage. How developmental and communitarian. In the next section, the sociopolitical and developmental fuse absolutely, for I take the 25-step model of discourse quality in the cognitive (mis)perception of the other that I constructed based on the current 25-step developmental model (presented in Chapter 7 and used in a study in Chapter 13), and analyze quotes by government officials in Ontario for the complexity of their dialogue with the public.

BABYHOOD TO PERSONHOOD
IN POLITICIANS' SPEECH:
THE CASE OF ONTARIO

Politicians constitute one of the most visible examples of the collective establishment. They play a preponderant role in shaping political discourse in society, and their words are reported in newspapers and on television to a public that consumes their printed words and sound bites. In the creation of cultural identity (in the IWEMEUS) their impact is important. In North America many governments at various levels in part are attempting to deal with their budgetary deficits by withdrawing support for social programs. Certain constituencies, in particular, react vehemently to these cuts, and government officials issue policy statements and speeches justifying their stance. In this regard, it is instructive to examine the particular justifications of politicians for decisions that are unpopular among a good portion of citizens.

In Table 14.1, I have taken selected quotes of government officials in

Table 14.1 Sample Quotes of Politicians Analyzed for Discourse Quality According to the Cognitive (Mis)perception of the Other[a]

Quote	Context of quote (and source)	Surface and deep scores[b]	Deep score explained
(We can) exaggerate problems in education by "creating a crisis."	From leaked tape of education minister's strategy speech about how to get acceptance for cuts in education. (*Toronto Star*, June 1, 1995)	Surface = 7 Deep = 7	Because the minister did not realize his speech would be taped and made public, surface level is at deep level already, revealing deep-level government intention.
Buy dented cans of food, buy in bulk … If children are going hungry, the Children's Aid Society might have to step in.	Social services minister denies that welfare cuts will be detrimental to families, that they can adapt; but then he threatens them if they cannot provide for their children. (*Toronto Star*, September 18 and 28, 1995)	Surface = 11 Deep = 6	The government is trying to channel, but does much more (it clearly manipulates, menaces).
(I was ordered to) use as much force as necessary.	Officer in charge of a security detachment justifies the use of force in controlling striking civil servants blocking politicians from entering legislature. Injuries resulted. (*Toronto Star*, June 7, 1996)	Surface = 11 Deep = 1	Although the officer says that he was just following orders, the orders permitted physical violence against protesters. In contrast, other detachments were restrained by their superiors.
Parasitic poverty pimps, welfare cheats, the mindless mantra of community policing apologists. … Fraud just incenses me.	Official in human services gives view on protesters of cuts in social assistance. (*Toronto Star*, May 19, 1996)	Surface = 13 Deep = 1	The official claims to want to help the "disadvantaged," but justifies across-the-board cuts by abusively invoking the case of welfare cheats and system apologists.
We want those counseling services to be coordinated within the community.	The minister for women's issues denies cuts to secondary services for women will jeopardize the safety of women fleeing abusive relationships. (*Globe and Mail*, October 5, 1995)	Surface = 13 Deep = 7	Although the minister sounds reasonable, he is asking for services to come from volunteerism, not paid work.
This review is not fiscally driven; it's driven by our intent to create a postsecondary education system that is of high quality for the future.	The education minister defends comprehensive review of educational system and its financing. (*Toronto Star*, July 17, 1996)	Surface = 13 Deep = 11	Given the track record of the government, deception behind the statement of concern for the citizen seems evident.

We are committed to helping the poor and downtrodden; that's why there is a need for your continued generosity and volunteerism. We are still committed to cutting costs.	The premier at a fundraising event, speaking after a direct confrontation by a participant about the needs of the poor. (*Toronto Star*, November 5, 1995)	Surface = 14 Deep = 11	The citizen's position is acknowledged, but the financial load is still passed on to citizens.
We're trying to build on gains. ... We'll try to sustain pay equity. ... [It] has meant a substantial cost.	Labor minister on changes to pay equity legislation. (*Toronto Star*, July 25, 1996)	Surface = 15 Deep = 11	Value of pay equity acknowledged, built upon, but provincial finances lead to bottom-line cuts once more.
Resources that are declining relative to the volume of work facing the judiciary must ultimately put pressure on the quality of justice. ... The rule of law is not a free good. It requires the expenditure of public resources, the amount of which must be adequate to maintain the quality of justice, and public confidence in the system of justice.	The Canadian chief justice warns the provincial government about budget cuts to the justice system. (*Toronto Star*, July 25, 1996)	Surface = 21 Deep = 21	One branch of government advises another in the interest of the public good. A public statement in which deep level is surface message.
We made a mistake on Bill 26, tried to do too much too fast. We needed to spend more time on the "how" of what we were going to do, not the "what". ... People need more time and are entitled to more consultation.	The premier expresses regret over having pushed through Bill 26. (*Toronto Star*, June 8, 1996)	Surface = 22 Deep = 11	Bill 26 gave the government broad authority to pass much legislation by bypassing normal government processes. After much criticism of lack of public consultation on the bill, a short consultative period was hastily arranged and proved ineffective. The premier's statement appears to suggest that the people's voice was heard, against the outcome.

[a]Analyzed using the scales in Chapter 7, as modified according to the text.
[b]See text for explanation of the surface appearance and deep interpretation scores.

Ontario and analyzed them for their level of complexity and sincerity. No attempt was made to be representative in the issues discussed, newspapers used, and the like, for the goal is to illustrate the applicability of the current developmental theory to political material. I analyzed the content of the quotes according to the 25-step developmental theory as it relates to the cognitive (mis)perception of the other (working with the 25-point scale presented in Chapter 7 and used in Chapter 13). In using the (mis)perception scale, the terms "government" and "citizen" replaced those of "parent" and "child." Some sentences were contextualized to the public domain or were dropped if they did not apply.

The quotes were analyzed at two levels using the scale. First, the *surface* appearance of the quotes in their contexts were analyzed according to the degree of dialogue and (mis)perception of the other, without bias or use of our knowledge of background issues and perceived motives. Second, a *deep* interpretation of the quotes was undertaken from the perspective of those most negatively affected by the government's decisions on the particular issues. The table provides the rationale that was used in determining the deep level in the quality of discourse in the cited quotes.

Table 14.1 gives only the most provocative examples that could be found over the last few years in Ontario. Except for a few examples, it is clear from the quotes in the table that the surface and deep judgments of the developmental levels of the quotes do not concur. In general, with respect to the specific quotes used on the contentious issues chosen, at the surface the government engages in a communicative style that is similar to the one parents would use with a school-age child. At a deeper level, from the perspective of those suffering from the decisions, the level of treatment of the citizen by the government appears less developmentally advanced, and can lapse into quite manipulative and controlling if not rejecting language. (I do not offer empirical statistics on the full range of quotes analyzed because of their nonrepresentative nature.)

Thus, it is possible to show that the level of political discourse in the public domain is not very advanced and that government officials may speak at one developmental level but act at another one less respectful of particular classes of citizens, at least from their perspective. As we know, politicians attempt to modulate the development of opinion and political identification toward their agendas.

At a broader level, the study suggests that the development of cultural identity is influenced by government. It suggests that a government's mindset about its citizen's filters its treatment of and dialogue with certain of its groups. When a government's goals are less than noble, when it resorts to subterfuge or worse in the treatment of its citizens, the pretense of its development toward a liberal, moderate communitarian, or any more advanced ethic is compromised. The advantage of the current (mis)perception scale is that it offers a very nuanced instrument to measure the degree to which this conjecture may be true for any one government or administrative entity.

The concept of the cognitive (mis)perception of the other that I developed as an outgrowth of the current developmental theory has produced a scale that has been used to analyze the quality of the dialogue between mothers and their adolescent sons (see Chapter 13). I have suggested that it is applicable not only to parental (mis)perceptions of their children but also to the (mis)perception of partners in couples and of citizens in collectives. Every week my psychotherapeutic work provides me with examples in support of the former, and the current preliminary investigation gives evidence in support of the latter.

CONCLUSION

Belenky and colleagues (Belenky et al., 1986, see Chapter 7) are applying their concept of women's epistemological ways of knowing to the issue of parental perceptions (Bond, Belenky, Weinstock, Cook, & Monsey, 1992; Bond, Belenky, Weinstock, & Cook, 1996). It will be recalled that I showed that Belenky et al.'s model is compatible with my concept of the cognitive (mis)perception of the other. Thus, it should be instructive to examine their model in comparison to my equivalent one of the cognitive (mis)perception of the other, presented in Table 7.1. As we have seen, they describe five ways of knowing—women of silence, received knowing, subjective knowing, procedural knowing, and constructivist knowing—which were shown to correspond to the five stages of development underscored in the current work, i.e., the reflexive, sensorimotor, perioperational, abstract, and collective intelligence periods. In Bond et al. (1996), these ways of knowing are hypothesized to influence consequent parental perception of the child and child-rearing practices.

According to Bond et al., silent women see their child as voiceless, mindless, without learning skills, and that any feelings that their child may have are not understood and are dangerous. Thus, in terms of parenting, raw power is used without listening, dialogue, or explanation, and the parents yell, enforcing absolute rules. For the woman manifesting the orientation of received knowing, their child is perceived as being capable of learning by listening, needing to be seen and not heard, in need of molding, etc. As for parenting, information is transmitted by lecturing, rules are imparted through teaching, rewards, and punishments, and the child is trained and modeled. Subjective parents believe that their child has an inner voice, is unique, and should show spontaneity. Their child is encouraged to think and speak with his or her own voice, and the parenting attitude is laissez-faire and nonjudgmental. Procedural parents emphasize the thinking and feeling processes that can be developed in their child, e.g., in problem solving. In terms of child rearing, these parents ask for and provide reasons and explanations and the family is encouraged to share the processes that underlie each other's thoughts. Finally, constructive knowing parents perceive their child to have the ability and responsibility to think through problems in order to invent solutions and make choices, by integrating cognition and emotion. Parenting involves questioning, challenging, drawing out, providing feedback, encouraging perspective-taking, planning, etc. Data in support of the model are provided for the first three of the five levels.

Although Bond et al. have developed a powerful model of the evolution of parenting practices, one that is highly compatible with the current approach. I believe that the type of parenting attributed to the subjective parenting style by Bond et al. does not fit as well with the nature of the subjective knower as compared to my own version. I emphasize that this type of parenting is more controlling and less benign than Bond et al. allow. Moreover, I have placed partial limits on the supportive parenting that Bond et al. describe for the procedural parent. In addition, the 25-point scale that I developed from the current theory (based on five substages within the five stages), permits a nuanced analysis of parental belief and practice compared to the five-level series offered by Bond et al. Finally, the theory and scales are phrased in a manner that permits application to the relationship between partners in a couple or even between governments and citizens, as we have seen. In conclusion, more work is needed in this area, and the two models under discussion seem to offer a beginning in this regard.

At this end to the book, it is worthwhile pondering how the current model of the cognitive (mis)perception of the other relates to the piagetian origins to which it is tied and which were described at the beginning of the book. Noam and K. W. Fischer (1996b) have edited a volume that allows us to examine this question. In this volume, Gouin Décarie and Ricard (1996) report on Piaget's (1954) views on the relationship between developing cognition and affectivity. He maintained that the two domains evidence a functional parallelism with no causal relationship. Thus, for example, emotions and social interactions have no direct influence or do not "affect the intellect as such" (Piaget 1967, p. 156).

The current theory respects this position, but tries to have emerge new concepts from it as well. For example, it admits that the steps in cognitive development prescribe upper limits on the development of parallel socio-emotional systems such as eriksonian stages, social cognition, the perception of the other, and the like. However, it adds that cognitive and socio-emotional development are equally integral in the epigenetic constitution of the individual. Cognitive development is embedded in the constitutive matrix of sociocultural contexts, as described by the model of coappropriation that I present in Chapter 8. The "open system" that is development (to which Piaget alluded especially later in his writings when he saw parallels in his work and that of dynamic systems theory; see Young, submitted) dictates that developmental trajectories are designed by all of the multiple components that are involved in it with none having primacy, whether they be putatively cognitive or emotional.

Piaget distinguished between cognitive structure and affective energetics, but it may be more fruitful to consider cognitive–emotional structures as we have done, e.g., in the coschemes that develop through coappropriation. Indeed, Piaget's writings reveal that even he was uncertain about the primacy of the cognitive steps he described, for he wrote that "a particular form of cognitive structure must correspond to every new level of affective conduct" (Piaget, 1954, p. 10, cited in Gouin Décarie and Ricard, 1996). Affectivity seems to be the developmental axis here. However, instead of an either/or stance, a both/and one seems preferable, to borrow a postmodern therapeutic concept presented above. Thus, both at the level of cognitive–emotional coschemes and the level of the integrated totalities of coschemes that constitute stages in development, a concept of integrated socioemotional–cognitive acquisitions seems appropriate.

A cognitive–socioemotional blending in phases of development is evident in other chapters in Noam and K. W. Fischer (1996b). Noam (1996) explores the nature of the development of psychological maturity and wisdom from the perspective of the later stages in stage theories such as Loevinger's (1976) and Erikson's (1980). He refers to the development of a continuous cycle of courage, vitality, greater flexibility, deeper insight, creative exploration, growth orientation, freedom to pursue new experiences, focusing on earlier vulnerabilities, commitment to the world, and so on. Almost all these characterizations of maturity englobe simultaneous cognitive and socioemotional processes. Levitt and Selman (1996) describe stages in the development of personal meaning as it relates to friendship and disputes in adolescence; again the development toward insight is emphasized. Gilligan (1996) and Benenson (1996) deal with the development of gender differences in relationships and are beginning to consider phases in this process and how they differ across the sexes (e.g., from a piagetian perspective in Gilligan; Benenson's developmental trajectories). Blatt and Blass (1996) develop a neoeriksonian model of personality development based on the developmental lines of stages in relatedness and self-definition, a process that is as much cognitive as socioemotional.

The work of Case (1996) and Fischer and Ayoub (1996) provide the most elaborate integration of stages in cognitive and socioemotional development. A prime focus of Young (submitted) is to examine their research in depth; nevertheless, their important work is presented here. It will be recalled that both Case and Fischer have developed a stage model of cognitive development in which substages cyclically recur within stages, with my own model being a modified version of theirs. Based upon the specific substage sequence that he proposes, Case shows that the development of attachment of the infant to the caregiver evolves with cognitive development and with the basic emotions such as anger, joy, and interest. Then he analyzes the working models that develop in the securely attached compared to the insecure avoidant infant. The defense mechanisms involved in the latter are traced right through to the adult, showing how relationships with romantic partner and offspring may reveal intergenerational transmission patterns. K. W. Fischer and Ayoub (1996) propose a similar model. They show how the working models of one particular couple in therapy had developed first separately in their developmental pasts and then together since meeting. The working models are shown to reflect Fischer's particular neopiagetian stage theory of cognitive development. Fischer and Ayoub document the influence on the development of the working couple's models an early loss of attachment in the case of the wife and hidden family violence in the case of the husband, respectively. For the adult period, working models are considered to form personality complexes, and examples are provided for the couple.

Despite the quality of Case's and Fischer's models, there are several limitations in this work that need to be noted (addressed further in Young, submitted). First, from the point of view of adult development, neither considers how working models develop in the postformal period. Their cognitive models either do not concern this period (Case) or do not see it as differentiating through substages (Fischer, who does not examine this period at all in the Fischer and Ayoub chapter). The current theory differs from those of Case and Fischer in its emphasis on the collective intelligence stage of adult development, and its substages and corresponding neoeriksonian systems. Second, the working models in attachment that Case and Fischer describe are treated as emanations of cognitive development, constrained by the characteristics of that development. Similarly, the other theories in the book by Noam and K. W. Fischer (1996b) may be more unidimensional than bidimensional in the sense that they fall on the other side of the fence by describing sequences in development from a socioemotional perspective without showing links to cognitive development, per se. The current theory addresses this imbalance by proposing that the parallel neopiagetian and neoeriksonian acquisitions that mark the developmental passage in its 25-step developmental model are quasi-independent though related, yet even though they may be described separately, they are simultaneous components of one dynamically developing system. In development, component coschemes are constructed conjoining cognition and socioemotion, person and environment, body and mind, past and present, and so on.

As far as I know, there is no other worker who has developed a neopiagetian substage recursion model of cognitive development and extended it by elaborating parallel stages in the socioemotional domain along the lines of Erikson, Loevinger, or the like. Kegan (1982, 1994) attempts the same but from a piagetian perspective in which substages are not treated, even if the postformal stage is included. Two equally weighted strands of development (the cognitive and the socioemotional) involving fractalized substage repetitions, with their seemingly separate routes coconstructed in the ensemble of conjoint living; ultimately, this vision informs the developmental model that I have described.

That is, developing individuals must traverse a multidimensional psychological space in the development of their social identity (see Figure 14.1). (1) Are they producing/receiving positive, directed goal-compatible behavior/output or, to the contrary, negative behavior/output (Positve----- Negative)? (2) How does the behavior/output vary with context, e.g., is the environment supportive/life-promoting or hostile/life-threatening (Supportive-----Nonsupportive)? (3) To what developmental level does the behavior/output speak both in its producer/author and in its target (Developmentally inappropriate-----Developmentally appropriate)? (4) Is it a product of an active, self-organized, freely chosen exploration/discovery or a passive, reactive imposition/control, (Active-----Reactive)? (5) Is it a turning to the self in individualism or to the other in collectivism/ communalism (Individual-----Collective)? (6) Finally, is the way of knowing underlying it subjective, intuitive, felt, evaluative, empirical, and mod-

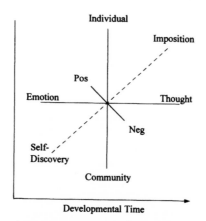

Figure 14.1. Contextual Variation in Underlying Dimensional Configuration Determines Identity Construction

ern (Subjective------Objective)? As well, these are the major dimensions underlying the IWEMEUS, and it was struck home to me in both a work in preparation by my wife (Lélia Young, personal communication, October 20, 1996), who independently arrived at many similar dimensions in describing the nature of language and a conversation with a teenage client who defined himself in terms of (1) more positive than negative behavior, (2) from a supportive but not fully understanding environment, (3) with his behavior/output being adultlike, (4) aimed at self-discovery, (5) individualistic, and (6) palpably emotional, not rational. (Figure 14.1 is presented in the simple oppositions that were convenient in my therapeutic work with this client.)

REFLECTIONS FOR ADULTS
IN TRANSITION OR CRISIS

Introduction

(*Appropriate clients are given the following essay. At the same time it serves as a metaphorical description of the postmodern therapeutic process.*) Clients enter the world of the therapist in a confused, vulnerable state, and they are rendered more confused when I ask them at the beginning of their first session to describe what they are doing right for themselves, or how they are sometimes controlling the bad habit that normally dominates them. This entry into their world of agency is a difficult one, because their past has imposed constraints that curtail jumps to freedom and growth. The present essay has been written to inspire emergent will to participate in the constant personal construction of new levels of psychological integration. Once begun, the process gathers momentum and moves from piecemeal redefinition and growth to more widespread metamorphosis.

In the Protoworld

Before timelessness, when worlds are formed, when we are formed, we navigate in a vast sea of potentials in which the only waves are the waves of hope, in which the only undercurrents are those of longing and belonging. We never lose our embryonic heart.

It hears us in our pain, feels our stuckness. When the river is dammed, waters well up behind and overflow. New pathways of flow form. When our developmental journey seems moribund, seems trapped in infinitesimal capillaries feeding tumored problems, seems imprisoned by inescapable realities, inexorable portents of change line one's projections in the future. Pessimism always knows optimism, even if hidden. Destined to grow, we do. Destined to find freedom, we seek. Destined to be unencumbered by the fetters of destiny, we submit.

Each self is more than self. Bred by two, we remain more than one. Birthed in magistral effort, nurtured by caregiving, infants give birth to caregiving. Giving care is the human birthright. We do not simply take oxygen from the air. We breathe the nutrient molecules of the common air and have them comingle with the molecules of our breathing apparatus. We live at the interface, are the interface of encounter. Boundaries are seamless barriers that are permeable to otherness. Otherness enters us and becomes us, and as we exhale our breath, our energy, our affection, we enrich the breath of others, are the otherness of others. Self is other for the self of other, and more.

In constant evolution, living becomes process. A swan alighting on a mirror lake at dusk merges with soft waters. Ripples marks its passage as it steers to underwater pastures. Rolling rings surround it, like chained memories of its displacement. They conjoin rings of other swans in larger circles that vibrate with new patterns of rhythm. The swan does not know the harmony it lives, but it participates in a primordial presence, an essence of being. There is no final staging ground to which the swan swims. It elegantly moves in stageness. If we take a photograph to capture its beauty, in examining it we sense both peace and inspiration, but the swan moves on.

Consciousness is not a thing. It has no address in our brain or in our mind. It is not a neuronal sequence but a living consequence. It is omnipresent, a state of our universe that we sense. It may be as large as the universe, for its scope is ours. The singularity is infinite. Its perception is not. We rush about seeking it, eyes open to its power, but it is a brook and not a torrent. We ponder its vastness in small thoughts, but it is a horizon existing between.

Who in the chain is more steel than space? One taurus cannot pass through the next when the oval is solid. Shapes cooperate to transfigure the whole. If a link is bent in a chain, its excision reduces the chain's size and decreases its resilience. Families and couples may resolve disputes by imposition or even excision, but inevitably inherent in its new chain will be metal fatigue.

Speaking begins with listening. Pure listening feels the other, allows the other to be fully self without judgment. In hearing the sensitivity and suffering behind words, both the congealing of union and the healing of its rifts are potentiated. Futures are built on pregnant presence.

Therapy is. Clients are. Words are reminders of impressions of presence on the clay of experience. They are accompanied by the contours of emotion that palpate the joint mind created in encounter. They express the pain of unwelcomed etchings, and the hope of projected pastiches. The therapist absorbs their reverberations, and in the security of echo new words of acceptance and adjustment emerge. Each therapist wishes that endless circles of growth leave the chambers of discourse for all parties in the conversation. Therapists are.

Conclusion

Clients learn that learning is forever, that growth is immutable, un-changing, that in visiting the attuned therapist they are visiting their path, that their path is an open one built not of solid bricks but of intangibles, that the unfelt feels, the undefined defines, the untruthed truths. Paths are not built alone or followed alone. They carry the memories of others or wishes about others, if not actual others. It is impossible to describe to someone the holding of hands, the links in humanity, simply by describing the shape of hands. It is impossible to induce hand-holding by pointing to or counting hands. Yet hands are perfectly shaped and placed to allow hand-holding, which thus is a natural emergent function in the life of hands. Similarly, hearts are perfectly shaped for love, and it does not reside in any one heart but in their union and the path of sharing that they trace in time.

References

Aarons, V. (1995). "Every window is a mother's mouth": Grace Paley's postmodern voice. In S. Trachtenberg (Ed.), *Critical essays on American postmodernism* (pp. 203–216). New York: Hall.

Adams-Westcott, J., Dafforn, T.A., & Sterne, P. (1993). Escaping victim life stories and co-constructing personal agency. In S. Gilligan & R. Price (Eds.), *Therapeutic conversations* (pp. 258–271). New York: Norton.

Ahadi, S.A., & Rothbart, M.K. (1994). Temperament, development, and the Big Five. In C.F. Halverson, G.A. Kohnstamm, & R.P. Martin (Eds.), *The developing structure of temperament and personality from infancy to adulthood* (pp. 187–207). Hillsdale, NJ: Erlbaum.

Aldous, J. (1990). Family development and the life course: Two perspectives on family change. *Journal of Marriage and the Family, 52,* 571–583.

Aloise-Young, P.A. (1993). The development of self presentation: Self-promotion in 6- to 10-year-old children. *Social Cognition, 11,* 201–222.

Alvarez de Lorenzana, J. (1993). Appendix: The constructive universe and the evolutionary systems framework. In S.N. Salthe, *Development and evolution: Complexity and change in biology.* Cambridge, MA: MIT Press.

Andersen, T. (1996). Language is not innocent. In F.W. Kaslow (Ed.), *Handbook of relational diagnosis and dysfunctional family patterns* (pp. 119–125). New York: Wiley.

Anderson, H. (1993). On a roller coaster: A collaborative language systems approach to therapy. In S. Friedman (Ed.), *The new language of change: Constructive collaboration in therapy* (pp. 323–344). New York: Guilford.

Anderson, H., & Galooshian, H.A. (1990). Beyond cybernetics: Comments on Atkinson and Heath's "Further thoughts on second-order family therapy." *Family Process, 29,* 157–163.

Angleitner, A., & Ostendorf, F. (1994). Temperament and the Big Five factors of personality. In C.F. Halverson, G.A. Kohnstamm, & R.P. Martin (Eds.), *The developing structure of temperament and personality from infancy to adulthood* (pp. 69–90). Hillsdale, NJ: Erlbaum.

Angus, L., & Hardtke, K. (1994). Narrative processes in psychotherapy. *Canadian Psychology, 35,* 190–203.

Arievitch, I., & van der Veer, R. (1995). Furthering the internalization debate: Gal'perin's contribution. *Human Development, 38,* 113–126.

Azmitia, M., & Hesser, J. (1993). Why siblings are important agents of cognitive development: A comparison of siblings and peers. *Child Development, 64,* 430–444.

Bacal, H.A. (1995). The essence of Kohut's work and the progress of self psychology. *Psychoanalytic Dialogues, 5,* 353–367.

Bader, V. (1995). Citizenship and exclusion: Radical democracy, community, and justice. Or what is wrong with communitarianism? *Political Theory, 23*, 211–246.

Bailey, C.E. (1996). Editcr's introduction: Postmodern practices in marriage and family therapy. *Journal of Marital and Family Therapy, 22*, 287–288.

Bakan, D. (1966). *The duality of human existence: An essay of psychology and religion.* Chicago: Rand McNally.

Baker-Brown, G., Ballard, E.J., Bluck, S., deVries, B., Suedfeld, P., & Tetlock, P.E. (1992). *Coding manual for conceptual/integrative complexity.* University of British Columbia, Vancouver, BC.

Baker-Senett, J., Matusov, E., & Rogoff, B. (1993a). Planning as developmental process. In H.W. Reese (Ed.), *Advances in child development and behavior* (Vol. 24; pp. 253–281). San Diego, CA: Academic.

Baker-Senett, J., Matusov, E., & Rogoff, B. (1993b). Sociocultural processes of creative planning in children's playcrafting. In P. Light & G. Butterworth (Eds.), *Context and cognition: Ways of learning and knowing* (pp. 93–114). Hillsdale, NJ: Erlbaum.

Bakhtin, M.M. (1973). *Problems of Dostoevesky's poetics* (R.W. Rostel, Trans.). Ann-Arbor, MI: Ardis. (Original work published 1929)

Bakhtin, M.M. (1981). *The dialogical imagination* (M. Holmquist, Ed.). Austin: University of Texas Press.

Bakhtin, M. (1990). *Art and answerability: Early philosophical essays.* Austin: University of Texas Press.

Bakhurst, D. (1995). On the social constitution of mind: Bruner, Ilyenkov, and the defence of cultural psychology. *Mind, Culture, and Activity, 2*, 158–171.

Baltes, P.B., & Standingers, J.M. (Eds.) (1996). *Interactive minds: Life-span perspectives.* New York: Cambridge University Press.

Bandura, A. (1986). *Social foundations of thought and action: A social-cognitive theory.* Englewood Cliffs, NJ: Prentice-Hall.

Bandura, A. (1989). Human agency in social cognitive theory. *American Psychologist, 44*, 1175–1184.

Barber, B. (1984). *Strong democracy: Participatory politics for a new age.* San Francisco: University of California Press.

Barker, P. (1986). *Basic family therapy* (2nd ed.). New York: Oxford University Press.

Barnhill, L.H., & Longo, D. (1978). Fixation and regression in the family life cycle. *Family Process, 17*, 469–478.

Barr, R.B., & Tagg, J. (1995). From teaching to learning: A new paradigm for undergraduate education. *Change*, (Nov–Dec), 13–25.

Basch, M.F. (1995). Kohut's contribution. *Psychoanalytic Dialogues, 5*, 367–375.

Bateson, G. (1972). *Steps to an ecology of mind.* New York: Ballantine.

Bateson, G. (1979). *Mind and nature: A necessary unity.* New York: Dutton.

Baudrillard, J. (1983). *Simulations.* New York: Semiotext(e).

Bauman, Z. (1996). On communications and human freedom or, How to square the circle. *Theory, Culture, & Society, 13*, 79–90.

Baumrind, D. (1991). Effective parenting during the early adolescent transition. In P.A. Cowan & M. H. Hetherington (Eds.), *Family transitions* (pp. 111–163). Hillsdale, NJ: Erlbaum.

Becvar, D.S., & Becvar, R.J. (1993). Story-telling and family therapy. *The American Journal of Family Therapy, 21*, 145–160.

Belenky, M.F., Clinchy, B.M., Goldberger, N.R., & Tartule, J.M. (1986). *Women's ways of knowing: The development of self, voice, and mind.* New York: Basic.

Benenson, J.F. (1996). Gender differences in the development of relationships. In G.G. Noam & K.W. Fischer (Eds.), *Development and vulnerability in close relationships* (pp. 237–261). Mahwah, NJ: Erlbaum.

Berg, I.K., & de Shazer, S. (1993). Making numbers talk: Language in therapy. In S. Friedman

(Ed.), *The new language of change: Constructive collaboration in therapy* (pp. 5–24). New York: Guilford.

Berkowitz, M.W., & Gibbs, J.C. (1983). Measuring the developmental features of moral discussion. *Merril Palmer Quarterly, 29*, 399–410.

Berkowitz, M.W., & Gibbs, J.C. (1985). The process of moral conflict resolution and moral development. *New Directions for Child Development, 29*, 71–83.

Berkowitz, M.W., & Keller, M. (1994). Transitional processes in social cognition: A longitudinal study. *International Journal of Behavioral Development, 17*, 447–467.

Bertens, H. (1995). *The idea of the postmodern: A history.* New York: Routledge.

Bevan, W., & Kessel, F. (1994). Plain truths and home cooking: Thoughts on the making and remaking of psychology. *American Psychologist, 49*, 505–509.

Bickhard, M.H. (1992). Scaffolding and self-scaffolding: Central aspects of development. In L.T. Winegar & J. Valsiner (Eds.), *Children's development within social context* (Vol. 2). *Research and methodology* (pp. 33–52). Hillsdale, NJ: Erlbaum.

Bidell, T.R. (1992). Beyond interactionism in contextualist models of development. *Human Development, 35*, 306–315.

Bidell, T.R., & Fischer, K.W. (1992). Beyond the stage debate: Action, structure, and variability in Piagetian theory and research. In R.J. Sternberg & C.A. Berg (Eds.), *Intellectual development* (pp. 100–140). New York: Cambridge University Press.

Billig, M. (1996). *Arguing and thinking: A rhetorical approach to social psychology* (2nd ed.). Cambridge, UK: Cambridge University Press.

Birch, J. (1991). Re-inventing the already punctured wheel: Reflections on a seminar with Humberto Maturana. *Journal of Family Therapy, 13*, 349–373.

Birchler, G.R. (1992). Marriage. In V.B. Van Hasselt & M. Hersen (Eds.), *Handbook of social development: A lifespan perspective* (pp. 397–419). New York: Plenum.

Bischoff, R.J., McKeel, A.J., Moon, S.M., & Sprenkle, D.H. (1996). Therapist-conducted consultation: Using clients as consultants. *Journal of Marital and Family Therapy, 22*, 359–379.

Blanchard-Fields, F. (1990). Postformal reasoning in a socioemotional context. In M.L. Commons, J.D. Sinnott, F.A. Richards, & C. Armon (Eds.), *Adult development* (Vol. 1). *Comparisons and applications of developmental models* (pp. 73–94). New York: Praeger.

Blasi, A., & Glodis, K. (1995). The development of identity. A critical analysis from the perspective of the self as subject. *Developmental Review, 15*, 404–433.

Blatt, S.J., & Blass, R.B. (1996). Relatedness and self-definition: A dialectic model of personality development. In G.G. Noam & K.W. Fischer (Eds.), *Development and vulnerability in close relationships* (pp. 309–338). Mahwah, NJ: Erlbaum.

Blatt, S.J. (in press). Representational structures in psychopathology. In D. Cicchetti & S. Toth (Eds.), *Representation, emotion, and cognition in developmental psychopathology.* Rochester, NY: University of Rochester Press.

Block, J. (1995a). A contrarian view of the Five-factor approach to personality description. *Psychological Bulletin, 117*, 187–215.

Block, J. (1995b). Going beyond the five factors given: Rejoinder to Costa and McCrae (1995) and Goldberg and Saucier (1995). *Psychological Bulletin, 117*, 226–229.

Bohart, A.C. (1995). Configurationism: Constructivism from an experiential perspective. *Journal of Constructivist Psychology, 8*, 317–326.

Bond, L.A., Belenky, M.F., Weinstock, J.S., Cook, T., & Monsey, T.V. (1992). Self-sustaining powers of mind and voice: Empowering rural women. In M. Kessler, S.E. Goldston, and J.M. Jaffee (Eds.), *The present and future of presentation: In honor of George V. Albee* (pp. 125–137). Newbury Park, CA: Sage.

Bond, L.A., Belenky, M.F., Weinstock, J.S., & Cook, T. (1996). Imagining and engaging one's children: Lessons from poor, rural, New England mothers. In S. Harkness & C.M. Super (Eds.), *Parents' cultural belief systems: Their origins, expressions and consequences* (pp. 467–493). New York: Guilford.

Bornstein, M.H. (1995). Form and function: Implications for studies of culture and human development. *Culture & Psychology, 1*, 123–137.

Bowlby, J. (1980). *Attachments and loss* (Vol. 3). *Loss, sadness, and depression*. New York: Basic.

Bourdieu, P. (1984). *Distinction: A social critique of the judgement of taste*. London: Routledge & Kegan Paul.

Bracken, P.J. (1995). Beyond liberation. Michel Foucault and the notion of a critical psychiatry. *Philosophy, Psychiatry, & Psychology, 2*, 1–13.

Bradley, B.S. (1993). A serpent's guide to children's "Theories of mind." *Theory and Psychology, 3*, 497–521.

Brainerd, C.J. (1996). Piaget: A centennial celebration. *Psychological Science, 7*, 191–195.

Brandtstädter, J., & Greve, W. (1994). The aging self: Stabilizing and protective processes. *Developmental Review, 14*, 52–80.

Brecher, S., & Friedman, S. (1993). In pursuit of a better life: A mother's triumph. In S. Friedman (Ed.), *The new language of change: Constructive collaboration in therapy* (pp. 278–299). New York: Guilford.

Bretherton, I. (1990). Open communication and internal working models: Their role in the development of attachment. In R.A. Thompson (Ed.), *Nebraska Symposium on Motivation* (Vol. 36). *Socioemotional development* (pp. 57–114). Lincoln, NB: University of Nebraska Press.

Brewster Smith, M. (1994). Selfhood at risk: Postmodern perils and perils of postmodernism. *American Psychologist, 49*, 405–411.

Brewster Smith, M. (1995). About postmodernism: Reply to Gergen and others. *American Psychologist, 50*, 393–394.

Broderick, M.A. (1996). A constructive-developmental approach to studying the "cancer-prone personality." In M.L. Commons, J. Demick, & C. Goldberg (Eds.), *Clinical approaches to adult development* (pp. 311–334). Norwood, NJ: Ablex.

Bronfenbrenner, U. (1993a). The ecology of cognitive development: Research models and fugitive findings. In R.H. Wozniak & K.W. Fischer (Eds.), *Development in context: Acting and thinking in specific environments* (pp. 3–44). Hillsdale, NJ: Erlbaum.

Bronfenbrenner, U. (1993b). Distancing theory from a distance. In R.R. Cocking & K.A. Renninger (Eds.), *The development and meaning of psychological distance* (pp. 63–77). Hillsdale, NJ: Erlbaum.

Brown, L.M. (1994). VII. Standing in the crossfire: A response to Tavris, Gremmen, Lykes, Davis, and Contratto. *Feminism & Psychology, 4*, 382–398.

Brown, L.M., & Gilligan, C. (1992). *Meeting at the crossroads: Women's psychology and girl's development*. Cambridge, MA: Harvard University Press.

Brown, L.M., & Gilligan, C. (1993). Meeting at the crossroads: Women's psychology and girl's development. *Feminism & Psychology, 3*, 11–35.

Brown, R. (1973). *A first language: The early stages*. Cambridge, MA: Harvard.

Bruner, J. (1990). *Acts of meaning*. Cambridge, MA: Harvard University Press.

Buber, M. (1970). *I and thou* (W. Kaufmann, Trans.). New York: Scribner. (Original work published 1923)

Buckley, W. (1967). *Sociology and modern systems theory*. Englewood Cliffs, NJ: Prentice-Hall.

Burgess, R.L. (1994). The family in a changing world: A prolegomenon to an evolutionary analysis. *Human Nature, 5*, 203–221.

Burman, E. (1994). *Deconstructing developmental psychology*. London, UK: Routledge.

Burtt, S. (1993). The politics of virtue today: A critique and a proposal. *American Political Science Review, 87*, 360–368.

Buss, D.M. (1994). The strategies of human mating. *American Scientist, 82*, 238–249.

Buss, D.M. (1995). Evolutionary psychology: A new paradigm for psychological science. *Psychological Inquiry, 6*, 1–30.

Buss, D.M., & Schmitt, D.P. (1993). Sexual strategies theory: An evolutionary perspective on human mating. *Psychological Review, 100,* 204–232.

Butterworth, G. (1990). Self-perception in infancy. In D. Cicchetti & M. Beeghly (Eds.), *The self in transition: Infancy to childhood* (pp. 119–137). Chicago: The University of Chicago Press.

Byng-Hall, J. (1991). The application of attachment theory to understanding and treatment in family therapy. In C.M. Parkes, J. Stevenson-Hinde, & P. Marris (Eds.), *Attachment across the life cycle* (pp. 199–215). New York: Routledge.

Byng-Hall, J. (1995). Creating a secure family base: Some implications of attachment theory for family therapy. *Family Process, 34,* 45–58.

Byng-Hall, J., & Stevenson-Hinde, J. (1991). Attachment relationships within a family system. *Infant Mental Health Journal, 12,* 187–200.

Caney, S. (1992). Liberalism and communitarianism: A misconceived debate. *Political Studies, 40,* 273–290.

Caney, S. (1993). Liberalisms and communitarianisms: A reply. *Political Studies, 41,* 657–660.

Canfield, R.L., & Ceci, S.J. (1992). Integrating learning into a theory of intellectual development. In R.J. Sternberg & C.A. Berg (Eds.), *Intellectual development* (pp. 278–300). New York: Cambridge University Press.

Carter, B., & McGoldrick, M. (Eds.) (1989). *The changing family life cycle* (2nd ed.). Boston: Allyn and Bacon.

Case, R. (1985). *Intellectual development: Birth to adulthood.* Orlando, FL: Academic.

Case, R. (1987). Neo-Piagetian theory: Retrospect and prospect. *International Journal of Psychology, 22,* 773–791.

Case, R. (1991a). *The role of primitive defenses in the regulation and representation of early attachment relations.* Paper presented at the biennial meeting of the Society for Research in Child Development Seattle, Washington, April.

Case, R. (1991b). Stages in the development of the young child's first sense of self. *Developmental Review, 11,* 210–230.

Case, R. (1996). The role of psychological defenses in the representation and regulation of close personal relationships across the life span. In G.G. Noam & K.W. Fischer (Eds.), *Development and vulnerability in close relationships* (pp. 59–88). Mahwah, NJ: Erlbaum.

Case, R., & Edelstein, W. (1993). Introduction: Structural approaches to individual differences. In R. Case & W. Edelstein (Eds.), *The new structuralism in cognitive development: Theory and research on individual pathways* (pp. 71–100). Basel: Karger.

Case, R., Okamoto, Y., Henderson, B., & McKeough, A. (1993). Individual variability and consistency in cognitive development: New evidence for the existence of central conceptual structures. In R. Case & W. Edelstein (Eds.), *The new structuralism in development: Theory and research on individual pathways* (pp. 1–10). Basel: Karger.

Cazden, C.B. (1993). Vygotsky, Hymes, and Bakhtin: From word to utterance to voice. In E.A. Forman, N. Minick, & C.A. Stone (Eds.), *Contexts for learning: Sociocultural dynamics in children's development* (pp. 197–212). New York: Oxford University Press.

Ceci, S.J. (1993). Contextual trends in intellectual development. *Developmental Review, 13,* 403–435.

Chang, J., & Phillips, M. (1993). Michael White and Steve de Shazer: New directions in family therapy. In S. Gilligan & R. Price (Eds.), *Therapeutic conversations* (pp. 95–111). New York: Norton.

Chang-Wells, G.L., & Wells, G. (1993). Dynamics of discourse: Literacy and the construction of knowledge. In E.A. Forman, N. Minick, & C.A. Stone (Eds.), *Contexts for learning: Sociocultural dynamics in children's development* (pp. 58–90). New York: Oxford University Press.

Chapman, M. (1988). *Constructive evolution: Origins and development of Piaget's thought.* New York: Cambridge University Press.

Cicchetti, D. (1991). Fractures in the crystal: Developmental psychopathology and the emergence of self. *Developmental Review, 11,* 271–287.

Clinchy, B.M. (1993). Ways of knowing and ways of being: Epistemological and moral development in undergraduate women. In A. Garrod (Ed.), *Approaches to moral development: New research and emerging themes* (pp. 180–200). New York: Teachers College Press.

Clinchy, B.M. (1995). Commentary. *Human Development, 38,* 258–264.

Cocking, R.R., & Renninger, K.A. (1993). Psychological distance as a unifying theory of development. In R.R. Cocking & K.A. Renninger (Eds.), *The development and meaning of psychological distance* (pp. 3–18). Hillsdale, NJ: Erlbaum.

Cole, M. (1992a). Context, modularity, and the cultural constitution of development. In L.T. Winegar & J. Valsiner (Eds.), *Children's development within social context* (Vol.2). *Research and methodology* (pp. 5–31). Hillsdale, NJ: Erlbaum.

Cole, M. (1992b). Culture in development. In M.H. Bornstein & M.E. Lamb (Eds.), *Developmental psychology: An advanced textbook* (3rd ed.) (pp. 731–789). Hillsdale, NJ: Erlbaum.

Cole, M. (1995a). Sociocultural–historical psychology: Some general remarks and a proposal for a new kind of cultural–genetic methodology. In J.V. Wertsch, P. del Río, & A. Alvarez (Eds.), *Sociocultural studies of mind* (pp. 187–214). New York: Cambridge University Press.

Cole, M. (1995b). Culture and cognitive development: From cross-cultural research to creating systems of cultural mediation. *Culture & Psychology, 1,* 25–54.

Cole, M., & Engström, Y. (1995) Commentary. *Human Development, 38,* 19–24.

Combrinck-Graham, L. (1985). A developmental model for family systems. *Family Process, 24,* 139–150.

Combs, G., & Freedman, J. (1994). Narrative intentions. In M.F. Hoyt (Ed.), *Constructive therapies* (pp. 67–91). New York: Guilford.

Commons, M.L. (1996). Preface, In M.L. Commons, J. Demick, & C. Goldberg (Eds.), *Clinical approaches to adult development* (pp. ix–xi). Norwood, NJ: Ablex.

Commons, M.L., Demick, J., & Goldberg, C. (Eds.) (1996), *Clinical approaches to adult development.* Norwood, NJ: Ablex.

Commons, M.L., & Grotzer, T.A. (1990). The relationship between Piagetian and Kohlbergian stage: An examination of the necessary but not sufficient relationship. In M.L. Commons, C. Armon, L. Kohlberg, F.A. Richards, T.A. Grotzer, & J.D. Sinnott (Eds.), *Adult development* (Vol. 2). *Models and methods in the study of adolescent and adult thought* (pp. 205–231). New York: Praeger.

Cook-Greuter, S.R. (1990). Maps for living: Ego development stages from symbiosis to conscious universal embeddedness. In M.L. Commons, C. Armon, L. Kohlberg, F.A. Richards, T.A. Grotzer, & J.D. Sinnott (Eds.), *Adult development* (Vol. 2). *Models and methods in the study of adolescent and adult thought* (pp. 79–104). New York: Praeger.

Costa, P.T., Jr., & McCrae, R.R. (1994). Stability and change in personality from adolescence to adulthood. In C.F. Halverson, G.A. Kohnstamm, & R.P. Martin (Eds.), *The developing structure of temperament and personality from infancy to adulthood* (pp. 139–150). Hillsdale, NJ: Erlbaum.

Costa, P.T., Jr., & McCrae, R.R. (1995). Solid grounds in the wetlands of personality: A reply to Block. *Psychological Bulletin, 117,* 216–220.

Costall, A. (1995). Socializing affordances. *Theory & Psychology, 5,* 467–481.

Coté, J.E. (1993). Foundations of a psychoanalytic social psychology: Neo-Eriksonian propositions regarding the relationship between psychic structure and cultural institutions. *Developmental Review, 13,* 31–53.

Crittenden, J. (1993). The social nature of autonomy. *The Review of Politics, 55,* 35–66.

Crittenden, P.M. (1990). Internal representational models of attachment relationships. *Infant Mental Health Journal, 11,* 259–277.

Crittenden, P.M. (1992). Quality of attachment in the preschool years. *Development and Psychopathology, 4,* 209–241.

Dallmayr, F. (1993). Heidegger and Freud. *Political Psychology, 14,* 235–253.

Dallos, R. (1995). Constructing family life: Family belief systems. In J. Muncie, M. Wetherell, R. Dallos, & A. Cochrane (Eds.), *Understanding the family* (pp. 173–211). London, UK: Sage.

Daly, M. (1994). *Communitarianism: A new public ethics.* Belmont, CA: Wadsworth.

Damon, W., & Hart, D. (1988). *Self-understanding in childhood and adolescence.* New York: Cambridge University Press.

Dannefer, D. (1996). Commentary. *Human Development, 39,* 150–152.

Danziger, K. (1991). *Psychology's construction of the subject.* Cambridge, UK: Cambridge University Press.

Darling, N., & Steinberg, L. (1993). Parenting style as context: An integrative model. *Psychological Bulletin, 113,* 487–496.

Dawkins, R. (1989). *The selfish gene* (2nd ed.). Oxford, UK: Oxford University Press.

Day, J.M., & Tappan, M.B. (1996). The narrative approach to moral development: From the epistemic subject to dialogical selves. *Human Development, 39,* 67–82.

Dean, A.L. (1994). Instinctual affective forces in the internalization process: Contributions of Hans Loewald. *Human Development, 37,* 42–57.

Dell, P.E. (1985). Understanding Bateson and Maturana: Toward a biological foundation for the social sciences. *Journal of Marital and Family Therapy, 11,* 1–20.

del Río, P. (1996). Building Identities in a mass-communication world: A commentary on Steve Miles's 'The cultural capital of consumption'. *Culture & Psychology, 2,* 159–172.

Demetriou, A., Efklides, A., & Platsidou, M. (1993). The architecture and dynamics of developing mind: Experiential structuralism as a frame for unifying cognitive developmental theories. *Monographs of the Society for Research in Child Development, 58* (5–6, Serial No. 234).

Demick, J. (1996a). Life transitions as a paradigm for the study of adult development. In M.L. Commons, J. Demick, & C. Goldberg (Eds.), *Clinical approaches to adult development* (pp. 115–144). Norwood, NJ: Ablex.

Demick, J. (1996b). Epilogue: What ARE clinical approaches to adult development? In M.L. Commons, J. Demick, & C. Goldberg (Eds.), *Clinical approaches to adult development* (pp. 335–356). Norwood, NJ: Ablex.

de Ribaupierre, A. (1993). Structural invariants and individual differences: On the difficulty of dissociating developmental and differential processes. In R. Case & W. Edelstein (Eds.), *The new structuralism in cognitive development: Theory and research on individual pathways* (pp. 11–32). Basel: Karger.

Derrida, J. (1986). The ends of man. In K. Baynes, J. Bohman, & T. McCarthy (Eds.), *After philosophy* (pp. 125–158). Cambridge, MA: MIT Press.

de Shazer, S. (1991). *Putting difference to work.* New York: Norton.

de Shazer, S. (1993a). Creating misunderstanding: There is no escape from language. In S. Gilligan & R. Price (Eds.), *Therapeutic conversations* (pp. 81–90). New York: Norton.

de Shazer, S. (1993b). Commentary: de Shazer and White: Vive la différence. In S. Gilligan & R. Price (Eds.), *Therapeutic conversations* (pp. 112–120). New York: Norton.

Desrochers, S., Ricard, M., & Gouin Décarie, T. (1995). Understanding causality in infancy: A reassessment of Piaget's theory. *Cahier de Psychologie Cognitive, 14,* 255–268.

de Vries, B., Birren, J.E., & Deutchman, D.E. (1990). Adult development through guided autobiography: The family context. *Family Relations, 39,* 3–7.

Dewey, J. (1916). *Democracy and education: An introduction to the philosophy of education.* New York: Macmillan.

Diaz, R.M., Neal, C.J., & Vachio, A. (1991). Maternal teaching in the zone of proximal development: A comparison of low- and high-risk dyads. *Merrill-Palmer Quarterly, 37,* 83–108.

Dickerson, V.C., & Zimmerman, J.L. (1993). A narrative approach to families with adolescents. In S. Friedman (Ed.), *The new language of change: Constructive collaboration in therapy* (pp. 226–250). New York: Guilford.

Digman, J.M. (1994). Child personality and temperament: Does the Big-Five factor model embrace both domains? In C.F. Halverson, G.A. Kohnstamm, & R.P. Martin (Eds.), *The developing structure of temperament and personality from infancy to adulthood* (pp. 323–338). Hillsdale, NJ: Erlbaum.

Dixon, R.A., & Lerner, R.M. (1992). A history of systems in developmental psychology. In M.H. Bornstein & M.E. Lamb (Eds.), *Developmental psychology: An advanced textbook* (3rd ed.) (pp. 3–58). Hillsdale, NJ: Erlbaum.

Donald, M. (1993). Précis of *Origins of the modern mind*: Three stages in the evolution of culture and cognition. *Behavioral and Brain Sciences, 16*, 737–791.

Dornbusch, S.M., Carlsmith, J.M., Bushwall, S.J., Ritter, P.L., Leiderman, H., Hastorf, A.H., & Gross, R.T. (1985). Single parents, extended households, and the control of adolescents. *Child Development, 56*, 326–341.

Dornbusch, S.M., Ritter, P.L., Liederman, P.H., Roberts, D.F., & Fraleigh, M.J. (1987). The relation of parenting style to adolescent school performance. *Child Development, 58*, 1244–1257.

Downing, L.A., & Thigpen, R.B. (1993). Virtue and the common good in liberal theory. *The Journal of Politics, 55*, 1046–1059.

Duncan, B.L., & Parks, M.B. (1988). Integrating individual and systems approaches: Strategic-behavioral therapy. *Journal of Marital and Family Therapy, 14*, 151–161.

Duncan, B.L., Parks, M.B., & Rusk, G.S. (1990). Eclectic strategic practice: A process constructive perspective. *Journal of Marital and Family Therapy, 16*, 165–178.

Dupré, L. (1993). The common good and the open society. *The Review of Politics, 55*, 687–712.

Duran, R.T., & Gauvain, M. (1993). The role of age versus expertise in peer collaboration during joint planning. *Journal of Experimental Child Psychology, 55*, 227–242.

Durrant, M., & Kowalski, K.M. (1993). Enhancing views of competence. In S. Friedman (Ed.), *The new language of change: Constructive collaboration in therapy* (pp. 107–137). New York: Guilford.

Duvall, E.M., & Hill, B.C. (1948). *When you marry*. Lexington, MA: Heath.

Eccles, J.S., Midgley, C., Wigfield, A., Buchanan, C.M., Reuman, D., Flanagan, C., & Mac Iver, D. (1993). Development during adolescence: The impact of stage-environment fit on young adolescents' experiences in schools and in families. *American Psychologist, 48*, 90–101.

Eckensberger, L.H. (1995). Activity or action: Two different roads towards an integration of culture into psychology? *Culture & Psychology, 1*, 67–80.

Eckert, P.A. (1993). Acceleration of change: Catalysts in brief therapy. *Clinical Psychology Review, 13*, 241–253.

Efran, J.S. (1994). Mystery, abstraction, and narrative psychotherapy. *Journal of Constructivist Psychology, 7*, 219–227.

Egendorf, A. (1995). Hearing people through their pain. *Journal of Traumatic Stress, 8*, 5–28.

Elias, N. (1971). Sociology of knowledge: New perspectives (Part Two). *Sociology, 5*, 355–370.

Elkind, D. (1996). Inhelder and Piaget on adolescence and adulthood: A postmodern appraisal. *Psychological Science, 7*, 216–220.

Ellis, A. (1990). Is rational-emotional therapy (RET) "rationalist" or "constructivist"? *Journal of Rational-Emotional and Cognitive-Behavior Therapy, 8*, 169–193.

Epston, D. (1993a). Internalizing discourses versus externalizing discourses. In S. Gilligan & R. Price (Eds.), *Therapeutic conversations* (pp. 161–177). New York: Norton.

Epston, D. (1993b). Internalizing other questioning with couples: The New Zealand version. In S. Gilligan & R. Price (Eds.), *Therapeutic conversations* (pp. 183–189). New York: Norton.

Epston, D. (1993c). Commentary. In S. Gilligan & R. Price (Eds.), *Therapeutic conversations* (pp. 231–236). New York: Norton.

Epston, D. (1994). Extending the conversation. *Family Therapy Networker, 18*(6), 30–37, 62–63.

Epston, D., & White, M. (1995). Termination as a rite of passage: Questioning strategies for a therapy of inclusion. In R.A. Neimeyer & M.J. Mahoney (Eds.), *Constructivism in psychotherapy* (pp. 339–354). Washington, DC: American Psychological Association.

Epston, D., White, M., & Murray, K. (1992). A proposal for re-authoring therapy: Rose's revisioning of her life and a commentary. In S. McNamee & K.J. Gergen (Eds.), *Therapy as social construction* (pp. 96–115). London, UK: Sage.

Erickson, G.D. (1988). Against the grain: Decentering family therapy. *Journal of Marital and Family Therapy, 14,* 225–236.

Erickson, M.F., Korfmacher, J., & Egeland, B.R. (1992). Attachments past and present: Implications for therapeutic intervention with mother-infant dyads. *Development and Psychopathology, 4,* 495–507.

Erikson, E.H. (1980). *Identity and the life cycle.* New York: Norton.

Etzioni, A. (1996). A moderate communitarian proposal. *Political Theory, 24,* 155–171.

Fairlamb, H.L. (1994). *Critical conditions: Postmodernity and the question of foundations.* New York: Cambridge University Press.

Falck, C. (1994) (2nd ed.). *Myth, truth, and literature: Towards a true post-modernism.* New York: Cambridge University Press.

Falicov, C.J. (1988). Family sociology and family therapy contributions to the family development framework: A comparative analysis and thoughts on future trends. In C.J. Falicov (Ed.), *Family transitions: Continuity and change over the life cycle* (pp. 3–51). New York: Guilford.

Feingold, A. (1994). Gender differences in personality: A meta-analysis. *Psychological Bulletin, 116,* 429–456.

Feinman, S. (1992). *Social referencing and the social construction of reality in infancy.* New York: Plenum.

Feixas, G. (1990). Personal construct theory and systemic therapies: Parallel or convergent trends? *Journal of Marital and Family Therapy, 16,* 1–20.

Feldman, D.H. (1993). Cultural organisms in the development of great potential: Referees, termites, and the Aspen music festival. In R.H. Wozniak & K.W. Fischer (Eds.), *Development in context: Acting and thinking in specific environments* (pp. 225–254). Hillsdale, NJ: Erlbaum.

Fernyhough, C. (1996). The dialogic mind: A dialogic approach to the higher mental functions. *New Ideas in Psychology, 14,* 47–62.

Fischer, C. T. (1992). A humanistic approach to lifespan development. In V.B. Van Hasselt & M. Hersen (Eds.), *Handbook of social development: A lifespan perspective* (pp. 113–130). New York: Plenum.

Fischer, K.W. (1980). A theory of cognitive development: The control and construction of hierarchies of skills. *Psychological Review, 87,* 477–531.

Fischer, K.W., & Ayoub, C. (1996). Analyzing development of working models of close relationships: Illustration with a case of vulnerability and violence. In G.G. Noam & K.W. Fischer (Eds.), *Development and vulnerability in close relationships* (pp. 173–199). Mahwah, NJ: Erlbaum.

Fischer, K.W., Bullock, D.H., Rotenberg, E.J., & Raya, P. (1993a). The dynamics of competence: How context contributes directly to skill. In R.H. Wozniak & K.W. Fischer (Eds.), *Development in context: Acting and thinking in specific environments* (pp. 93–117). Hillsdale, NJ: Erlbaum.

Fischer, K.W., & Granott, N. (1995). Beyond one-dimensional change: Parallel, concurrent, socially distributed processes in learning and development. *Human Development, 38,* 302–314.

Fischer, K.W., & Hencke, R.W. (1996). Infants' construction of actions in context: Piaget's contribution to research on early development. *Psychological Science, 7*, 204–210.

Fischer, K.W., Knight, C.C., & Van Paris, M. (1993b). Analyzing diversity in developmental pathways: Methods and concepts. In R. Case & W. Edelstein (Eds.), *The new structuralism in cognitive development: Theory and research on individual pathways* (pp. 33–56). Basel: Karger.

Fish, V. (1996). [Letter to the editor]. *Journal of Marital and Family Therapy, 22*, 407–409.

Fisk, M. (1993). Community and morality. *The Review of Politics, 55*, 593–616.

Flam, F. (1991). Beating a fractal drum. *Science, 254*, 1593.

Flaskas, C., & Humphreys, C. (1993). Theorizing about power: Intersecting the ideas of Foucault with the "problem" of power in family therapy. *Family Process, 32*, 35–47.

Flemons, D.G., Green, S.K., & Rambo, A.H. (1996). Evaluating therapists' practices in a postmodern world: A discussion and a scheme. *Family Process, 35*, 43–56.

Fogel, A. (1993). *Developing through relationships: Origins of communication, self, and culture*. Chicago: University of Chicago Press.

Forman, E.A., & McPhail, J. (1993). Vygotskian perspective on children's collaborative problem-solving activities. In E.A. Forman, N. Minick, & C.A. Stone (Eds.), *Contexts for learning: Sociocultural dynamics in children's development* (pp. 213–229). New York: Oxford University Press.

Forman, E.A., Minick, N., & Stone, C.A. (1993). *Contexts for learning: Sociocultural dynamics in children's development*. New York: Oxford University Press.

Foucault, M. (1980). *Michel Foucault, power/knowledge, selected interviews, and other writings 1972–1977* (Ed., C. Gordon). Hemel Hempstead, UK: Harvester.

Fowers, B.J., & Richardson, F.C. (1996). Individualism, family ideology and family therapy. *Theory and Psychology, 6*, 121–151.

Fox, D.R. (1993). Psychological jurisprudence and radical social change. *American Psychologist, 48*, 234–241.

Framo, J.L. (1994). The family life cycle: Impressions. *Contemporary Family Therapy, 16*, 87–117.

Freedman, D.G., & Gorman, J. (1993). Attachment and the transmission of culture—An evolutionary perspective. *Journal of Social and Evolutionary Systems, 16*, 297–329.

Freedman, J., & Combs, G. (1993). Invitations to new stories: Using questions to explore new possibilities. In S. Gilligan & R. Price (Eds.), *Therapeutic conversations* (pp. 291–303). New York: Norton.

Freeman, J.C., & Lobowits, D. (1993). The turtle with wings. In S. Friedman (Ed.), *The new language of change: Constructive collaboration in therapy* (pp. 188–225). New York: Guilford.

Freeman, M. (1995). Groping in the light. *Theory & Psychology, 5*, 353–360.

Friedman, M. (1995). Constructivism, psychotherapy, and the dialogue of touchstones. *Journal of Constructivist Psychology, 8*, 283–292.

Friedman, S. (1993). Escape from the furies: A journey from self-pity to self-love. In S. Friedman (Ed.), *The new language of change: Constructive collaboration in therapy* (pp. 251–277). New York: Guilford.

Friedman, S. (1994). Staying simple, staying focused: Time-effective consultations with children and families. In M.F. Hoyt (Ed.), *Constructive therapies* (pp. 217–250). New York: Guilford.

Frosh, S. (1995). Postmodernism versus psychotherapy. *Journal of Family Therapy, 17*, 175–190.

Funk, J.D. (1990). Postformal cognitive theory and developmental stages of musical composition. In M.L. Commons, J.D. Sinott, F.A. Richards, & C. Armon (Eds.), *Adult development* (Vol. 1). *Comparisons and applications of developmental models* (pp. 3–32). New York: Praeger.

Furman, B., & Ahola, T. (1994). Solution talk: The solution-oriented way of talking about problems. In M.F. Hoyt (Ed.), *Constructive therapies* (pp. 41–66). New York: Guilford.

Gadamer, H.-G. (1975). *Truth and method.* (G. Barden and J. Cumming, Trans.). New York: Continuum. (Original work published 1960)

Gadamer, H.-G. (1988). *Philosophical hermeneutics* (Ed., D.E. Linge). Berkeley,CA: University of California Press.

Galinsky, E. (1981). *Between generations: The six stages of parenthood.* New York: Berkeley.

Gallimore, R., & Goldenberg, C. (1993). Activity settings of early literacy: Home and school factors in children's emerging literacy. In E.A. Forman, N. Minick, & C.A. Stone (Eds.), *Contexts for learning: Sociocultural dynamics in children's development* (pp. 315–335). New York: Oxford University Press.

Galooshian, H.A., & Anderson, H. (1992). Strategy and intervention versus nonintervention: A matter of theory? *Journal of Marital and Family Therapy, 18,* 5–15.

Gardiner, M. (1996). Alterity and ethics: A dialogical perspective. *Theory, Culture, & Society, 13,* 121–143.

Garton, A.F. (1992). *Social interaction and the development of language and cognition.* Hillsdale, NJ: Erlbaum.

Gauvain, M. (1993). The development of spatial thinking in everyday activity. *Developmental Review, 13,* 92–121.

Gelcer, E., & Schwartzbein, D. (1989). A piagetian view of family therapy: Selvini-Palazzoli and the invariant approach. *Family Process, 28,* 439–456.

Gergen, K.J. (1994a). The communal creation of meaning. In W.F. Overton, & D.S. Palermo (Eds.), *The nature and ontogenesis of meaning* (pp. 19–39). Hillsdale, NJ: Erlbaum.

Gergen, K.J. (1994b). Exploring the postmodern: Perils or potentials? *American Psychologist, 49,* 412–416.

Gergen, K.J. (1994c). *Realities and relationships: Soundings in social construction.* Cambridge, MA: Harvard University Press.

Gergen, K. (1995). Postmodern psychology: Resonance and reflection. *American Psychologist, 50,* 394.

Gergen, K.J., Hoffman, L., & Anderson, H. (1996). Is diagnosis a disaster? A constructionist trialogue. In F.W. Kaslow (Ed.), *Handbook of relational diagnosis and dysfunctional family patterns* (pp. 102–118). New York, Wiley.

Gergen, K.J., & Kaye, J. (1992). Beyond narrative in the negotiation of therapeutic meaning. In S. McNamee & K.J. Gergen (Eds.), *Therapy as social construction* (pp. 166–185). London, UK: Sage.

Gergen, M. (1995). Postmodern, post-cartesian positionings on the subject of psychology. *Theory & Psychology, 5,* 361–368.

Gibson, E.J. (1982). The concept of affordances in perceptual development: The renascence of functionalism. In W.A. Collins (Ed.), *The Minnesota Symposia on Child Psychology* (Vol. 15) (pp. 55–81). Hillsdale, NJ: Erlbaum.

Gilligan. C. (1982). *In a different voice: Psychological theory and women's development.* Cambridge, MA: Harvard University Press.

Gilligan, C. (1994). XI. Afterward: The power to name. *Feminism & Psychology, 4,* 420–424.

Gilligan, C. (1996). The centrality of relationship in human development: A puzzle, some evidence, and a theory. In G.G. Noam & K.W. Fischer (Eds.), *Development and vulnerability in close relationships* (pp. 237–261). Mahwah, NJ: Erlbaum.

Glass, J.M. (1993). Multiplicity, identity, and the horrors of selfhood: Failures in the postmodern position. *Political Psychology, 14,* 255–278.

Glassman, M. (1995). The difference between Piaget and Vygotsky: A response to Duncan. *Developmental Review, 15,* 473–482.

Globus, G.G. (1995). *The postmodern brain.* Philadelphia: Benjamins.

Goldberg, C. (1996). Introduction: The approach to positive adult development. In M.L.

Commons, J. Demick, & C. Goldberg (Eds.), *Clinical approaches to adult development* (pp. 1–7). Norwood, NJ: Ablex.

Goldberg, L.R. (1994). Resolving a scientific embarrassment: A comment on the articles in this special issue. *European Journal of Personality, 8*, 351–356.

Goldberg, L.R., & Rosolack, T.K. (1994). The Big Five factor structure as an integrative framework: An empirical comparison with Eysenck's P-E-N model. In C.F. Halverson, G.A. Kohnstamm, & R.P. Martin (Eds.), *The developing structure of temperament and personality from infancy to adulthood* (pp. 7–35). Hillsdale, NJ: Erlbaum.

Goldberg, L.R., & Saucier, G. (1995). So what do you propose we use instead? A reply to Block. *Psychological Bulletin, 117*, 221–225.

Goldin-Meadow, S., Alibali, M.W., & Church, R.B. (1993). Transitions in concept acquisition: Using the hand to read the mind. *Psychological Review, 100*, 279–297.

Goldner, V. (1993). Power and hierarchy: Let's talk about it! *Family Process, 32*, 157–162.

Gonçalves, Ó.F. (1995). Hermeneutics, constructivism, and cognitive-behavioral therapies: From the object to the project. In R.A. Neimeyer & M.J. Mahoney (Eds.), *Constructivism in psychotherapy* (pp. 195–230). Washington, DC: American Psychological Association.

Göncü, A. (1993). Development of intersubjectivity in social pretend play. *Human Development, 36*, 185–198.

Goodnow, J.J. (1990a). The socialization of cognition: What's involved? In J. Stigler, R. Schweder, & G. Herdt (Eds.), *Cultural psychology* (pp. 259–286). Chicago: University of Chicago Press.

Goodnow, J.J. (1990b). Using sociology to extend psychological accounts of cognitive development. *Human Development, 33*, 81–107.

Goodnow, J.J. (1993). Afterword: Direction of post-vygotskian research. In E.A. Forman, N. Minick, & C.A. Stone (Eds.), *Contexts for learning: Sociocultural dynamics in children's development* (pp. 357–368). New York: Oxford University Press.

Gopnik, A. (1996). The post-Piaget era. *Psychological Science, 7*, 221–225.

Gouin Décarie, T. (1962). *Intelligence et affectivité chez le juene enfant.* Neuchâtel: Delachaux et Niestlé.

Gouin-Décarie, T., & Ricard, M. (1996). Revisiting Piaget revisited or the vulnerability of Piaget's infancy theory in the 1990's. In G.G. Noam & K.W. Fischer (Eds.), *Development and vulnerability in close relationships* (pp. 113–132). Mahwah, NJ: Erlbaum.

Granott, N. (1993). Patterns of interaction in the co-construction of knowledge: Separate minds, joint effort, and weird creatures. In R.H. Wozniak & K.W. Fischer (Eds.), *Development in context: Acting and thinking in specific environments* (pp. 183–207). Hillsdale, NJ: Erlbaum.

Granott, N., & Gardner, H. (1994). When minds meet: Interactions, coincidence, and development in domains of ability. In R.J. Sternberg & R.K. Wagner (Eds.), *Mind in context: Interactionist perspectives on human intelligence* (pp. 171–201). Cambridge, UK: Cambridge University Press.

Greenberg, L.S. (1986). Change process research. *Journal of Consulting and Clinical Psychology, 54*, 4–9.

Greenberg, L.S. (1991). Research on the process of change. *Psychotherapy Research, 1*, 3–16.

Greenberg, L., & Pascual-Leone, J. (1995). A dialectical constructivist approach to experiential change. In R.A. Neimeyer & M.J. Mahoney (Eds.), *Constructivism in psychotherapy* (pp. 169–191). Washington, DC: American Psychological Association.

Greenberg, L.S., Rice, L.N., & Elliot, R. (1993). *Facilitating emotional change: The moment-by-moment process.* New York: Guilford.

Greenspan, S.I., & Lieberman, A.F. (1988). A clinical approach to attachment. In J. Belsky & T. Nezworksi (Eds.), *Clinical implications of attachment* (pp. 387–414). Hillsdale, NJ: Erlbaum.

Greenwood, J.D. (1994). A sense of identity: Prolegomena to a social theory of personal identity. *Journal for the Theory of Social Behavior, 24*, 25–46.

Gribbon, J. (1994). Is the universe alive? *New Scientist, 141*, 38–40.

Griffin, P., Belyaeva, A., Soldatova, G., & The Velikhov-Hamburg Collective. (1993). Creating and reconstituting contexts for educational interactions, including a computer program. In E.A. Forman, N. Minick, & C.A. Stone (Eds.), *Contexts for learning: Sociocultural dynamics in children's development* (pp. 120–152). New York: Oxford University Press.

Griffith, J.L., & Griffith, M.E. (1993). Language solutions for mind-body problems. In S. Gilligan & R. Price (Eds.), *Therapeutic conversations* (pp. 309–323). New York: Norton.

Griffith, J.L., Griffith, M.E., & Slovik, L.S. (1990). Mind-body problems in family therapy: Contrasting first- and second-order cybernetics approaches. *Family Process, 29*, 13–28.

Guidano, V.F. (1995). Constructivist psychotherapy: A theoretical framework. In R.A. Neimeyer & M.J. Mahoney (Eds.), *Constructivism in psychotherapy* (pp. 93–108). Washington, DC: American Psychological Association.

Guisinger, S., & Blatt, S.J. (1994). Individuality and relatedness: Evolution as a fundamental dialectic. *American Psychologist, 49*, 104–111.

Gülerce, A. (1995a). An interview with K.J. Gergen (Part I). Culture and self in postmodern psychology: Dialogue in trouble? *Culture & Psychology, 1*, 147–159.

Gülerce, A. (1995b). An interview with K.J. Gergen (Part II). Culture and psychology in postmodernism: A necessary dialog. *Culture & Psychology, 1*, 299–308.

Guttierez, J., & Sameroff, A.J. (1990). Determinants of complexity in Mexican-American and Anglo-American mothers' conceptions of child development. *Child Development, 61*, 384–394.

Hagekull, B. (1994). Infant temperament and early childhood functioning: Possible relations to the five-factor model. In C.F. Halverson, G.A. Kohnstamm, & R.P. Martin (Eds.), *The developing structure of temperament and personality from infancy to adulthood* (pp. 227–240). Hillsdale, NJ: Erlbaum.

Halford, (1993). *Children's understanding: The development of mental models.* Hillsdale, NJ: Erlbaum.

Halonen, J.S. (1995). Demystifying critical thinking. *Teaching of Psychology, 22*, 75–81.

Halverson, C.F., Jr., Kohnstamm, G.A., & Martin, R.P. (Eds.) (1994). *The developing structure of temperament and personality from infancy to adulthood.* Hillsdale, NJ: Erlbaum.

Hand, S. (Ed.) (1989). *The Lévinas reader.* Oxford, UK: Blackwell.

Handlin, D. (1993). Structuring the silence: An interview with Mary Belenky and Blythe Clinchy. *New Ideas in Psychology, 11*, 245–251.

Harré, R. (1995). The necessity of personhood as embodied being. *Theory & Psychology, 5*, 369–373.

Harris, A. (1987). The rationalization of infancy. In J. Broughton (Ed.), *Critical theories of psychological development* (pp. 31–59). New York; Plenum.

Harris, J.R. (1995). Where is the child's environment? A group socialization theory of development. *Psychological Review, 102*, 458–489.

Hart, D., Mahoney, J., & Damon, W. (1990). Une perspective développementale sur l'identité personelle et le sens de soi. *Psychologie Française, 35*, 35–41.

Harter, S. (1983). Developmental perspectives on the self system. In E.M. Hetherington (Ed.), *Handbook of child psychology* (4th ed.) (Vol. 4). *Socialization, personality, and social development* (pp. 275–385). New York: Wiley.

Hatfield, T., & Hatfield, S.R. (1992). As if your life depended on it: Promoting cognitive development to promote wellness. *Journal of Counseling and Development, 71*, 164–167.

Hatano, G. (1993). Time to merge vygotskian and constructivist conceptions of knowledge acquisition. In E.A. Forman, N. Minick, & C.A. Stone (Eds.), *Contexts for learning: Sociocultural dynamics in children's development* (pp. 153–166). New York: Oxford University Press.

Heath, A., Evans, G., & Martin, J. (1994). The measurement of core beliefs and values: The development of balanced socialist/laissez-faire and libertarian/authoritarian scales. *British Journal of Political Science, 24*, 115–158.

Heatherington, L., & Friedlander, M.L. (1990). Applying task analysis to structural family therapy. *Journal of Family Psychology, 4*, 36–48.

Hecht, M.L., Marston, P.J., & Larkey, L.K. (1994). Love ways and relationship quality in heterosexual relationships. *Journal of Social and Personal Relationships, 11*, 25–43.

Heidegger, M. (1927/1962). *Being and time* (J. Macquarrie & E. Robinson, Trans.). Oxford, U.K.: Blackwell. (Original work published 1927)

Held, B.S. (1990). What's in a name? Some confusions and concerns about constructivism. *Journal of Marital and Family Therapy, 16*, 179–186.

Held, B.S. (1992). The problem of strategy within the systemic therapies. *Journal of Marital and Family Therapy, 18*, 25–34.

Held, B.S. (1995a). *Back to reality: A critique of postmodern theory in psychotherapy*. New York: Norton.

Held, B.S. (1995b). The real meaning of constructivism. *Journal of Constructivist Psychology, 8*, 305–315.

Helgeson, V.S. (1994). Relation of agency and communion to well-being: Evidence and potential explanations. *Psychological Bulletin, 116*, 412–428.

Helson, R., & Roberts, B.W. (1994). Ego development and personality change in adulthood. *Journal of Personality and Social Psychology, 66*, 911–920.

Hendricks-Jansen, H. (1996). *Catching ourselves in the act: Situated activity, interactive emergence, evolution, and human thought*. Cambridge, MA: MIT Press.

Henggeler, S.C., Borduin, C.M., & Mann, B.J. (1993). Advances in family therapy: Empirical foundations. In T.H. Ollendick & R.J. Prinz (Eds.), *Advances in Clinical Child Psychology* (Vol. 15) (pp. 207–241). New York: Plenum.

Hermans, H.J.M. (1995a). From assessment to change: The personal meaning of clinical problems in the context of the self-narrative. In R.A. Neimeyer & M.J. Mahoney (Eds.), *Constructivism in psychotherapy* (pp. 247–271). Washington, DC: American Psychological Association.

Hermans, H.J.M. (1995b). The limitation of logic in defining the self. *Theory & Psychology, 5*, 375–382.

Hermans, H.J.M. (1996a). Voicing the self: From information processing to dialogical interchange. *Psychological Bulletin, 119*, 31–50.

Hermans, H.J.M. (1996b). Opposites in a dialogical self: Constructs as characters. *Journal of Constructivist Psychology, 8*, 1–26.

Hermans, H.J.M., & Kempen, H.J.G. (1993). *The dialogical self: Meaning as movement*. Orlando, FL: Academic.

Hermans, H.J.M., & Kempen, H.J.G. (1995). Body, mind and culture: The dialogical nature of mediated action. *Culture & Psychology, 1*, 103–114.

Hermans, H.J.M., Kempen, H.J.G., & van Loon, R.J.P. (1992). The dialogical self: Beyond individualism and rationalism. *American Psychologist, 47*, 23–33.

Hill, G. (1993). Citizenship and ontology in the liberal state. *The Review of Politics, 55*, 67–84.

Hill, P. (1993). Recent advances in selected aspects of adolescent development. *Journal of Child Psychology and Psychiatry, 34*, 39–93.

Hoffmann, L. (1990). Constructing realities: An art of lenses. *Family Process, 29*, 1–12.

Hoppe-Graffe, S. (1993). Individual differences in the emergence of pretend play. In R. Case & W. Edelstein (Eds.), *The new structuralism in cognitive development: Theory and research on individual pathways* (pp. 57–70). Basel: Karger.

Hoyt, M.F. (1994). Introduction: Competency-based future-oriented therapy. In M.F. Hoyt (Ed.), *Constructive therapies* (pp. 1–10). New York: Guilford.

Hoyt, M.F. (Ed.) (1996a). *Constructive therapies: Vol. 2*. New York: Guilford.

Hoyt, M.F. (1996b). Introduction: Some stories are better than others. In M.F. Hoyt (Ed.), *Constructive therapies: Vol. 2* (pp. 1–32). New York: Guilford.

Hoyt, M.F. (1996c). Postmodernism, the relational self, constructive therapies, and beyond: A conversation with Kenneth Gergen. In M.F. Hoyt (Ed.), *Constructive therapies: Vol. 2* (pp. 347–368). New York: Guilford.

Hoyt, M.F., & Combs, G. (1996). On ethics and the spiritualities of the surface: A conversation with Michael White. In M.F. Hoyt (Ed.), *Constructive therapies: Vol. 2* (pp. 33–59). New York: Guilford.

Hutchins, E. (1995). *Cognition in the wild.* Cambridge, MA: MIT Press.

Hutchins, E. (1996). Response to reviewers. *Mind, Culture, and Activity, 3,* 64–68.

Israelstam, K.V. (1989). Interacting individual belief systems in marital relationships. *Journal of Marital and Family Therapy, 15,* 53–63.

Jacoby, S. & Ochs, E. (1995). Co-construction: An introduction. *Research on Language and Social Interaction, 28,* 171–183.

Jankowicz, A.D. (1995). Negotiating shared meanings of the management process: A discourse in two voices. *Journal of Constructivist Psychology, 8,* 117–128.

John, O.P., Caspi, A., Robins, R.W., Moffitt, T.E., & Stouthamer-Loeber, M. (1994). The "Little Five": Exploring the nomological network of the Five-Factor model of personality in adolescent boys. *Child Development, 65,* 160–178.

Kail, R., & Bisanz, J. (1992). The information processing perspective on cognitive development in childhood and adolescence. In R.J. Sternberg & C.A. Berg (Eds.), *Intellectual development* (pp. 229–260). New York: Cambridge University Press.

Karmiloff-Smith, A. (1992). *Beyond modularity: A developmental perspective on cognitive science.* Cambridge, MA: MIT Press.

Karney, B.J., & Bradbury, T.N. (1995). The longitudinal course of marital quality and stability: A review of theory, method, and research. *Psychological Bulletin, 118,* 3–34.

Kauffman, S.A. (1993). *The origins of order.* New York: Oxford University Press.

Keating, D.P. (1991). Constructivism and diversity. In D.P. Keating & H. Rosen (Eds.), *Constructivist perspectives on developmental psychopathology and atypical development* (pp. 1–10). Hillsdale, NJ: Erlbaum.

Kegan, R. (1982). *The evolving self: Problem and process in human development.* Cambridge, MA: Harvard University Press.

Kegan, R. (1986). The child behind the mask: Sociopathy as developmental delay. In W.H. Reid, D. Dorr, J.I. Walker, & J.W. Bonner (Eds.), *Unmasking the psychopath: Antisocial personality and related syndromes* (pp. 45–77). New York: Norton.

Kegan, R. (1994). *In over our heads: The mental demands of modern life.* Cambridge, MA: Harvard University Press.

Kelly, G.A. (1955). *The psychology of personal constructs.* New York: Norton.

Kitchener, K.S., Lynch, C.L., Fischer, K.W., & Wood, P.K. (1993). Developmental range of reflective judgment: The effect of contextual support and practice on developmental stage. *Developmental Psychology, 29,* 893–906.

Klahr, D. (1992). Information processing approaches to cognitive development. In M.H. Bornstein & M.E. Lamb (Eds.), *Developmental psychology: An advanced textbook* (3rd ed.) (pp. 273–335). Hillsdale, NJ: Erlbaum.

Kohlberg, L. (1981). *Essays on moral development: Vol. 1. The psychology of moral development.* San Francisco: Harper & Row.

Kohlberg, L. (1984). *Essays on moral development: Vol. 2. The psychology of moral development.* San Francisco: Harper & Row.

Kohlberg, L., & Ryncarz, R.A. (1990). Beyond justice reasoning: Moral development and consideration of a seventh stage. In C.N. Alexander & E.J. Langer (Eds.), *Higher stages of human development: Perspectives on adult growth* (pp. 191–207). New York: Oxford University Press.

Koplowitz, H. (1990). Unitary thought: A projection beyond Piaget's formal operational stage. In M.L. Commons, F.A. Richards, & C. Armon (Eds.), *Beyond formal operations: Late adolescent and adult cognitive development* (pp. 272–293). New York: Praeger.

Kozulin, A. (1991). Life as authoring: The humanistic tradition in Russian psychology. *New Ideas in Psychology, 9*, 335–351.

Kozulin, A. (1993). Apes, primitives, children and ... translators. *Human Development, 36*, 368–372.

Krieglstein, W. (1995). From domination to partnership in a self-organizing universe: Building the smallest democracy at the heart of society. *Dialogue and Universalism, 3*, 106–120.

Kruger, A.C. (1992). The effect of peer and adult-child transactive discussions on moral reasoning. *Merrill-Palmer Quarterly, 38*, 191–211.

Kruger, A.C. (1993). Peer collaboration: Conflict, cooperation or both? *Social Development, 2*, 165–182.

Kuhn, D. (1991). *The skills of argument.* Cambridge, UK: Cambridge University Press.

Kuhn, D. (1992). Cognitive development. In M.H. Bornstein & M.E. Lamb (Eds.), *Developmental psychology: An advanced textbook* (3rd ed.) (pp. 211–272). Hillsdale, NJ: Erlbaum.

Kuhn, D. (1993). Connecting scientific and informal reasoning. *Merrill-Palmer Quarterly, 39*, 74–103.

Kurtines, W.M., Azmitia, M., & Alvarez, M. (1992). Science, values, and rationality: Philosophy of science from a critical co-constructivist perspective. In W.M. Kurtines, M. Azmitia, & J.L. Gewirtz (Eds.), *The role of values in psychology and human development* (pp. 3–29).

Kvale, S. (Ed.). (1992). *Psychology and postmodernism.* Newbury Park, CA: Sage.

Laboratory of Comparative Human Cognition (1983). Culture and cognitive development. In P.H. Mussen (Series Ed.), *Handbook of child psychology* (4th ed.) (Vol. 1). W. Kessen (Vol. Ed.), *History, theory, and methods* (pp. 295–365). New York: Wiley.

Labouvie-Vief, G. (1992). A neo-Piagetian perspective on adult cognitive development. In R.J. Sternberg & C.A. Berg (Eds.), *Intellectual development* (pp. 197–228). Cambridge, UK: Cambridge University Press.

Labouvie-Vief, G. (1996). Commentary. *Human Development, 39*, 173–180.

Labouvie-Vief, G., Orwoll, L., & Manion, M. (1995). Narratives of mind, gender, and the life course. *Human Development, 38*, 239–257.

LaLane, J. (1996). Teaching, as in learning, in practice. *Mind, Culture, and Activity, 3*, 149–164.

La Llave, J., & Commons, M.L. (1996). Comparing psychodynamic, cognitive-developmental, and behavior-developmental views of psychological boundaries. In M.L. Commons, J. Demick, & C. Goldberg (Eds.), *Clinical approaches to adult development* (pp. 175–209). Norwood, NJ: Ablex.

Landsmann, L.T. (Ed.) (1991). *Culture, schooling and psychological development.* Norwood, NJ: Ablex.

Lapsley, D.K. (1996). Commentary. *Human Development, 39*, 100–107.

Larner, G. (1995). The real as illusion: Deconstructing power in family therapy. *Journal of Family Therapy, 17*, 191–217.

Larson, R., & Ham, M. (1993). Stress and "storm and stress" in early adolescence: The relationship of negative events with dysphoric affect. *Developmental Psychology, 29*, 130–140.

Lash, S. (1996). Postmodern ethics: The missing ground. *Theory, Culture, & Society, 13*, 91–104.

Lautrey, J. (1993). Structure and variability: A plea for a pluralistic approach to cognitive development. In R. Case & W. Edelstein (Eds.), *The new structuralism in cognitive development: Theory and research on individual pathways* (pp. 101–114). Basel: Karger.

Lawrence, J.A., & Valsiner, J. (1993). Conceptual roots of internalization: From transmission to transformation. *Human Development, 36*, 150–167.

Lax, W.D. (1992). Postmodern thinking in clinical practice. In S. McNamee & K.J. Gergen (Eds.), *Therapy as social construction* (pp. 69–85). London, UK: Sage.

Leont'ev, A.N. (1981). The problem of activity in psychology. In J.V. Wertsch (Ed.), *The concept of activity in Soviet psychology* (pp. 37–71). Armonk, NY: Sharpe.

Lester, D. (1993–1994). On the disunity of the self: A systems theory of personality. *Current Psychology: Developmental, Learning, Personality, Social, 4*, 312–325.

Levenson, M.R., & Crumpler, C.A. (1996). Three models of adult development. *Human Development, 39*, 135–149.

Lévinas, E. (1985). *Ethics and infinity.* Pittsburgh, PA: Duquesne University Press.

Levitt, M.Z., & Selman, R.L. (1996). The personal meaning of risk behavior: A developmental perspective on friendship and fighting in early adolescence. In G.G. Noam & K.W. Fischer (Eds.), *Development and vulnerability in close relationships* (pp. 201–233). Mahwah, NJ: Erlbaum.

Lewin, R. (1992). *Complexity: Life at the edge of chaos.* New York: Macmillan.

Lewis, M. (1990). The development of intentionality and the role of consciousness. *Psychological Inquiry, 1*, 231–247.

Lewis, M.D. (1995). Cognition-emotion feedback and the self-organization of developmental paths. *Human Development, 38*, 71–102.

Lieberman, A.F. (1992). Infant–parent psychotherapy with toddlers. *Development and Psychopathology, 4*, 559–574.

Light, P., & Butterworth, G. (Eds.) (1993). *Context and cognition: Ways of learning and knowing.* Hillsdale, NJ: Erlbaum.

Lillard, A.S. (1993). Pretend play skills and the child's theory of mind. *Child Development, 64*, 348–371.

Lillienfeld, S.O., & Marino, L. (1995). Mental disorder as a Roschian concept: A critique of Wakefield's "Harmful dysfunction" analysis. *Journal of Abnormal Psychology, 104*, 411–420.

Litowitz, B.E. (1993). Deconstruction in the zone of proximal development. In E.A. Forman, N. Minick, & C.A. Stone (Eds.), *Contexts for learning: Sociocultural dynamics in children's development* (pp. 184–196). New York: Oxford University Press.

Loevinger, J. (1976). *Ego development: Conceptions and theories.* San Francisco: Jossey-Bass.

Loevinger, J. (1987). *Paradigms of personality.* San Francisco: Freeman.

Loevinger, J. (1993). Measurement of personality: True or false. *Psychological Inquiry, 4*, 1–16.

Loevinger, J. (1994). In search of grand theory. *Psychological Inquiry, 5*, 142–144.

Loewald, H. (1980). *Papers on psychoanalysis.* New Haven, CT: Yale University Press.

Lourenço, O. (1996). Reflections on narrative approaches to moral development. *Human Development, 39*, 83–99.

Lourenço, O., & Machado, A. (1996). In defense of Piaget's theory: A reply to 10 common criticisms. *Psychological Review, 103*, 143–164.

Lund, W.R. (1993). Communitarian politics and the problem of equality. *Political Research Quarterly, 46*, 577–600.

Lyddon, W.J. (1995). Forms and facets of constructivist psychology. In R.A. Neimeyer & M.J. Mahoney (Eds.), *Constructivism in psychotherapy* (pp. 69–92). Washington, DC: American Psychological Association.

Lyddon, W.J., & McLaughlin, J.T. (1992). Constructivist psychology: A heuristic framework. *The Journal of Mind and Behavior, 13*, 89–107.

Lyotard, J.-F. (1984). *The postmodern condition.* Manchester: Manchester University Press.

Lykken, D.T., McGue, N., Tellegen, A., & Bouchard, T.J. (1992). Emergenesis: Genetic traits that may not run in families. *American Psychologist, 47*, 1565–1577.

Macdonald, S. (1994). *Complexity of political reasoning and discourse in the context of a neo-piagetian framework.* Unpublished manuscript, York University, Toronto.

Maddox, J.E. (1995). Yes, people can change, but can psychotherapists? *Contemporary Psychology*, *40*, 1047–1048.

Madigan, S.P. (1992). The application of Michel Foucault's philosophy in the problem externalizing discourse of Michael White. *Journal of Family Therapy*, *14*, 265–279.

Madigan, S.P. (1993). Therapeutic rituals: Passages into new identities. In S. Gilligan & R. Price (Eds.), *Therapeutic conversations* (pp. 237–252). New York: Norton.

Madigan, S. (1994). Body politics. *Family Therapy Networker*, *18*(6), 27.

Mahoney, M.J. (1995). The psychological demands of being a constructivist psychotherapist. In R.A. Neimeyer & M.J. Mahoney (Eds.), *Constructivism in psychotherapy* (pp. 385–399). Washington, DC: American Psychological Association.

Mahrer, A.R. (1995). A solution to an illusory problem: Clients construct their worlds versus there really is a reality. *Journal of Constructivist Psychology*, *8*, 327–337.

Main, M. (1991). Metacognitive knowledge, metacognitive monitoring, and singular coherent vs. multiple (incoherent) model of attachment: Findings and direction for future research. In C.M. Parkes, J. Stevenson-Hinde, & P. Morris (Eds.), *Attachment across the life cycle* (pp. 199–215). New York: Routledge.

Mair, M. (1988). Psychology as story-telling. *International Journal of Personal Construct Psychology*, *1*, 125–138.

Mair, M. (1989). *Between psychology and psychotherapy*. London: Routledge.

Martin, R.P., Wisenbaker, J., & Huttunen, M. (1994). Review of factor analytic studies of temperament measures based on the Thomas-Chess structural model: Implications for the Big Five. In C.F. Halverson, G.A. Kohnstamm, & R.P. Martin (Eds.), *The developing structure of temperament and personality from infancy to adulthood* (pp. 157–172). Hillsdale, NJ: Erlbaum.

Marvin, R.S. (1992). Attachment- and family systems-based intervention in developmental psychopathology. *Developmental and Psychopathology*, *4*, 697–711.

Mascolo, M.F., & Dalto, C.A. (1995). Self and modernity on trial: A reply to Gergen's *Saturated Self*. *Journal of Constructivist Psychology*, *8*, 175–191.

Matthews, E. (1995). Moralist or therapist? Foucault and the critique of psychiatry. *Philosophy, Psychiatry, & Psychology*, *2*, 19–30.

Maturana, H.R. (1991). Response to Jim Birch. *Journal of Family Therapy*, *13*, 349–373.

May, R. (1983). *The discovering of being*. New York: Norton.

McCrae, R.R., & Costa, P.T., Jr. (1994). The stability of personality: Observations and evaluations. *Current Directions in Psychological Science*, *3*, 173–175.

McGillicuddy-De Lisi, A.V. (1992). Correlates of parental teaching strategies in families of children evidencing normal and atypical development. *Journal of Applied Developmental Psychology*, *13*, 215–234.

McNaughton, S. (1996). Ways of parenting and cultural identity. *Culture & Psychology*, *2*, 173–201.

Meacham, J.A. (1993). Where is the social environment? A commentary on Reed. In R.H. Wozniak & K.W. Fischer (Eds.), *Development in context: Acting and thinking in specific environments* (pp. 255–267). Hillsdale, NJ: Erlbaum.

Meltzoff, A.N., & Moore, M.K. (1989). Imitation in newborn infants: Exploring the range of gestures initiated and the underlying mechanisms. *Developmental Psychology*, *25*, 954–962.

Mercer, N. (1993). Culture, context, and the construction of knowledge in the classroom. In P. Light & G. Butterworth (Eds.), *Context and cognition: Ways of learning and knowing* (pp. 28–46). Hillsdale, NJ: Erlbaum.

Miles, S. (1996). The cultural capital of consumption: Understanding "postmodern" identities in a cultural context. *Culture & Psychology*, *2*, 139–158.

Miller, J.L. (1994). Linguistic tools for intellectual work: A review. *New Ideas in Psychology*, *12*, 61–71.

Miller, M.B. (1993). Comment on Lykken et al. *American Psychologist, 48*, 1295–1297.

Mills, S.D., & Sprenkle, D.H. (1995). Family therapy in the postmodern era. *Family Relations, 44*, 368–376.

Minick, N.J. (1985). L.S. Vygotsky and Soviet activity theory: New perspectives on the relationship between mind and society. Unpublished doctoral dissertation, Northwestern University, Evanston, IL.

Minick, N., Stone, N., & Forman, E.A. (1993). Introduction: Integration of individual, social, and institutional processes in accounts of children's learning and development. In E.A. Forman, N. Minick, & C.A. Stone (Eds.), *Contexts for learning: Sociocultural dynamics in children's development* (pp. 3–16). New York: Oxford University Press.

Misra, G. (1993). Psychology from a constructionist perspective: An interview with Kenneth J. Gergen. *New Ideas in Psychology, 11*, 399–414.

Mittelmeier, C.M., & Friedman, S. (1993). Toward a mutual understanding: Constructing solutions with families. In S. Friedman (Ed.), *The new language of change: Constructive collaboration in therapy* (pp. 158–181). New York: Guilford.

Moll, I. (1994). Reclaiming the natural line in Vygotsky's theory of cognitive development. *Human Development, 37*, 333–342.

Moll, L.C. (Ed.) (1990). *Vygotsky and education: Instructional implications and applications of sociohistorical psychology*. New York: Cambridge University Press.

Moll, L.C., & Whitmore, K.F. (1993). Vygotsky in classroom practice: Moving from individual transmission to social practice. In E.A. Forman, N. Minick, & C.A. Stone (Eds.), *Contexts for learning: Sociocultural dynamics in children's development* (pp. 19–42). New York: Oxford University Press.

Morss, J.R. (1992). Making waves: Deconstruction and developmental psychology. *Theory and Psychology, 2*, 445–465.

Moshman, D. (1995). The construction of moral rationality. *Human Development, 38*, 265–281.

Moss, B.F., & Schwebel, A.I. (1993). Defining intimacy in romantic relationships. *Family Relations, 42*, 31–37.

Moss, E. (1992). The socioaffective context of joint cognitive activity. In L.T. Winegar & J. Walsiner (Eds.), *Children's development within social context* (Vol. 2), *Research and methodology* (pp. 117–154). Hillsdale, NJ: Erlbaum.

Mounoud, P. (1986). Similarities between developmental sequences at different age periods. In I. Levin (Ed.), *Stage and structure: Reopening the debate* (pp. 40–58). Norwood, NJ: Ablex.

Mundy, P., Kasari, C., & Sigman, M. (1992). Nonverbal communication, affective sharing, and intersubjectivity. *Infant Behavior and Development, 15*, 371–381.

Murdoch, I. (1992). *Metaphysics as guide to morals*. London: Penguin.

Neimeyer, R.A. (1993). An appraisal of constructivist psychotherapies. *Journal of Consulting and Clinical Psychology, 61*, 221–234.

Neimeyer, R.A. (1994). The role of client-generated narratives in psychotherapy. *Journal of Constructivist Psychology, 7*, 229–242.

Neimeyer, R.A. (1995a). Constructivist psychotherapies: Features, foundations, and future directions. In R.A. Neimeyer & M.J. Mahoney (Eds.) (1995), *Constructivism in psychotherapy* (pp. 11–38). Washington, DC: American Psychological Association.

Neimeyer, R.A. (1995b). Limits and lessons of constructivism: Some critical reflections. *Journal of Constructivist Psychology, 8*, 339–361.

Neimeyer, R.A., & Feixas, G. (1990). Constructivist contributions to psychotherapy integration. *Journal of Integrative and Eclectic Psychotherapy, 9*, 4–20.

Neimeyer, R.A., Neimeyer, G.J., Lyddon, W.J., & Hoshmand, L.T. (1994). The reality of social construction. *Contemporary Psychology, 39*, 458–463.

Neisser, V. (1991). Two perceptually given aspects of the self and their development. *Developmental Review, 11*, 197–209.

Nesse, R.A. (1991). What good is feeling bad? The evolutionary benefits of psychic pain. *The Sciences, 31*(6), 30–37.

Newberger, C. (1980). The cognitive structure of parenthood: Designing a descriptive measure. In R. Selman & R. Yando (Eds.), *Clinical developmental psychology: New directions for child development* (pp. 45–67). San Francisco: Jossey Bass.

Newman, F., & Holtzman, L. (1993). *Lev Vygotsky: Revolutionary scientist.* New York: Routledge.

Nichols, M.P., & Schwartz, R.C. (1991). *Family therapy: Concepts and methods* (2nd ed.). Boston: Allyn & Bacon.

Nichols, W.C., & Pace-Nichols, M.A. (1993). Developmental perspectives and family therapy: The marital life cycle. *Contemporary Family Therapy, 15*, 299–315.

Nicolopoulou, A. (1993). Play, cognitive development, and the social world: Piaget, Vygotsky, and beyond. *Human Development, 36*, 1–23.

Nicolopoulou, A., & Cole, M. (1993). Generation and transmission of shared knowledge in the culture of collaborative learning: The fifth dimension, its play world, and its institutional contexts. In E.A. Forman, N. Minick, & C.A. Stone (Eds.), *Contexts for learning: Sociocultural dynamics in children's development* (pp. 283–314). New York: Oxford University Press.

Niebuhr, H.R. (1978). *The responsible self.* New York: Harper & Row.

Noam, G.G. (1992). Development as the aim of clinical intervention. *Development and Psychopathology, 4*, 679–696.

Noam, G.G., & Dill, D.L. (1996). Developmental dimensions of psychological symptoms and treatment preferences in adult outpatients. In M.L. Commons, J. Demick, & C. Goldberg (Eds.), *Clinical approaches to adult development* (pp. 267–293). Norwood, NJ: Ablex.

Noam, G.G., & Fischer, K.W. (Eds.) (1996). *Development and vulnerability in close relationships.* Mahwah, NJ: Erlbaum.

Nordquest, D.A. (1994). Lonergan's cognitional theory: Toward a critical human science. *The Review of Politics, 56*, 71–100.

Nylund, D., & Thomas, J. (1994). The economics of narrative. *Family Therapy Networker, 18*(6), 38–39.

Offer, D., & Shonert-Reichl, K.A. (1992). Debunking the myths of adolescence: Findings from recent research. *Journal of the American Academy of Child and Adolescent Psychiatry, 32*, 1003–1014.

O'Hanlon, W.H. (1994). The third wave. *Family Therapy Networker, 18*(6), 18–26, 28–29.

O'Hanlon, W.H., & Hudson, P.O. (1994). Coauthoring a love story: Solution-oriented marital therapy. In M.F. Hoyt (Ed.), *Constructive therapies* (pp. 160–188). New York: Guilford.

O'Hara, M. (1995). Is it time for clinical psychology to deconstruct constructivism? *Journal of Constructivist Psychology, 8*, 293–303.

Oppenheimer, L. (1991). Determinants of action: An organismic and holistic approach. In L. Oppenheimer & J. Valsiner (Eds.), *The origins of action: Interdisciplinary and international perspectives* (pp. 37–63). New York: Springer-Verlag.

Orr, R., & Luszcz, M. (1994). Rethinking women's ways of knowing: Gender communalities and intersections with postformal thought. *Journal of Adult Development, 1*, 225–233.

Overton, W.F. (1994a). The arrow of time and the cycle of time: Concepts of change, cognition, and embodiment. *Psychological Inquiry, 5*, 215–237.

Overton, W.F. (1994b). Interpretationism, pragmatism, realism, and other ideologies. *Psychological Inquiry, 5*, 260–271.

Oyama, S. (1993). How shall I name thee? The construction of natural selves. *Theory and Psychology, 3*, 471–496.

Packer, M.J. (1992). Toward a postmodern psychology of moral action and moral development. In W.M. Kurtines, M. Azmitia, & J.J. Gewirtz (Eds.), *The role of values in psychology and human development* (pp. 30–59). New York: Wiley.

Packer, M.J. (1993). Away from internalization. In E.A. Forman, N. Minick, & C.A. Stone (Eds.), *Contexts for learning: Sociocultural dynamics in children's development* (pp. 254–265). New York: Oxford University Press.

Palincsar, A.S., Brown, A.L., & Campione, J.C. (1993). First-grade dialogues for knowledge acquisition and use. In E.A. Forman, N. Minick, & C.A. Stone (Eds.), *Contexts for learning: Sociocultural dynamics in children's development* (pp. 43–57). New York: Oxford University Press.

Pam, A. (1993). Family systems theory—A critical review. *New Ideas in Psychology, 11,* 77–94.

Paré, D.A. (1995). Of families and other cultures: The shifting paradigm in family therapy. *Family Process, 34,* 1–19.

Paré, D.A. (1996). Culture and meaning: Expanding the metaphorical repertoire of family therapy. *Family Process, 35,* 21–39.

Parry, A. (1993). Without a net: Preparations for postmodern living. In S. Friedman (Ed.), *The new language of change: Constructive collaboration in psychotherapy* (pp. 428–459). New York: Guilford.

Parry, A., & Doan, R.E. (1994). *Story re-visions: Narrative therapy in the post-modern world.* New York: Guilford.

Pascual-Leone, J. (1990). Emotions, development and psychotherapy: A dialectical constructivist perspective. In J.D. Safran & L.S. Greenberg (Eds.), *Emotion, psychotherapy and change* (pp. 302–335). New York: Guilford.

Pascual-Leone, J. (1991). Reflections on life-span intelligence. Consciousness and ego development. In C.N. Alexander and E.J. Langer (Eds.), *Higher stages of human development: Perspectives on adult growth* (pp. 258–285). New York: Oxford University Press.

Pascuale-Leone, J. (1995). Learning and development as dialectical factors in cognitive growth. *Human Development, 38,* 338–348.

Pascual-Leone, J., & Baillargeon, R. (1994). Developmental measurement of mental attention. *International Journal of Development, 17,* 161–200.

Pascual-Leone, J., & Irwin, R.R. (1994a). Non-cognitive factors in high-road/low-road learning I: The modes of abstraction in adulthood. *Journal of Adult Development, 1,* 73–89.

Pascual-Leone, J., & Irwin, R.R. (1994b). Non-cognitive factors in high-road/low-road learning II: The will, the self and modes of instruction in adulthood. *Journal of Adult Development, 1,* 153–168.

Penn, P. (1992). By the light of the never-before-said. *The Family Therapy Networker, 16*(1), 13–14.

Penn, P., & Frankfurt, M. (1994). Creating a participant text: Writing, multiple voices, narrative multiplicity. *Family Process, 33,* 217–231.

Perry, W.B. (1970). *Forms of intellectual and ethical development in the college years.* New York: Holt, Rinehart & Winston.

Persons, J.B. (1993). The process of change in cognitive therapy: Schema change or acquisition of compensatory skills. *Cognitive Therapy and Research, 17,* 123–137.

Pérusse, D. (1994). Mate choice in modern societies: Testing evolutionary hypotheses with behavioral data. *Human Nature, 5,* 255–278.

Pervin, L.A. (1994a). A critical analysis of current trait theory. *Psychological Inquiry, 5,* 103–114.

Pervin, L.A. (1994b). Further reflections on current trait theory. *Psychological Inquiry, 5,* 169–178.

Peterson, C., & McCabe, A. (1993). Parental styles of narrative elicitation: Effect on children's narrative structure and content. *First Language, 12,* 299–321.

Peterson, C., & McCabe, A. (1994). A social interactionist account of developing decontextualized narrative skill. *Developmental Psychology, 30,* 937–948.

Peterson, C., & McCabe, A. (1993). Parental styles of narrative elicitation: Effect on children's narrative structure and content. *First Language, 12,* 299–321.

Phillips, J. (1996). Key concepts: Hermeneutics. *Philosophy, Psychiatry, & Psychology, 3,* 61–69.

Piaget, J. (1954). *Les relations entre l'affectivité et l'intelligence dans le développement mental de l'enfant* [Relations between affectivity and intelligence in the mental development of the child]. Paris: "Les cours de Sorbonne"; Centre de documentation universitaire.

Piaget, J. (1967). *Etudes sociologiques* [Sociological studies]. Geneva: Droz.

Piaget, J. (1970). Piaget's theory. In. P.H. Mussen (Ed.), *Carmichael's manual of child psychology* (3rd ed.). *Vol. 1* (pp. 703–732). New York: Wiley.

Piaget, J. (1978). *Behavior and evolution* (D. Nicholson-Smith, Trans.). New York: Random House.

Pinsof, W.M. (1995). The efficacy of marital and family therapy: An empirical overview, conclusions, and recommendations. *Journal of Marital and Family Therapy, 21,* 585–613.

Pocock, D. (1995). Searching for a better story: Harnessing modern and postmodern positions in family therapy. *Journal of Family Therapy, 17,* 149–173.

Poirié, F. (1987). *Emmanuel Lévinas: Qui étes-vous?* Lyon, France: La Manufacture.

Polkinhorne, D.E. (1995). Piaget's and Derrida's contributions to a constructivist psychotherapy. *Journal of Constructivist Psychology, 8,* 269–282.

Popp, N. (1996). Dimensions of a psychological boundary development in adults. In M.L. Commons, J. Demick, & C. Goldberg (Eds.), *Clinical approaches to adult development* (pp. 145–174). Norwood, NJ: Ablex.

Portes, P.R. (1991). Assessing children's cognitive environment through parent-child interactions. *Journal of Research and Development in Education, 24*(3), 30–37.

Pratt, M.W., Green, D., MacVicar, J., & Bountrogianni, M. (1992). The mathematical parent: Scaffolding, parental style, and learning outcomes in long-division mathematics homework. *Journal of Applied Developmental Psychology, 13,* 17–34.

Pratt, M.W., Hunsberger, B., Pancer, S.M., Roth, D., & Santolupo, S. (1993). Thinking about parenting: Reasoning about developmental issues across the lifespan. *Developmental Psychology, 29,* 585–595.

Prest, L.A., & Carruthers, W.K. (1991). The cast of the Sneaky Sleep Thief: White's externalizing technique within a broad strategic frame. *Journal of Strategic and Systemic Therapies, 10*(3–4), 66–75.

Price, R. (1993). If you really knew me: An exploration of therapeutic concerns in collaborating with the "damaged" self. In S. Gilligan & R. Price (Eds.), *Therapeutic conversations* (pp. 277–286). New York: Norton.

Prochaska, J.O., Norcross, J.C., & DiClemente, C.C. (1994). *Changing for good: The revolutionary program that explains the six stages of change and teaches you how to free yourself from bad habits.* Morrow: New York.

Puka, B. (1996). Commentary. *Human Development, 39,* 108–116.

Pynchon, T. (1973). *Gravity's rainbow.* New York: Viking Penguin.

Raethel, A. (1994a). Symbolic production and coherence. *Mind, Culture, and Activity, 1,* 69–88.

Raethel, A. (1994b). The look back into history prolongs the stretches of travel still lying before us. *Mind, Culture, and Activity, 1,* 89–101.

Rast, M., & Meltzoff, A.N. (1995). Memory and representation in young children with Down syndrome: Exploring deferred imitation and object permanence. *Development and Psychopathology, 7,* 393–407.

Real, T. (1990). The therapeutic use of self in constructionist/systemic therapy. *Family Process, 29,* 252–272.

Redekop, F. (1995). The "problem" of Michael White and Michel Foucault. *Journal of Marital and Family Therapy, 3,* 309–318.

Reed, E.S. (1993). The intention to use a specific affordance: A conceptual framework for psychology. In R.H. Wozniak & K.W. Fischer (Eds.), *Development in context: Acting and thinking in specific environments* (pp. 45–76). Hillsdale, NJ: Erlbaum.

Resnick, L.B. (1994). Situated rationalism: Biological and social preparation for learning. In L.A. Hirschfeld & S.A. Gelman (Eds.), *Mapping the mind: Domain specificity in cognition and culture* (pp. 474–493). Cambridge, UK: Cambridge University Press.

Ricard, M., & Gouin Décaire, T. (1990). A matter of definition. *Psychological Inquiry, 1,* 261–262.

Richards, F.A., & Commons, M.L. (1990). Postformal cognitive-developmental theory and research: A review of its current status. In C.N. Alexander & E.J. Langer (Eds.), *Higher stages of human development: Perspectives on adult growth* (pp. 139–160). New York: Oxford.

Ricoeur, P. (1981). *Hermeneutics and the human sciences* (J. Thompson, Trans.). Cambridge: Cambridge University Press.

Robbins, M. (1990). *Midlife women and the death of mother.* New York: Peter Lang.

Roberts, R.N., & Barnes, M.L. (1992). "Let momma show you how": Maternal–child interactions and their effects on children's cognitive performance. *Journal of Applied Developmental Psychology, 13,* 363–376.

Robinow, P. (Ed.) (1994). *The Foucault reader.* New York: Pantheon.

Robins, R.W., John, O.P., & Caspi, A. (1994). Major dimensions of personality in adolescence: The Big Five and beyond. In C.F. Halverson, G.A. Kohnstamm, & R.P. Martin (Eds.), *The developing structure of temperament and personality from infancy to adulthood* (pp. 267–292). Hillsdale, NJ: Erlbaum.

Rochat, P. (1993). Connaisance de soi chez le bébé. *Psychologie Française, 38,* 41–51.

Rogoff, B. (1990). *Apprenticeship in thinking: Cognitive development in social context.* New York: Oxford University Press.

Rogoff, B. (1992). Three ways to relate person and culture: Thoughts sparked by Valsiner's review of *Apprenticeship in thinking. Human Development, 35,* 316–320.

Rogoff, B. (1993). Children's guided participation and participatory appropriation in sociocultural activity. In R.H. Wozniak & K.W. Fischer (Eds.), *Development in context: Acting and thinking in specific environments* (pp. 121–135). Hillsdale, NJ: Erlbaum.

Rogoff, B. (1994). Developing understanding of the idea of communities of learners. *Mind, Culture, and Activity, 1,* 209–229.

Rogoff, B. (1995). Observing sociocultural activity on three planes: Participatory appropriation, guided participation, and apprenticeship. In J.V. Wertsch, P. del Río, and A. Alvarez (Eds.), *Sociocultural studies of mind* (pp. 139–164). New York: Cambridge University Press.

Rogoff, B., & Chavajay, P. (1995). What's become of research on the cultural basis of cognitive development? *American Psychologist, 50,* 859–877.

Rogoff, B., Chavajay, P., & Matusov, E. (1993). Questioning assumptions about culture and individuals. *Behavioral and Brain Sciences, 16,* 533–544.

Rogoff, B., Mosier, C., Mistry, J., & Göncü, A. (1993). Toddlers' guided participation with their caregivers in cultural activity. In E.A. Forman, N. Minick, & C.A. Stone (Eds.), *Contexts for learning: Sociocultural dynamics in children's development* (pp. 230–253). New York: Oxford University Press.

Rosen, H. (1991). Constructivism: Personality, psychopathology, and psychotherapy. In D.P. Keating & H. Rosen (Eds.), *Constructivist perspectives on developmental psychopathology and atypical development* (pp. 149–172). Hillsdale, NJ: Erlbaum.

Rosen, H. (1994). Commentary. *Human Development, 37,* 58–60.

Rosmarin, L. (1991). *Emmanuel Lévinas: Humaniste de l'autre homme.* Toronto: GREF.

Roth, S., & Epston, D. (1996). Consulting the problem about the problematic relationship: An exercise for experiencing a relationship with an externalized problem. In M.F. Hoyt (Ed.), *Constructive Therapies: Vol. 2* (pp. 148–162). New York: Guilford.

Russell, R.L., & Gaubatz, M.D. (1995). Contested affinities: Reaction to Gergen's (1994) and Smith's (1994) postmodernisms. *American Psychologist, 50,* 389–390.

Sachs, M. (1993). *Relativity in our time: From physics to human relations*. London: Taylor & Francis.

Safran, J.D., & Segal, L.V. (1990). *Interpersonal process in cognitive therapy*. New York: Basic.

Salthe, S.N. (1993). *Development and evolution: Complexity and change in biology*. Cambridge, MA: MIT Press.

Sameroff, A.J. (1989). Commentary: General systems and the regulation of development. In M.R. Gunnar & E. Thelen (Eds.), *The Minnesota Symposia on Child Psychology* (Vol. 22). *Systems and development* (pp. 219–235). Hillsdale, NJ: Erlbaum.

Sameroff, A.J., & Feil, L. (1985). Parental concepts of development. In I.E. Sigel (Ed.), *Parental belief systems: The psychological consequences for children* (pp. 84–104). Hillsdale, NJ: Erlbaum.

Sameroff, A.J., & Feise, B.H. (1992). Family representations of development. In I.E. Sigel, A.V. McGillicuddy-DeLisi, & J.J. Goodnow (Eds.), *Parental belief systems: The psychological consequences for children* (2nd ed.) (pp. 347–369). Hillsdale, NJ: Erlbaum.

Sameroff, A.J., Seifer, R., Baldwin, A., & Baldwin, C. (1993). Stability of intelligence from preschool to adolescence: The influence of social and family risk factors. *Child Development, 64*, 80–97.

Sameroff, A.J., Seifer, R., Barocas, R., Zax, M., & Greenspan, S. (1987). Intelligence quotient scores of 4-year-old children: Social environmental risk factors. *Pediatrics, 79*, 343–350.

Sander, L.W. (1975). Infant and caretaking environment. In E.J. Anthony (Ed.), *Explorations in child psychiatry* (pp. 129–166). New York: Plenum.

Santolupo, S.S., & Pratt, M.W. (1994). Age, gender, and parenting style variations in mother-adolescent dialogues and adolescent reasoning about political issues. *Journal of Research in Adolescence, 9*, 240–260.

Santostefano, S. (1991). Coordinating outer space with inner space: Reflections on developmental psychopathology. In D.P. Keating & H. Rosen (Eds.), *Constructivist perspectives on developmental psychopathology and atypical development* (pp. 11–40). Hillsdale, NJ: Erlbaum.

Saxe, G.B. (1991). *Culture and cognitive development: Studies in mathematical understanding*. Hillsdale, NJ: Erlbaum.

Saxe, G.B. (1994). Studying cognitive development in sociocultural context: The development of a practice-based approach. *Mind, Culture, and Activity, 1*, 135–157.

Scheib, J.E. (1994). Sperm donor selection and the psychology of female mate choice. *Ethology and Sociobiology, 15*, 113–129.

Scholnick, E.K., & Wing, C.S. (1992). Speaking deductively: Using conversation to trace the origins of conditional thought in children. *Merrill Palmer Quarterly, 38*, 1–20.

Schneider, B.H. (1993). *Children's social competence in context: The contributions of family, school, and culture*. Oxford: Pergamon.

Schneuwly, B. (1993). Cultural learning is cultural. *Behavioral and Brain Sciences, 16*, 534.

Schwartz, R.C., Barrett, M.J., & Saba, G. (1985). Family therapy for bulimia. In D. Gardner & P. Garfinkel (Eds.), *The handbook of psychotherapy for anorexia nervosa and bulimia* (pp. 280–307). New York: Guilford.

Schwartz, R.C. (1994). *Internal family systems therapy*. New York: Guilford.

Selman, R.L. (1980). *The growth of interpersonal understanding: Developmental and clinical analyses*. New York: Academic.

Selman, R.L., & Demorest, A.P. (1986). Putting thoughts and feeling in perspective: A developmental view on how children deal with interpersonal disequilibrium. In D.J. Bearison & H. Zimiles (Eds.), *Thought and emotion: Developmental perspectives* (pp. 93–128). Hillsdale, NJ: Erlbaum.

Selvini-Palazzoli, M. (1980). Why a long interval between sessions? The therapeutic control of the family-therapy suprasystem. In M. Andolfi & I. Zwerling (Eds.), *Dimensions of family therapy* (pp. 161–168). New York: Guilford.

Serpell, R. (1993). Interface between sociocultural and psychological aspects of cognition. In E.A. Forman, N. Minick, & C.A. Stone (Eds.), *Contexts for learning: Sociocultural dynamics in children's development* (pp. 357–368). New York: Oxford University Press.

Shapiro, J.K. (1995). Dr. Kohlberg goes to Washington: Using congressional debates to teach moral development. *Teaching of Psychology, 22,* 245–247.

Shaugnessy, E.A., & Carey, J.C. (1996). Validation of a cognitive-developmental model of clinical supervision. In M.L. Commons, J. Demick, & C. Goldberg (Eds.), *Clinical approaches to adult development* (pp. 223–238). Norwood, NJ: Ablex.

Shotter, J. (1993a). Vygotsky: The social negotiation of semiotic mediation. *New Ideas in Psychology, 11,* 61–75.

Shotter, J. (1993b). Harré, Vygotsky, Bakhtin, Vico, and Wittgenstein: Academic discourses and conversational realities. *Journal for the Theory of Social Behavior, 23,* 459–482.

Shotter, J. (1995a). In conversation: Joint action, shared intentionality, and ethics. *Theory & Psychology, 5,* 49–73.

Shotter, J. (1995b). A "show" of agency is enough. *Theory & Psychology, 5,* 383–390.

Shweder, R.A. (1995). The confessions of a methodological individualist. *Culture & Psychology, 1,* 115–122.

Siegler, R.S. (1988). Individual differences in strategy choices: Good students, not-so-good students. *Child Development, 59,* 833–851.

Siegler, R.S. (1991). *Children's thinking* (2nd ed.). Englewood Cliffs, NJ: Prentice-Hall.

Siegler, R.S., & Ellis, S. (1996). Piaget on childhood. *Psychological Science, 7,* 211–215.

Sigel, I.E. (1992). The belief-behavior connection: A resolvable dilemma? In I.E. Sigel, A.V. McGillicuddy-DeLisi, & J.J. Goodnow (Eds.), *Parental belief systems: The psychological consequences for children* (pp. 433–456). Hillsdale, NJ: Erlbaum.

Sigel, I.E. (1993). The centrality of a distancing model for the development of representational competence. In R.R. Cocking & K.A. Renninger (Eds.), *The development and meaning of psychological distance* (pp. 141–158). Hillsdale, NJ: Erlbaum.

Sigel, I.E., Stinson, E.T., Kim, M.-I. (1993). Socialization of cognition: The distancing model. In R.H. Wozniak & K.W. Fischer (Eds.), *Development in context: Acting and thinking in specific environments* (pp. 211–224). Hillsdale, NJ: Erlbaum.

Sigel, I.E., & Vandenberg, B. (1994). Book review essay of Wertsch's *Voices of the Mind*: Voice and context. *Psychological Inquiry, 5,* 344–353.

Silberman, M.A., & Snarey, J. (1993). Gender differences in moral development during early adolescence: The contribution of sex-related variations in maturation. *Current Psychology: Developmental, Learning, Personality, Social, 12,* 163–171.

Sinott, J.D. (1994). Development and yearning: Cognitive aspects of spiritual development. *Journal of Adult Development, 1,* 91–59.

Sluzki, C.E. (1992). Transformations: A blueprint for narrative changes in therapy. *Family Process, 31,* 217–230.

Smith, C.U.M. (1994). Homo sapiens and human being. *Journal of Social and Evolutionary Systems, 17,* 413–434.

Smith, R.J. (1993). Eating disorders and the production-consumption dialectic. *New Ideas in Psychology, 11,* 95–104.

Smolak, L. (1993). *Adult development.* Englewood Cliffs, NJ: Prentice-Hall.

Snyder, C.R. (1996). Construing more workable realities and revising our personal stories, or vice versa. [Review of the book *Constructivism in psychotherapy*]. *Contemporary Psychology, 41,* 658–659.

Sonnert, G. (1994). Limits of morality: A sociological approach to higher moral stages. *Journal of Adult Development, 1,* 127–134.

Speed, B. (1991). Reality exists, O.K.? An argument against constructivism and social constructionism. *Journal of Family Therapy, 13,* 395–409.

Speed, B. (1994). A comment on "Contemporary family therapy in the United States." *Journal of Family Therapy, 16*, 25–29.

Spellman, D., & Harper, D.J. (1996). Failure, mistakes, regret and other subjugated stories in family therapy. *Journal of Family Therapy, 18*, 205–214.

Sperry, R.W. (1988). Psychology's mentalist paradigm and the religion/science tension. *American Psychologist, 43*, 607–613.

Sperry, R.W. (1991). In defense of mentalism and emergent interaction. *Journal of Mind and Behavior, 12*, 221–248.

Squire, L.R. (1987). *Memory and brain.* New York: Oxford University Press.

Sroufe, L.A. (1990). An organizational perspective on the self. In D. Cicchetti & M. Beeghly (Eds.), *The self in transition: Infancy to childhood* (pp. 281–207). Chicago: University of Chicago Press.

Sroufe, L.A. (1996). *Emotional development: The organization of emotional life in the early years.* New York: Cambridge University Press.

St. Aubin, E. de, & McAdams, D.P. (1995). The relations of generative concern and generative action to personality traits, satisfaction/happiness with life, and ego development. *Journal of Adult Development, 2*, 99–112.

Strayer, J. (1996). Trapped in the mirror: Psychosocial reflections on mid-life and the queen in Snow White. *Human Development, 39*, 155–172.

Stern, D.N. (1985). *The interpersonal world of the infant: A view from psychoanalysis and developmental psychology.* New York: Basic.

Sternberg, R.J. (1994). PRSVL: An integrative framework for understanding mind in context. In R.J. Sternberg & R.K. Wagner (Eds.), *Mind in context: Interactionist perspectives on human intelligence* (pp. 218–232). Cambridge, UK: Cambridge University Press.

Sternberg, R.J., & Wagner, R.K. (Eds.) (1994). *Mind in context: Interactionist perspectives on human intelligence.* Cambridge, UK: Cambridge University Press.

Stevenson-Hinde, J. (1990). Attachment within family systems: An overview. *Infant Mental Health Journal, 11*, 218–227.

Stevenson-Hinde, J., & Shouldice, A. (1995). Maternal interactions and self-reports related to attachment classifications at 4.5 years. *Child Development, 66*, 583–596.

Stewart, J.E. (1995). Metaevolution. *Journal of Social and Evolutionary Systems, 18*, 113–147.

Stewart, L., & Pascual-Leone, J. (1992). Mental capacity constraints and the development of moral reasoning. *Journal of Experimental Child Psychology, 54*, 251–287.

Stilwell, B.M., Galvin, M., Kopta, S.M., & Norton, J.A. (1994). Moral-emotional responsiveness: A two-factor domain of conscious functioning. *Journal of the American Academy of Child and Adolescent Psychiatry, 33*, 130–139.

Stock, G. (1993). *Metaman: The merging of humans and machines into a global superorganism.* Toronto: Doubleday.

Stone, C.A. (1993). What is missing in the metaphor of scaffolding? In E.A. Forman, N. Minick, & C.A. Stone (Eds.), *Contexts for learning: Sociocultural dynamics in children's development* (pp. 169–183). New York: Oxford University Press.

Stratton, P. (1988). Spirals and circles: Potential contributions of developmental psychology to family therapy. *Journal of Family Therapy, 10*, 207–231.

Suedfeld, P., Bluck, S., Loewen, L., & Elkins, D.J. (1994). Sociopolitical values and integrative complexity of members of student political groups. *Canadian Journal of Behavioural Science, 26*, 121–141.

Szapocznik, J., & Kurtines, W.M. (1993). Family psychology and cultural diversity: Opportunities for theory, research, and application. *American Psychologist, 48*, 400–407.

Tahir, L. (1996). Growth through opposition: The development of a point of view in young Bernard Shaw. In M.L. Commons, J. Demick, & C. Goldberg (Eds.), *Clinical approaches to adult development* (pp. 29–53). Norwood, NJ: Ablex.

Tappan, M.B., & Brown, L.M. (1992). Hermeneutics and developmental psychology: Toward and ethic of interpretation. In W.M. Kurtines, M. Azmitia, & J.L. Gewirtz (Eds.), *The role of values in psychology and human development* (pp. 105–130). New York: Wiley.

Taylor, C. (1989). *Sources of the self: The making of modern identity.* Cambridge, MA: Harvard University Press.

Taylor, C.E. (1995). "You think it was a *fight?*": Co-constructing (the struggle for) meaning, face, and family in everyday narrative activity. *Research on Language and Social Interaction, 28*, 283–317.

Terrell, C.J., & Lyddon, W.J. (1996). Narrative and psychotherapy. *Journal of Constructivist Psychology, 8*, 27–44.

Terwee, S.J.S. (1990). *Hermeneutics in psychology and psychoanalysis.* Berlin: Springer-Verlag.

Tharp, T. (1993). Institutional and social context of educational practice and reform. In E.A. Forman, N. Minick, & C.A. Stone (Eds.), *Contexts for learning: Sociocultural dynamics in children's development* (pp. 269–282). New York: Oxford University Press.

Thelen, E. (1990a). Dynamical systems and the generation of individual differences. In J. Colombo & J. Fagen (Eds.), *Individual differences in infancy: Reliability, stability, prediction* (pp. 19–43). Hillsdale, NJ: Erlbaum.

Tomasello, M., Kruger, A.C., & Ratner, H.H. (1993). Cultural learning. *Behavioral and Brain Sciences, 16*, 495–552.

Tomm, K. (1987a). Interventive interviewing: Part I. Strategizing as a fourth guideline for the therapist. *Family Process, 26*, 3–13.

Tomm, K. (1987b). Interventive interviewing: Part II. Reflexive questioning as a means to enable self-healing. *Family Process, 26*, 167–183.

Tomm, K. (1988). Interventive interviewing: Part III. Intending to ask circular, strategic or reflexive questions. *Family Process, 27*, 1–15.

Tomm, K. (1989). Externalizing the problem and internalizing personal agency. *Journal of Strategic and Systemic Therapies, 8*, 54–59.

Tomm, K. (1991). *Alternative ethical postures in therapy.* Paper presented at a meeting of the Ontario Psychological Association, Toronto, February.

Tomm, K. (1993). The courage to protest: A commentary on Michael White's work. In S. Gilligan & R. Price (Eds.), *Therapeutic conversations* (pp. 62–80). New York: Norton.

Tomm, K., Suzuki, K., & Suzuki, K. (1990). The Kan-No-Mushi: An inner externalization that enables compromise? *The Australian and New Zealand Journal of Family Therapy, 11*, 104–107.

Trachtenberg, S. (Ed.) (1995). *Critical essays on American postmodernism.* New York: Hall.

Tudge, J.R.H. (1992). Processes and consequences of peer collaboration: A vygotskian analysis. *Child Development, 63*, 1364–1379.

Tudge, J.R.H., & Winterhoff, P.A. (1993). Vygotsky, Piaget, and Bandura: Perspectives on the relations between the social world and cognitive development. *Human Development, 36*, 61–81.

Tulving, E., & Schacter, D.L. (1990). Priming and human memory systems. *Science, 247*, 301–306.

Valsiner, J. (1987). *Culture and the development of children's action.* New York: Wiley.

Valsiner, J. (1988). Epilogue: Ontogeny of co-construction of culture within socially organized environmental settings. In J. Valsiner (Ed.), *Child development within culturally structured environments* (Vol. 2). *Social construction and environmental guidance in development* (pp. 283–297). Norwood, NJ: Ablex.

Valsiner, J. (1991). Construction of the mental: From the "cognitive revolution" to the study of development. *Theory & Psychology, 1*, 477–494.

Valsiner, J. (1992). Social organization of cognitive development: Internalization and externalization of constraint systems. In A. Demetriou, M. Shayer, & A. Efklides (Eds.), *Neo-Piagetian theories of cognitive development: Implications and applications for education* (pp. 65–78). London, UK: Routledge.

Valsiner, J., & Gupta, S. (1995). Comment on Leyendecker et al. (1995). Rediscovering realities of social worlds: But can they be adequately explained? *Social Development, 4*, 207–213.

Valsiner, J., & Leung, M.-C. (1994). From intelligence to knowledge construction: A sociogenetic process approach. In R.J. Sternberg & R.K. Wagner (Eds.), *Mind in context: Interactionist perspectives on human intelligence* (pp. 202–217). Cambridge, UK: Cambridge University Press.

Valsiner, J., & van der Veer, R. (1993). The encoding of distance: The concept of the zone of proximal development and its interpretations. In R.R. Cocking & K.A. Renninger (Eds.), *The development and meaning of psychological distance* (pp. 35–62). Hillsdale, NJ: Erlbaum.

Valsiner, J., & Winegar, L.T. (1992). Introduction: A cultural-historical context for social "context." In L.T. Winegar & J. Valsiner (Eds.), *Children's development within social context* (Vol. 1). *Metatheory and theory* (pp. 1–14). Hillsdale, NJ: Erlbaum.

Vandenberg, B. (1991). Is epistemology enough? An existential consideration of development. *American Psychologist, 46*, 1278–1288.

Vandenberg, B. (1993). Existentialism and development. *American Psychologist, 48*, 296–297.

van der Veer, R., & Valsiner, J. (1991). *Understanding Vygotsky: A quest for synthesis.* Oxford, UK: Blackwell.

van der Veer, R., & Valsiner, J. (1994). *The Vygotsky reader.* Oxford, UK: Blackwell.

Vandervert, L.R. (1991). A measurable and testable brain-based emergent interactionism: An alternative to Sperry's mentalist emergent interactionism. *The Journal of Mind and Behavior, 12*, 201–220.

Vandervert, L.R. (1992). The emergence of brain and mind amid chaos through maximum-power evolution. *World Futures, 33*, 253–273.

Vandervert, L.R. (1995a). Chaos theory and the evolution of consciousness and mind: A thermodynamic-holographic resolution to the mind-body problem. *New Ideas in Psychology, 13*, 107–127.

Vandervert, L.R. (1995b). Chaos theory and Neurological Positivism—Clarifications: A reply to Newman, Bickhard, Alexander and Globus. *New Ideas in Psychology, 13*, 143–148.

Vandervert, L.R. (1996). From *idiots savants* to Albert Einstein: A brain-algorithmic explanation of savant and everyday performance. *New Ideas in Psychology, 14*, 81–92.

van Geert, P. (1994). Vygotskian dynamics of development. *Human Development, 37*, 345–365.

Verba, M. (1994). The beginnings of collaboration in peer interaction. *Human Development, 37*, 125–139.

Vogel, D. Narrative perspectives in theory and therapy. *Journal of Constructivist Psychology, 7*, 243–261.

Vygotsky, L.S. (1978). *Mind in society.* Cambridge, MA: Harvard University Press.

Vygotsky, L.S. (1981a). The genesis of higher mental functions. In J.V. Wertsch (Ed.), *The concept of activity in Soviet psychology* (pp. 144–188). Armonk, NY: Sharpe.

Vygotsky, L.S. (1981b). The instrumental method in psychology. In J.V. Wertsch (Ed.), *The concept of activity in Soviet psychology* (pp. 134–143). Armonk, NY: Sharpe.

Vygotsky, L.S. (1985). *Pensée et langage.* Paris: Editions Sociales.

Vygotsky, L.S. (1987). *The collected works of L.S. Vygotsky* (Vol. 1). *Problems of general psychology including the volume Thinking and Speech* (R.W. Reiber & A.S. Carton, Eds., and N. Minick, Trans.). New York: Plenum.

Vygotsky, L.S. (1993). *The collected works of L.S. Vygotsky* (Vol. 2). *The fundamentals of defectology (Abnormal psychology and learning disabilities).* (R.W. Reiber & A.S. Carton, Eds., and J.E. Knox & C. Stevens, Trans.). New York: Plenum.

Vygotsky, L.S., & Luria, A.R. (1993). *Studies on the history of behavior: Ape, primitive, and child* (V.I. Golod & J.E. Knox, Eds. and Trans.). Hillsdale, NJ: Erlbaum. (Original work published in 1930)

Wachs, T.D. (1992). *The nature of nurture.* Newbury Park, CA: Sage.

Wallon, H. (1942). *De l'acte à la pensée.* Paris: Flammarion.

Walter, J.W., & Peller, J.E. (1994). "On track" in solution-focused brief therapy. In M.F. Hoyt (Ed.), *Constructive therapies* (pp. 111–125). New York: Guilford.

Williams, W.M., & Sternberg, R.J. (1988). Group intelligence: Why some groups are better than others. *Intelligence, 12,* 351–377.

Wapner, S. (1993). Parental development: A holistic, developmental systems-oriented perspective. In J. Demick, K. Bursik, & R. DiBiase (Eds.), *Parental development* (pp. 3–37). Hillsdale, NJ: Erlbaum.

Warren, M.E. (1993). Can participatory democracy produce better selves? Psychological dimensions of Habermas's discursive model of democracy. *Political Psychology, 14,* 209–234.

Wertsch, J.V. (1991). *Voices of the mind: A sociocultural approach to mediated action.* Cambridge, MA: Harvard University Press.

Wertsch, J.V. (1993). Commentary. *Human Development, 36,* 168–171.

Wertsch, J.V. (1994a). Commentary. *Human Development, 37,* 343–345.

Wertsch, J.V. (1994b). The primacy of mediated action in sociocultural studies. *Mind, Culture, and Activity, 1,* 202–208.

Wertsch, J.V. (1995a). Sociocultural research in the copyright age. *Culture & Psychology, 1,* 81–102.

Wertsch, J.V. (1995b). The need for action in sociocultural research. In J.V. Wertsch, P. del Río, & A. Alvarez (Eds.), *Sociocultural studies of mind* (pp. 56–74). New York: Cambridge University Press.

Wertsch, J.V. (1995c). Commentary. *Human Development, 38,* 127–130.

Wertsch, J.V., & Bevins, J.A. (1993). The social origins of individual mental functioning: Alternatives and perspectives. In R.R. Cocking & K.A. Renninger (Eds.), *The development and meaning of psychological distance* (pp. 203–218). Hillsdale, NJ: Erlbaum.

Wertsch, J.V., del Río, P., & Alavarez, A. (1995). Sociocultural studies: History, action, and mediation. In J.V. Wertsch, P. del Río, & A. Alvarez (Eds.), *Sociocultural studies of mind* (pp. 1–34). New York: Cambridge University Press.

Wertsch, J.V., & Kanner, B.G. (1992). A sociocultural approach to intellectual development. In R.J. Sternberg & C.A. Berg (Eds.), *Intellectual development* (pp. 328–349). New York: Cambridge University Press.

Wertsch, J.V., & Sohmer, R. (1995). Vygotsky on learning and development. *Human Development, 38,* 332–337.

Wertsch, J.V., Tulviste, P., & Hagstrom, F. (1993). A sociocultural approach to agency. In E.A. Forman, N. Minick, & C.A. Stone (Eds.), *Contexts for learning: Sociocultural dynamics in children's development* (pp. 336–356). New York: Oxford University Press.

West, M.L., & Sheldon-Keller, A.E. (1994). *Patterns of relating: An adult attachment perspective.* New York: Guilford.

White, D., & Wang, A. (1995). Universalism, humanism, and postmodernism. *American Psychologist, 50,* 392–393.

White, M. (1984). Pseudo-encopresis: From avalanche to victory, from vicious to virtuous cycles. *Journal of Family Systems Medicine, 2*(2), 150–160.

White, M. (1985). Negative explanation, restraint, and double description: A template for family therapy. *Family Process, 25,* 169–184.

White, M. (1991). Deconstruction and therapy. *Dulwich Centre Newsletter, 3,* 1–22.

White, M. (1993a). Deconstruction and therapy. In S. Gilligan & R. Price (Eds.), *Therapeutic conversations* (pp. 22–61). New York: Norton.

White, M. (1993b). Commentary: The histories of the present. In S. Gilligan & R. Price (Eds.), *Therapeutic conversations* (pp. 121–135). New York: Norton.

White, M. (1993c). Commentary: Systems of understanding, practices of relationships, and practices of self. In S. Gilligan & R. Price (Eds.), *Therapeutic conversations* (pp. 190–196). New York: Norton.

White, M. (1994). The politics of therapy. *Context, 18*, 28–34.

White, M., & Epston, D. (1990). *Narrative means to therapeutic ends.* New York: Norton.

Widdershoven, G.A.M. (1994). Identity and development: A narrative perspective. In H.A. Bosma, T.L.G. Graafsma, H.D. Grotevant, & D.J. de Levita (Eds.), *Identity and development: An interdisciplinary approach* (pp. 103–117). Thousand Oaks, CA: Sage.

Wilson, J.Q. (1993). The moral sense. *American Political Science Review, 87*, 1–11.

Winegar, L.T., & Valsiner, J. (1992). Recontextualizing context: Analysis of metadata and some further elaborations. In L.T. Winegar & J. Valsiner (Eds.), *Children's development within social context* (Vol. 2). *Research and methodology* (pp. 249–266). Hillsdale, NJ: Erlbaum.

Wolff, P.H. (1960). The developmental psychologies of Jean Piaget and psychoanalysis. *Psychological Issues, 2*(1).

Wood, D. (1980). Teaching the young child: Some relationships between social interaction, learning, and teaching. In D.R. Olson (Ed.), *The social foundations of learning and teaching* (pp. 281–296). New York: Norton.

Wozniak, R.H. (1992). Co-constructive, intersubjective realism: Metatheory in developmental psychology. In W.M. Kurtines, M. Azmitia, & J.L. Gewirtz (Eds.), *The role of values in psychology and human development* (pp. 89–94). New York: Wiley.

Wozniak, R.H. (1993). Co-constructive metatheory for psychology: Implications for an analysis of families as special social contexts. In R.H. Wozniak & K.W. Fischer (Eds.), *Development in context: Acting and thinking in specific environments* (pp. 77–91). Hillsdale, NJ: Erlbaum.

Wozniak, R.H., & Fischer, K.W. (1993). Development in context: An introduction. In R.H. Wozniak & K.W. Fischer (Eds.), *Development in context: Acting and thinking in specific environments* (pp. xi–xvi). Hillsdale, NJ: Erlbaum.

Wylie, M.S. (1994a). Panning for gold. *Family Therapy Networker, 18*(6), 40–48.

Wylie, M.S. (1994b). Policing our lives. *Family Therapy Networker, 18*(6), 48–49.

Yeates, K.O., Schultz, L.H., & Selman, R.L. (1990). Bridging the gaps in child-clinical assessment: Toward the application of social-cognitive development. *Clinical Psychology Review, 10*, 567–588.

Yoder, P.J., & Munson, L.J. (1995). The social correlates of co-ordinated attention to adult and objects in mother infant interaction. *First Language, 15*, 219–230.

Young, C.M. (1995). *The portrayal of motherless female characters in Disney film.* Unpublished manuscript. Newtonbrook Secondary High School, Toronto.

Young, G. (1990a). Early neuropsychological development: Lateralization of functions—hemispheric specialization. In C.-A. Hauert (Ed.), *Developmental psychology: Cognitive, perceptuo-motor and neuropsychological perspectives* (pp. 113–181). Amsterdam: North Holland.

Young, G. (1990b). The development of hemispheric and manual specialization. In G.E. Hammond (Ed.), *Cerebral control of speech and limb movements* (pp. 79–139). Amsterdam: North Holland.

Young, G. (submitted). *The stages of life: Co-fractalization in development and therapy.* York University, Toronto.

Young, G., & Young, L.B. (in preparation). *Cohesion in normal and nonstandard discourse acquisition: Laterality effects.* Norwood, NJ: Ablex.

Young, T.R. (1995). Chaos theory and social dynamics: Foundations of postmodern social science. In R. Robertson & A. Combs (Eds.), *Chaos theory in psychology and the life sciences* (pp. 217–233). Mahwah, NJ: Erlbaum.

Youniss, J. (1994). Vygotsky's fragile genius in time and place: Essay review of *Understanding Vygotsky: A quest for synthesis* by Rene van der Veer and Jaan Valsiner. *Human Development, 37*, 119–124.

Zazzo, R. (1993). *Reflets de miroir et autres doubles.* Paris: Presse Universitaire de France.

Zazzo, R., & Zazzo, B. (1968). Conduites et conscience. *Théorie et pratique en psychologie.* Neuchâtel: Delachaux et Niestlé.

Zimmerman, J.K. (1993). Developmental and conceptual issues in *Women's ways of knowing*: A response to Handlin's interview with Belenky and Clinchy. *New Ideas in Psychology, 11,* 259–265.

Zimmerman, J.L., & Dickerson, V.C. (1993). Bringing forth the restraining influence of pattern in couples therapy. In S. Gilligan & R. Price (Eds.), *Therapeutic conversations* (pp. 197–214). New York: Norton.

Zimmerman, J.L., & Dickerson, V.C. (1994a). Tales of the body thief: Externalizing and deconstructing eating problems. In M.F. Hoyt (Ed.), *Constructive therapies* (pp. 295–318). New York: Guilford.

Zimmerman, J.L., & Dickerson, V.C. (1994b). Using a narrative metaphor: Implications for theory and clinical practice. *Family Process, 33,* 233–245.

Index